Windows on the House of Islam

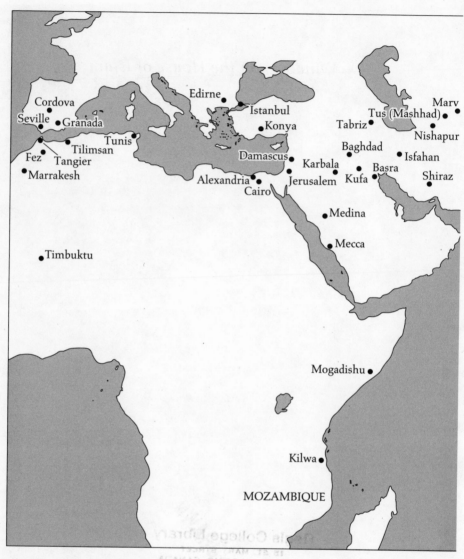

Map of key places mentioned in text.

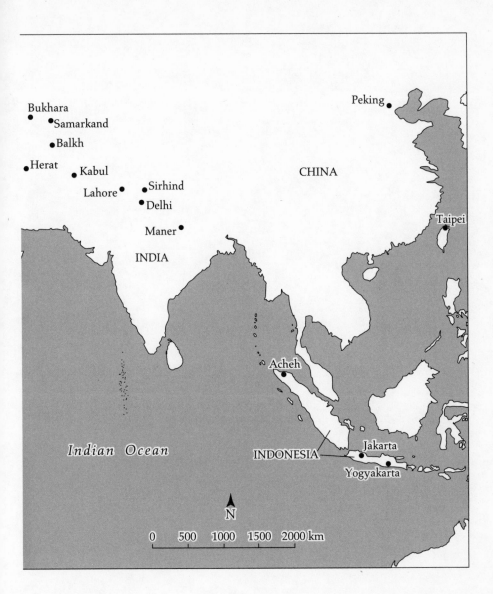

Bukhara
Samarkand
Balkh
Herat
Kabul
Lahore
Sirhind
Delhi
Maner

INDIA

CHINA

Peking

Taipei

Acheh

Indian Ocean

INDONESIA
Jakarta
Yogyakarta

N

0   500   1000 1500 2000 km

Windows on the House of Islam

Muslim Sources on Spirituality and Religious Life

Edited by
JOHN RENARD

University of California Press

BERKELEY   LOS ANGELES   LONDON

Selections from the following sources are reprinted with permission:

David B. Edwards, *Heroes of the Age: Moral Fault Lines on the Afghan Frontier* (Berkeley: University of California Press, 1996), pp. 126–28.

Richard T. Antoun, *Muslim Preacher in the Modern World* (Princeton: Princeton University Press, 1989), revised from pp. 75–81, 85.

Wheeler M. Thackston, trans., *A Century of Princes*, Aga Khan Program for Islamic Architecture (Cambridge, Mass., 1989), pp. 213–15, 370–72, 375.

R. Stephen Humphreys, "Women as Patrons of Religious Architecture in Ayyubid Damascus," *Muqarnas* 11 (1994), p. 47. Published by the Aga Khan Program for Islamic Architecture (Cambridge, Mass.).

R. W. J. Austin, trans., *Sufis of Andalusia* (Berkeley: University of California Press, 1971), copyright Allen and Unwin, rights held by HarperCollins, London, excerpts from pp. 142, 145–46, 154–55.

University of California Press
Berkeley and Los Angeles, California

University of California Press, Ltd.
London, England

©1998 by
The Regents of the University of California

Library of Congress Cataloging-in-Publication Data

   Windows on the house of Islam: Muslim sources on spirituality
and religious life / edited by John Renard.
      p. cm.
   Includes bibliographical references (p.   ) and index.
   ISBN 0–520–20976–1 (cloth: alk. paper). — ISBN 0–520–21086–7
(pbk.: alk. paper)
      1. Religious life—Islam—Sources.   2. Islam—Sources.   I. Renard,
John, 1944–   .
   BP161.2.W57   1998
   297.5'7—dc21
                                                        97–9853
                                                        CIP

Printed in the United States of America
9 8 7 6 5 4 3 2 1

Contents

List of Illustrations   *xiii*

Preface   *xvii*

ONE   FOUNDATIONS: PROPHETIC REVELATION   1

TEXTS FROM THE QUR'AN / 2

    Surat ar-Rahman, The Merciful   2

    Writing Sacred Text   5

    Surat Yusuf   6

    Hadith: Prophetic and Sacred   24

    Sacred Text and Architecture   26

VARIETIES OF QUR'AN INTERPRETATION / 28

    Three Commentaries on Surat al-Fatiha, The Opening   29

    Ibn Taymiya: *Treatise on the Principles of Tafsir*   35

    Sacred Text and the Mihrab   43

    Al-Ghazali: *The Canons of Ta'wil*   48

EXPERIENCING QUR'AN / 55

    Nawawi: Etiquette in Recitation   55

TWO   DEVOTION: RITUAL AND PERSONAL PRAYER   59

ON THE FIVE PILLARS / 59

    Sharaf ad-Din Maneri: On the Necessity of Proper Intention   59

    Nurcholish Madjid: Worship as an Institution of Faith   65

    Tabari: Hadith on the Five Daily Ritual Prayers   74

    Ritual and Creed in Moses' Conversation with God   78

    Hamka: Qur'an Commentary on Pilgrimage Ritual   85

DEVOTION BEYOND DUTY   /   92

   Prayers of Holy Women   92

   Rites of Passage and Popular Practice   95
      Marthiya: Imam Husayn's Conversation with God   95

      Madih: Three Contemporary Poems Honoring Imam Riza   98

      Na't: Poem in Praise of Muhammad   102

      Ginan: Isma'ili Petition of a Yearning Soul   103

   Sermon for a Special Occasion   107
      A Radio *Mawlid* Sermon   107

THREE   INSPIRATION: EDIFICATION AND ETHICS   119

EXEMPLARY MODELS   /   119

   The Prophet: From Devotion to Edification   119
      Acrostic Poem in Praise of Muhammad   120

      Na't in Praise of Muhammad   123

      Taha Hussein: Interpreting Muhammad's Life in Modern
      Times   124

   Collections of Holy Lives   130
      Asiya, an Exemplary Woman in Tha'labi's *Stories
      of the Prophets*   130

      Munawi's Life of Rabi'a al-'Adawiya   132

      Three Women of Iberia   135

      Holy Women of Morocco and Egypt   137

      The Life of Sufi Badhni   139

      Jabarti's Account of 'Ali al-Bayyumi   141

WISDOM LITERATURE   /   144

   The Qur'anic Paradigm of Wisdom: Surat Luqman   144

   Morals for the Masses   149
      Aphorisms of 'Ali   149

      Sayings Attributed to Mu'in ad-Din Chishti   155

ENCOUNTERING THE EXEMPLARY PERSONS   /   159

   Storytelling as Entertainment   159
      Telling Tales: A Miracle of Mulla Hadda   159

      Edifying Anecdotes: Ziya' ad-Din Nakhshabi   162

FOUR   AESTHETICS: FROM ALLEGORY TO ARABESQUE   169

LITERATURE AND SPIRITUALITY / 169

  Interpreting Religious Poetry   170
    Mir 'Ali-Shir Nawa'i: A Poet's Intentions   170
    Shams ad-Din Lahiji: Commentary on Shabistari's *Garden of Mystery*   172

  Allegory   180
    Yahya Suhrawardi Maqtul: Allegory of Beauty and Love   180

PRINCIPAL POETIC FORMS / 184

  Didactic Poetry   185
    Sana'i of Ghazna: Two Teaching Parables   185
    Mude Kala: Gayo Didactic Religious Poetry   189

  Lyric Poetry   194
    Ibn al-Farid: *Ruba'iyat, Ghazal, Qasida*   194
    Munawi's Literary Hagiography of Ibn al-Farid   202
    Jalal ad-Din Rumi: *Ghazal*   208
    Muhammad Shirin Maghribi: *Ghazal*   209
    Nuri and Shad: *Na'ts*   212
    Bibi Hayati: *Ghazal*   214

FIVE   COMMUNITY: SOCIETY, INSTITUTIONS, AND PATRONAGE   217

SOCIAL AND HISTORICAL CONTEXTS / 217

  Religion, Society, and Culture   217
    Shaykh Luqman: A Contemporary Life in a Traditional Context   218

INSTITUTIONAL TEXTS / 223

  Public Support   223
    Historical Epigraphy of Mamluk Sultan Faraj ibn Barquq   223
    Two *Waqf* Documents: Sultan Barquq and Khwaja Ahrar   226
    Mamluk Sultan Barquq's *Waqf*   226
    A Central Asian *Waqf* of Naqshbandi Sufi Master Khwaja Ahrar   231

  Private Discipline   235
    Shihab ad-Din 'Umar Suhrawardi: Treatises on Sufi Chivalry   235

PATRONAGE AND THE ARTS /   244

Women as Patrons of Architecture   244
   Sitt ash-Sham of Damascus   244

   Works of Timurid and Ottoman Women   245

Building Community and Community Patronage   249
   Architectural Past, Present, and Future in America   249

Chronicles of Royal Patronage   250
   Ibn Marzuq: Sultan Abu 'l-Hasan 'Ali's Architectural
   Patronage   250

   Khwandamir: The Rediscovery and Refurbishment of 'Ali's
   Tomb   261

   Sultan-Husayn Mirza: Apologia   265

SIX   PEDAGOGY: FANNING SPARK INTO FLAME   269

ADVANCED INTERPRETATION OF FOUNDATIONAL ISSUES   /   269

   Teaching Islam in Medieval Iran: Ahmad Sam'ani's
   Refreshment of Spirits   269

Teaching across Cultures   278
   Islam in China: Wang Daiyu's *Real Commentary on the True
   Teaching*   278

   From Arabic into Javanese: *The Gift Addressed to the Spirit
   of the Prophet*   283

FROM THE GREAT TEACHERS   /   286

Between Sermon and Seminar   286
   Women as Scholars and Teachers   286

   Teaching with Pictures: Three Paintings of Bawa
   Muhaiyaddeen   290

Borrowed Notes   296
   Muhammad Husayni Gesu Daraz on Love   297

Keeping in Touch   298
   Shaykh Husayn: A Letter on the True Names of God   298

REQUIRED READING FOR MYSTICS / 301

Advice for Inexperienced Travelers   301
    Majd ad-Din Baghdadi: Treatise on Journeying   301

Mystical Geography   311
    Vahidi: The Seven Invocations and the Seven Journeys   311

Languages of the Spirit   317
    Sayyid Ja'far Sajjadi: Lexicon of Mystical Terms   317

SEVEN   EXPERIENCE: TESTIMONY, PARADIGM, AND CRITIQUE   325

HEART SPEAKS TO HEART / 325

Soul on Pilgrimage   325
    The Diary of Ahmad Wahib   325

Muhammad as Mystical Model   336
    Tabari: Muhammad's Night Journey and Ascension   336

BEYOND STORYTELLING / 345

Saying the Unsayable   345
    Rabi'a's Dream   346

    Amir Khusraw of Delhi's Poetic Vision   347

    Gesu Daraz's Vision of Jesus   349

    Visionary Experiences of 'Ali al-Bayyumi   350

    Ahmad Wahib's Dream   352

Explaining the Unexplainable   353
    Tabari: The Correct Interpretation of the Mi'raj Narrative 353

    Al-Ghazali: *Treatise on the Intimate Knowledge of God*   355

EVALUATING EXPERIENCE / 359

The Science of Hearts   359
    Sharaf ad-Din Maneri: A Letter on the Qualities
    of Spiritual Guides   359

    Sayyid Ahmad Khan: Treatise on Visualizing the Shaykh   368

Traveling Companions   375
    Hasan Palasi's Encounter with Shaykh Kujuji   375

Appendix 1: Text Distribution   385

Appendix 2: Art Program Distribution   389

Notes   393

Suggestions for Further Reading   405

About the Contributors   409

Index of Qur'anic Citations   413

General Index   417

Illustrations

MAP OF KEY PLACES MENTIONED IN TEXT   *frontis*

FIGURES

1. Dome of the Sultan's mosque in Shah Alam, Malaysia, 1980s   xxii
2. Qur'an page, Iraq (?), ninth century   6
3. Qur'an page, Egypt, fourteenth century (Mamluk)   7
4. Taj Mahal, Agra, India, 1632–1654 (Mughal)   27
5. Mosque of Shaykh Lutfullah, Isfahan, Iran, 1603–1619 (Safavid)   28
6. *Qibla* dome mosaics, Great Mosque of Cordova, Spain, 961 (Umayyad)   29
7. Tile mihrab, Isfahan, Iran, ca. 1354   44
8. Mihrab, Rustem Pasha Mosque, Istanbul, 1561–1562 (Ottoman)   45
9. Stucco mihrab, Congregational Mosque of Isfahan, Iran, 1310 (Il-Khanid)   46
10. Mihrab of Fatima Khatun, Iran, twelfth century   47
11. Mosque of Selim II, Edirne, Turkey, 1568–1575 (Ottoman)   58
12. Prayer Rug, Turkey, early nineteenth century (Ottoman)   66
13. Brass mosque candlestick, Iran, 1300–1350 (Il-Khanid)   67
14. Kalyan Minaret, Bukhara, Uzbekistan, 1127 (Saljuqid)   75
15. Jami Masjid, Kuala Lumpur, Malaysia, 1897   76
16. Pilgrim's plan of Ka'ba, guidebook, Mecca, 1582 (Ottoman)   86
17. Pilgrims' banner, North Africa, 1683   88
18. "Du'a' Lady," calendar poster, India, 1994   93
19. Son grieves for his father, from *Mantiq at-tayr* by 'Attar, Herat, Iran, 1483 (Timurid)   99
20. Marble tombstone, Iran, twelfth century   104

xiii

21. Mausoleum, Bukhara, Uzbekistan, tenth century (Samanid)   108

22. Muhammad at the Ka'ba, miniature painting, Turkey, seventeenth century (Ottoman)   118

23. Dome of the Rock, Jerusalem, 692 (Umayyad)   139

24. Tile panel, Syria, seventeenth century (Ottoman)   150

25. Tomb of Mu'in ad-Din Chishti, calendar poster, India, 1994   156

26. Prophet Joseph with his bride Zulaykha, from *Haft Awrang*, by Jami, Iran, 1556–1565 (Safavid)   163

27. Manuscript frontispiece illumination, Iran, sixteenth century (Safavid)   168

28. Funerary complexes of Sultan Inal (1451–1456) and Qurqumas (1506–1507), Cairo, Egypt (Mamluk)   180

29. Complex of Amir Khayrbak, Cairo, 1520–1521 (Mamluk/Ottoman)   181

30. Gur-i Mir, Samarkand, Uzbekistan, ca. 1400–1404 (Timurid)   190

31. Congregational Mosque of Isfahan, Iran, eighth–seventeenth centuries (Saljuqid, Timurid, Safavid)   191

32. Tomb of Akbar, main gate, Sikandra, India, 1605–1613 (Mughal)   201

33. Congregational Mosque, Delhi, India, 1644–1658 (Mughal)   202

34. Mosque of Bayezid II, Edirne, Turkey, begun 1484 (Ottoman)   210

35. Mosque of Selim II, Edirne, Turkey, 1569–1575 (Ottoman)   211

36. Madar-i Shah Madrasa, Isfahan, Iran, ca. 1706–1715 (Safavid)   216

37. Mevlevi *tekke* courtyard, Konya, Turkey, thirteenth–sixteenth century (Ottoman)   245

38. Mausoleum, Samarkand, Uzbekistan, ca. 1425 (Timurid)   246

39. Mosque of Bibi Khanum, Samarkand, Uzbekistan, begun 1399 (Timurid)   247

40. Mihrimah Sultan Mosque, Istanbul, 1565–1570 (Ottoman)   248

41. Yeni Valide Mosque, Istanbul, ca. 1625–1650 (Ottoman)   249

42. Early mosque, Toledo, Ohio, mid–twentieth century   250

43. Islamic Center of Greater Toledo, Perrysburg, Ohio, 1980s   251

44. Mosque of Selim I, Istanbul, 1522 (Ottoman)   252

45. Model, Islamic Center of Greater Toledo, Perrysburg,
    Ohio, 1980s   253

46. 'Ubbad Mosque prayer hall, Tlemcen, Algeria, fourteenth
    century (Marinid)   256

47. 'Ubbad Mosque portal dome, Tlemcen, Algeria, fourteenth
    century (Marinid)   258

48. Madrasa, Sale, Morocco, fourteenth century (Marinid)   259

49. Dara Shikoh with Mian Mir and Mulla Shah, album
    painting, India, ca. 1635 (Mughal)   268

50. Great Mosque, Taipei, Taiwan, mid–twentieth century   279

51. Karatay Madrasa, Konya, Turkey, 1253 (Saljuqid)   287

52. Shir Dar Madrasa, Registan, Samarkand, 1616–1636 (Uzbek)   288

53. Madrasa Madar-i Shah, Isfahan, Iran, 1706–1715 (Safavid)   289

54. *The Inner Heart*, Bawa Muhaiyaddeen, U.S.A.,
    twentieth century   292

55. *Four Steps to Pure Iman*, Bawa Muhaiyaddeen, U.S.A.,
    twentieth century   294

56. *The Rocky Mountain of the Heart*, Bawa Muhaiyaddeen,
    U.S.A., twentieth century   296

57. "The Valley of the Quest," marginal image, from *Divan* by
    Sultan Ahmad Jalayir, Tabriz, Iran, ca. 1406–1410 (Jalayirid) 312

58. Sa'di visited by angels, from *Haft Awrang*, by Jami,
    Mashhad, Iran, 1556–1565 (Safavid)   324

59. Muhammad's Ascension, from *Falnama*, Tabriz or Qazwin,
    Iran, ca. 1550 (Safavid)   338

60. Lusterware plate by Shams ad-Din al-Hasani, Kashan,
    Iran, 1210 (Saljuqid)   346

61. Angels and houris, ink drawing, Iran, sixteenth
    century (Safavid)   348

62. Joseph interprets dreams, album painting, India, early
    seventeenth century (Mughal)   351

63. Dervish meditating, Iran, ca. 1580 (Safavid)   360

64. Dervishes dancing, from *Divan* by Hafiz, Iran,
    ca. 1490 (Timurid)   365

65. Dervish seated, album painting, Iran, late fifteenth
    century (Timurid)   373

66. Seeker receiving spiritual direction, album painting, India,
    1605–1627 (Mughal)   376

Preface

The followers of Muhammad's way, by the pure light of that first and
last master, have opened a window in the house of devotion, so that the
rays of the sun of truth may fall into the house and clean the interior
with the sanctity of that sacred world.

Majd ad-Din Baghdadi, *Treatise on Journeying*

In the spacious House of Islam there has always been room for enormous
variety. More than a billion people live here, people from scores of ethnic,
linguistic, national, cultural, and social backgrounds. Before Islam was
barely a century old as a religious community, it was already a house whose
inhabitants viewed their world from many vantage points.

Over the centuries and across the globe, Muslim authors and artists have
given brilliant and moving testimony to their experience of being members
of the Islamic community. They have spoken clearly about how to interpret
the foundational sources, the Qur'an and Hadith, and argued persuasively
about the way good Muslims ought to live. They have raised eloquent monuments, both great and small, in praise of God and reminisced poignantly
about the exemplary figures and formative moments in their individual lives
and in the larger sweep of Islamic history. In their verbal and visual arts
Muslims have taught one another the core of a great spiritual legacy and
have sought to share the insight and intimate knowledge at the heart of their
manifold experience of religious truth.

Since the global phenomenon called Islam is enormously rich and complex, it is important to note that neither any individual selection or category of items nor even the collection as a whole can begin to present anything like a definitive picture of Islam. The materials presented here have
been chosen in the hope of offering a small sample of the vast array of textual and visual documentation that, taken together, begins to suggest something of the amazing spiritual patrimony of the ancient and now earth-
encircling community of Muslims. I have attempted not to paint a picture
of some "normative" Islam, but to sketch the outlines of a phenomenon that
actually includes several "Islams." Muslims are in general agreement about
their tradition's most basic tenets; but about many of the finer details of
personal conviction, experience, and daily practice there is considerable lat-

itude. The purpose of this anthology is to celebrate that immense variety and to offer a wide spectrum of representative contributions.

Unlike many previous books of its kind, this anthology divides its material into seven parts meant to suggest aspects of experience rather than the historical or theoretical categories with which readers interested in the study of religious traditions may be more familiar. It begins, as have many books on Islam, with foundational texts and the various ways in which Muslims have interpreted them; but from there it moves through a series of broadly thematic sections that revolve around the Muslim experience of devotion, sources of ethical and religious inspiration, the aesthetic appreciation of the religious arts, community, instruction in Islam's more demanding teachings, and finally the communication and interpretation of religious experience itself.

CHOICE OF MATERIALS

Choosing specific items for an anthology as expansive as this presents several challenges. The overall goal of the collection has been to achieve the broadest possible coverage with respect to geography, chronology, theme, and language of origin, and to arrange the material so that it would not only stand alone but also function as a companion volume to *Seven Doors to Islam: Spirituality and the Religious Life of Muslims*.[1] To help readers and teachers take maximum advantage of the anthology's breadth, the two appendixes offer tables outlining the distribution of materials: of texts by century, location, language, and literary form; and of visual documentation by century, location, form, and function.

I have kept several other considerations in mind as well. The first has been to include as much newly translated material as possible. About two-thirds of the texts appear here for the first time in English, and of those, about half have never before been translated into a European language, so far as I can tell. Of the remainder, about half are reprinted from sources now out of print or very hard to find; and half are newly translated, mostly of texts first published in English long ago or in need of fresh renderings. Most of the visual documentation has been published previously and studied carefully by historians of Islamic art. I include those works here in the belief that one can appreciate their explicitly religious implications fully only in the context of a study of religion and spirituality.

My second consideration has been to offer as much depth in a few areas as a sweeping sample would allow. To that end I have sought to include a number of integral longer texts along with whole shorter texts, such as poems, and assorted excerpts of much longer works.

Add practical constraints of size and the need to keep the price afford-
able, and the net result is that some major authors (such as Shah Wali Allah and Hafiz) and languages of origin (such as Sindhi, Punjabi, and Ben-
gali) could not be included. In the particular instance of Hadith texts, some
readers will understandably expect a larger selection under the heading "Hadith" in part 1; I provide only a few examples there because dozens more
hadith appear scattered among larger texts throughout the anthology.

Finally, a brief explanation about the segments devoted to works by and
about women is in order. Sections on prayers, lives, and architectural patronage of Muslim women stand alone for the simple reason that the prayers,
lives, and patronage of Muslim men are already richly represented in various other texts and images. In addition, I know of no existing anthologies
of Islamic materials that pointedly showcase the works and daily lives of
important women, with the possible exception of the mystic Rabi'a. The net
result has been the presumption that there simply is not much available in
literary or visual form to testify to the accomplishments of Muslim women.
The pieces included here offer at least a glimpse at the materials now becoming increasingly available.

PRACTICALITIES AND ACKNOWLEDGMENTS

In the interest of keeping the table of contents as clear and readable as possible, names of contributors are not included there but appear at each selection.

In *Seven Doors to Islam*, the photos functioned specifically as illustrations
to the text. Here the photos generally serve a different purpose: in most instances they function as primary sources, with textual commentary attached.
In parts 1, 4, 5, and 6 I have clustered photos together with their commentary; elsewhere illustrations appear individually, with relevant data provided
in captions. Except where otherwise acknowledged, all photos and commentary on visual documentation are by the editor.

Foreign technical terms are italicized on first occurrence, and thereafter
only for purposes of further definition. Footnotes include information
meant to aid uninterrupted reading; all other information is in endnotes.
Brief equivalents of technical terms are included in the index. Suggestions
for further reading include only books in English. I have converted some
translators' use of "gnosis" and "gnostic" to render variations on the Arabic root *'arafa*, to "intimate knowledge" [of God] (*ma'rifa*) and "mystic"
(*'arif*). Cross references to *Seven Doors to Islam* will be as follows: for illustrations, SD fig. *n*; for pages, SD followed by page number. Unless otherwise specified, all parenthetical numbers in the text refer to Qur'an sura

and verse, e.g. 24:35. Introductions to individual selections appear under the translators' names; but for editorial reasons of consistency and balance, the responsibility for their final form, as well as for that of foot- and endnotes, is mine. Editorial concern for inclusive language and contemporary usage has in some instances required me to introduce very minor changes into translated texts.

For the completion of this project, I am indebted first of all to the active interest and generous collaboration of more than thirty scholars from all over the world. For permission to reproduce excerpts of previously published material I thank the University of California Press, Princeton University Press, the Aga Khan Program for Islamic Architecture, and HarperCollins Publishers. For reproductions of their holdings I am grateful to the St. Louis Art Museum, the Walters Art Gallery, Harvard University Art Museums, the Freer and Sackler Galleries of the Smithsonian Institution, the Metropolitan Museum of Art, and the Bawa Muhaiyaddeen Fellowship.

I am particularly grateful to Michael Spath of Saint Louis University for his invaluable help in collating, editing, revising, and proofreading. Special thanks also to David Vila of Saint Louis University for his assistance in the later phases of the project, especially in proofreading and indexing, and to Mindi Grieser for proofreading. To Saint Louis University, its College of Arts and Sciences and Department of Theological Studies, I express my thanks for providing extra time through the Hotfelder Professorship in the Humanities; and for additional resources through a Mellon Faculty Development Grant and a Graduate School Summer Research Award. I am grateful to editor Douglas Abrams Arava, of the University of California Press, for supporting this project from the start and for his advocacy at the Press throughout its several-year history. Thanks also to Rachel Berchten for her superb work on both volumes and to Anne Canright for her fine copyediting of this one. Finally, as always, I thank my ever-patient companion, Mary Pat, for her humor and encouragement.

Figure 1.   Sultan's mosque, Shah Alam, Malaysia (1980s).

1 Foundations
Prophetic Revelation

The House of Islam rests on the threefold foundation of a sacred scripture, the prophetic sayings of Muhammad, and a sophisticated tradition of exegesis, or interpretation of the sacred texts. All aspects of Islamic faith and practice begin with the sacred scripture, the Qur'an ("recitation"), understood as the literal word of God revealed directly to Muhammad and, through him, to the community. Texts of two complete suras, or chapters, of the Qur'an, ar-Rahman (55, The Merciful) and Yusuf (12, Joseph), appear here in new translations.

Muslims regard Muhammad's own words and deeds as wholly distinct from those of the Qur'an and preserved in a large body of literature known as Hadith. They consider both Qur'an and Hadith to be divinely revealed; the major theological distinction is that although the content of the Hadith is ultimately from God, the precise words are those of Muhammad. A second major category of Hadith comprises sayings attributed to God but still considered distinct from the Qur'an. These "sacred hadith" appear almost exclusively in the context of Muhammad's sayings; for example: Muhammad is reported to have said that God said. . . . This chapter offers a small sample of hadith of both types; subsequent texts in this and later chapters include many more examples, including several hadith attributed to Shi'i Imams.

Muhammad's sayings provide a wealth of material helpful in the interpretation of scripture. The third section of this chapter offers two types of exegetical literature that make extensive use of prophetic traditions. Three different interpretations of Sura 1, Al-Fatiha, provide the entire text of a chapter, along with examples of different approaches to its interpretation. Then two of Islam's most influential religious scholars, Abu Hamid al-Ghazali (d. 1111) and Ibn Taymiya (d. 1328), analyze the principles behind the two major exegetical types, the relatively straightforward *tafsir* and the often esoteric *ta'wil*. Visual illustrations will focus on three themes: styles of calligraphy, sacred text in inscriptions on architecture generally, and epigraphy on the unique visual focus called the *mihrab*, or niche.

TEXTS FROM THE QUR'AN

The Qur'an's 114 chapters (suras) offer a wide array of literary styles, lengths, tones, themes, and textures. Some of the earliest suras, dating from the first years of Muhammad's public ministry (610–615), are only a few verses in length— Sura 112, for instance: "Say: He, God, is one; God is everlasting; he does not beget and he is not begotten, and there is none like him"; or Sura 110: "When the help of God and victory arrive, and you see humankind entering God's religion in throngs, then break forth with praise of your Lord and seek his forgiveness, for he is ever turning back [to forgive]." After the community left Mecca for Medina in 622, the qur'anic texts gradually shifted in style and tone from more poetic and exhortatory to more prosaic, and in content from pedagogical narrative and apocalyptic imagery to regulatory and practical instruction.

The two complete suras that follow represent the early and later Meccan periods; both are particularly suitable for recitation even in translation. Surat ar-Rahman (55), presented first, needs to be read aloud to be appreciated, while Surat Yusuf (12) offers an excellent opportunity for group dramatization. It is the only sura dedicated entirely to a single narrative, and Joseph is the only one of the prophets whose story the Qur'an tells without interruption.

✳   Surat ar-Rahman, The Merciful

ANTHONY H. JOHNS

From the litany of divine blessings in this expansive paean one gets a vivid sense of the earliest Muslim teaching about the creator and sustainer of all, about this world as a theater of God's revelation, and about the ultimate consequences of faith and unbelief. Intensity builds with the insistent refrain.

1   The Merciful

2   He taught the Qur'an.

3   He created the human being.

4   He taught him speech.

5   Sun and Moon follow their courses.

6   Creeping plants and trees both bow before Him.

7   He has raised up the heavens and set the Scale of Justice

8   [so firmly] that you cannot play it false.

9   Apply this scale with justice;
    you must not give short measure by this scale.

10 The earth God has set out for His creatures;

11 in it are fruits of every kind

12 and date palms packed with blossom,
    unwinnowed grain and fragrant herbs

13 —which then of your Lord's blessings can you deny?

14 He fashioned the human being like earthen ware from potter's clay;

15 He fashioned the jinn from fire with smokeless flame

16 —which then of your Lord's blessings can you deny?

17 He is Lord of the furthest points of the sun's rising
        and its setting

18 —which then of your Lord's blessings can you deny?

19 He has let the two great waters flow to a point of meeting,

20 yet between them rests a barrier they cannot breach

21 —which then of your Lord's blessings can you deny?

22 From them come forth pearls and coral

23 —which then of your Lord's blessings can you deny?

24 His are the ships on the sea with sails aloft like mountains

25 —which then of your Lord's blessings can you deny?

26 Everything upon the earth is to perish,

27 yet the face of your Lord will remain
        full of might and honor

28 —which then of your Lord's blessings can you deny?

29 Everything in the heavens and on earth is supplicant to Him;
        every day He is attentive [to them]

30 —which then of your Lord's blessings can you deny?

31 We have ample time to deal with you,
        you and your burdens

32 —which then of your Lord's blessings can you deny?

33 You, company of jinn and humankind,
    try, if you can, to enter the regions of heaven and earth,
    try to enter them!
    Enter them you shall not other than with the power

[We alone can give]

34   —which then of your Lord's blessings can you deny?

35   Smokeless flame and flameless smoke will be hurled against you;
      no help shall reach you

37   —which then of your Lord's blessings can you deny?

38   Then when the heaven is sundered and glows rose like tanned hide

39   —which then of your Lord's blessings can you deny?

40   on that day neither human creatures nor jinn need be questioned of
         their sins

41   —which then of your Lord's blessings can you deny?

42   Evildoers will be known by the marks they bear, then will they
         be seized by
      their feet and forelocks.

43   —which then of your Lord's blessings can you deny?

44   Here is the hell the evildoers denied.
      They circle between it and scalding water

45   —which then of your Lord's blessings can you deny?

46   But for one who fears his encounter before his Lord
      there are two gardens

47   —which then of your Lord's blessings can you deny?

48   in each of them boughs giving shade

49   —which then of your Lord's blessings can you deny?

50   in each of them two flowing springs

51   —which then of your Lord's blessings can you deny?

52   in each of them of every fruit two kinds

53   —which then of your Lord's blessings can you deny?

54   as they recline on couches, lined with
         thick textured silk,
      and the fruit of both gardens at hand hanging low

55   —which then of your Lord's blessings can you deny?

56   In them are maidens of modest gaze
      neither man nor jinn having yet touched them

57   —which then of your Lord's blessings can you deny?

58   their beauty like that of jacinth and coral

59   —which then of your Lord's blessings can you deny?

60   Can goodness receive aught but goodness?

61   —which then of your Lord's blessings can you deny?

62   And below them both are two other gardens

63   —which then of your Lord's blessings can you deny?

64   both of deep green

65   —which then of your Lord's blessings can you deny?

66   In each of them two springs abundantly flowing

67   —which then of your Lord's blessings can you deny?

68   In them are fruit, with date palms and pomegranates

69   —which then of your Lord's blessings can you deny?

70   In them are virtuous women beautiful of face

71   —which then of your Lord's blessings can you deny?

72   clear black their eyes, set apart in pavilions

73   —which then of your Lord's blessings can you deny?

74   no man nor jinn having yet touched them

75   —which then of your Lord's blessings can you deny?

76   reclining on green cushions and rich carpets

77   —which then of your Lord's blessings can you deny?

78   Blessed be the name of your Lord, full of grace and honor.

✳   Writing Sacred Text

A number of exquisite calligraphic styles developed during the early centuries of Islamic history, largely for the purpose of writing the sacred word. Kufic script, named after the Iraqi city of Kufa, was the first important style. Its chief distinguishing mark is bold, thick letters with flat bottoms that do not descend much below the horizontal line; Kufic's low profile lends itself to a horizontal format. Figure 2 displays the text of Qur'an 2:111–112. Noting that Christians and Jews assert that only they will be saved, the text picks up: "Say [to them]: Give proof if you are correct. On the contrary, anyone who surrenders wholly to God and does good will be rewarded in his Lord's presence, and no fear will beset them [and they will not grieve]." The small medallion in the middle of the page is a device used to indicate divisions in the text. Bold dots distinguish various otherwise similar consonants from each other. As later ilustrations will show, Kufic

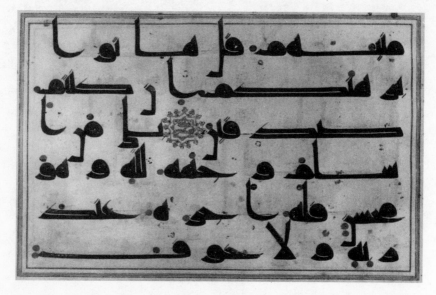

Figure 2.   Ninth-century Qur'an page, possibly from Iraq. St. Louis: St. Louis Art Museum, 32:1948.

script developed in a number of stylistic variations but retained its characteristic angularity.

More graceful cursive styles of script, whose elongated forms look best on pages of vertical format, developed alongside of Kufic. Figure 3 displays two of the many "rounded" scripts, showing the end of one sura (83:18–36) and the beginning of another (84:1–3). The Qur'anic text itself is written in *rayhani* script. The title panel below, in *tawqiʿ* script, reads, "Surat al-Inshiqaq [The Sundering], 25 verses, Meccan," and is followed by the phrase "In the name of God, the Compassionate, the Merciful," which occurs at the head of all but one of the 114 suras. The small roundels in the text mark the ends of verses; the medallion in the right margin indicates one of the standard liturgical divisions of the Qur'an; and the small markings above and below the lines of text indicate vowels, added out of a concern for maximum accuracy in reciting the sacred text.

✳ Surat Yusuf

JAMES W. MORRIS

This "literal" version of the twelfth sura of the Qur'an, "The Most Beautiful of Tales," is designed to convey a more accurate sense of the actual experience of

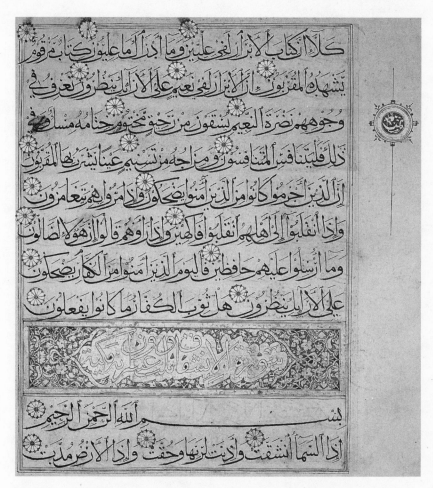

Figure 3.   Fourteenth-century Qur'an page from Mamluk Egypt. New York: Metropolitan Museum of Art, Pickering 69.149.

reading the Arabic text. Many of the most distinctive rhetorical, structural, and metaphysical features of the Qur'an become strikingly apparent when one studies this text in comparison with the long biblical narrative of Joseph and his brothers (Genesis 37–50).[1] One of the most difficult challenges in translating the Qur'an is to bring out the unifying themes, symbols, and vocabulary that are so evident to Arabic readers. To help convey this richness in English, the most important of what are essentially untranslatable spiritual terms have been presented throughout in small capitals and in "literal" form, to remind readers of their mysterious, multivalent nature. The text lends itself beautifully to dramatic recitation, with parts read by four or more participants. The four basic "levels" or "frames" of discourse are indicated thus: I = Narrator; II = Divine "We"; III = Various Actors; IV = Inner "Asides." Frame III can then be further divided among the various individual characters indicated.

IN THE NAME OF GOD,
THE ALL-LOVING, THE ALL-COMPASSIONATE

I.   [1] Alif Lam Ra: Those are the SIGNS of the BOOK making-clear.

II.   Indeed, We have sent It down, as a Qur'an [lit., recitation] in Arabic, so that you all might understand. We, We are recounting to you the most good and beautiful of tales through what We have inspired to you, this Qur'an—even though before It you were among the heedless ones.

I.   When Joseph said to his father:

III.   "O my dear father, I indeed, I have seen eleven planets and the sun and the moon: I saw them to me bowing down!"

I.   [5] He said:

III.   "O my dear son, do not recount your vision to your brothers, for they are devising a scheme against you. The Shaytan is indeed for INSAN* an enemy making-clear!"

III.   [Jacob to Joseph? or possibly "We"/Narrator (to whom)?]: And that is how your RABB† picks you out, and causes you to KNOW‡ through

---

* Throughout Q, the term *insan* refers to the spiritual reality of every human being, the manifestation of the divine "Breath/Spirit of God" fully realized in the prophets and "friends of God"; always contrasted with the created, part-animal mortal form of "clay," referred to as *bashar*.

† The term *rabb* is used over a thousand times in Q, usually as an emotionally charged form of address evoking our "personal," most powerfully real and intimate existential relationship to some aspect of the divine. This Arabic root evokes images of a parent lovingly and devotedly "raising" or "taking care of" and educating a dependent child.

‡ "Knowing" as divinely inspired spiritual awareness (*'ilm*); a central spiritual virtue in Q (used nearly nine hundred times). The different verb and noun forms of this term usually refer to direct (nonconceptual) human awareness of God and the spiritual world, of the inner nature of things and ultimate realities underlying the phenomenal and historical world; located in the Heart (*qalb, lubb*); term also intimately connected with the central symbolic families of images of Sight and Light.

FINDING THE INNER MEANING of what comes to be,* and fulfills His blessing upon you and upon the people of Jacob, as He fulfilled His blessing upon your two fathers before, Abraham and Isaac. Indeed your RABB is ALL-KNOWING, ALL-WISE.

I.   [Narrator?/"We"?]: So in Joseph and his brothers there was surely a SIGN for those who question and plead. When they said:

III.   "Now Joseph and his brother are more dearly beloved by our father than we, though we are a tight-knit bunch: Certainly our father is clearly gone astray!"

IV.   [Who? Shaytan? One of the brothers?]: "Kill Joseph! Or toss him out on some earth, [so that] your father's regard may be left for you all alone. And after that you all can be a group DOING WHAT IS RIGHT!"†

I.   [10] One of them, speaking, said:

III.   "Don't kill Joseph, but throw him in the hidden depths of the well, [so that] some caravan may pick him up, if you all are indeed doing [what you propose]."

I.   They said:

III.   "O our father, why do you not have FAITH‡ in us regarding Joseph, though surely we are sincerely meaning him well!? Send him with us tomorrow, [so that] he may run around and play. Certainly we are protecting him!"

I.   He said:

III.   "As for me, it does make me sad for you all to take him with you. And I am afraid that the wolf may eat him up while you all are heedless in regard to him!"

I.   They said:

---

* *Ta'wil al-ahadith*: The first term of this key phrase means "taking (things) back to the First," to their ultimate source, while the second refers to whatever "comes to be."

† The Arabic root *s-l-h* ordinarily means whatever is "right," but the qur'anic usage consistently joins and precedes references to the "right things" (*as-salihat*) with the essential precondition of "having FAITH."

‡ *Iman* refers to the condition of faith, inner peace and absolute assurance, implicit confidence and total trust, granted by God. Its most frequently mentioned "contents" or perceptions include the reality and presence of God, the angels, and all the divine "Books" and Messengers.

III.   "If the wolf were to eat him up, while we're such a tight-knit bunch, then we would be the ones suffering loss!"

II.   [15] Then when they took him with them and agreed together that they would put him in the hidden depths of the well, We inspired in him: "Surely you will inform them of this affair of theirs, while they are [still] unaware!"

I.   And they came to their father in the night [or: night-blind, dim-sighted], crying. They said:

III.   "O our father, we, we went off trying to get ahead of one another, and we left Joseph back with our possessions. So the wolf ate him up!"

IV.   "But you don't have FAITH in us, even if we were SPEAKING TRUTHFULLY!"*

I.   And they came with lying blood upon his shirt. He said:

III.   "No, on the contrary: your souls† have seduced you into some affair!"

IV.   "So SABR‡ is beautiful. And it is God [alone] Whose Help must be sought against what you all describe!"

I.   And a caravan came along. So they sent their water-man, and he let down his vessel. He said:

III.   "O what GOOD NEWS! This is a young man!"§

I.   And they kept him hidden, as trading goods.

II.   But God is ALL-KNOWING of what they are doing.

---

* *Sidq* (along with related epithets such as *as-Siddiq*, later applied to Joseph) means acknowledging the truth of what is real—and therefore discerning the divine presence and intentions behind appearances.

† Like the English expression "the self," the Arabic term *nafs* has many meanings in Q. This passage and verse 53 below became the locus classicus for later Islamic references to the psycho-spiritual aspect of the nafs as the "carnal soul" manifesting the reprehensible qualities of the human animal (*bashar*, rather than *insan*).

‡ *Sabr*, exemplified in Q above all by Jacob, refers to faithful perseverance in allegiance to the divine Truth in the midst of difficult circumstances.

§ Ordinarily, the term *ghulam* means simply a boy or youth; however, in Q it usually refers to the spiritual state of a young future prophet, visible as such only to those family members, like Jacob here, who are specially inspired by God (Abraham, Mary, Zacharia). Likewise, the water-drawer's reference to his caravan's serendipitous "good news" (*bushra*) contains a similar irony: in Q that same Arabic root is always used more specifically (several dozen times) to refer to the divine "good news" brought by the prophets and Messengers.

I.   [20] And they sold him for a cheap price, a number of dirhams—
for they were among those considering him of little value. And the one
from Egypt who bought him said to his wife:

III.   "Honor his dwelling place. Perhaps he may be useful to us and
we may adopt him as a son."

II.   And that is how We established a place for Joseph upon the earth,
and so that We might cause him to KNOW through FINDING THE INNER
MEANING of what comes to be.

I.   [Narrator?/"We"?]: And God is prevailing in his affair—but most
of the people do not know!

II.   And then when he reached his mature strength We brought him
WISE JUDGMENT* and [divine] KNOWING: That is how We reward the
MUHSINUN.†

I.   And the [woman] in whose house he was tried to entice him away
from himself. She locked the doors and said:

III.   "Come here!"

I.   He said:

III.   "May God protect [me]! He is my RABB, who has made good and
beautiful my dwelling place. He does not cause the wrongdoers to truly
flourish!"

I.   Now she was longing for him, and he was longing for her, were it
not that he saw the Proof of his RABB.

II.   That is how [it was], so that We might keep away from him evil
and indecency. He is indeed among OUR WHOLLY DEVOTED SERVANTS.‡

I.   [25] So they each tried to reach the door first and she ripped his
shirt in back, and at the door they met her master. She said:

---

* Divinely inspired wisdom (*hikma*), or the inspired right-judgment and spiritual authority (*hukm*) concerning particular circumstances that flows from such inspired Knowing, are mentioned as human spiritual virtues almost a hundred times
in Q. See part 3 below for a discussion of wisdom in Surat Luqman.

† *Muhsinun* are "those who do *ihsan*," one of the highest spiritual states, typi-
fied by the greatest prophets. Meaning literally "doing/making-what-is-good-and-
beautiful," its qur'anic usage stresses the deeper, divinely inspired awareness necessary to know concretely what is truly good-and-beautiful.

‡ The virtue of *ikhlas* refers to purity of intention, doing whatever one does entirely for God's sake. In Q it is often connected specifically with the spiritual state
of the prophets and Friends of God.

III.   "What is the recompense for someone who intended evil for your family, if not that he be imprisoned or [receive] a painful torment!?"*

I.   He [Joseph] said:

III.   "She tried to entice me away from myself!"

I.   And a witness from her people testified:

III.   "If his shirt is ripped in front, then she spoke truthfully and he is among the liars. But if his shirt is ripped in back, then she has lied and he is among THOSE SPEAKING TRUTHFULLY."

I.   So when he [her husband] saw his shirt was ripped in back, he said:

III.   "This is from your [fem. pl.] scheming, for your scheming is indeed tremendous!"

"O Joseph, turn away from this!"

[To his wife]: "And you, seek forgiveness for your offense: surely you were among the erring ones!"

I.   [30] And some women in the city said:

III.   "The wife of the DEAR/MIGHTY ONE† is trying to entice her young servant away from himself. He's made her fall madly in love. Indeed, we see she's clearly gone astray!"

I.   So when she heard about those women's sly devising she sent to them and prepared for them a cushion, and she brought a knife to every one of them and said [to Joseph]:

III.   "Come out before them!"

I.   And when the women saw him they glorified him and they all cut their hands [in astonishment], and they said:

III.   "God preserve [us]! This is no ordinary mortal‡—this can only be a majestic angel!"

* *'Adhab alim*: Used some seventy times in Q, this term means the sufferings or punishments of Gehenna and the "Fire"; the root referring to "prison" throughout this section (*s-j-n*) also refers to a fearful level of Gehenna in many key eschatological passages. Thus Zulaykha's threat here has powerful eschatological resonances that openly set the stage for a more symbolic, metaphysical "reading" of this drama and Joseph's predicament.

† *Al-'Aziz*: one of the more common divine Names in Q, appearing more than a hundred times. Joseph turns out to have this same semiregal title when he is later addressed by his brothers.

‡ *Bashar*, in contrast with the spiritual *insan*; cf. verse 5, and above, notes on pages 8 and 10.

I.   She said:

III.   "So there for you all is the one because of whom you were reproaching me! I did try to entice him away from himself, only he resisted."

IV.   [To herself?] "But if he doesn't do what I order him to, he will most certainly be imprisoned, and then he will surely be among the lowly ones!"

I.   He said:

III.   "My RABB! Prison is more lovable to me than what they [masc. pl.] are calling me to—and if You do not turn their [fem. pl.] scheming away from me I will give in to them [fem. pl.] and become one of the ignorant and foolish ones!"

I.   So his RABB did respond to him and turned their scheming away from him. Surely He is the ALWAYS LISTENING, the ALL-KNOWING. [35] Next, it appeared [right] to them [masc. pl.], after they had seen the SIGNS, to imprison him until a certain time.

And two young servants entered the prison with him. One of the two said:

III.   "I am seeing myself squeezing out wine."

I.   And the other one said:

III.   "I am seeing myself carrying above my head a loaf of bread from which the birds are eating."

[Both of them]: "Inform us both about the INNER MEANING of it. For we see you among the MUHSINUN."

I.   He said:

III.   "There does not come to you two any nourishment that is bestowed as your SUSTENANCE,* but that I have already told both of you the INNER MEANING of it, before it comes to you both. That, for you both, is among what my RABB has caused me to KNOW. I have

---

* *Rizq* (sustenance) almost always refers to the universal divine activities of creating and bestowing all the forms of God's "grace" and "bounty," including much more than food and extending ultimately to the very existence of all creatures and forms of manifestation.

indeed forsaken the MILLA* of a group who do not have FAITH in God
and who reject† THE OTHERWORLD!

"And I have followed the MILLA of my fathers, Abraham and Isaac
and Jacob: it was not for us to associate any thing with God. That was
through God's favor for us and for [all] the people—and yet most of
the people are not giving thanks!

"O two companions [or 'masters'] of the Prison: Are disparate/
separate lords [pl. of *rabb*] better—or God THE ONE, THE
OVERPOWERING?!"

I. [40] ["We"? Narrator? Muhammad?]:‡ "What you all are
worshipping/serving besides Him are nothing but names that you
all have named, you and your fathers! God has not sent down for
them any authority. Certainly the DECISIVE JUDGMENT is only for
God! He commanded that you all not worship/serve any but Him
alone: That is THE UPRIGHT RELIGION§—and yet most of the people
do not know!"

III.   [Joseph]: "O two companions of the Prison: As for one of
you, he is pouring wine for his lord to drink. And as for the other
one, he is crucified, so that the birds are eating from his head.‖ The
matter has [already] been decreed which you are seeking to have
me explain."

---

* The term *milla* is usually used in Q specifically in connection with the particular monotheistic religious "way" or path of Abraham (or his descendants).

† The root *k-f-r*, here meaning to reject, cover over, or be ungrateful for, often
denotes the contrary of faith and mindfulness, as well as of gratitude or thankful-
ness to God.

‡ The "addressees" here are in the indefinite plural rather than the explicitly dual
form used repeatedly in the preceding verses, making it unclear who is speaking to
whom or in what situation and time frame.

§ *Ad-din al-qayyim* (also in 9:36, 30:30, and 30:43) affirms the unchanging unity
of "religion" (*ad-din*) as the proper relation between God and the human soul, the
spiritual state of true "worship-and-divine-service" (*ʿibada*, on which see text by
Madjid in part 2) exemplified by the prophets and Friends of God.

‖ The image of "pouring wine" for one's Lord evokes the eschatological symbolism of "banquets" (fountains, cupbearers, etc.) in the heavenly Garden and the
related symbolism of the divine "Court" that is continued in the next few verses.
Similarly, symbolism involving birds often suggests the spiritual states of souls or
other spiritual beings.

I.   And he said to the one of the two who he suspected was being saved:*

III.   "Mention/remember me in the presence of your lord [*rabb*]!"

I.   Then the Shaytan made him forget mentioning/remembering his RABB, so he lingered in the Prison several years. And THE KING[+] said:

III.   "Surely I am seeing seven fat cows that seven thin ones are eating, and seven green ears [of grain], and other dry ones. O you dignitaries,[‡] explain to me about my vision, if you are [capable of] interpreting the vision!"

I.   They said:

III.   "Mixed-up dreams! And we are not, with regard to FINDING THE INNER MEANING of dreams, among those who know."

I.   [45] And he said, the one of the two who was saved and [only now] remembered after some time:

III.   "I [intend to] inform you of its INNER MEANING, so send me out." [Then at the Prison he said]:

"Joseph, O you TRUTHFULLY SPEAKING ONE [*as-siddiq*]: Explain to us regarding seven fat cows that seven thin ones are eating, and seven green ears and other dry ones, so that I might return to the people, so that perhaps they might know!"

I.   He said:

III.   "You all plant for seven years, tirelessly. But of what you all have harvested, leave it on the ear except for a very little, from which you eat. Then there come after that seven hard ones eating up what you all have prepared for them, except for a very little from what you all are preserv-

---

   * As in God's "saving" the prophets and the righteous in an explicitly spiritual or eschatological sense. Likewise, Joseph's parting words here clearly evoke the imagery of the eschatological intercession (*shafa'a*) of the prophets in the divine "Court" alluded to in Q and described in greater detail in many well-known hadith.

   + "The King" or "Possessor" (*al-malik*) of all creation, is one of the most frequent of the divine Names. Curiously, this sura never mentions "Pharaoh" (*fir'awn*), the usually pejorative title for the Egyptian ruler in the rest of the stories of Q.

   ‡ *Al-mala*: A term also used in Q (and the hadith) to refer to the highest angels or archangels around the divine "Throne."

ing. Then there comes after that a year in which the people are abundantly helped out, and in it they are pressing [much oil]."

I. [50] And the KING said:

III. "Bring him to me!"

I. Then when the messenger came to him, he said:

III. "Return to your lord and ask him: 'What was the problem with
those women who cut their hands?'"

IV. [To himself?] "Certainly my RABB is WELL KNOWING about their
schemes!"

I. He [the King] said [to those women]:

III. "What was going on with you all when you tried to entice Joseph
away from himself?!"

I. They said:

III. "God forbid—we didn't know any wrong of him!"

I. The wife of the DEAR/MIGHTY ONE said:

III. "Now the Truth has become clear: I did try to entice him away
from himself, and surely he is among the TRUTHFULLY SPEAKING ONES."

IV. [Joseph—apparently to himself]: "That is so that he* might
know that I did not betray him regarding the UNSEEN, and that God
does not guide the scheming of those who betray. And I am not absolving
my NAFS:† Surely the NAFS is commanding [us] to do wrong, except to
the extent that my RABB has MERCY. Indeed my RABB is MOST FORGIVING,
MOST LOVING AND MERCIFUL!"

I. And the KING said:

III. "Bring him to Me, so that I may have him WHOLLY DEVOTED to
Myself!"

I. Then once He had spoken with him, He said:

III. "Today you are in Our presence, well settled and well trusted!"‡

---

* Or "He": may refer to Zulaykha's husband, the King, or perhaps to God. In favor of the latter possibility is the fact that in Q the recurrent expression for "the
unseen (spiritual) world" (*al-ghayb*) has to do with realities far broader (and quite
different from) mere worldly "secrecy" and discretion.

† See note on page 10 (to verse 18) above.

‡ This phrase evokes eschatological images of people in the presence of the divine judge. Moreover, both the epithets bestowed on Joseph here (*amin, makin*) are
often applied to Muhammad as divine Messenger.

I. [55] He [Joseph] said:

III. "Place me over the TREASURIES OF THE EARTH. Indeed I am WELL PROTECTING, WELL KNOWING!"*

II. And that is how We established Joseph on the earth, settling down upon it wherever he wishes. We bestow Our LOVING MERCY on whomever We wish. And We do not neglect the reward of the MUHSINUN!

I. [Narrator?/"We"?]: And surely the reward of THE OTHERWORLD is best, for those who had FAITH and were MINDFUL [of God]!†

I. And Joseph's brothers came. Then they entered before him and he knew them, while they were DENYING‡ him. And when he had provided them with their supplies he said:

III. "Bring me from your father a [certain] brother of yours. Don't you all see that I fill up the measure and I am the best of those who give hospitality?!" [60] "But if you don't bring him to me, then there is no measure for you with me—and you may not come near me!"

I. They said:

III. "We will try to entice his father from [holding on to] him: Certainly we are doing [that]!"

I. And he said to his young servants:

III. "Put their trading goods back in their saddlepacks, so that they may recognize them when they have gone back to their family—that perhaps they may return."

I. So when they returned to their father they said:

III. "O our father, the measure [of grain requested] was forbidden to us. So send our brother with us that we may be given the measure. Surely we are protecting him!"

---

* The terms *hafiz* and *'alim*, both of which appear often as divine Names, here suggest Joseph's "investiture" with full prophetic attributes. Likewise, the word "treasuries" always refers elsewhere in Q to God's Treasuries (e.g., at 63:7).

† "Those who do *taqwa*" (mindfulness, which could be rendered as "active God-awareness"): it is the consciousness of God's Presence, an inner mindfulness of the divine at every instant, combined with an eager, attentive orientation to do what that spiritual awareness demands.

‡ The term translated here as "denying" (*munkir*) connotes a person pretending not to know something that he or she really does know. The Arabic roots of the word convey a broader reference to spiritual "blindness"; here, too, it points by way of contrast to Joseph's inspired recognition of theophany (the divine "Signs").

I.   He said:

III.   "Can I have faith in you regarding him—except as I had faith in you regarding his brother before!?"

IV.   [To himself?] "For God is BEST IN PROTECTING, and He is the MOST LOVING OF THOSE SHOWING LOVING MERCY!"

I.   [65] But when they opened their possessions they found their trading goods returned to them. They said:

III.   "O our father, what [more] do we desire? These are our own trading goods returned to us! And we will provide for our family and protect our brother and increase [our provisions] by the measure of a camel load. That is an easy measure!"

I.   He said:

III.   "I will never send him with you all until you give me a pledge from God that you will most surely bring him back to me, unless you are surrounded!"

I.   So when they had given him their pledge he said:

III.   "God is TRUSTEE for what we are saying!"

I.   And he said:

III.   "O my sons, don't go in through a single gate, but enter through separate gates! And I cannot help you, in place of God, with regard to any thing. The DECISIVE JUDGMENT is only for God: in Him have I trusted, and on Him should rely all those who trust!"*

I.   And when they entered in the way their father had commanded them, that was not of any help to them, in place of God, with regard to any thing—except as a need in Jacob's NAFS, which he satisfied. And surely he is a possessor of [divine] KNOWING through what We have made him KNOW—and yet most of the people do not know! And when they entered before Joseph, he made his brother his [special] guest. He said:

III.   "Indeed, I myself am your own brother! So do not be upset about what they have been doing."

---

* *Tawakkul*: the spiritual station of total trust and confidence in God, the inner attitude of sincerely "handing things over" totally to Him, as a departing traveler or pilgrim would entrust his family and affairs to a servant or steward (*wakil*, as in the previous verse).

I. [70] Then when he had provided them with their supplies, he put the drinking cup in his brother's saddlebag. Next a herald called out:

III. "O you of the caravan, indeed you all are surely thieves!"

I. They said, as they came [back] close to them:

III. "What is it you are missing!?"

I. They said:

III. "We are missing the King's chalice!

[Joseph]: "For whoever brings it there is a camel's load [in reward], and I am responsible for it."

I. They said:

III. "By God, you all surely know we didn't come to do harm in the earth and we haven't been thieves!"

I. They said:

III. "Then what are the amends for it, if you all have been lying?"

I. [75] They said:

III. "The amends for it are the person in whose saddlebag it is found—let him be the compensation for it: that is how we repay the wrongdoers!"

I. So he began with their sacks before his brother's sack, and then he brought it out of his brother's sack.

II. That is how We contrived for Joseph: he would not have taken his brother according to the religion of the King, except that God wishes [it]. We raise up by degrees whomever We wish, and above every possessor of knowledge is ONE ALL-KNOWING!!*

I. They said:

III. "If he is stealing, then a brother of his had stolen before!"

I. But Joseph kept it secret within himself and did not reveal it to them. He said [to himself]:

IV. "You yourselves are in a far worse situation, and God is MORE KNOWING about what you describe!"

I. They said:

---

* This famous last phrase may refer either only to God (as translated here), or to the existence of much wider earthly and/or spiritual hierarchies of religious or other knowledge. In Q these frequently mentioned "degrees" or "ranks" (*darajat*) usually refer specifically to spiritual qualities, functions, or rewards in the otherworld.

III.   "O DEAR/MIGHTY ONE, he has a father, an extremely old man,*
so take one of us instead of him. Certainly we see you are among the
MUHSINUN!"

I.   He said:

III.   "God forbid that we should take anyone except the person with
whom we found our things! Otherwise we would surely be wrongdoers!"

I.   [80] So then, when they had despaired of [persuading] him, they
went away to talk in secret. The oldest of them said:

III.   "Don't you all know that your father took a pledge from you
with God, and before how you were so remiss with regard to Joseph?!
So I will never leave [this] earth until my father gives me permission
or God judges for me, for He is the BEST OF THOSE WHO JUDGE! You
all return to your father and say: 'O our father, your son has certainly
stolen. And we have only given witness to what we have come to know:
we were not protecting the UNSEEN!' And ask the village where we were
and the caravan in which we came back: indeed, we are surely SPEAKING
TRUTHFULLY!"

I.   He [Jacob] said:

III.   "No, on the contrary: your carnal souls [pl. of *nafs*] have seduced
you into some affair! So SABR is beautiful. Perhaps God may bring them
to me all together. For He is THE ALL-KNOWING, THE ALL-WISE."

I.   And he turned away from them and said:

IV.   "O my grief for Joseph!"

I.   And his eyes had become white [i.e., blind] from sorrow, for he was
restraining himself.

[85] They said:

III.   "By God, you won't stop remembering Joseph until you waste
away, or join those who pass away!"

I.   He said [to himself?]:

IV.   "I only complain to God of my grief and my sorrow. And I KNOW
from God what you all do not know."

III.   "O my sons, go and try to find out about Joseph and his brother.

* Or "a great shaykh."

And do not despair of THE SPIRIT OF GOD! No one despairs of THE SPIRIT OF GOD, but the group who reject [God]."

I.   So when they entered before him they said:

III.   "O DEAR/MIGHTY ONE, we and our family have been beset by hardship, and we have brought unworthy goods! So fill up the measure for us, and be charitable with us: surely God rewards those who are charitable!"

I.   He said:

III.   "Did you all know what you did with Joseph and his brother, when you were foolish and ignorant?"

I.   [90] They said:

III.   "Is it really you who are Joseph?!"

I.   He said:

III.   "I am Joseph, and this is my brother. God has been generous with us."

I.   [Narrator?/"We"?/Joseph to himself?]: "For whoever is MINDFUL [of God] and shows SABR, surely God does not neglect the reward of the MUHSINUN."

They said:

III.   "By God, God has preferred you over us, though we were certainly erring ones."

I.   He said:

III.   "No blame for you today! God forgives you—and He is the MOST LOVING OF THOSE SHOWING LOVING MERCY. Go all of you, with this shirt of mine, then place it on my father's face, that he may come SEEING.* And come to me with your family, all together!"

I.   And when the caravan started out, their father said:

III.   "Surely I do feel the smell† of Joseph—even if you think I'm losing my mind!"

---

* *Basir* is used more than a hundred times, with related forms, in Q to refer to spiritual "vision," insight, and discernment, often described as a divinely given grace or inspiration.

† *Rih* (smell) is closely related to the divine "Spirit" or "Breath" (*ruh Allah*) of verse 87 and elsewhere.

I.   [95] They said:

III.   "By God, certainly you are in your old error!"

I.   Then when the bearer of good news arrived, he placed it [the shirt] on his face, so that he was returned to BEING-SEEING. He said:

III.   "Didn't I tell you that I KNOW from God what you all do not know?"

I.   They said:

III.   "O our father, ask for our sins to be forgiven for us—indeed we were erring ones!"

I.   He said:

III.   "I will ask my RABB to forgive you. Certainly He is THE MOST FORGIVING, THE MOST MERCIFUL!"

I.   Then when they entered before Joseph, he received both his parents as his [special] guests, and he said:

III.   "Enter Egypt, if God wishes, in security!"

I.   [100] And he raised up both his parents upon the Throne, and they [the brothers] fell down bowing before him. And he said:

III.   "O my dear father, this is the INNER MEANING of my vision from before! My RABB did make it real and true. And He was good to me when He pulled me out of the Prison and He brought you all in from the desert, after the Shaytan had incited conflict between me and my brothers. Surely my RABB is MOST GRACIOUS to whatever He wills! Indeed, He is THE ALL-KNOWING, THE ALL-WISE! O my RABB, You have brought to me some [worldly] dominion and You have caused me to KNOW through FINDING THE INNER MEANING of what comes to be! O CREATOR of the heavens and the earth! You are my PROTECTING FRIEND [*Wali*] in this world and the otherworld. Come to receive me surrendered [to You],* and include me with THOSE WHO DO WHAT IS RIGHT!"

II.   That was from the disclosures of the UNSEEN We inspire in you. You were not present with them when they agreed together about their affair, while they were slyly devising. And most of the people, even though you greatly desire [it], do not have FAITH.

---

* "Surrendered," from *tawaffa*, refers to the divine or angelic "reception" of each soul at the moment of death.

Nor do you ask of them any reward for it. It is only a REMINDER to the worlds!

[105] And how many a SIGN there is in the heavens and the earth which they pass on by, turning away! And most of them have no FAITH in God, except while they are associating [other appearances with the One]. So do they feel safe from their being overwhelmed by a dark shroud of punishment from God, or from the HOUR suddenly overcoming them while they are not even aware?!

Say: "This is my Path: I am calling/praying to God with CLEAR INSIGHT,* myself and whoever followed me. And Praise be to God! I am not among those who associate [others with the One]."

And We did not send [any as Messenger] before you except for some men whom We inspire among the people of the towns. Have they not traveled through the earth, that they might observe how the ultimate end of those before them has been?! Indeed the Abode of the otherworld is best, for THOSE WHO ARE MINDFUL! So then do you all still not understand?! [110] Until, when the Messengers despaired and supposed that they had been rejected, there came to them Our TRIUMPHANT SUPPORT and whoever We wish was saved. Nor can Our Affliction be kept from those who do harm.

I.   Surely in the tales about them there was a deep lesson for THOSE WHO HAVE HEARTS!† It was not a made-up story, but a confirmation of what was [already] before him, and a proper distinguishing of every thing, and RIGHT GUIDANCE and LOVING MERCY to a people who have FAITH.

---

* *'Ala basira* (clear insight) refers to the divine guidance of prophets and Friends of God; it recalls Jacob's restored "vision" or spiritual insight above (*basir*, at v. 96; see first note on page 21).

† The phrase "those who have hearts" (*ulu 1-albab*) occurs sixteen times in Q, always in reference to those who are ready to realize the spiritual virtues, who alone are truly capable of recognizing the divine "Signs" and thereby "remembering" and returning to God.

✳   ## Hadith: Prophetic and Sacred

JOHN RENARD

Since later texts will include scores of thematically apposite examples from the massive treasure trove of hadith, I include only a few samples of the genre; and I locate them here rather than later in part 1 because of the prominent role of hadith in exegetical commentary.

MUHAMMAD'S SAYINGS

Sayings of Muhammad cover a vast gamut of topics, from the most mundane to the most ethereal. In the thousands of sayings attributed to the Prophet, Muslims have a nearly inexhaustible source of examples and guidance. Some hadiths function as miniature commentaries on individual texts of the Qur'an. In the following example I include the complete chain of transmitters (the *isnad*) for illustrative purposes; other examples will omit the isnad. The final link in the chain of transmitters here is Abu Dharr (d. 653), a man known for his lofty piety:

> Muhammad ibn Yusuf stated that Sufyan had narrated, from al-A'mash, from Ibrahim at-Tamimi, from his father, from Abu Dharr, may God be pleased with him, who said: The Prophet, may God bless him and give him peace, said to Abu Dharr: "When the sun sets, do you know where it goes?" I [Abu Dharr] said, "God and his messenger know better." He [Muhammad] said: "It goes until it prostrates itself beneath the Throne [of God], then it seeks permission [to rise], and it is given leave [to do so]. But [one day] when it is about to offer prostration, [the gesture] will not be accepted from it. It will seek leave [to go forward] but permission will not be granted. Instead it will be told: Return whence you came, so that it will rise in its setting place (i.e., the west). And that is [the meaning of] the saying of the Most High: And the sun follows a course set for it—that is the determination of the Mighty, the Knowing One" (36:38).[2]

Many hadith speak of the spiritual and moral responsibilities of Muslims toward one another. Abu Hurayra (d. 678) was one of Muhammad's foremost companions and transmitters of hadith. He reported these two sayings:

> The Messenger of God, may God bless him and give him peace, said: Let one who believes in God and the Last Day be hospitable to his guest; let one who believes in God and the Last Day be considerate of his neighbor; and let one who believes in God and the Last Day speak positively or hold his tongue.[3]

And again, a saying beautiful and moving in its simplicity:

The Messenger of God, may God bless him and give him peace, said: A man used to loan money to people, and would say to his employee, "When you come to a person on hard times, go easy on him; perhaps God will go easy on us." [Muhammad] said [further]: And when he came to meet God, God went easy on him.[4]

SACRED SAYINGS

Tradition ascribes some sayings not to Muhammad but directly to God. Some allude to God's transcendent unity by playing on Arabic words. For example, to understand the saying "I am Ahmad without the *m*," one has to know that Ahmad is an alternate title of Muhammad and that the word *ahad* means "one" in Arabic. Similarly, the saying "I am 'Arab without the *'ayn*" means that if one removes the initial consonant (*'ayn*) and its vowel sound (a) from the word *'arab*, what remains is *rab*[*b*] or Lord.

Other sayings suggest aspects of God's relationship to human beings, conveying the essence of some interaction between God and the servant. "Were it not for you [Muhammad], I would not have created the heavens," for example, hints at Muhammad's critical importance in God's own motives for action. Others are more inclusive: "I and my faithful servant are united in in undiluted goodness: even as I am removing his soul from within him, he praises me"; and "For my devout servants I have in store what no eye has seen, no ear has heard, and what has not occurred to any human heart"; and "Those who love each other in me, and who keep each other's company in me, and who visit each other in me, and who share unstintingly with each other—these are entitled to my love." In a slightly longer saying, God speaks to the whole community:

> A thousand years before he created the universe, God inscribed a text on his Throne and declared: Observe, O Community of Muhammad, that my mercy comes before my anger. Before you ask, I bestow; before you seek forgiveness, I forgive you. I will usher into Paradise each of you who comes before me and says, "There is no god but God and Muhammad is the Messenger of God."

Finally, a charming hadith combines key aspects of these first two kinds of sacred sayings. God says he has divided the first sura, al-Fatiha, between himself and his servant, recalling sacred hadith that refer to God's own qualities as well as those that describe the human servant's relationship to God. According to that hadith, the first three verses of the sura belong to God:

> Praise belongs to God, Lord of all beings,

The Merciful, the Compassionate,
Ruler of the Judgment Day.

The fourth, or middle verse—"Only You do we serve; only from You do we seek aid"—belongs to both because of its reference to asking and granting. And the last three verses belong to the servant:

Guide us along the straight path
The path of those whom you have blessed
Not those against whom You have sent Your wrath, nor those who are
　astray.[5]

✳ Sacred Text and Architecture

Architectural inscriptions of both Qur'an and hadith texts have long revealed how Muslims interpret both their religious structures and their sacred texts. Facades and domes are the most visible features of major religious buildings. Sometimes even lengthy suras of the Qur'an appear in their entirety on facades, as in figure 4. The Taj Mahal's extensive qur'anic inscriptions in monumental *thuluth* script are of inlaid black stone; here on the east arch is the end (verses 67–83) of Sura 36 (Ya Sin), whose full text begins on the south arch and continues around the west and north sides. Around the doorway within the *iwan* is the full text of Sura 98, al-Bayyina (The Clarification), on the eschatological theme of final accountability, all in keeping with a funerary monument.

Shorter complete texts also occasionally appear on the exteriors of domes, as in figure 5. Three Qur'an texts in thuluth script encircle the upper register of the drum of the dome of the Safavid mosque of Shaykh Lutfullah. In three pairs of contrasting natural phenomena (sun/moon, day/night, heaven/earth), Sura 91, al-Shams (The Sun), calls the created world to witness to God's power, then refers to the individual soul's capacity for moral discernment. Then Sura 76, ad-Dahr (Time), explores the theme of contrast between people who opt for good and those who prefer evil. Finally, Sura 108, al-Kawthar (Abundance), the shortest sura of all, reminds believers to acknowledge God's beneficence with prayer. Larger Kufic inscriptions on the drum give repeating texts of the kind often found on Timurid and Safavid monuments: "Noble one, Merciful one, Compassionate one"; and "God is supreme, to God belongs sovereignty, praise God, God, Muhammad and 'Ali."

Sometimes, as in figure 1, a text on the dome is chosen because of its explicit reference to mosques and their religious significance. Monumental thuluth script, with some upright Arabic letters over ten feet in height, around the drum

Figure 4.   Taj Mahal, Agra, India (1632–1654, Mughal). The four *pishtaq* facades and two-tiered arcades of the Taj Mahal adapt Iranian forms (see fig. 31), but achieve an entirely different effect by using white marble as basic building material and inlaid semiprecious stones for decoration.

of the dome of the Sultan's mosque (seen from half a mile away through a long lens) in Shah Alam, Malaysia, reads: "They will maintain God's mosques who believe in God and in the last day, and observe the ritual prayer, and give alms, and fear only God. It is these who are among the guided. Do you regard offering drink to pilgrims or the upkeep of the Mosque of the Sanctuary [in Mecca] as on a par with [the devotion of] those who believe in God and the last day and [who] strive in the way of God? They are not on a par in God's opinion; and God does not guide people who countenance injustice" (9:18–19).

Inside the mosque as well, the dome over the niche that marks the direction toward Mecca (mihrab) often receives special inscriptions (fig. 6). In glittering mosaic, Qur'an texts in foliated Kufic script on the interior of the dome of the Great Mosque of Cordova emphasize God's sovereignty and power to forgive, as befits a spectacular dome: "On no soul does God place a burden greater than it can bear. Each receives every good earned, and likewise every evil earned. Our Lord, do not condemn us if we should become heedless or fall into error. . . . Blot out our sins and forgive us; have mercy on us for you are our Protector; aid us against those who deny the faith" (2:286). Built on the site of a former Christian church in the midst of a society long Christian, the mosque also features

Figure 5.   Mosque of Shaykh Lutfullah, Isfahan, Iran (1603–1619). Thanks to Jonathan Bloom for identifying the texts. (Further on Safavid architecture, see figs. 36, 53 below; and SD fig. 23.)

texts that distinguish Islamic from Christian notions of deity: "It is not fitting that God should beget a son. Glory to Him. When He decides on an affair He merely says 'Be' and it is" (19:35). And "To Him belong the origins of heaven and earth; how can he have a son when he has no wife? He created everything and knows all things completely. That is God your Lord. There is no god but He, the Creator of all; so worship Him who is in charge of all matters" (6:101–102). Finally, the dome recalls the goal of human existence and reminds believers of the appropriate demeanor: "Those who hold up God's Throne and who surround it sing 'Glory and Praise' to their Lord, believe in Him and ask forgiveness for believers: Our Lord, your control extends over all things in mercy and knowledge. Therefore forgive those who repent and follow your way and save them from the Fire's torments; give them, Lord, entry to the Garden . . . " (40:7–9).

VARIETIES OF QUR'AN INTERPRETATION

Qur'an interpretation occurs in many contexts. Sayings of Muhammad sometimes function as occasions for a reflection on the meaning of a particular brief text, as in the hadith cited above. Sermons, too, provide a natural setting for the

Figure 6.   Great Mosque of Cordova, Spain (ca. 961), *qibla* dome mosaics.

elucidation of a revealed text. But Muslim exegetes have also produced countless volumes dedicated to the interpretation of their scripture and to the principles of exegesis. Here are, first, three brief examples of *tafsir* by different exegetes on the Qur'an's first sura, al-Fatiha (The Opening); then a treatise by Ibn
Taymiya on the principles of tafsir; and finally, a study by Abu Hamid al-Ghazali on the more rarefied art of esoteric interpretation called *ta'wil*. Frequent citation of hadith gives ample evidence of the foundational importance of Muhammad's sayings in scriptural interpretation.

✳ Three Commentaries on Surat al-Fatiha, The Opening

ANDREW RIPPIN

The commentary on the Qur'an by Muqatil ibn Sulayman is probably the earliest existing complete example of this exegetical genre. Muqatil provides an edifying narrative to accompany the reading of the text, with little interest in the
Qur'an's grammar and textual details. Muqatil was born in Balkh, lived in Marv,
Baghdad, and Basra, and died at an old age in the year 767.[6]

"In the name of God, the Merciful, the Compassionate."
   "Praise belongs to God": that is, thanks to God.

"Lord of all beings": that is, the jinn and mankind; this is similar to God's saying in 25:1: "So that he may be a warner to all beings."

"The Merciful, the Compassionate": two names of compassion, one of which is more compassionate than the other. "The Merciful" relates to the sense of being merciful, while "the Compassionate" means to be inclined toward the giving of mercy.

"Ruler of the Judgment Day": that is, the day of reckoning, just as God said in 37:53: "Are we the ones to be judged?" that is, those subject to the reckoning. Concerning this it is said that the kings of the world will rule the earth and He will inform them that no one other than Him will rule over the day of resurrection. That is contained in His saying in 82:19: "That day the command belongs to God."

The saying of God: "Only You do we serve": that is, we declare your unity, just as in God's saying in 66:5: "Those who worship," that is, those who declare the unity of God.

"Only from You do we seek aid": in Your worship.

"Guide us [*ihdina*] along the straight path": that is, the religion of Islam because there is no guidance in any religion other than Islam. According to the variant reading of Ibn Masʿud the text reads *arshidna*, "guide us."

"The path of those whom You have blessed": that is, We have indicated the way of those whom We have blessed, that is, the proofs of those whom God has blessed with prophethood, just as in God's saying in 19:58: "Those were from among the prophets whom God blessed," among whom was Abraham.

"Not those against whom You have sent Your wrath": that is, a religion other than the Jewish one, against which God was wrathful. Monkeys and pigs were made from them.

"Nor those who are astray": God is saying: "And not the religion of the polytheists," that is, the Christians.

The narrator said: ʿUbayd Allah informed me that his father told him on the authority of Hudhayl from Muqatil from Murtadd from Abu Hurayra that the Messenger of God, may the prayers and peace of God be upon him, said: "God, Most Exalted and Most High, said: 'This sura arose between Me and My servant in two halves.' When the servant said:

'Praise belongs to God, Lord of all beings,' God said: 'My servant thanks Me.' When he said: 'The Compassionate, the Merciful,' God said: 'My servant praises Me.' When he said: 'Ruler of the Judgment day,' God said: 'I will praise My servant and the rest of the sura shall be for him.' So when he said: 'Only from You do we seek aid,' God said: 'This is for My servant who seeks aid only from Me.' So when he said: 'Guide us on the straight path,' God said: 'This is for My servant.' And when he said: 'The path of those whom You have blessed,' God said: 'This is for My servant. "And not those who are astray": this is for My servant alone.'"

The narrator said: 'Ubayd Allah told me that his father told him that Hudhayl told him on the authority of Muqatil who said: "Whenever one of you is reading this sura and reaches its conclusion saying: 'And not those who are astray,' he should say 'Amen'. Indeed, the angels are believers and if the saying of 'Amen' by the angels coincides with the saying of it by people, the previously committed sins of the people will be forgiven."

The narrator said: 'Ubayd Allah told me that his father told him that Hudhayl told him on the authority of Waqi' from Mansur from Mujahid who said that when Sura 1 was revealed, the Devil wailed.

The narrator said: 'Ubayd Allah said that his father told him on the authority of Abu Salih from Waqi' from Sufyan ath-Thawri from as-Suddi from 'Abd Khayr from 'Ali, may God be pleased with him, concerning the words of God in 15:87, "The seven *mathani*," that he said that they are the seven verses of Sura 1.

The following text of commentary is frequently ascribed to Ibn 'Abbas, although in its present form it probably originated in the ninth or tenth century. Ibn 'Abbas (d. ca. 687) is the source of much Qur'an commentary and is considered one of the best informed of all early authorities, even though he was quite young when Muhammad died. The work is characterized by little narrative embellishment, but considerable attention to difference of opinion as expressed via the connecting phrase "it is also said."[7]

This is a Medinan sura, although some say it is Meccan.
"In the name of God, the Merciful, the Compassionate."

With its chain of transmission from Ibn ʿAbbas concerning the saying of God most High, "Praise be to God": He is saying "Thanks to God." He it is who made His created beings, so they praise Him. It is also said [that it means]: "Thanks to God" for his abundant blessing on His servants whom He guides to faith. It is also said that it means thanks and testifies that unity and divinity belong to God, who has no offspring, partner, supporter, or helper.

"Lord of the worlds": Lord of all possessors of spirit moving on the face of the earth and of all the inhabitants of heaven. It is also said that it means: Master of the jinn and of humanity. It is also said that it means: Creator of the created beings for whom He provides the subsistence and whom He takes from one condition of faith to another.

"The Merciful": the One who feels mercy [*raqiq*], which is derived from *al-riqqa*, mercy, and that is kindness [*rahma*].

"The Compassionate": the One who is a true companion.

"Ruler of the day of religion": Judge on the day of religion [*din*], which is the day of reckoning and destiny on which He shall divide up His creatures. That is, the day on which people shall be repaid [*yudanu*] for their deeds. There is no judge other than Him.

"Only You do we serve": to You do we profess our belief in Your oneness and to You do we yield.

"Only from You do we seek aid": with You do we seek aid in our performance of Your worship and from You we receive trust to perform in Your obedience.

"Guide us along the straight path": direct us to the steadfast religion which pleases You, which is Islam. It is also said that this means: strengthen us in it. It is also said that it means it is the book of God such that He is saying: "Guide us in its categories of permitted and forbidden and in an explication of what is in the book."

"The path of those whom You have blessed": the religion of those to whom You have shown favor by means of religion. They are the followers of Moses [before the blessings of God changed against them (cf. 8:53)], when clouds put them in the shadow and manna and quail were sent down to them in the desert [cf. 2:57]. It is also said [that the people who have been favored are] the prophets.

"Not those against whom You have sent your wrath": other than the religion of the Jews against whom You have been wrathful and have abandoned and have not preserved their hearts in order for them to become [true?] Jews.

"Nor those who are astray": nor the religion of the Christians, who err away from Islam.

"Amen": thus, His community will come into being. It is also said that it means: So be it thus. It is also said that it means: O our Lord, do with us as we ask of You. God knows best.

Jalal ad-Din as-Suyuti (d.1505) is the likely author of the following commentary on Sura 1. It is part of *The Commentary of the Two Jalals* (*Tafsir al-Jalalayn*), so called because it was begun by Jalal ad-Din al-Mahalli (d. 1459) and completed by Suyuti. As-Suyuti was a prolific writer who collected material from a vast number of sources and presented it both concisely and in a variety of forms. There is little room in the tafsir for expression of differences of opinion or for elaborations of narratives. This work has been quite popular in the Muslim world because of its precise nature and grammatical focus.[8]

This is a Meccan sura with seven verses, if one counts the *basmala* ("In the name of God, the Merciful, the Compassionate") as a verse and counts the seventh verse as starting with "The path of those whom" until the end of the sura. If one does not consider the basmala a verse, then the seventh verse starts with "Not those against whom you have sent your wrath" to the end of the sura. One needs to understand the word "say" at the beginning of the sura because of the statements that precede "Only You do we serve." This is in keeping with the sura being a statement repeated by the worshippers.

"In the name of God, the Merciful, the Compassionate."

"Praise be to God": this is a predicative sentence, which intends thereby praising God such that the sentence affirms that the Most High is the possessor of all the praise from His creation. Or, it is the praise which He deserves because they should praise Him. Allah is the personal name of Him who is worthy of worship.

"Lord of the worlds": that is, ruler of all creation including humanity,

the jinn, the angels, the animals, and other creatures, all of whom may
be said to be endowed with intelligence. It is also said that it means those
intelligent members of humanity and those intelligent members of the
jinn and so forth. The plurality [of "worlds"] with the *ya'* and the *nun*
[i.e., the masculine sound plural ending of "worlds"] indicates the
supremacy of those who possess knowledge over all others. The word
'alamin, "worlds," is derived from *'alama*, meaning "mark, sign, or
characteristic" because the world provides a sign of its Creator.

"The Merciful, the Compassionate": that is, the possessor of mercy,
which entails intending good for His people.

"Ruler of the day of religion": that is, the day of requital, which is the
day of the resurrection. The day is singled out for mention because there
is no ruler in reality for anyone on that day other than God Most High,
as indicated by "To whom is the rulership of the day? To God!" (40:16).
Those who read *malik* [with an *alif* in its spelling] understand it to mean
the ruler of the entire affair on the day of resurrection; that is, He is
characterized in that way ceaselessly, in the same way that He is the
One who pardons sin. The occurrence of *malik* with *alif* is sound, for
it indicates a characteristic of knowledge.

"Only You do we serve; Only from You do we seek aid": that is, we
devote only to You acts of Islamic worship and the like. We request help
only from You in the acts of worship and the like.

"Guide us along the straight path": that is, lead us to the path, which
is grammatically substituted by the following phrase [in the accusative
case].

"The path of those whom You have blessed": with guidance. The
resumptive pronoun ["those whom"] is then substituted in the next
phrase by *ghayr* ["not," which is in the genitive case, being governed
by the preposition *'ala* of this phrase].

"Not those against whom You have sent your wrath": who are the
Jews.

"Nor": and other than [and thus equivalent to the preceding *ghayr*].

"Those who are astray": and they are the Christians. The subtlety of
the substitution is that it is an indication that those who are guided are
not Jews or Christians. And God knows best what is right.

✳   Ibn Taymiya
Treatise on the Principles of Tafsir

JANE DAMMEN MCAULIFFE

Taqi ad-Din ibn Taymiya, whose father and paternal grandfather were also
deeply learned in the religious sciences, was born in the northern Syrian city
of Harran in 1263. Fleeing the Mongol incursions, his family eventually moved
to Damascus, where Ibn Taymiya was educated, earned acclaim as a Hanbali
scholar-activist, and, in 1328, died imprisoned in the Citadel. He spent a total of
more than six years in prison, both in Mamluk Egypt and in Damascus, condemned by his adversaries for his relentless attacks on what he deemed to be
unacceptable innovations in Muslim thought and practice. Ibn Taymiya was a
prolific author and his published works continue to exert a strong influence.
What follows is an excerpt from his short hermeneutical treatise on the proper
approach to the exegesis and explication of the Qur'an, *Introductory Treatise on
the Principles of Tafsir*.⁹

PROLOGUE

One of the brethren asked me to write for him an introductory treatise
that would include comprehensive rules prescribed for understanding the
Qur'an, for knowing its interpretation and its meanings, for distinguishing—in both what has been handed down about it and what is the result
of reasoning—between the truth and various kinds of falsehood, and
for drawing attention to the decisive argument [*dalil*] that distinguishes
correct opinions from incorrect. For the books composed about Qur'anic
interpretation are laden with lean and fat, with obvious falsehood and
evident truth. Now, true knowledge lies either in a trustworthy transmission [*naql*] from one who is protected from error [*ma'sum*] or in a
statement for which there is a clearly understood argument. Anything
else is either [a transmission] rejected as a forgery or remains in "suspen-
sion," neither recognized as spurious nor ever critically tested. There is
a palpable need for the Muslim community to understand the Qur'an,
which is "God's strong rope, the wise remembrance, the straight path,
which passions cannot divert nor tongues confuse. Despite frequent
repetition, it never wears out; its wonders never cease, and learned men
never become satiated with it. Whoever professes it speaks the truth;

whoever acts upon it is rewarded; whoever judges by it acts justly; whoever summons [others] to [follow] it is [himself] guided to a straight path. Whoever arrogantly abandons it, God shall deal him a mortal blow. Whoever seeks guidance in anything else, God shall lead astray." . . . [10]

THE BEST METHODS OF INTERPRETATION: INTERPRETING THE QUR'AN THROUGH THE QUR'AN AND INTERPRETING IT THROUGH THE SUNNA

If someone asks, "What is the best method of interpretation?" the answer is that the soundest method is that whereby the Qur'an is interpreted through the Qur'an. For what is summarily expressed in one place is expatiated upon in another. What is abridged in one place is elaborated upon in another.

If that defeats your efforts, then you should resort to the Sunna, for the Sunna is what explains the Qur'an and elucidates it. Imam Abu 'Abdallah Muhammad ibn Idris ash-Shafi'i* has even said, "God's Messenger based his adjudications entirely upon what he understood of the Qur'an." God said, "We sent down to you the book with truth so that you may judge between people according to what God has shown you; do not, then, side in dispute with those who are faithless" [4:105]. And God said, "We sent down on you the remembrance so that you may make clear to people what has come down to them and perhaps they may reflect" [16:44]. And God said, "We only sent down the book on you so that you may clarify for them those matters on which they hold divergent views and [that it may be] a guidance and mercy for a people who believe" [16:64]. Because of this God's Messenger said, "Truly I was given the Qur'an and its like together," meaning the Sunna. The Sunna, too, came down upon him by inspiration, just like the Qur'an, except that the Sunna was not recited [to him] as was the Qur'an. Imam ash-Shafi'i and other leading scholars have drawn many inferences from that [hadith], but this is not the place [to discuss them].

The point is that you should seek the interpretation of the Qur'an

---

* Ash-Shafi'i (d. 820) stressed prophetic hadith as, along with the Qur'an, fundamental to the elaboration of Islamic jurisprudence.

from the Qur'an itself, and if you do not find it there, then from the
Sunna. As God's Messenger said to Mu'adh when he sent him to Yemen:
"On the basis of what will you judge?" Mu'adh answered, "By the book
of God." "And if you do not find anything [there]?" Muhammad pressed.
Mu'adh responded, "By the Sunna of God's Messenger." "And if you still
do not find anything?" Mu'adh replied, "I will give my own considered
opinion." Then God's Messenger tapped Mu'adh's chest and exclaimed,
"Praise belongs to God, who grants success to the messenger of God's
Messenger in satisfying the Messenger of God." This hadith can be found
in the various collections [*fi 'l-masanid wa 's-sunan*] with a flawless
chain of transmitters.

INTERPRETING THE QUR'AN THROUGH THE STATEMENTS OF THE COMPANIONS

Then when you do not find the interpretation in the Qur'an or in the
Sunna, you should have recourse to the statements of the Companions.
This is because they are particularly knowledgeable in such matters,
given what they actually witnessed with regard both to the Qur'an and
to those circumstances of which they alone have cognizance. It is also
because of their complete understanding and sound knowledge, especially
that of the most learned and prominent among them, such as the four
rightly guided and rightly guiding caliphs, and 'Abdallah ibn Mas'ud.*
Imam Abu Ja'far Muhammad ibn Jarir at-Tabari[†] stated that Abu Kurayb
related that Jabir ibn Nuh transmitted from al-A'mash, on the authority
of Abu 'd-Duha [Muslim ibn Sabih], that Masruq reported 'Abdallah, that
is Ibn Mas'ud, to have said: "I swear by the one and only God, no verse
from the book of God came down for which I was not the most knowledgeable about when it came down and where. If I knew where there was
anyone, whom riding beasts could reach, more knowledgeable about the
book of God than I, I would go to him." Al-A'mash also, on the authority

---

* Ibn Mas'ud (d. 653) was a Companion of the Prophet and a famous Kufan reciter of the Qur'an.

† At-Tabari (d. 923) is renowned for both his massive commentary on the Qur'an
and his history of the world from creation to his own times. Samples of his work
appear below in parts 2 and 7.

of Abu Wa'il [Shaqiq ibn Salama], reported Ibn Mas'ud to have said: "When any one of us had learned ten verses, he would not go beyond them until he knew what they meant and how to put them into practice."

Among them (that is, those particularly knowledgeable in interpretation) stands the learned man and scholar 'Abdallah ibn 'Abbas,* cousin of God's Messenger and expositor of the Qur'an by virtue of the blessing obtained for him by the supplication of God's Messenger when he prayed, "O God, give him understanding in religion and teach him the interpretation [ta'wil] of the Qur'an.". . . .

Yet sometimes sayings which they used to recount from the "people of the Book"† are transmitted on the Companions' authority, [a practice] which was approved by God's Messenger when he said, "Convey on my authority even a single verse and narrate [traditions] about the Banu Isra'il [i.e., Jews and Christians] without constraint. But whoever tells lies against me intentionally, let him take his seat in the Fire." Al-Bukhari related this on the authority of 'Abdallah ibn 'Amr [ibn al-'As].

Because of this, on the day of [the battle of] Yarmuk 'Abdallah ibn 'Amr acquired two camel loads of books belonging to the "people of the Book." He then used to transmit information from them, based on what he understood of this hadith to be the permission to do so.

Yet these Jewish and Christian accounts [al-ahadith al-isra'iliyat] should only be mentioned for purposes of attestation, not as a basis for belief. These accounts are essentially of three kinds. The first kind is what we know to be true because we already possess that which attests to its authenticity. That kind is sound. The second sort is that which we know to be untrue because of what we possess which contradicts it. The third type is that about which nothing can be said, being neither of the first kind nor the second. We should neither believe it nor declare it to be false. It is permissible to recount it, given what has just been said, but most of it provides no benefit in matters religious.

Among the "people of the Book" the scholars themselves disagree

* Ibn 'Abbas (d. 686), whose comments on Sura 1 were given above, was perhaps the most prominent early exegete.

† This expression—*ahl al-kitab* in Arabic—is a common qur'anic designation for Jews and Christians as possessors of earlier revelations.

greatly in such matters and consequently disagreement is conveyed through the interpreters of the Qur'an [who utilize *isra'iliyat*]. . . .

The best thing to do in reporting matters about which there is disagreement is this: all of the views pertinent to that case should be included; the reader should be made aware of those that are valid and the erroneous ones should be refuted; and the extent to which the diversity of opinion is useful or fruitful should be mentioned lest prolonged controversy and disagreement over useless matters distract one from what is more important.

Anyone who reports a disputed question without including everything that people have said about it is acting deficiently, since the correct view may be in what he ignores. Whoever simply reports disputed matters and lets it go at that, without drawing attention to which views are sound, also acts deficiently. If he deliberately defines as sound what is not, he has supported falsehood. If he does so out of ignorance, then he has committed an error. The same can be said for one who generates disagreement about useless matters or transmits statements under many different wordings, the gist of which conveys but one or two views as far as sense is concerned. He, too, has certainly wasted his time and made much of what is unsound. He is like someone dressed in "the two garments of a lie" [*thawbay zur*].* But God is the One who leads us to the right answer.

INTERPRETING THE QUR'AN THROUGH
THE STATEMENTS OF THE FOLLOWERS

When you find the interpretation in neither the Qur'an nor the Sunna, nor on the authority of the Companions, in that case much that is reported on the authority of the leading scholars goes back to the statements of the Followers, for example Mujahid ibn Jabr,† for he was a prodigy [*aya*] in interpretation. Muhammad ibn Ishaq recounted from Aban ibn Salih that Mujahid said, "I spread out the *mushaf* [i.e., the text

---

* This expression, which can refer to someone who pretends to have more than he possesses, occurs in a Prophetic hadith recorded in the collections of both al-Bukhari and Muslim.

† Mujahid (d. ca. 720) was a famous reciter and exegete of the Qur'an among the "Followers," the generation after that of the Companions.

of the Qur'an] before Ibn 'Abbas three times, from its opening sura to
its concluding one. At each and every verse I stopped him and asked him
about it." At-Tirmidhi included a report about it from al-Husayn ibn
Mahdi al-Basri, who received it from 'Abd ar-Razzaq, who was told by
Mu'ammar that Qatada said, "There is no verse in the Qur'an about
which I have not heard something [significant]."* At-Tirmidhi also
included a report about it from Ibn Abi 'Umar, who received it from
Sufyan ibn 'Uyayna on the authority of al-A'mash, who heard Mujahid
say, "If I had read Ibn Mas'ud's version of the *mushaf* [*qira'ata Ibn
Mas'ud*], I would not have needed to ask Ibn 'Abbas about many of the
Qur'anic matters on which I sought information." Ibn Jarir [at-Tabari]
reported from Abu Kurayb, who related from Talaq ibn Ghannam on
the authority of 'Uthman al-Makki, that Ibn Abi Mulayka said, "I saw
Mujahid, with his slates in hand, asking about the interpretation of the
Qur'an. [Whenever he posed a question] Ibn 'Abbas said to him, 'Write.'
This went on until Mujahid had asked Ibn 'Abbas about the interpretation
of the whole text." For this reason Sufyan ath-Thawri used to say,
"When interpretation comes to you from Mujahid, it is sufficient
for you."

[After listing a number of Followers, he continues:] You may mention
their statements about a particular verse. But when a difference of
wording occurs in what they have expressed, the unknowledgeable person
counts it as a divergence of opinion and conveys it as a plurality of views.
That, however, is not the case. For among this group are those who express something in its exact wording [*bi-lazimihi*], or the equivalent of
that [*nazirihi*], and those who render the essence of it [*bi-'aynihi*]. Taken
as a whole, this amounts to a single idea expressed in many [different]
passages. The intelligent person should certainly understand that. God,
however, is the supreme Guide.

Shu'ba ibn al-Hajjaj and others said, "In legal stipulations [*al-furu'*]
the statements of the Followers do not constitute sufficient proof [*hujja*],
so how can they do so in matters of interpretation?" That is to say, they

* In the *Sunan* of at-Tirmidhi this hadith from Qatada (d. 735), another noted
exegete of the Followers' generation, is also inserted among the accounts from
Mujahid.

are not considered a sufficient proof against the statements of other
Followers who disagree with them. This, in fact, is a sound argument.
When the Followers are in agreement, it unquestionably constitutes
sufficient proof. If, however, they disagree, the statement of one does not
disprove either the statement of another Follower or that of succeeding
generations. In that situation one must resort to the language of the
Qur'an or to the Sunna or to Arabic usage generally or to the statements
of the Companions about the matter.

INTERPRETING THE QUR'AN
ON THE BASIS OF PERSONAL OPINION

Interpreting the Qur'an solely on the basis of personal opinion [ra'y]
is strictly forbidden. . . . Ibn 'Abbas reported, "God's Messenger said,
'Whoever speaks about the Qur'an without knowledge will assuredly take
his seat in the Fire.'" Jundab related, "God's Messenger said, 'Whoever
speaks about the Qur'an on the basis of his personal opinion, even if he
gets it right, has still erred.'" . . .

Similarly, it has been reported that some scholars, both Companions
and others, spoke harshly about the interpretation of the Qur'an without
well-founded knowledge. No one should suggest, however, that to say
Mujahid, Qatada, and other such scholars interpreted the Qur'an means
that they spoke about the Qur'an or interpreted it without well-founded
knowledge or on their own accord. What, in fact, has been recounted
of them definitely confirms what we have said, that is, that they did not
speak of their own accord or without knowledge. Whoever *does* speak
about the Qur'an on the basis of his own personal opinion feigns a knowledge that he does not possess and acts contrary to the command he
has been given. Even if, in actuality, he were to get the meaning right,
he would still be erring, because he did not come at the matter in the
proper way.

The same can be said for anyone who, in a state of ignorance, judges
between people. He, too, is in the Fire, even if, in actuality, his judgment
accords with the right one. Still, he is less blameworthy than one who
makes a wrongful judgment. God, however, knows best. In similar fashion
did God call those who make slanderous accusations liars when He said,

"Since they did not bring witnesses, in God's eyes they are liars" [24:13]. For one who utters slander is a liar, even were he to slander someone who has actually committed adultery. That is because he has made a statement about something on which he has no right to comment, and because he has feigned a knowledge which he does not possess. But, again, God knows best.

For this reason a group of our distinguished predecessors refrained from any interpretation of which they had no knowledge. . . . Abu Bakr as-Siddiq* exclaimed, "What earth would support me and what heaven would overshadow me were I to say about the book of God what I knew not." . . .

Ayyub, Ibn 'Awn, and Hisham ad-Dastawa'i reported that Muhammad ibn Sirin said, "I asked 'Abida as-Salmani about a verse of the Qur'an and he replied, 'Those who know why the Qur'an was sent down (that is, the circumstances of revelation) have died, so fear God and follow the right course."

Abu 'Ubayd related from Mu'adh, who transmitted from Ibn 'Awn that 'Ubaydallah ibn Muslim ibn Yasar reported that his father said, "When you speak about God stop to consider the premises and the consequences of what you say."

Hashim related from Mughira that Ibrahim said, "Our associates have always feared and dreaded interpreting the Qur'an."

Shu'ba related from 'Abdallah ibn Abi as-Safar that ash-Sha'bi said, "By God, there is not a single verse about which I have not asked, and yet it is God's own transmission!"

Abu 'Ubayd reported from Hashim, who related from 'Umar ibn Abi Za'ida on the authority of ash-Sha'bi that Masruq said, "Beware of interpreting the Qur'an because it is nothing less than God's own transmission!"

These and other well-founded reports, which come down to us from our leading predecessors, are concerned with their refusal to say anything

---

* Abu Bakr (d. 634) was the first caliph of the Muslim community after the death of Muhammad.

of which they have no knowledge about the interpretation of the Qur'an. There is no objection, however, to one who speaks from a basis of [sound] linguistic and legal knowledge.

There is no contradiction, consequently, in the fact that statements about the interpretation of the Qur'an have been reported from these and others, because they talked about what they knew and kept quiet about what they did not know. This is what everyone should do. Just as one should remain silent about what he knows not, one should speak when asked about what he knows. This is supported by God's saying, "You shall expound it to people and not suppress it" (3:187), and by the hadith that is handed down through various lines of transmission: "Whoever is asked about something he knows but suppresses it, will be bridled on the Day of Resurrection with a bridle of fire."

Ibn Jarir [at-Tabari] reported from Muhammad ibn Bashshar, who transmitted from Mu'ammal on the authority of Sufyan who reported from Abu 'z-Zinad that Ibn 'Abbas said, "Interpretation of the Qur'an is of four kinds: a kind that the Arabs recognize on the basis of their [native] speech; interpretation that no one can be excused for not knowing; interpretation that the scholars [alone] know; and interpretation that only God knows." For God, may He be exalted and glorified, is all-knowing.

✳ Sacred Text and the Mihrab

In many mosques the primary visual focus is the niche (mihrab) that indicates the *qibla*, the ritual orientation to Mecca. Around the outer edges of the tile mihrab shown in figure 7 runs the same text featured on the drum of the Sultan's mosque in Shah Alam, near Kuala Lumpur, Malaysia (9:18–19; see fig. 1), in *muhaqqaq* script, but here the inscription also includes the following three verses (20–22) encouraging believers to emigrate (lit., "make a *hijra*") and strive "in the cause of God" in sure hope of eternal reward. Around the inner arch runs a hadith, in Kufic script, about the five pillars; and at the center of the niche another brief hadith declares: "The mosque is the house of every God-fearing person."[11]

The inscription in thuluth script above the mihrab of the Rustem Pasha mosque (1561–1562) built by Sulayman the Magnificent's chief architect,

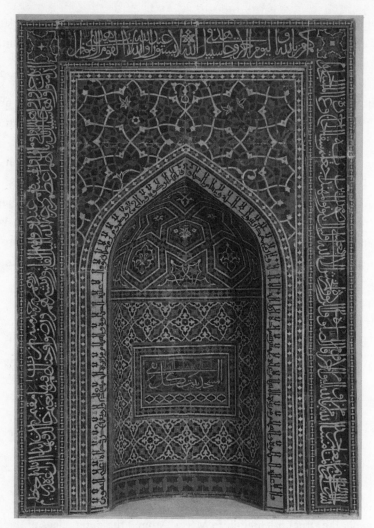

Figure 7.   Tile mihrab, Isfahan, Iran (ca. 1354). New York: Metropolitan Museum of Art, Harris Brisbane Dick Fund, 1939 (39.20).

Sinan, is an example of the most literal kind of epigraphic exegesis—the implied interpretation of a text by association with a visual setting (fig. 8). The text (3:37) appears often on Turkish mihrabs, apparently because it contains the word *mihrab*, even though the text uses the word in the sense of "private chamber" rather than Mecca-oriented niche: "God the Most High, to whom be praise, said: Every time Zacharia went in to her [Mary] in the chamber [he found her (miraculously) supplied with provisions]." In other words, the mere appearance

Figure 8.   Rustem Pasha Mosque, mihrab, Istanbul (1561–1562).

of a word seems to have dictated the choice of inscription. (The flanking brass candlesticks are similar to the one shown in fig. 13.)

Some mihrabs function in a commemorative or votive capacity in addition to serving their principal ritual role of liturgical orientation. A stucco mihrab dated 1310 (fig. 9) in a "side chapel" of the Congregational Mosque of Isfahan (see fig. 31) was in part a commemorative gift to acknowledge the conversion (in 1309) of the Il-Khanid ruler Uljaytu to Twelver Shi'ism. Several extended

Figure 9. Mihrab of Uljaytu, Congregational Mosque of Isfahan, Iran (1310). (On votive mihrabs, see also fig. 10, SD fig. 3.)

texts, almost entirely in thuluth script, include hadith about the Imams, obvious evidence of Shiʿi patronage. One long hadith provides a commentary on Qurʾan 4:59: When Muhammad uttered the just-revealed words "O you who believe, obey God and obey the Messenger and those who hold authority among you," a listener named Jabir asked who those in authority might be. Muhammad responded by naming the twelve Imams, ʿAli and his two sons Hasan and Husayn, and the nine yet to come. A second Prophetic hadith reminds would-be patrons that "anyone who builds a mosque, be it as small as the Prophet of God's dovecote, will have a house in paradise." Finally, a saying attributed to ʿAli recalls that anyone who comes to the mosque will receive one of eight rewards, including guidance on the straight path and freedom from fear. Taken together, the inscriptions provide an interpretation of the mihrab as part of the renovation of an existing structure now under the care of Shiʿi leaders.[12]

Men of royal blood were not the only people to fund such offerings. A twelfth-century Iranian woman named Fatima Khatun also commissioned a votive or commemorative mihrab (fig. 10). Its historical inscription in Kufic on the horizontal panel above the inner arch indicates that "the Khatun Fatima bint Zahir ad-Din ordered its [construction]." Two qurʾanic texts are cited: the first, in Kufic around the three outer edges, "Perform ritual prayer at the

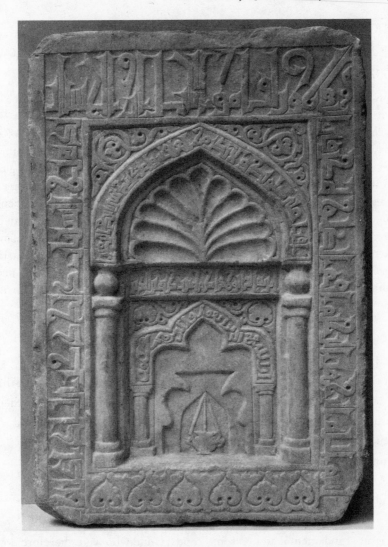

Figure 10.   Votive mihrab of Fatima Khatun, Iran (12th cent.). New York: Metropolitan Museum of Art, Macy Fund, 31.50.1. (See also SD figs. 2, 3.)

two ends of the day and as night approaches" (11:114); and the second, in Naskhi around the innermost arch, "Indeed God is with the God-fearing and those who do good" (16:128). A devotional Kufic text around the upper arch reads: "Occupy yourself with prayer and do not be among the heedless; serve your Lord generously."[13]

✳ Al-Ghazali
The Canons of Ta'wil

NICHOLAS HEER

Now for a very different approach, one that assesses the value of reason as a principle of interpretation. The text of Abu Hamid al-Ghazali's (d. 1111) *The Canons of Ta'wil (Qanun at-ta'wil)* translated here is the middle section of an essay in which Ghazali responds to a number of questions regarding scriptural passages that deal with Satan, the jinn, the angels, and certain eschatological matters. In this section Ghazali explains that the interpretation of scripture is necessary because there often appears to be a contradiction between statements found in the Qur'an or the traditions of the Prophet and what is known to be true through reason. He describes the approaches five different groups have taken with respect to this issue, pointing out that only one is correct. He concludes the section with a set of three recommendations for those who may want to interpret scriptural passages for the purpose of reconciling them with reason.[14]

At first glance one's superficial impression is that there is a conflict between reason [*ma'qul*] and scripture [*manqul*]. Those who deal with this issue have split up into (1) those who, at one extreme, have confined their studies to scripture, (2) those who, at the other extreme, have confined their studies to reason, and (3) those moderates in between who seek to unite and reconcile [reason and scripture].

The moderates, in turn, have split into (1) those who made reason fundamental and scripture secondary, and who consequently were not very concerned with the study of scripture, and (2) those who made scripture fundamental and reason secondary, and who were therefore not greatly concerned with the study of reason, and (3) those who made both reason and scripture equally fundamental and strove to bring together and reconcile the two.

There are thus five groups. The first group consists of those who confined their studies to scripture. They stand at the first stage of the way, being content with what they already understand of the apparent meaning of scripture. They have accepted as true what scripture contains both in its details and in its fundamentals. If they are asked to explain a contradiction in the apparent meaning of scripture and to give an interpretation [*ta'wil*] [of it], they decline, saying that everything is within the power of God. If one asks them, for example, how the person of Satan can be seen at the same time in two places and in two different forms, they reply that nothing is amazing in view of the power of God, for God has power over all things. And perhaps they would not even shrink from saying that a person's being in two places at once is within the power of God.

The second group distanced themselves from the first [taking a position] at the opposite extreme from them. They confined their studies to reason and did not concern themselves with scripture. If they hear something in scripture [*ash-shar'*] that is agreeable to them, they accept it. On the other hand, if they hear something that is in conflict with their reason, they claim that it is something that has been imagined by the prophets, for the prophets were required to descend to the level of ordinary people, and sometimes it was necessary for them to describe things in a way that did not conform with reality. Thus anything that did not agree with their reason they interpreted in this way. They exaggerated rationality to the extent of becoming unbelievers inasmuch as they ascribed lying to the prophets, may God's blessing and peace be upon them, for the sake of the general welfare. There is no disagreement within the [Islamic] community that whoever sanctions such a thing with respect to the prophets should have his head cut off.*

As for the first group, their shortcoming was in seeking safety from the danger of interpretation and investigation. They ended up in the domain of ignorance but felt secure there. Nevertheless, the position of this first group is closer [to safety] than that of the second group. The first group sought refuge from difficulties by saying that everything is within the power of God and that we cannot fathom the wonders of God's command. The second group sought refuge by saying that the Prophet, for the sake of the general welfare, described things as other than the way he knew them to be. It is evident how much difference there is between these two kinds of refuge with respect to danger and safety!

* That is, ascribing lying to the prophets amounts to apostasy, and the punishment for that is death.

The third group made reason fundamental and investigated it at length. However, they paid little attention to scripture, and did not encounter those passages that at first glance and initial impression seem to be contradictory and in conflict with each other or contrary to reason. They did not plunge into the heart of the problem, but when they did hear passages that conflicted with reason they rejected and ignored them or accused their transmitters of lying, except when the transmission was by *tawatur*,* like the Qur'an, or when the words of the hadith were easy to interpret. They rejected what they found difficult to interpret in order to avoid making far-fetched interpretations. It is clear how dangerous this position is in its rejection of sound traditions that have been transmitted by those trustworthy persons through whom scripture has reached us.

The fourth group made scripture fundamental and dealt with it at length. They were familiar with a large number of scriptural passages [*zawahir*], but they avoided reason and did not plunge into it. The conflict between reason and scriptural passages was apparent to them only in some fringe areas of the rational sciences. However, since their involvement with reason was not extensive nor did they plunge into it, rational impossibilities were not obvious to them, for some impossibilities are perceived only after careful and extended investigation built on many successive premises.

One must add here another point, and that is that they believed that they could consider anything to be possible as long as it was not known to be impossible. They did not realize that there are three categories [to be taken into account]: (1) a category whose impossibility is known by a proof, (2) a category whose possibility is known by a proof, and (3) a category neither the possibility nor impossibility of which is known. It was their custom to judge this third category to be possible, since its impossibility was not apparent to them. This is a mistake, just as it is a mistake to conclude that something is impossible because its possibility is not apparent. Indeed, there is a third category, namely, the category

---

* Transmission by *tawatur* (repetition, frequency) is transmission that involves so many transmitters at each stage of transmission that it is inconceivable that the transmitters could have conspired together on a falsehood.

that is neither known to be possible nor known to be impossible, either because it is beyond[15] reason and cannot be comprehended by human ability, or because of the shortcoming of an individual investigator due to his inability to discover the proof himself or his not having someone to point the proof out to him.

An example of the first, from the sense of sight, is the inability of the visual sense to determine whether the number of stars is even or odd or, because of their distance, to apprehend their real sizes. An example of the second, which is the shortcoming of the individual [investigator], is the inability of some people to perceive the stations of the Moon[16] and the visibility of fourteen of them at any given time [of the night] and the concealment of fourteen of them opposite the course of the [visible] stations as they rise and set, as well as other things that some people grasp with the sense of sight and others cannot. Such differences [in ability] also extend to the intellect's faculty of apprehension.

Since these (that is, the fourth group), did not plunge deeply into the rational sciences, they did not encounter many of these impossibilities. They were therefore spared the great effort of making most interpretations, for they were not aware of any need for interpretation. They resemble someone who does not know that God's being in a location is impossible and who can therefore dispense with the interpretation of "above" and "mounting" and all such words that indicate location.*

The fifth group is the intermediate group who combined the study of reason and scripture. They made each of them an important fundamental and denied that there was a real conflict between reason and scripture. One who denies reason denies scripture as well, since it is only through reason that the truth of scripture is known. Were it not for the truthfulness of the evidence of reason, we should not know the difference between the true prophet [*nabi*] and the false [*mutanabbi*], nor between the truthful person and the liar. How can reason be denied by scripture, when scripture can only be proven true by reason?

---

* This is a reference to such verses in the Qur'an as "The Hand of God is above their hands" (48:10) and "God it is who raised up the heavens without visible supports, then mounted the Throne" (13:2).

These constitute the group who are in the right. They have followed a proper procedure. Nevertheless, they have climbed to a difficult level, have sought an exalted goal, and have traveled an arduous road. How difficult is the goal they have sought, and how rugged is the road they have traveled! It may be level and easy in some places, but it is arduous and difficult in most.

Indeed, one who has dealt with the sciences at length and who has been involved in them extensively will be able to reconcile reason and scripture in most cases with simple interpretations. Nevertheless, there inevitably remain two situations [in which interpretation is difficult]: the first is the situation in which one is forced to employ far-fetched interpretations from which [rational] minds shrink, and the other is the situation in which one cannot determine how to make any interpretation at all. This latter situation is a problem similar to that of the letters mentioned at the beginning of some of the suras [of the Qur'an],[17] since no correct explanation of them has been transmitted [to us]. Anyone who thinks that he has escaped from these two situations does so either because of his deficiency in the rational sciences and his ignorance of rational impossibilities, so that he considers possible what he does not know to be impossible, or because of his deficiency in reading traditions, so that he has not encountered many individual traditions which contradict reason. I should therefore like to make three recommendations:

The first recommendation is that one not aspire to know all of that,* and this was the purpose to which I was directing my discourse. Such knowledge is not something to be aspired to, and one should recite [the verse from the Qur'an in which] God says, "And of knowledge you have been vouchsafed but little" [17:85].

The second recommendation is that one should never deny the testimony of reason, for reason does not lie. Were reason to lie, it might lie in establishing scripture, for it is by reason that we know scripture to be true. How can the truthfulness of a witness be known through the testimony of a lying character witness? Scripture is a witness for the details, and reason is the character witness for scripture. If, then,

---

* That is, that one not aspire to a complete understanding of scripture.

it is necessary to believe reason, one cannot dispute [the fact that] location and form must be denied to God. If you are told that works are
weighed,* you will recognize that works are an accident that cannot be
weighed, and that interpretation is therefore necessary.

If you hear that death is brought in the form of a fat ram which is then
slaughtered,[18] you will know that [such a statement] requires interpretation. The reason for this is that death is an accident, and as such it cannot
be brought, for bringing constitutes movement, which is impossible for
an accident. Moreover, death does not have the form of a fat ram, since
accidents cannot be transformed into bodies. Nor is death slaughtered,
for slaughtering involves separating the neck from the body, and death
has neither a neck nor a body. Death is an accident, or the absence of an
accident in the opinion of those who believe that it is the absence of life.
Therefore, interpretation [of this statement] is inescapable.

The third recommendation is that one refrain from specifying an interpretation when the [various] possibilities [of interpretation] are incompatible. Judgment concerning the intention of God or of His Prophet by
means of supposition and guessing is dangerous. One knows the intention of a speaker only when he reveals his intention. If he does not reveal
his intention, how can one know it, unless the various possibilities are
limited and all but one of them is eliminated. This one [intention] is
then demonstrably specified. Nevertheless, the various possibilities in
the speech of the Arabs and the ways of expanding upon them are many,
so how can they be limited? Refraining from interpretation is therefore
safer.

For example, if it is clear to you that works cannot be weighed, and the
tradition concerning the weighing of works comes up, you must interpret
either the word "weighing" or the word "works." It is possible that the
word used metaphorically is "works," and that it was used in lieu of the
register of works, in which they are recorded, and it is these registers of
works which are weighed. On the other hand, it is also possible that the

---

* A reference to weighing human works in the Balance as an indication of who
will be the inhabitants of the Garden and who the inhabitants of the Fire. See 7:8–9,
23:101–104, 101:6–11.

word used metaphorically is "weighing," and that it was used in lieu of
its effect, that is, the determination of the amount of work, since that is
the utility of weighing, and weighing and measuring are ways of deter-
mining [amounts]. If you conclude at this time that what is to be interpreted is the word "works" rather than the word "weighing," or "weighing" rather than "works," without relying on either reason or scripture,
you are making a judgment about God and His intention by guessing,
and guessing and supposition are tantamount to ignorance.

Guessing and supposition are permitted as necessary for the performance of acts of worship, piety, and other works that are ascertained
by *ijtihad*.* Nevertheless, matters unrelated to any action belong in the
same category as abstract sciences and beliefs, so on what basis does one
dare to make judgments in these matters by supposition alone? Most of
what has been said in the way of interpretation consists of suppositions
and guesses. The rational person has the choice either of judging by
supposition or of saying: "I know that its literal meaning is not what
is intended, because it contains what is contrary to reason. What exactly
is intended, however, I do not know, nor do I have a need to know, since
it is not related to any action, and there is no way truly to uncover
[its meaning with] certainty. Moreover, I do not believe in making
judgments by guessing." This is a safer and more proper choice for
any rational person. It also provides more security for the day of
resurrection, since it is not improbable that on the day of resurrection
he will be questioned [about his judgments] and held accountable for
them and be told, "You made a judgment about Us by supposition."
He will not, however, be asked, "Why did you fail to discover Our
obscure and hidden meaning [in a passage] in which there was no
command for action? You have no obligation with respect to belief in
it except absolute faith and general acceptance of its truth." This means
that one should say, "We believe therein; the whole is from our Lord"
[3:7].

---

* *Ijtihad*: independent investigation as conducted by a religious scholar with requisite training, called a *mujtahid*.

EXPERIENCING QUR'AN

✳ Nawawi
Etiquette in Recitation

FREDERICK M. DENNY

Imam Abu Zakariya Yahya ibn Sharaf ad-Din an-Nawawi (1233–1278), from
Damascus, rose to a respected position through his scholarship on a wide range
of Islamic subjects, but he was especially noted for his commentary on Muslim's collection of Hadith. His *Exposition of the Code of Behavior for Those Who
Bear the Qur'an (at-Tibyan fi adab hamalat al-Qur'an)*, from which the following selections come, contains many Qur'an and Hadith texts on the subject
of those who learn, recite, and teach the Qur'an. Its concern for sincerity, humility, responsible awareness, and God-fearing respect in all dealings with the
scripture underscores the devotional aspect of experiencing the Qur'an.

[GENERAL MATTERS]

The first thing incumbent on the scholars and performers of recitation is
to aspire to the pleasure of God Most High. As God Most High has said:
"And they have been commanded no more than to serve God, being
devoted to him, people of pure faith; to establish regular prayer; and to
pay the alms—that is the religion of the truly upright" [98:5]. [This is
true concerning] any religious community. In the two sound hadith
collections [of Muslim and Bukhari], according to the Messenger of God,
peace be upon him, "Acts are judged by their intentions; however, for
everyone is what was intended."

. . . First, sincerity is required of the reciter . . . and compliance with
the etiquette of the Qur'an. It is also necessary that he call to mind in his
soul that he is confiding in God Most High. And it is said concerning the
case of one who sees God Most High, that he does not see [God], but God
Most High does see him.

[RECITING WITH A CLEAN MOUTH]

It is required that at the beginning of recitation that the mouth be
cleansed with a toothbrush of some kind or other. This tooth cleaner

should preferably be a stick of the arak tree. However, it is permissible to use twigs of other woods for cleaning, such as rough scraps of saltwort and so forth. . . .

[RECITATION AND RITUAL PURITY]

It is meritorious, when reciting, to be in a state of ritual purity, although recitation in the state of minor impurity is permissible, according to the consensus of Muslims, and many hadith concur. The Imam al-Haramayn [al-Juwayni, d. 1085] said: "It is not to commit a sin of reprehensible conduct; rather it is to omit a better way." If water is not available, then purify using clean sand or stone. . . . However, the person with major impurity and the menstruating woman are forbidden to recite the Qur'an, even just a verse or part of one. But it is permitted for them to apply the Qur'an in their heart rather than uttering it out loud. It is permitted for them to look at the book as it influences the heart. The Muslims agree that glorification, rejoicing, praise, exclaiming "God is most great," and blessing of the Prophet are permitted, among other things concerning pious utterances of the ritually impure individual and the menstruating woman. . . .

[WHERE RECITATION MAY TAKE PLACE]

It is recommended that recitation be performed in a select, clean location. With respect to that, the majority of legal scholars prefer recitation in the mosque, because it is generally clean and dignified. And it is there that takes place another excellent practice, namely secluded spiritual retreat. Moreover, in that case, it is first required that the reciter's entry into the mosque include the formal intention of retreat and the etiquette of careful attention to it. . . . However, with regard to recitation in the bath, the pious forebears differ as to whether it is legally reprehensible. Our companions say: "It is not reprehensible." . . . [But others have declared that] "recitation in three places is disliked: in the baths, in the hashish dens, and in the mills when they are grinding." As Abu Maysara has declared: "Recite only in a nice place."

As for recitation in the street, it is permitted, not disliked [so long as nothing inappropriate is connected with it]. But if there is, then it is reprehensible, as when the Prophet disapproved the recitation performance of a drowsy person for fear of confusion. [Even] outside the formal *salat* [daily ritual] prayer, it is [nevertheless] preferable for the reciter to face the qibla direction of Mecca. . . .

[TAKING REFUGE WITH GOD]

At the point of beginning the recitation [the reciter] says: "I take refuge with God from Satan the accursed." The generality of religious scholars say to do that. But some of the scholars specify that refuge should be taken after the recitation. According to the speech of God Most High: "When you recite the Qur'an, take refuge with God from Satan the accursed" [16:98]. . . .

[CONCERNING REFLECTION DURING THE RECITATION]

When the reciter begins reciting, his state is humble submission and reflection on the matter being recited. . . . God said: "Will they not reflect on the Qur'an?" [4:82]. God Most High also said: "We caused the Book to be revealed to you, full of blessing, so that they may ponder its verses" [38:30]. There are also many hadith concerning [reflection]. . . .

[WEEPING DURING RECITATION]

God Most High has said: "They prostrate on their faces and weep and humility increases in them" [17:109]. The Prophet said: "Recite the Qur'an and weep, and if you do not weep, then induce tears in yourselves. . . . " Imam [Abu Hamid] al-Ghazali declared: "Weeping is recommended with recitation and in its presence."[19]

Figure 11.   A view through the courtyard of the Mosque of Ottoman Sultan Selim II in Edirne, Turkey (1568–1575), built by Sinan, showing the ablution fountain and prayer hall entrance. (On Ottoman architecture, see also figs. 34, 35, 40, 41, 44, 50; and SD fig. 19.)

2 Devotion
Ritual and Personal Prayer

Muslim writers and artists have invested enormous energy in celebrating, teaching, and interpreting the devotional aspects of their tradition. From the complex of rituals expected of all, to the practices of smaller populations that vary from one region to another, to the aspirations of the individual who prays in silence, recent scholarship has made the riches of that tradition increasingly accessible. In this section Muslims past and present from all over the world offer their views on the core of the believer's response to God's initiatives. Visual themes will feature the ritual settings of daily liturgical prayer, pilgrimage, and funerary rites.

ON THE FIVE PILLARS

We begin with a fourteenth-century letter from India on the prerequisite of all devotion, right intention, and a contemporary Indonesian theologian's analysis of the relationship between ritual and faith. A hadith describes how Muslims came to pray five ritual prayers daily (see figs. 11–15); a recently discovered Swahili religious epic recounts a conversation between God and Moses on the requirements of the life of devotion; and a selection from a modern Indonesian *tafsir* explores various aspects of pilgrimage (see Figs. 16, 17).

✳ ## Sharaf ad-Din Maneri
On the Necessity of Proper Intention
PAUL JACKSON

Ahmad son of Yahya Bibi Razia was born in 1290 in Maner, not far west of Patna, the capital of the state of Bihar, India. He left home at age fourteen to study in Bangladesh; after nineteen years there he headed for home, but soon journeyed to Delhi in search of a spiritual guide. After nearly ten years with a shaykh of the Firdawsi order, Najib ad-Din, Ahmad again returned to Maner; but on the way he decided to spend some time in solitude in a cave near Rajgir. His reputation for sanctity and sage advice spread abroad. So many people sought his counsel that he ended up remaining there nearly fifty years, until his death in 1381. Given the name Sharaf ad-Din (Eminence of the Religion), the shaykh developed a large correspondence with disciples unable to visit in person. The Shaykh 'Umar to whom this letter is addressed probably lived in the Gaya district. Maneri's hundreds of letters are sprinkled with citations of Persian poetry. His topic here is no less than the bedrock of devotional response to God's revelation: purity of intention.[1]

Brother, Shaykh 'Umar, prayerful greetings from the writer of these lines, Ahmad Yahya Maneri!

You must know that the position of the Law is: "On the Day of Resurrection, people will be raised according to the purity of their intention." If the desire and quest of God predominates within you, you will be raised up among the lovers and seekers of God. Their reward is: "Our Lord will shine forth radiantly." What room is there for heaven and hell here?

> There is no room for heaven or hell:
> Whatever you know serves but to veil Me.

If your desire and quest is mainly for heaven, you will be counted among the virtuous, for whom the reward is: "Gardens of paradise descend." 'Ayn al-Qudat* says: "Here we have eating and drinking, and there we have eating and drinking. God forbid that simply by eating and drinking we are the same as brute beasts!" Behold the boldness of the intrepid!

> A spiritless dog searches for bones:
> A lion cub pursues living marrow.

If your predominant passion is a desire and quest for the world, you will be counted among the worldly. Their reward is: "And a gulf is set between them and what they desire" (34:54). Here, dust has to be thrown

---

* 'Ayn al-Qudat al-Hamadhani: a Persian Sufi executed in Baghdad in 1132 because of statements some judged heretical.

on the head, and one should grieve for oneself, and the same thing should be said as was mentioned by a luckless one:

> Where shall I seek medicine for this pain?
>> My life is done: how can I grieve?
> I am a plaything of the age, no matter what I do:
>> Nothing comes to completion, no matter what I do.

Look within yourself to see what is there. Do love and affection for God predominate? Or love and affection for paradise? Or love and affection for the world? Realize that whatever predominates now has its significance explained in the following couplet:

> Whatever captures your attention in this world
>> Will be your path to union for eternity.

This is the meaning of the one who said: "God does not look at your faces or your works: He looks at your hearts and your intentions." The impact of this news on the souls of the righteous is similar to that of hell on the souls of the unbelievers and foolish people.

> Until one experiences this work of seeking God,
>> What does he know about love and pain?
> You know not this work, nor are you a lover:
>> You are dead! How are you fit to love?

O brother, asking questions about the state of the work takes its birth from you and me. If you are serious, correct your intention and desire, for the work of a believer cannot but be one. If he goes on pilgrimage to Mecca, he cannot keep trying to please his mother. If he does not go because he wants to please his mother, he simply cannot go on pilgrimage. The same applies to other works. By his intention he reaches out to all sorts of good deeds and acts of submission. The recompense for any good work performed by the believer has to be limited because the work is limited, while the recompense for a believer's good intention is unlimited, for there can be no limit to the intention of performing acts of submission and good deeds. "The good intention of a believer is better than his work." This would mean that if someone has a good intention and desire but for some reason is unable to perform the work—as, for example, a sick person is unable to perform the pilgrimage; a weak man cannot go out to fight on the way of God; and a poor person cannot bestow alms—the reward and recompense would certainly be the same as that of the person who performs all these works.

It is related that the Messenger set out on the jihad of Tabuk during which the Muslims had to undergo many labors and trials. He said: "It is perfectly true that there are some people in Medina who have not seen this desert, nor have they defrayed any of the expenses involved, nor have they suffered any trial or sorrow on the way of God. Nevertheless, they are participating in all things along with us."

People said: "O Apostle of God, how could this be? They are still in Medina." He replied: "There was an excuse for their remaining. They are accounted as present with us because of the perfection of their intention." From this it is proved that the work is of the heart, not of clay, and there is an enormous distance between clay [*gil*] and heart [*dil*]. The abode of intention is the heart, not clay. Here one needs to be careful so that negligence finds no entrance. That is the meaning of the words

> From the door of the body to the Ka'ba of the heart,
>   There are, for lovers, a thousand and one stages.
> Along this way, befriend your heart:
>   Make provision for a hundred thousand stages.

O brother, the science of intention is exceedingly refined and subtle. Not everyone is capable of traveling along that road. Whatever a master of the heart does is in accordance with his intention, for the intention of each person is a measure of his faith. The faith of someone who follows others is rooted in imitation; that of the rationalist, in proof; while that of a mystic flows from personal experience. Look at the astonishing work of the renowned Righteous One [Abu Bakr]! He left his wife and children behind in Mecca and migrated from Mecca together with the Chosen One [Muhammad]. Khwaja Uways Qarani* did not leave his mother behind. When you examine their intention, both are correct.

---

* Uways Qarani: a legendary figure of Yemen during Muhammad's time, after whom a group of religious seekers, guided solely by God's grace without aid of a spiritual guide, is named (Uwaysis).

There were a number of people from earlier generations who abandoned submission to God because they did not have a correct intention therein. Ibn Sirin* did not recite the funeral prayer for Khwaja Hasan Basri.† He said: "This is not my intention." Thus it is that renowned men say that it is possible that his not saying the prayers was better than their recital by others, as far as merit was concerned. What do you know about why people pray, or why they do not pray? What do you know about their motive for going on pilgrimage to Mecca, or for not going? Do you know why people fast or not? The heads of those addicted to habit and custom spin at this stage. Inevitably, habit and custom are one thing, while the way of the prophets and saints is something else.

> When can you travel along this way, O friend?
> Can a spider hope to travel like an elephant?

Nowadays everybody finds contentment in foolish ideas and feels satisfied with false opinions. If religion were as easy as people think it is, then prophets and saints would not have grown anxious, nor would the brave have become faint hearted. . . .

You should know that the behavior of the world is one thing, while lovers form a different category. They do not have the strength to wait. They seek the Promised One here and now. Intoxicated with love they all say:

> Either give me what I want, or free me of my desire:
> Don't talk about tomorrow's promise! Do this or that.

Rabi'a of Basra‡ was asked why she did not wish for paradise. She said: "First the neighbor, then the house." Look at the firm resolve of this wearer of a skirt and grieve over your fine dress and turban-sash and know that, in reality, you are neither a man nor a woman. Simply ask, "What am I?"

On one occasion Imam Shibli§ disappeared. His disciples went looking

---

* Ibn Sirin (d. 728): a Hadith scholar and renowned interpreter of dreams.
† Hasan al-Basri (d. 728): an early ascetic and a father figure of Sufism.
‡ Rabi'a (d. 801): a poetess and the most famous woman Sufi; see Rabi'a's hagiography in part 3, and her dream account in part 7.
§ Abu Bakr ash-Shibli (d. 945): an early Sufi of Baghdad and friend of Hallaj.

for him. They saw him in the garb of hermaphrodites and seated in their midst, looking just like one of them. They threw dust upon their heads and cried out: "O Leader of the Age, what is this all about?" He replied: "I saw that I could not be called a man, nor did I have the features of a woman. Thus I could not be anything else than a hermaphrodite. And what could be better for a hermaphrodite than to be among kindred folk?" Khwaja 'Attar* says:

> When a madman seeks with such artful boasting,
> Don't blindly rush to do battle with him.
> Keep your tongue far from his enticing words:
> Hold excused a lover in his madness.
> Wise people experience the difficulty of the Law,
> While those without hearts love being honored.
> Without doubt a madman, even if at fault,
> Speaks arrogantly, no matter what he says.

In short, O brother, each action that a person performs cannot be bereft of intention and purpose. If he is interiorly filled with love of this world, his intention and purpose will be of this world and, in his actions, the same will apply. No matter how much he prays, fasts, goes on pilgrimage, or gives alms, it will all be tinged with worldliness. On the other hand, if his inner disposition is that of a love for what lies in store for him, and that is the purpose and intention of his actions, then, whether it be eating or drinking, it will be related to the world to come. "From each vessel the contents will appear" is a well-known adage.

There is another group of people known for being royally audacious. Whatever they do is done purely for His sake. "My prayer, my worship, my life, and my death are for God, the Lord of the worlds" would be attributed to them. Their splendor is: "They seek His face," with their feet in this world and their heads in the next. They do not lower them until they hear from the Friend: "You are, in truth, My favorites."

---

* Farid ad-Din 'Attar (d. 1220): a Persian poet, author of the didactic religious epic *The Conference of the Birds*.

✳ Nurcholish Madjid
Worship as an Institution of Faith

THOMAS MICHEL

A contemporary Indonesian discussion of the question of ritual prayer's place in the larger context of Muslims' faith and worship now builds on Maneri's foundational reflections on intention. Muslim authors all over the world continue to write books on Islamic doctrine for the purpose of reinterpreting the tradition in ever-changing circumstances. Dr. Nurcholish Madjid's "Worship as an Institution of Faith" ("Ibadat Sebagai Institusi Iman") is part of a much larger treatise on Islamic doctrine and ethics.[2]

THE PROBLEMATIC OF THE RELATIONSHIP
BETWEEN WORSHIP AND FAITH

Touching upon the connection between worship and faith is not simply a hypothetical question, for people often raise the question, "Isn't it enough for someone to have faith and do good works, without also having to worship?" Einstein has been quoted, for example, as saying that he believed in God and the necessity of doing good, without feeling a need to join a formal religion such as Judaism or Christianity, which he considered useless.

In passing, we might note that a question of this type suggests an attitude both logical and reasonable. Moreover, the Holy Book itself always speaks about faith and good works as two associated values that people must possess. However, if we examine the matter more closely, the question can raise various problems. First, in historical reality, no system of beliefs has ever appeared that has not introduced, to a greater or lesser extent, rituals. Even a view of life that has absolutely no pretense to religiosity, including those like communism that strive to eliminate religion, has its own ritual system. Through the use of ritual, seen both in the show of respect to the party symbol and in a dogmatic living-out of party doctrines and ideology, a communist strengthens his commitment and dedication to its [the system's] profession of life as well as to its ideals. Similarly, Javanese mystical [*kebatinan*] teachings and informal spiritualities, such as those of theosophical movements and Freemasonry,

Figure 12. All traditional prayer rugs depict a two-dimensional version of the mihrab. In this early-nineteenth-century Turkish design, geometry nearly overpowers floral elements; stylized ewers in the spandrels (above the arch on both sides) may allude to the ablution required before every ritual prayer. St. Louis: St. Louis Art Museum, 108:29.

Figure 13. A fourteenth-century Iranian brass engraved, silver- and gold-inlaid, mosque candlestick holder, one of a pair designed to flank the mihrab (as in fig. 8). It is inscribed to the patron: "Glory to our master, the lofty king, the sultan, the magnificent, the wise, the just." St. Louis: St. Louis Art Museum, 43:1926.

have introduced certain forms of ritual for their members. At the very minimum there is a process of initiation of members, with a ceremony of profession and the pronouncement of a pledge of faithfulness as a type of oath of allegiance.

The second problem connected with the notion of faith without worship is that, unlike scientific systems or philosophies that have only a rational dimension, faith always possesses a suprarational or spiritual dimension that expresses itself in devotional actions by means of a system of worship. Such devotional acts not only have the effect of strengthening the feeling of belief and producing a higher consciousness concerning the implications of faith in the matter of deeds, but they also prepare one for an experience of holiness that has no little meaning for a feeling of joy. Such an experience of holiness, for example, is the feeling of closeness to God, the Object of Worship, the One Lord who is humankind's reason for existence and goal of life.

The third problem is that while it is true that what is important is faith and good works, that is, a combination of the two values of which the one [faith] is the basis for the other [good works], in order for abstract faith to move someone in the direction of performing good works, it must possess a warmth and intimacy in the soul of a believer, and this can be achieved by way of the activity of worship. There is even a general understanding that the reality of a religious life is always found connected with forms of worship activities.

It would seem clear from the above that worship systems are a continuation of the logic of any faith system. Otherwise, faith would become a kind of abstract formulation without the ability to motivate the individual inwardly to do something at the level of genuine sincerity. Thus, the act of faith must be institutionalized in worship as an expression of a person's servanthood before the Lord, the Center of meaning and the Goal of life.

WORSHIP BETWEEN FAITH AND GOOD WORKS

The above-mentioned problem can be taken as the basis for discussing the place of worship as an institution of faith, or an institution that links faith and its consequence, that is, good works.

As an interior attitude, faith or belief can exist at a very high level of abstraction so that it is difficult to understand its relationship to evident daily behavior. Every heavenly religion emphasizes salvation through faith. This emphasis is especially found in the Abrahamic religions—that is, Judaism, Christianity, and Islam—because they go back in the central elements of their teaching to that of their ancestor, the prophet Abraham

in the eighteenth century before Christ. These religions strongly emphasize the connection or internal consistency between faith and works or
deeds in favor of humankind. For those heavenly religions, the Lord is not
understood to be found in things (totemism) or ceremonies (sacramental-
ism) as in some other religions, but rather in that which goes beyond the
world. At the same time, the Lord demands that humanity pass through
life following a specific path whose measure is the goodness of every
member of human society. In other words, the Lord, in addition to being
of a wholly transcendent and august nature, is, according to the perception of the heavenly religions, also by nature ethical, in the sense that
God intends for humankind behavior that is *akhlaqi*, that is, ethical or
moral.

The link between abstract faith and behavior or concrete good deeds
is acts of worship. Worship, as a kind of concretizing of the sense of faith,
bears the intrinsic meaning of closeness to the Lord (*taqarrub*) [see 96:19
and 9:99]. In worship, a servant of the Lord (or *ʿabd Allah*) feels a spiritual intimacy with the Creator. This experience of holiness is something
that can be said to be the essence of religious feeling or religiosity, which
in the view of the mystics such as Sufis possesses the highest level of
legitimacy. (Sufis even tend to hold that religious feeling must always
have an inner dimension, while stressing that every exoteric [*lahiriah*]
act is legitimate only if it leads someone to this esoteric [*batiniah*]
experience.)

However, in addition to its intrinsic meaning, worship also bears
an instrumental meaning, for it can be seen as an effort of private
and communitarian education leading to a commitment or an interior
adherence to moral behavior [see 29:45]. The assumption is that by way
of worship, a believer nourishes and increases his individual and collective
behavior in regard to his personal and social duties so as to enable the
best possible life together in this world. The root of that awareness is a
deep realization of one's responsibility for every deed before the Lord in
the unavoidable Divine Judgment, at which a person appears strictly as an
individual [see 2:28 and 31:33]. Thus because of its very personal nature
(as a relationship between a servant and his Lord), worship can become a
very deep and effective instrument of moral and ethical education. In the

Holy Book the hope is clearly expressed that an important effect of worship is the growth of a kind of social solidarity. It is even emphasized that, without the growth of that social solidarity, worship is not only worthless and incapable of bringing one to salvation, but is in fact cursed by the Lord.

From this perspective, worship can be called a framework and institutionalization of faith that manifests itself in forms of behavior and concrete deeds. Moreover, in addition to being a manifestation of faith in practice, worship also functions as an effort at nourishing faith and making it grow. Faith is not something static that appears once and for always. Faith, rather, is of a dynamic character that knows both the rhythm of negative development (decreasing, failing, becoming weak) and positive growth (increasing, deepening, becoming stronger). Positive growth requires continuous efforts at fostering and nourishing faith [see 48:4].

HUMAN NATURE AND WORSHIP

As a declaration of servanthood before the Lord, worship, which also bears the meaning of glorifying God, is truly a natural thing. That is, it is something that is inherently found in the native tendency of humankind and as a natural phenomenon in its own right. For this reason changing from one form of worship activity to another can be seen as simply a case of substitution. This is because in the living reality of humans there is almost no individual who is absolutely without some form of expression of worshipful or devotional character. If someone does not carry out a normative act of worship (such as salat in Islam), that person will nevertheless certainly carry out some other form of worship activity (such as, as we have mentioned, the strong tendency of communists to glorify their leaders.)

Thus, as with every other natural tendency, the human tendency to perform acts of worship must be properly channeled. The key test of the correctness of an act of worship is that it must raise the status and human dignity of the individual involved in it. True worship will certainly not result in fettering and restraining the worshipper as happens in mythological systems.

This means that worship must be directed only toward the Most
Exalted Presence, who is truly "superior" to humankind because He is
our Creator, while human beings are His creatures (even though, and
precisely because, they are the pinnacle of His creation.) Moreover, the
act of worship must be directed toward Him who, when one has certitude,
consciousness, and an experience of His presence in life, produces the
sincere desire to do something to earn his "pleasure," that is, good works.

From this perspective, worship can be seen as the symbol of a servant's
glorifying his Creator as well as the declaration of the servant's accepting
His moral demands. Through worship, a servant hopes that the Creator
will help and guide his life to follow the path toward truth. In standing
before Him, an individual becomes aware that in confronting the unavoidable challenge of leading a moral life he needs mercy and grace (in
Arabic, *fadl*), for human beings cannot fully and perfectly seek and find
the path of truth without His guidance [see 24:21].

WORSHIP AND RELIGIOSITY

The Qur'an recounts the story of the prophet Jacob (Ya'qub), who held
the title *Isra'il*, that is, *'abd Allah*, Servant of God, probably because
he was very assiduous in his worship, who asked his sons when he was
on the point of death: "What will you worship after I am gone?" They
answered: "We shall worship your God and the God of your forefathers
Abraham, Ishmael, and Isaac: God alone! We surrender ourselves to
Him" [2:133]. That account in the Sacred Book shows that an act of
worship must be accompanied by an attitude of total self-surrender
toward the One who is worshipped, that is, God the One Lord. Performing an act of worship without accompanying it with a sincere attitude
of self-surrender nullifies the meaning of the act itself as an approach
to and intimacy with al-Khaliq, the Great Creator.

This experience is the basis for a "leap" in the soul of a believer every
time the name of the Lord is mentioned and arouses in the believer's
heart a deep attitude of appreciation each time an expression of religion,
such as God's word [in the Qur'an] is heard. It is this "leap" that arouses
in the believer a longing to entrust and pledge one's entire life to God,

Creator and Protector [see 8:2]. In the consciousness of the presence of the Creator Lord in one's life, a human person finds his or her proper nature.

One form of worship in Islam that is highly symbolic of an awareness of the presence of the Lord in the life of humankind is salat. Making "contact" with the Lord is the highest purpose of salat (that is, its intrinsic purpose, as has been shown above). This is clear in the command of the Lord to the prophet Moses [see 20:14]. The Arabic word *salat* literally means "to call upon," the same meaning as is carried by the Arabic word *du'a'*, that is, the crying out of a servant to the Lord, Creator of the universe.

Furthermore, salat, defined as "a collection of readings and actions that begin with a proclamation of God's greatness (*takbir*) and conclude with the greeting of peace (*taslim*)," is highly symbolic of the submission and surrender (*islam*) of a person to the Lord. In the salat, after the opening takbir the person is commanded to direct his every attitude and attention exclusively to the object of his cry, that is, the Creator of the entire universe, in his position as a servant who is encountering his Lord. Any attitude, whether exterior or interior, that is not relevant to his situation of encountering the Lord is forbidden (thus the first takbir is called the *takbirat al-ihram*, that is, the takbir by which one enters the sacred state). In this way, at the moment of salat, a person, being totally overcome by his contact with the Lord in the vertical dimension, is free from the horizontal dimension of his life, including the social aspects of that life.

At the moment of salat, a servant should experience as deeply as possible the presence of the Lord in his life, [as in the hadith] "as if you see Him, and even if you do not see Him, truly He sees you." With the bodily positions of bowing (*ruku'*) and prostration (*sujud*), which is performed by touching the forehead on the surface of the earth, accompanied by sacred readings which serve to prepare a dialogue with Him, humble obedience and submission to the Lord are shown most clearly. It is not an exaggeration to hold that properly performed salat, that is, when performed with devotion and attention and accompanied by the tranquillity of every member of the body, is a perfect declaration of faith, as has been said by ʿAli Ahmad al-Jurjawi.[3] Salat creates a highly elevated feeling of religion or religiosity.

Moreover, that religiosity can have broad implications in this life, both in one's external life and in the interior. This is owing to the peacefulness of soul that comes about through communication with the Lord [see 13:28], so the person who performs salat with reverence will have a soul that is more balanced, full of hope, but not losing awareness of himself or becoming haughty, for he "does not despair if misfortune strikes, and does not become puffed up while he is experiencing good fortune" [see 70:19–23].

Thus, salat will be effective in producing an impact of forming an inner disposition that is free from the misplaced worries of facing life. This is not only because faith is always joined with hope, as the Sacred Book affirms, just as denying the Lord, or unbelief, is linked with despair [see 12:87], but also because a person truly grows in stability in orienting one's life to attain the pleasure of the Lord alone. One result of imbibing the meaning of salat is that "the angels will come down upon them [saying]: 'Do not fear or feel saddened, and rejoice in word about the Garden which you have been promised! We are your companions during worldly life and in the Hereafter'" [41:30].

Religiously, the experience of "being accompanied by angels" must be lived as a reality. Even though the Muslim philosophers tended to interpret this metaphorically, that experience nevertheless has concrete implications in daily life. It is clear that experience is a continuation or consequence of hoping in the Lord and His protection. Thus, even though such a person must suffer, he sees his suffering as a common human experience that can happen to anyone, while he himself, in his sufferings, keeps on believing and hoping in the Lord. This is an attitude that another person would not have [see 4:104].

From all that we have tried to explain above, we can conclude that salat, as well as other forms of worship such as, for example, fasting and the pilgrimage, are strongly connected with a strength of soul and resoluteness of heart in facing life, because there is hope in the Lord. At the same time, hope in the Lord is one aspect of faith that, among other

things, gives birth to a sense of security: faith (*al-iman*) gives birth
to security (*al-amn*) [see 6:82]. Furthermore, that sense of security and
of being under the protection of the Lord will equip someone to aspire
to lead a moral life, that is, a life that is inspired by the highest social
awareness. (That social awareness, for example, is symbolized by the
greeting of peace at the conclusion of the salat to the persons on the right
and left, by the *zakat fitra* at the end of the month of Ramadan, and by
the white robes worn equally by all during the pilgrimage (*hajj*) and the
devotional visitation of Mecca (*'umra*), as well as in fulfilling the obligation of paying the *zakat* (alms). As we have seen, worship that does not
give birth to social awareness, clearly one of the most important manifestations of a moral life, would lose its true meaning, to the point that
someone who performs any type of formal worship without social
awareness is cursed by the Lord.

Because of its effects in producing resoluteness and peace of soul, the
foundations of optimism in facing a life that is not always easy, worship,
particularly salat, is a source of spiritual strength in facing difficulties, as
is the case also with mental courage and endurance [see 2:153]. Creativity,
inventive power, and resourcefulness in seeking to resolve the problems
of life, for example, will grow even stronger in the individual who has
found stability through sincere devotion (*taqwa*) [see 65:2]. Thus, worship as a manifestation of journeying the path of life toward the Lord,
if it is performed with full consciousness and consistency, will result in a
life of total well-being [see 72:16], because of the sense of security based
on faith. In this way, worship is the institutionalization of faith.

✳ Tabari
Hadith on the Five Daily Ritual Prayers
REUVEN FIRESTONE

Islamic tradition includes a treasury of lore about the divine origins of ritual
practices, such as the following hadith about the five rounds of daily salat. Abu
Ja'far Muhammad ibn Jarir at-Tabari (d. 923) grew up in Tabaristan, a northern
province in today's Iran. He traveled in search of learning and became a brilliant legalist, qur'anic scholar, historian, and collector of hadith, spending most
of his adult life in the center of the civilized world of his day, Baghdad. He fol-

Figure 14. Fifteen stories tall, the Kalyan Minaret in Bukhara (1127) exemplifies the ornate geometric design in baked brick characteristic of early medieval Iran and Central Asia.

lowed the Shafiʿite legal school until founding a legal school of his own known as the Jariri school, which, perhaps because of its strong similarity to that of Shafiʿi, did not long survive. Many of his works are lost, but his great world history and his enormous Qurʾan commentary survive. Both are popular among Muslims and are considered extremely important among critical scholars of Islam. His Qurʾan commentary includes the following tradition concerning the

Figure 15.   The classic Jami Masjid (1897) in Kuala Lumpur, Malaysia, shows influence of Mughal architectural style in its ogival arches as well as in the triple ogival domes over the prayer hall and the use of *chattri* pavilions on roofline and minarets. (See also figs. 32, 33; and SD fig. 24.)

way in which the Muslim community came to the practice of five daily ritual prayers. Cast as a conversation between Muhammad, during his Ascension and journey through the various heavens, and Moses, its tone is reminiscent of Abraham's bargaining with God over Sodom and Gomorrah. The story's repetitive nature is a common characteristic of texts that began as oral tradition.[4]

[Muhammad] said: He enjoined upon me fifty prayers, but when I returned to Moses he said: How many were you commanded, Muhammad? I said: Fifty prayers. He said: Go back to your Lord and ask for a reduction, for your community is the weakest of communities, and I have met resistance among the Children of Israel [against imposing such religious requirements]. [The narrator] continued: So the Prophet returned to his Lord, asked for a reduction, and they were reduced by ten. Then he returned to Moses, who asked: How many were you commanded? He answered: Forty. He said: Go back to your Lord and ask for a reduction, for your community is the weakest of communities, and I have met resistance among the Children of Israel. [The narrator] continued: So the Prophet returned to his Lord, asked for a reduction, and they were reduced by ten. Then he returned to Moses, who asked: How many were you commanded? He answered: Thirty. Moses said to him: Go back to your Lord and ask for a reduction, for your community is the weakest of communities, and I have met resistance among the Children of Israel. [The narrator] continued: So the Prophet returned to his Lord, asked for a reduction, and they were reduced by ten. Then he returned to Moses, who asked: How many were you commanded? He answered: Twenty. He said: Go back to your Lord and ask for a reduction, for your community is the weakest of communities, and I have met resistance among the Children of Israel. [The narrator] continued: So the Prophet returned to his Lord, asked for a reduction, and they were reduced by ten. Then he returned to Moses, who asked: How many were you commanded? He answered: Ten. He said: Go back to your Lord and ask for a reduction, for your community is the weakest of communities, and I have met resistance among the Children of Israel. [The narrator] continued: So the Prophet returned to his Lord, asked for a reduction, and they were reduced by five. Then he returned to Moses, who asked: How many were you commanded? He answered: Five. He said: Go back to your Lord and ask for a reduction, for your community is the weakest of communities, and I have met resistance among the Children of Israel. [Muhammad] said: I [began to] go back to my Lord, but I was embarrassed and did not go back to Him. So he was told: Just as you had patience for [accepting] five prayers [daily], they will serve as the equivalent of fifty prayers, and every good deed will be considered as ten good deeds. [The narrator] said: Muhammad was overwhelmingly satisfied.* Moses was very harsh toward [Muhammad] when he [intended to] pass by [with a large number of prayers], and very good to him when he returned to [ask for a reduction from] God.

---

* The tradition ends here. The following line is appended.

✳ Ritual and Creed in Moses' Conversation with God

JAN KNAPPERT

Moses' conversation with Muhammad is well known, but Moses is still more renowned as the *Kalim Allah*: the one who conversed with God. The Swahili *Epic of Moses* (*Utenzi wa Musa*) is the first literary work yet discovered in northern Mozambique, evidence that a lively Islamic culture existed far from the major cities of East Africa long ago.[5] Tentatively dated to the late nineteenth century, the text may have been written in Kenya. About 330 stanzas in length, the poem recounts an intriguing conversation (*munajat*) between the prophet Moses and God, offering important insights into both the spirituality and theological views of early modern Muslims in East Africa. Topics include the full range of basic religious duties and elements of the creed, as well as a rare "first-person" description of how God created the world. It opens with Moses slaughtering a goat, possibly recalling Leviticus 9:3, but here the prophet seems motivated by a desire to receive a revelation; God obliges. We have here a rare example of a Swahili text that describes a most intimate spiritual experience, similar to but less mythical in tone than accounts of Muhammad's Ascension (see part 7 below). In this story, even the prophet Moses needs encouragement to perform the fundamental religious observances. After a brief invocation, the poet continues:

One day when Moses was in a state of ritual purity [after ritual ablutions], he heard a voice in the air and he knew it was a sign from God. It gave him strength and he fasted for forty days in the mountains. Then he heard again the voice of God: "O ye mountains! Today I need Moses the son of Amram. I am the Lord without equal. Moses, hasten to come to me! I want you so that we may see each other and speak words to each other."

God's voice shook the mountains, but the Prophet Moses went up and climbed higher and higher. Up to the Mountain of Tur [i.e., Sinai] he climbed, thinking only of God. He made great efforts climbing the steep rocks until he reached the summit at the end of the path. There he prayed a salat of two cycles of prostration, and God on his throne saw it. Moses heard God's voice; it was like thunder and already he received insight. God spoke to his prophet: "I am your God. I am alone. There is no other.

Listen to me, Moses my messenger, I am God the Absolute, I am the First and the Last. Listen to me, beloved of my heart, I will give you my words."

Moses heard God's words while he was in the act of prostration, and he increased the intensity of his prayers. Then the Lord spoke: "Rise from your prayer. I am the Knower of all secrets: I can hear the date palms rustling in the orchards, I can see all that happens in the shadows of the night." While God spoke the earth shook, and Moses fainted for a long hour. When he came to, he stood up and prayed: "O merciful Lord!" God answered [with a phrase uttered by pilgrims to Mecca]: "At your service!" When Moses heard this he fell down on his face, and God asked him: "When I answer you, you fall down! What is the matter, my prophet?" Moses gave the Lord his answer: "O my Lord, when you answer me with 'At your service,' I feel I am falling and losing my senses." God answered: "My prophet! Hear my words: Every day, when a servant of mine calls me, mentioning my name with true intentions and a pure heart, I answer quickly: 'At your service,' I answer. Whenever a person calls me, I can hear him wherever he is; even if there are many, I will hear their prayers at once. Now, Moses, if you have a wish, speak!"

Moses spoke to his Lord: "My Lord! I wish to see you!" And Moses saw what seemed like a valley of bright light. He fainted again, so strong was the light; he heard hundreds of angels calling him: "Moses! You have sinned! The Lord God cannot be seen!" And Moses felt as if the mountains were crumbling and the earth was sinking away. But on the third day God relented and restored his brain to complete consciousness and light. The Lord gave him grace because he had become humble.

And Moses spoke to the Lord: "Lord, next time please warn me, may I receive right guidance in time, that I may continue to be humble." The Lord spoke to him: "Avoid the wrath of your Lord. Speak: There is no god but God, and adhere to that conviction. Have no doubt nor any alternative views ever! Doubt will make you want to see, and doubting God is sin. Repeat 'There is no god but Allah' with reverence. When the heart is upright, the soul will not be condemned on the Day of Reckoning. With my mercy you will be carried across to the Garden of Bliss, there to live forever. Until the end of time repeat: There is no god but Allah. Mercy comes after wrath.* Make your prayers numerous at every hour. Pray also for my final prophet Muhammad the Intercessor for his community. Remember to keep the fast and make the pilgrimage to Mecca. Do not neglect to pay the zakat [alms] regularly."

When the Lord had finished speaking to his faithful prophet, Moses suddenly saw how his arms were growing wings, seven on each side, beautiful wings decorated with pearls, and holy scripture was engraved on the feathers: the Torah and the Psalms. But when Moses heard the Lord praise his final prophet, Muhammad, Moses' heart was spoiled by envy and anger as well.† Jealousy entered his heart so that he lost all reason. Strength left his hands and the lovely wings disappeared from his arms. So Moses asked God the Compeller: "That Muhammad, what kind of person will he be?"

The Lord answered him: "I have given him beauty and I have given him the world, for the entire world will one day accept Muhammad's word and the religion of Islam. I swear by me that he will be mentioned after my name is mentioned in the *shahada*.‡ If it had not been for Muhammad, I would not have created the world,§ there would be no moon, nor a sun to give light, nor a sky nor an earth, nor paradise nor hell, nor life nor death, if it had not been for my favorite Prophet whom I decided to create first. The prophets would not have existed, nor the animals nor birds, nor the waters, salt or fresh, Adam and Eve would never have been created, nor the forbidden fruit nor any tree or plant, not even the angel Jibril, if it had not been for the Intercessor.

"Now Moses, I tell you, choose between this world and the next. If you choose this world you will surely regret it. Choose between God and the world, Moses; meditate and reflect, avoid hellfire, it has dangerous snakes on every floor. Beware! Every serpent is as long as a year's walk. These terrifying snakes are everywhere in the houses of the wicked, the

---

* Inverting a sacred hadith; later in the conversation, God says the opposite.
† Swahili literature provides many examples of one prophet "envying" another's loftier state.
‡ "There is no god but God and Muhammad is the Messenger of God."
§ A near quotation of a popular sacred hadith.

oppressors, those who worshipped false gods as well as the eaters of
forbidden food, the wine drinkers and drunkards. I have placed snakes
ready for the man who rebels against his father and lies with his mother.

"And for the merchant who does not give alms when breaking the fast
and for the fornicator I have lit a great fire in hell. Do not doubt it: those
who cut their beards and those who pray while weeping will receive
no pardon: Amru Rabani, the angel of the fire, will have their trembling
souls to roast. The drunkard will not be able to pronounce the confession
of faith in the grave, so my snakes will creep all over him.⁶ I warn all
people, do not be tempted to slander others; fear me! Do not increase my
wrath by even thinking about atheism [*kufr*]. An angry heart without
faith [*iman*] will follow the Devil.

"The gift for those who long for me," thus spoke the kind Lord
further, "is knowledge of the divine qualities, the lauding words by which
I am praised. He that fears me with goodness, I will fill him with mercy
and I will decide in his favor on Judgment Day. Night and day I observe
everyone, and whoever repeats my name while doing good things, I will
fill him with mercy, and punishment will be removed from him. Remember death day and night: it may come at any time, and when it comes
there is no delay. My messenger of death will take his soul, so a person
has no other worry in life than to think of the last hour. If a person makes
his thoughts pure, I will forgive his sins. The digger of graves will live in
heaven, and the one who buries his mother with love will live in a palace
in paradise. The one who carries the bier with a heart eager to please, his
sins will be forgiven. And the one who pays for the funeral and feeds the
poor need not worry and will avoid all suffering later.

"Give meals to the poor and let them be good meals. Feed also my
fakirs* and do not despise them." At that point Moses asked: "Lord,
what is a fakir?" God the Giver spoke: "A fakir is a lonely man who is
disliked by the people; he is never treated like a neighbor, people take no
notice of him. They will invite a rich man to their homes, but they will
ignore a fakir. If you invite my fakir with honor and give him a good

---

*From the Arabic *faqir*, lit. mendicants, beggars, perhaps referring to Sufis; one
of many Arabic terms used in Swahili, like *iman* and *kufr* above.

meal, then on the Day of Resurrection I will remove your sins from your record.

"Furthermore, never be angry because in your anger there is Satan's footstep. Every dead body must be buried, even the slaves; it is honorable to be buried by all people together. Do not dwell in the company of a miser, nor of a greedy man, for he will not leave you your house. Avoid liars and do not speak evil of people nor reveal their disgrace. Never lie. Beware of adultery. On the day when the souls emerge there will be anxiety and pain, and the rich will be reduced.

"Moses! Your people must always repeat my name and my greatness, then an angel will come [at Judgment] and purify all the people with compassion, those who have remembered me all their lives with gratitude. Their sins will be removed."

Moses spoke and asked the Generous One: "What did you do to Adam? What were his sins?" The Rich One spoke: "Adam rebelled against me to follow the Devil instead of what I had told him. I placed him in the Garden; he could not eat from all the trees, but he ate from the forbidden tree knowingly. A quarrel does not end soon. I had to expel him from heaven. My commandments must never be questioned. I am the Giver. Wrath comes after mercy."

God the Giver spoke: "I will always stay close to my believers. My visiting will be in their hearts. There I will stay. I am as close as that which throbs in your throat" [50:16].

Then faithful Moses asked: "How can I know who is a believer?" Spoke the Exalted One, answering his good prophet: "The one who abandons the forbidden and does what is allowed and loves the law for my sake." Further Moses inquired: "Where do you live? What is your true abode?" The Lord God the Giver revealed to him: "I live up there above all else on the Throne. But there is more that I will disclose: even though I reside on my throne, it is not there alone that I live. My existence spreads across the skies" [see 2:255]. And Moses asked: "Who are you? Please explain yourself to me." The Powerful One answered: "I am I, with the angels."

Then Moses asked: "Who is righteous [*salih*]?" The Lord spoke: "A righteous person keeps my commandments by night as well as by day.

He is my beloved and I shall recognize him [on the Day of Judgment]."
Then Moses asked: "Where is your abode? If it is not only on the Throne,
where are you?" The Majesty spoke: "You want to know my first existence? Then listen: In the beginning I created something with the likeness
of an egg, and the whole creation in one, the very first, but it was invisible. It was a hundred thousand years long and as much in width. Then I
made the elements: light, fire, water, and earth. I created the earth out of
foam. I created the rocks, and I placed one rock in Jerusalem as a good gift.
It will await the Resurrection when the masses meet there. The throngs
of the risen will converge there.* That will be the moment of luck or
disgrace and joy for the good. I accompany the clouds, I reveal by my
power, I am my power, there is nothing that can stop it." The Lord spoke:
"All things people wish for will be given to them in this life and the
hereafter."

All the Majesty spoke further: "You want to know my first? Hear,
we will tell you: My first is to love the thing I begin to do, and that is
creating the heart of a human being, for what is more useful than the
heart? The length of a human heart is eight finger breadths across, and
yet I dwell inside it.† Every heart, trustworthy one, is rounded, soft and
weak, more so than any other thing on earth. These hearts, my prophet,
a mustard seed of faith inside one will be sufficient for salvation. Each
heart, my prophet, I give it a soul inside it, like a little bird with green
feathers. When you die that bird will fly back to me. It will show me if
there was a mustard seed of true faith in a person's heart at the time of
his death, so that he did not have to fear death. No one has to fear death
and yet they cry when death approaches, but I do not prolong their lives.
The body dies. I created all souls out of the first light. Half of this light
in my hand I made into the soul of my prophet Muhammad. I placed this
light-substance in front of my face for a thousand years until it began to
spread and the soul worshipped me. Then it rose up and stood before me.

"Ten thousand angels prostrated themselves worshipping the light,

---

* An apparent reference to the Dome of the Rock (see fig. 23).
† An allusion to a sacred hadith that says that although heaven and earth cannot
contain God, the human heart can.

performing the salat of noon. Only then did I create my throne of light, the lesser angels, the human souls, and many other things: the wind that carries voices, the palanquin of the starry sky, the bright light of the sun and the full moon. The skies with their mists, the clouds and the earth, and the ocean full of waves. I created mountains, my prophet, and the true paradise full of good things. I adorned it with jewels, pearls and gemstones, with red gold and fine silver.

"I will place all human souls in it who have not worshipped idols but have followed the truth of God, thus keeping sin away from themselves. This paradise, Confessor, I will place in it the Muslims who have worshipped me unceasingly, praying the good prayers; and those who have kept the vigils, who have never harmed other people nor envied anyone, nor coveted anything they saw. But everyone who rebels and follows the devil, the seducer of souls, will go into the fire forever. Having created all those things, I then created the jinns and placed them in the wells; there they live.

"After that, Confessor, I created Adam, who would rule the jinns and make them his subjects. Listen carefully: this is not *your* Adam who was your ancestor, it was not the same person. This Adam lived for a thousand and ten years, then I took him away and replaced him with another king of the jinns. Many years later I created the human Adam and his wife, Eve. All their descendants will die at an unknown time, so remember to repent your sins daily, keep the fast in Ramadan, pray to the Lord day and night, love your parents, respect your neighbor, be generous to the poor and to the orphans, and live in peace with all people. I will reward you later.

"Let there be no corruption, accept the commandment to pray, submit yourselves to my law, purify your souls, and read my book. Contemplate my mercy: on the Day of Resurrection your sins will be forgiven. The one who worships me sincerely according to my religion of praying, I will reduce his pain on the day his soul is taken."

Think, human being! Be honest, never lie! Pray God that he lighten the suffering in the afterlife and forgive you your sins. God of grace! Help us with your power. Be merciful toward us obedient Muslims! This is my last wish in this life.

✳ Hamka
Qur'an Commentary on Pilgrimage Ritual

ANTHONY H. JOHNS

Pilgrimage to Mecca is the fifth of the "pillars" of Islam. As numerous visual reminders make clear (see figs. 16 and 17),[7] over the centuries Muslims have expended enormous effort preparing for the event and enjoyed reminiscing about it afterward. The following example of modern *tafsir* from Indonesia discusses an important ritual aspect of the required religious practice of hajj, pilgrimage to Mecca. During hajj, pilgrims commemorate Hagar's frantic search for water for her baby Isma'il; this commentary explains a key verse related to the practice, 2:158.

Hamka is the acronym of Haji Abdul Malik Karim Amrullah (1908–81). His father, Karim Amrullah, belonged to the first generation of Sumatran *'ulama'* who returned from study in the Middle East at the turn of the nineteenthth century to spread the reformist ideas of Muhammad 'Abduh and Rashid Rida in the then Dutch East Indies. Hamka was born in 1908, in central Sumatra. He studied with his father (of whom he wrote a biography), with other outstanding local *'ulama'*, and at local religious schools. He first made the pilgrimage in 1927 (he was to make it seven times). He became a leading figure in the Reformist Muhammadiya (a social welfare and educational organization), and in addition became widely known as a novelist. After the Japanese occupation he became a national figure, and from 1959 on regularly denounced Sukarno's increasing reliance on the Indonesian Communist Party. He was arrested in 1964 and held in detention until 1966, being rehabilitated in 1967. While in prison he wrote the tafsir from which this excerpt comes. When the Council of Indonesian *'ulama'* was established in 1975, he was elected its first general chairman.[8]

"Safa and Marwa [two hills now within the precincts of the Ka'ba] too are among the signs of God. So whoever makes the Hajj or the 'Umra [lesser pilgrimage] to the House, there is no objection that he makes the round between them. Whoever adds to a good deed, then God is indeed one who responds to gratitude, one who is all-knowing" [Q 2:158].

According to Muhammad 'Abduh in the explanation he gives in his tafsir, this verse continues the matters presented in the verses on the change of *kiblat* [i.e., qibla, facing Mecca] [2:144–145: "Turn your face then toward the Sacred Mosque . . . "], although other tafsir do not make

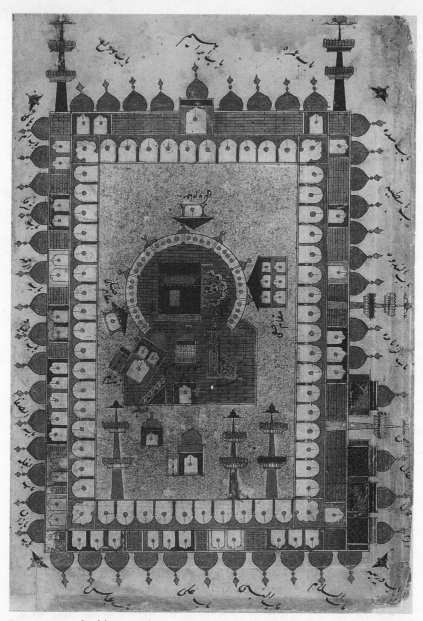

Figure 16.   A leaf from a Pilgrimage guidebook shows the Kaʿba in both plan and elevation and indicates the various sacred sites within the sanctuary, especially the "station of Abraham," where the prophet is said to have stood and prayed, and the well of Zamzam at lower left of the Kaʿba. Written in Mecca in 1582 after the Ottoman conquest of the central Middle East, the diagram also indicates places assigned to the four Sunni law schools and the names of all gates into the sanctuary. Cambridge, MA: Harvard University Art Museums, Arthur M. Sackler Museum, The Edwin Binney, 3rd, Collection of Turkish Art, 1985.265A. (See also fig. 22.)

this connection. It mentions the hastening to and fro (*sa'y*) between Safa and Marwa after giving a reminder of the need for prayer and patience [2:153: "ask help with prayer and patience"] and the endurance of trials of various kinds later to receive the fullness of God's blessing [2:157: "It is such who receive blessings and mercy from their Lord"].

This verse then gives hope that a time will come when they will be able to make the round between Safa and Marwa. No matter how hard are present difficulties they now face, there must always be hope, especially when it is God Himself who gives this hope.

"Safa and Marwa too are among the signs of God" [2:158, first words]. We have enriched our Indonesian language with the word *shi'ar*, for we regularly speak of the *syi'ar* of Islam. *Shi'ar* means sign. Its plural form is *sha'a'ir*. *Sha'a'irullah* means signs of devotion to God. Many such signs are included in the performance of the Hajj. The napes of the necks of the camels and cattle to be sacrificed on the conclusion of the Hajj are incised as a sign. This incision is called a *shi'ar*. Prayer at the tomb of Abraham is another of these *sha'a'ir* of devotion. Circumambulation of the Ka'ba, the station at 'Arafat, and also the hastening to and fro between Safa and Marwa mentioned in this verse are also among these *sha'a'ir*, and likewise the stoning of Jumra [pillars representing the Devil] at Mina.

These rituals are classed as acts of devotion (*ta'abbud*), as opposed to acts of understanding (*ta'aqqul*). *Ta'abbud* means an act of religious devotion, but why it is performed as it is is not accessible to reason. *Ta'aqqul* is an act of understanding. We can understand by the use of reason why we perform the ritual prayer, but we cannot understand why for the midday (*zuhr*) prayer there should be four cycles of prostration (*rak'a*) and for the dawn (*subh*) prayer two cycles. These are acts of devotion. We can understand why the Hajj should be performed at least once in a lifetime. This is an act of understanding. But we cannot understand why there should be a command to stone Jumra with small stones seven times. This is an act of devotion. All such *sha'a'ir* are acts of devotion.

"So whoever makes the Hajj or 'Umra to the House, there is no objection that he makes the round between them." The House referred to here is the *bayt Allah* (the House of God, the Ka'ba). Now the Hajj is

Figure 17.   Above a field of talismanic geometric shapes (stars, circles, octagons) on this North African pilgrims' banner (1683), a large horizontal band of Kufic script quotes Q 48:1–3: "Truly we have granted you [Muhammad] a decisive victory victorious, [namely] that God might forgive your sins [both] past and future, bring his grace to fulfillment in you, and guide you on a straight path; and that God might assist you with redoubtable aid." The twin blades of 'Ali's sword, Dhu 'l-Faqar, repeat those verses in the more flowing Naskhi script, adding part of verse 4: "He it is who sent down peace upon the hearts of the believers. . . . " In the rectangular panel directly below the upper inscription, an Arabic poem in Maghribi script mentions several of the rituals and sites integral to the hajj, as well as the name 'Abd al-Qadir al-Jilani (d. 1166), suggesting that members of the Qadiriya *tariqa* carried the banner. Cambridge, MA: Fogg Art Museum, Gift of John Goelet, 1958.20.

performed on a prescribed date, commencing on the ninth [*sic*] of the month Dhu 'l-Hijja (the twelfth lunar month) and continuing until the completion of the halt at Mina, on the twelfth or thirteenth of Dhu 'l-Hijja. The 'Umra, on the other hand, is an obligation that may be fulfilled any time, including during the Hajj season. It does not involve the station at 'Arafat and the halting at Muzdalifah and Mina. Both the Hajj and the 'Umra, however, require putting on the garment of *ihram* and the circumambulation of the Ka'ba, and both require the hastening to and fro (*sa'y*) between the hills of Safa and Marwa.

Safa and Marwa are two small hills not far from the Sacred Mosque. The distance between them is about 760.5 cubits [circa 200 m]. After the most recent renovations to the Masjid al-Haram (1957), both are within the mosque precinct. The sa'y, that is, the going to and fro around these two hills seven times, is part of both the Hajj and the 'Umra. It is performed after completion of the circumambulation. After this, divestiture [*tahallul*], that is, the cutting of the hair and taking off of the garment of ihram, is permissible. With this divestiture the ceremonies of the pilgrimage are complete.

According to a hadith reported by Bukhari and Muslim on the authority of Ibn 'Abbas, this shi'ar of hastening to and fro commemorates Hajar (the second wife of Abraham). After she had given birth to Isma'il, Abraham left her alone in the desert because he had to continue his journey to Syria. Their supply of water was finished, her breasts were almost dry, and there was no well in that place. Her child Isma'il had been crying with hunger until his throat was hoarse. Full of anxiety, Hajar hastened to and fro seven times between the two hills looking for water, while her child remained alone, in her tent in the lower valley.

Suddenly she heard a voice, and saw a bird flying. At the same time, she could hear the voice of her child crying for milk. After her hastening to and fro seven times, she ran back to where she had left her child. There she saw an angel digging the earth at its feet, and water appeared. Anxiously she scooped up the water in her hands exclaiming, "Zam! Zam!," which means, "Gather round! Gather round!"

By chance at the same time, a caravan of the people of Jurhum passed by looking for water. This became the well of Zamzam, and this was how "the barren valley" [Q 14:37: "Our Lord, I have set some of my posterity to dwell in a barren valley next to your Sacred House"] became populated and developed into a city. This was the origin of Mecca.

So Hajar's hastening to and fro became one of the shi'ar of the Hajj and the 'Umra, and the verse that we are explaining acknowledges her as indeed a shi'ar of devotion to God. A special sign of religious devotion.

Why should there be or not be anything wrong if one wishes to hasten to and fro between these two hills as is required?

According to a hadith reported by Bukhari and Muslim, 'Urwa ibn Zubayr one day expressed to 'A'isha,* Mother of the Believers, his opinion that from the wording of the verse the hastening to and fro between Safa and Marwa is not obligatory, for if it said there is no objection if one hastens to and fro between these two hills, then there is certainly no objection if one does not do so. 'Urwa's opinion was aptly answered by 'A'isha, "It is not as you understand it, my sister's son."

[The hadith continues:] "The hastening to and fro between Safa and Marwa is one of the sha'a'ir of devotion. The reason why the verse says there is no objection to the practice is that, during the Time of Ignorance,† if any of the Ansar‡ went to Mecca to perform the Hajj or 'Umra, they were sure to encounter a huge, menacing statue of Manat§ placed between the two hills. After they had become Muslims, they had doubts as to whether they should still perform the hastening to and fro between the two hills while the statue of Manat was still there. This verse makes it clear that there was no objection to their hastening to and fro even though the statue was still there." Such is a summary of the hadith in Bukhari and Muslim.

The verse continues, "Whoever adds to a good deed, then God is indeed one who responds to gratitude, who knows all things" [2:158, end]. Performance of the Hajj or 'Umra is required only once in a life-

---

* 'A'isha (d. 678): Muhammad's youngest wife and a transmitter of numerous traditions.

† Time of Ignorance: the age of *jahiliya,* prior to the advent of Islam.

‡ The Ansar ("Helpers") were citizens of Medina who become Muslims after the hijra.

§ Manat was one of the three pre-Islamic deities called "daughters of Allah." Muhammad forbade belief in them, of course.

time. However, if one wishes to repeat it, doing a good deed willingly [and not out of obligation—by *tatawwu*] by adding another performance of the Hajj or the 'Umra, up to as many times as one goes to Mecca, God will respond to the pious act and reward the good deed. God knows every good deed one does.

So it seems that this verse is indeed connected with the command to change the direction of the kiblat and the hope it gives for a future victory. At a time to come, Muhammad's followers in Medina will indeed be able to perform the 'Umra. Even though at the time of the revelation of this verse there was still an idol between the hills of Safa and Marwa, and there were still statues lining the walls of the Ka'ba, there was no objection to their continuing their act of devotion, because it had no connection with the idols.

Some time later, the Messenger of God dreamt that he and his companions would be able to go to Mecca to perform the 'Umra, and then they would go together. But when in year 6 of the Hijra they reached Hudaybiya, the Quraysh* prevented them from going further. The treaty of Hudaybiya† was made, and they did not go that year. It was not until the following year, year 7, that the 'Umra of Qadha took place. They were able to perform the 'Umra in full. They circumambulated the Ka'ba, although it still contained idols, and they did the hastening to and fro between Safa and Marwa, although there was still a statue of Manat there. They paid no attention to these idols. They carried out the sha'a'ir of the ceremony in full.

Then, a year later, in year 8, because the Quraysh had dishonored the treaty, the city of Mecca was conquered, and all the idols were swept away. Before they achieved this, the Muslims endured sufferings of many kinds, shortages of material possessions and loss of friends who died as martyrs on the field of battle in jihad, but at the end came the fullness of the blessings that God had promised. And God repaid with victory in this world and happiness in the hereafter all the efforts they had made and the good deeds they had done.

* The Quraysh were the ruling tribe in Mecca.
† In the treaty of Hudaybiya, a place ten miles from Mecca, the Quraysh agreed to allow the Muslims to visit the holy city.

Concerning this hastening to and fro between Safa and Marwa, all the 'ulama' whose authority we accept agree that it is one of the rituals of the pilgrimage. They only differ concerning the way it is defined according to the norms of *fiqh* [religious law]. Malik, Shafi'i, and Ibn Hanbal are of the view that it is a component [*rukn*] of the Hajj. Abu Hanifa is of the view that its performance is obligatory for the Hajj.

DEVOTION BEYOND DUTY

In addition to the required observances suggested by the term "Five Pillars," Muslims the world over have engaged in a variety of devotional activities that often manifest distinctive regional or local characteristics. We begin with personal prayers (*du'a'*) attributed to a number of holy women of the classical and middle periods of Islamic history. Then a series of poems offers a taste of four poetic genres—*marthiya* (lamentation), *madih* (praise of a holy person), *na't* (laud of Muhammad), and *ginan* (love song)—that have played important roles in popular piety, especially in the Middle East and the Indian subcontinent. A radio sermon preached in an Egyptian village celebrating the birthday of a local holy person provides a sample of how the mosque sermon (*khutba*) continues to function in popular experience. Themes of devotion (fig. 18) and rites of passage such as those associated with death, mourning, and burial are also vividly expressed in art and architecture (figs. 19–21).

*   Prayers of Holy Women

JOHN RENARD

In his hagiographical anthology *Shining Stars of the Biographies of the Masters of Sufism* (*Al-kawakib ad-durriya tarajim as-sadat as-sufiya*), 'Abd ar-Ra'uf al-Munawi (1545–1621) includes biographical notices on thirty-five women renowned for piety and learning. Many of his notices feature brief prayers attributed to their subjects. Here is a sample of their heartfelt aspirations.

Barada of [the Yemeni valley of] Sarim lived during the second Islamic century. She used to keep long night vigils and keep herself awake by saying "with a voice of longing": "Eyes are at rest as the stars are

Figure 18.   An Indian woman at prayer appears on this calendar poster, with the Ka'ba and Muhammad's mosque/tomb in Medina in the background. Courtesy of Carl Ernst.

setting. Every lover is alone with his beloved. And I am alone with you, O Beloved! Do you not see how you torture me while your love is in my heart, O Beloved."[9]

After the night salat, Habiba al-'Adawiya (8th–9th c.) used to stand on a balcony and pray: "My God, the stars have set; eyes are closed in sleep; kings have barred their gates. But your gate is open: every lover is alone with his beloved, and this is my place [lit., (mystical) station] in your presence." At the break of dawn, she would say: "O God, this night has slipped away and this day has unveiled itself. If only I knew: Has my night pleased you, so that I might rejoice? Or have you rejected it, so that I must suffer? For it is by your power that I persevere and by your eternal tirelessness that you give me staying power. And if by your power you would drive me away, may I never depart from your door; and let nothing but your generosity and bounty descend upon my heart."[10]

Rabi'a al-'Adawiya (d. 801) of Basra (Iraq) was also fond of praying after the night salat: "Eyes are heavy with sleep, unaware of their forgetfulness. And still Rabi'a the sinner abides in your presence in the hope that You might look on her with a gaze that will keep sleep from diminishing her service of You. By your power and majesty, may I not slacken in serving You either night or day until I meet You [in death]."[11]

Ruqayya of Mosul (Iraq, 8th c.) prayed: "My God and my Master, if You tormented me with your full punishment, loss of your nearness would be more severe; and if You blessed me with all the delights of the people of the Garden, your love in my heart would be still greater [pleasure]." And "I love my Lord with a fierce love; should he order me to the Fire, I would feel none of its heat for [the heat of] His love."[12]

Rayhana (8–9th c.), whom some called "the Madwoman," embroidered this prayer in verse on her gown:

> You are my confidant, my desire and my joy
>> my heart knows how to love only you.
> O my beloved, my desire and my longing
>> my yearning stretches on till I meet You.
> I ask not the delights of the Garden
>> but only to see you, O my greatest desire.

At dawn she prayed: "Darkness has left with closeness and familiarity / O that darkness would come again with its intimacy!"[13]

'A'isha (d. 762), daughter of the sixth Shi'i Imam, Ja'far as-Sadiq (d. 765), prayed: "By your glory and your magnificence, should you send me to the Fire, I would brandish my faith in your unity and would go about among the damned saying, 'People of the Fire, I have believed only in His Oneness yet He punishes me!'"[14]

Zahra' the Mournful (9th c.) prayed: "You whose powers are without limit, you the Munificent and Eternal, make the eyes of my heart rejoice in gardens of your power. Join my anxious care to your tender largess, O Gracious One. In your majesty and splendor take me away from the paths of the arrogant [lit., those who make a show of power], O Compassionate one. Make me a servant and a seeker. And be, O light of my heart and ultimate desire, my Friend."[15]

Rites of Passage and Popular Practice

✳ *Marthiya*
Imam Husayn's Conversation with God

ALI ASANI

Annual Shi'i rituals of mourning for the proto-martyr Husayn are symbolic of much more than the love and attachment the Shi'a feel toward Husayn and their Imams.[16] Around these rituals has developed a theological doctrine, unique in the history of Islamic thought, that of redemptive suffering. According to this doctrine, the Prophet's legitimate descendants, the Shi'i Imams and their families, will intercede on the Day of Resurrection for those faithful who have participated in their sorrows and afflictions. God has granted them the status of intercessors by virtue of their sufferings in this world, and in the case of Husayn, by virtue of his martyrdom. Implicit is the doctrine of salvation through faith, for only those who have faith (love) for the Shi'i Imams, and hence suffer with them, will be redeemed. The various rituals in the month of Muharram therefore provide important means for the Shi'a community to participate symbolically in the sufferings of the Imams and ensure their intercession.

The following elegy (*marthiya*) is commonly attributed to Anis (1803–1875), one of the most renowned elegists in the Urdu language. The poem is widely recited among Shi'i communities in South Asia. Its six-line verses are characteristic of the marthiya as it developed in the nineteenth century in northern India. Since the elegy deals with the final moments preceding Imam Husayn's martyrdom in 680, it is usually recited on the tenth day of Muharram, the anniversary of the Imam's death, at the climax of the mourning rituals. Its widespread popularity as a religious poem is due to its unusual format as a final conversation between Imam Husayn and God just before the enemy forces behead him.[17]

1. After seventy-two bodies had perished in the path of God
   The King of Martyrs [Husayn] remained all alone in the field of
       affliction.
   The Imam of the two worlds had no more strength in his body;
   And not one among the king's companions and friends survived.

Neither the glory of his dignity nor that of his court remained;

All that remained [to be done] was the plunder of his women-folk and this chieftain's demise.

2. Holding the corpse of [his son] Asghar "Little One" in his arms, he repeated:

"O Lord, this unworthy offering, may it be accepted!

How can I adequately express my gratitude to You, O my just Sovereign?

You have bestowed on my 'Little One' the highest rank.

He sacrificed his life for the children of my [followers] the Shi'a;

Although a mere babe of six months, his obedience to God was absolute.

3. "I am not saddened by this tragedy; [rather] I rejoice in happiness.

I do not care about my head, nor do I fear anyone.

Yes! Husayn, son of 'Ali, does have a single request:

May I not see the Prophet's granddaughter disgraced.

When she is stripped of her veil, may it be after I lie [dead] on the ground.

And [God] if that truly be Your will, may I not even be lying unburied!

4. "You gave me an army, a family, and also a house.

You made me a leader and also gave me a head.

You gave me a son who resembled the Prophet.

You gave me this resolution, this heart and also this courage;

I am proud to give up my dear ones in the path of God

For it is Your bounty that I have sacrificed for You.

5. "Did I have the strength [to endure] having my entire household plundered?!

Or to bring forth Asghar 'The Little One' in my arms when Akbar 'The Elder One' was murdered?!

He was writhing in my arms, but I said not a word!

Even if my arms were to be cut off, I would still not abandon [lit., remove my hand from] my people.

No one [else] could have been happy [as I am] at this assault of
　destruction.
Without the grace of God, I, the lowly one, would not have been
　capable of [enduring] all of this.

6. "Well known is Adam's lament at being exiled from paradise;
But I set out from Yathrib [Medina] cheerful and happy.
When Jacob's son was taken from him,
He cried so much that his eyes went blind.
But I, the lowly one, have received [such] support from the Almighty
That the sacrifice of [my son] Akbar was a festival [*'id*].

7. "Do not You abandon me as the community has!
You are pure; remove me from the world in purity.
Abandoned by all, I journey to paradise alone.
O Lord, protect me from the grief of the grave.
In the gloom of the pauper's grave
May I see from every direction Your splendor.

8. "I need not a house; the door of Your felicity is enough for me.
I need not a head; my only concern is You.
I need not a bed; Your grace is my pillow [lit., support].
I need not an army; I want Your assistance.
May the agonies of death be easy for my Shi'a;
May whatever befalls me be in requital for my devotees."

9. Suddenly a voice issued from [behind] the veil of divine omnipotence:
"Well done! You have demonstrated perfectly submission and
　willingness.
O servant! We made you a divine representative.
In this manner do God's chosen exemplify loyalty and fidelity.
You have sacrificed your dear ones as well as your companions.
Only one head was pledged; you have offered seventy-two!

10. "Enough! enough! O Shabbir*, for your God is embarrassed.
Why are you afraid, O Shabbir, to enter My presence?

* Shabbir: an alternate name for Husayn.

O Shabbir, I covet the gift you bring.

O Shabbir, I like humility among my servants;

You have considered Our court the gift of forgiveness.

By understanding your [special] status, one understands the Almighty."

11. When the holy one heard the Divine command in its entirety,

He spontaneously turned toward the infidels and cried out:

"Where is the murderer? Let him come and remove my head!"

From the ladies' tent, the sister cried, "May I be sacrificed for you!

Brother, to whom will the Sayyid* women lament in their pain?

These sisters of yours, bereft of a mother, will be looted!"

12. From yonder the tyrants suddenly advanced the line of entrenchment,

Casting a cloudlike shadow on Fatima's† moon.

The arrow of oppression was fired so that it pierced through the chest.

The spears were flung so that they penetrated the vitals.

As the blood of the King's body flowed from his wounds,

Came forth from his mouth, continuously, "I trust in God."

✴ *Madih*

Three Contemporary Poems Honoring Imam Riza

FATEMEH KESHAVARZ

Celebration of the spiritual status of the Prophet, the Imams, or other holy persons is deeply rooted in Persian poetic discourse.[18] But the passage of time has not left this genre obsolete. A recent edition of contemporary poems, *The Seventh Qibla*, demonstrates the relevance of this kind of poetic tribute in modern Iran. A significant number of such poems are dedicated to ʿAli ar-Riza (d. 818), known as Imam Riza, the eighth successor to Muhammad according to the "Twelver" Shiʿa.

Imam Riza is a special figure in Iranian religious culture. His tomb, located in the city of Tus (now known as Mashhad) in northeast Iran (see map), is the site of regular pilgrimage and is associated with many miracles in popular belief. Imam Riza's appointment by the Abbasid caliph al-Maʾmun as the heir to

---

* Sayyid: a title used to refer to any descendant of the Prophet Muhammad, especially through his grandson Husayn.

† Fatima (d. 633): Husayn's mother, and daughter of the Prophet Muhammad.

Figure 19.　Excessive grief of a son at the burial of his father. In his *Conference of the Birds* (*Mantiq at-tayr*), 'Attar tells how a son walked ahead of his father's coffin, grieving disconsolately. The panels of text on the upper right and lower left of this 1483 Persian miniature relate how a Sufi (here pictured at the gate) reminds the mourner that he should heed the lesson of his father's mortality rather than dwell on his own sorrow: "Though you long to sit on a kingdom's throne, your hand will grasp only the wind." On the banner is a reminder that "God is the best of trustees, the best of patrons, and the best of helpers"; the pennants around the upper grave read "O God!" New York: Metropolitan Museum of Art, Fletcher Fund, 63.210.35r.

the caliphate in the year 816 brought the Shi'a two uncharacteristically jubilant years. However, his untimely death on Iranian soil, attributed to al-Ma'mun's rivalry, resonates in Shi'i memory with the passionate injured feelings of an oppressed minority. He has acquired the unofficial status of the patron saint of travelers, sick and needy persons, and even captive animals.[19] Note especially how these twentieth-century poets use imagery of pilgrimage, implicitly likening Mashhad to Mecca.

The first selection is called "The Heart's Hope" ("Umid-i dil"), by Muhammad Husayn Bihjati, a.k.a Shafaq, "Twilight":

In Riza's domain the soul is purified.
    The heart, here, opens up to God's light.
O dejected one, turn to Riza,
    For this king accepts beggars graciously.
Go to him humbly, for he receives his pilgrims
    At the table of his generosity.
His kindness is boundless like the sea,
    He accepts the sinful and the righteous alike.
His unhampered charity is open to all,
    He accepts friends and strangers alike.
If you are in pain, come to his door,
    For every pain finds a remedy here.
O [Riza] my heart's hope! Look in my direction,
    For my heart will be purified in your gaze.
Ask God to forgive my sins,
    For whatever you ask, God will accept.
O Shafaq! burn all your longings!
    For the Beloved accepts the heart which has no desires.[20]

In a poem entitled "The Ka'ba of the Heart" ("Ka'ba-i dil"), 'Ali Khaliliyan, whose poetic pen name is Raja', "Hope," writes:

Come to the Ka'ba of the heart! Zamzam and Safa are here.
    The true house of God's singular glory is here.
If the journey to the house of Ka'ba did not bear fruit,

Do not look in vain, the essence of faith is here.
If your false [human] insight did not solve the problem
There is no need [for that insight], for the knot-opening hand is here.
Do not despair needlessly because of your sins,
If you have lost hope, this is your true mistake.
Say, O Raja, to the one suffering from the ailment of sin:
"Be happy!" for the best remedy for your pain is here.[21]

The last example is an excerpt from a relatively long poem in rhyming couplets by Rahi Mu'ayyiri, well known for his rich variations on the traditional Persian *ghazal*. This poem, entitled "The Light of Riza" ("Nur-i Riza"), is a nocturnal meditation over a problem that the poet feels was solved through supplication to Imam Riza. The portion translated here is the middle section and consists entirely of praise of the Imam:

Behold the light of this bright star!
Behold the splendor of the king of Khurasan!*
See the mirror depicting the unseen!
Abandon yourself and [in the mirror] see God!
Whoever has been immersed in Riza's light
Has found in his own heart the gem of contentment.†
The shadow of the king is a source of respite.
The domain of Riza is the domain of happiness.
What is the Ka'ba where circumambulating his [Riza's] house is
concerned?
What is musk where the aroma of the breeze from his land is
concerned?
Dust turns into gold under his feet
And musk gains aroma in his presence.
Who am I? One among his many slaves
Pleading for help to his generosity.
[Who am I?] A speck of dust revolving around the sun of love
A dead person who, in love, has found eternal life.

* King of Khurasan: A common epithet of Imam Riza.
† A pun on the word Riza, which means contentment.

To the king of Khurasan, I am but a doorkeeper.

To the king of Khurasan, I am the dust spread on the threshold.[22]

✳ *Na't*
Poem in Praise of Muhammad
ALI ASANI

Muslims have composed verses praising the virtues of their Prophet since the seventh century. As expressions of personal piety and feeling, these poems often contain ideas that do not necessarily conform with "official" theological doctrines. Perhaps the most important theme in these poems is love for Muhammad. He appears as a father figure, a revered family elder, a close relative, or a dear friend to whom one would turn for assistance. Indeed, it has become customary for many Muslims to beseech the Prophet for guidance in solving every problem, no matter how mundane. Some poets even express their feelings for the Prophet with language borrowed from the profane realm of human romance, seeing themselves as intoxicated with Prophetic love and yearning to be with their beloved. It is in this context that the poet Lutf (d. 1881) expresses his longing for Medina, the site of the Prophet's final resting place.[23]

Intercessor for mankind, O intercessor for mankind,

Forgive me, O intercessor for mankind.

To whom else should I plea, O redresser of grievances,

But to you, O intercessor for mankind.

O king, where should he go, abandoning your door,

This supplicant of yours, O intercessor for mankind.

My every sin you will have

Forgiven by God, O intercessor for mankind.

In both worlds, yours is the protection,

There is none other, O intercessor for mankind.

For God's sake, don't forget me

On the day of recompense, O intercessor for mankind.

Save me from [the torments of] hell,

For God's sake, O intercessor for mankind.

Lord, may I die in Medina,

That is my prayer, O intercessor for mankind.

In my grave, too, assist me;

    O my Mustafa,* O intercessor for mankind.

You are aware of what I desire;

    What [else] can I request, O intercessor for mankind.

Lord, this is my heart's desire,

    This is my hope, this is my passion, praise God, O intercessor for
        mankind:

As in this life I have enthusiasm for

    Composing poems for you, O intercessor for mankind,

May I continue after death in paradise

    For ever and always, O intercessor for mankind.

In the Qur'an, in place after place,

    God Himself praises you, O intercessor for mankind.

Let aside humans, even angels cannot compose

    Praise poems worthy of you, O intercessor for mankind.

Call Lutf to Medina now,

    So that he does not have go from door to door [like a beggar],

        O intercessor for mankind.

---

* *Ginan*
Isma'ili Petition of a Yearning Soul

ALI ASANI

The Nizari Isma'ilis are well known in the contemporary Muslim world as members of a small Shi'i Muslim community whose spiritual leader (Imam) is the Aga Khan. The ginan translated here is an excellent example of the use of the *virahini*, the yearning young woman or bride tormented by the absence of her husband. This symbol of the soul and the associated concept of *viraha*, "longing in separation," has enjoyed great popularity in a wide variety of South Asian religious literatures, including the Hindu, Sikh, and Islamic Sufi traditions. The hymn, attributed to the sixteenth-century preacher Sayyid Khan (d. 1572), employs a mixture of three Indian languages, Hindi, Braj Bhasha, and Gujarati, and is sung in a suitably plaintive melody.

    Here the virahini is typically affected by the fiery pangs of yearning for the

---

* Mustafa: Chosen One, an epithet of the Prophet.

Figure 20. This white marble tombstone of an Iranian named Abu Saʿd ibn Muhammad, who died in 1150, includes inscriptions in both Kufic and Naskhi scripts. Within the mihrab form a Kufic inscription gives information on the deceased; just beneath that is the name of the sculptor. A qurʾanic text (3:18) about God's transcendent unity, power, and justice appears around the three sides of the inner rectangular frame. New York: Metropolitan Museum of Art, Rogers Fund, 1933 (33.118).

vision (*darshan* or *didar*) of her beloved Imam. Love for the Imam has driven her to distraction, for she knows she can no longer survive without him. In this state, worldly existence has become a cage from which the Imam is the refuge. To emphasize the humility of the disciple before the spiritual guide, the virahini is not only willing to sacrifice everything for her love but is also conscious of her inferiority and sinfulness. These, she fervently hopes, the beloved will overlook out of loving kindness and mercy. Because the relationship between the seeker (*murid*) and the Imam is spiritual, the composer avoids explicitly erotic or sensual imagery, portraying the virahini's love instead in a strictly spiritualized manner. Hence, the ginan contains references to meditational practices, usually performed early in the morning, during which the disciple repeats, preferably with total concentration, the special name (the *ism-i a'zam* or Greatest Name) given by the Imam for spiritual progress. It is through meditation, ethical conduct, and complete devotion to the guide that the Imam's devotees can attain the goal of their quest, the vision of spiritual light.[24]

1. I thirst for a glimpse [*darshan*] of you, O my Beloved!
   Fulfill my heart's desire, O my Beloved!
   I thirst with desire for you;
   Why do you not show concern for me?
   I serve you with the utmost dedication,
   Why do you then turn away [from me] in anger, O my Beloved?

2. Listen to me, my Lord, and grant me what I ask;
   Do not be so indifferent to me, your wife.
   Grant me, my Lord, grant me what I ask; I suffer immensely.
   Beloved, fulfill my heart's desire, so I can be joyously happy.

3. Like a fish without water, how can one live without the beloved?
   For the sake of its beloved, it gives away its life;
   Without water the fish is lost, see how it writhes [in agony];
   It writhes and leaps in vain but [alas] the fisherman shows no mercy!

4. Consider false the love of the bee;
   It certainly is not the way to get a glimpse [*darshan*] of the beloved!
   Consider false the love of the bee;
   It flits from flower to flower sucking nectar.

Such are negligent and blinded people, lacking virtue,
who will not sacrifice their lives for the beloved's sake.

5. Consider true the love of the moth;
    For it is in this manner in which one may glimpse the beloved:
    True love is that of the moth that deliriously sacrifices its body;
    For the sake of a single candle, so many moths give up their lives.

6. I have sacrificed everything for my Beloved,
    For all that is precious should be offered to him.
    Throw aside this hesitation; make up your mind to say something;
    Show mercy, O master, and protect me; pay heed to this my prayer.

7. One who sees the Lord wishes
    Never to leave Him and thinks not of anyone else.
    The heart of one who sees [the Lord] is so attached
    That day by day love grows;
    Recite [His] name with complete concentration;
    For in this way one has a glimpse of the beloved.

8. Do not treat this destitute [female] devotee so,
    If I have faults, consider them to be virtues.
    I am a devotee of yours, although sinful.
    Why are you not concerned about me?
    If I have faults, consider them to be virtues; pay heed to this
        my prayer.

9. One who becomes nothing [i.e., of no significance] is called your
        [female] devotee
    In this manner one pleases the Lord;
    One who becomes nothing is called your [female] devotee,
    Wakes up regularly [for meditation] and grows in her love.
    Reciting [the Lord's] name with complete concentration,
    Burns away in this way the body [i.e., material ties].

10. Stay with the Lord in complete concentration,
    Coloring yourself with the color of love.
    Stay with the Lord in complete concentration,

Loving Him intensely.
Only the one who sacrifices life out of love
Can catch a glimpse of the beloved.

11. Nothing have I seen that compares to [this] love;
Do whatever pleases your Master.
One who dies the death of love
Has led a worthwhile life in this world;
Perform good deeds, and the Master will redeem you.

12. Though sinful, yet I am your creature;
Remember me soon, O Lord.
My Lord has remembered me;
So rejoice, my friends.
By the grace of the Master, says Sayyid Khan,
All difficulties and troubles have fled!

Sermon for a Special Occasion

✳ A Radio *Mawlid* Sermon

PATRICK D. GAFFNEY

Sermons (*khutba*) are preached every Friday at the noon prayer, but special cel-ebrations are also occasions for preaching. The following text is a sermon that fits both descriptions: it occurred on a Friday that fell during a *mawlid*, a cele-bration of a local holy person's birthday, in the village of Shuha in northern Egypt. Note how in the midst of his call for social justice the preacher makes several suggestions meant to diminish emphasis on the cult of an individual holy per-son. The radio announcer, by contrast, hints in his opening remarks that he is surprised at the negative attitude of some preachers toward such popular devotion.

In its standard format, the radio transmission of the Friday noon prayer ser-vice opens with Qur'an recitation, solemn chanting that lasts for approximately twenty minutes. The reciter (*muqri'*) signals the end of this portion of the ser-vice by intoning the opening sura of the Qur'an, al-Fatiha, which the congre-gation recites in unison. The radio announcer also shares in this recitation. Those gathered in the mosque then wait in reverent silence, while the announcer pro-ceeds with introductory remarks to the radio audience.[25]

Figure 21.   An early example of monumental funerary architecture, the tenth-century tomb of Isma'il the Samanid in Bukhara, Uzbekistan, shows elaborate baked brick decoration similar to that of fig. 14. (For further development of funerary architecture in central Asia, see figs. 30, 38.)

[Radio announcer:]

Fellow believers, the village of Shuha contains a number of facilities that make it a sort of model village. Its enterprises include farming activities such as the production of cotton, corn, wheat, and rice, alongside other related agricultural works. Among its industrial endeavors is a factory that makes matches and a dairy that supplies milk products to Mansura. Its educational opportunities consist of a secondary school, a preparatory school, a religious institute, and four primary schools, in addition to a kindergarten.

There are more than seven mosques located here, plus a village hospital and a social center. There is also a women's education organization and a training institute serving the meat and milk industry as well as poultry breeding. The village has also sponsored a number of publications in the areas of science and culture. But generally, what one notices here is the expanse of green fields, which our country needs, and it is easy to see that most hands are engaged in cultivating these crops.

[The muezzin chants the call to prayer.]

[Radio announcer resumes:]

Fellow believers, yesterday thousands came to this mosque from throughout the governorate of Daqahliya and from other governorates as well. They came to attend the "small night" of the feast day [*mawlid*] of Sidi 'Abd ar-Rahman 'Uthman ash-Shahawi. Thousands more are now joining them today for yet another celebration, the "big night," which starts this evening.

They have been leaving their ordinary affairs behind, what they call their wealth and their property, in order to gather here around this mosque in the village of Shuha. Countless legends and stories are told about this man of saintly deeds and pious learning. No sooner do these crowds converge than the stories about him begin to spread as though he were alive. People can see and hear what he has done from the many accounts his devotees relate about him.

But if we are so inspired by their portrayal and by the example of this holy man and others like him, about whom we hear such remarkable stories, then why do certain preachers hold themselves aloof and even disapprove of these blessed ones? Why do they treat these saintly figures, their teachings, and their followers so unjustly? For it is the duty of us all to preserve religion from any stain and to rescue scholars from their cleverness when they would close certain beautiful and hospitable mosques all on account of the simplicity of some people. It is incumbent on us to save such persons from their own misguided views and to warn them as best we can in these matters. We should inform them about the truth of their noble religion and about the true role to be fulfilled by those entrusted with learning.

May God bestow upon us what is good and the goodness of our religion. May he make us indeed the best community to have come from humankind, bidding to what is right and shunning evil.

Fellow believers, we turn now to the congregation gathered in this mosque of Sidi 'Abd ar-Rahman 'Uthman ash-Shahawi in the village of Shuha, in the district of Mansura, for the performance of prayer services. The Friday sermon, entitled "Religion and Social Life," will be delivered by Shaykh Mahmud 'Abd as-Salam Muhammad Ibrahim.

[The Preacher:]

May the peace and mercy of God be with you.

[The muezzin again chants the call to prayer.]

[The Preacher:]

Praise to God, the Great, the Most High, the Generous, the Omnipotent. He was pleased to make Islam our religion as we too are pleased with it and we have taken it as our pattern for living. We praise Him and we thank Him, although no praise or thanksgiving can match His greatness. I profess that there is no god but God and that Muhammad is His servant, His messenger, and His chosen one. God sent him with guidance and the religion of truth and he strove in the way of God for the instruction of His creatures. The prayers and peace of God be upon him, his family, his companions, and those called by his summons who follow his path up until the Day of Judgment.

Now then, Islam is the religion of guidance and instruction, while the Prophet is peace for every time and place. His motto proclaims a respect for rights and a reverence for authority. He exhorts to truth and honesty in action. He has laid down guarantees that assure its protection and that defend its harmony. Here he established the basis for order in the dealings of people with one another. He urges them to hold to standards of justice and to solid principles. They should do nothing that is unfair, nor try to cover up unseemly things. They are to refrain from deception, exert no pressure, avoid oppression, not engage in hoarding, nor behave in a hostile manner. And he endorses this type of behavior in a wise and sturdy expression, as the Lord says: "O you who believe, you should not play false with one another in your business affairs" [4:29].

Indeed, this holy text has laid down the foundation upon which their lives were established, just as it has fixed the basic arrangements for their institutions. Then, when some occasion arose for making financial profit involving a variety of operations and an assortment of procedures, all serving to multiply life's demands and to entangle the interests of different people, it was the law [*shari'a*] that looked after those who lacked experience to assure right conduct in the dealings of people with one another.

And when it comes to the exchange of goods between them, God set down the law as the basis upon which they were to handle their affairs. Thus, they were to devote themselves to the construction of a society out of the storms of contention that had left their cities seething in crime and hatred. God spurred them on to act in this righteous fashion, adding His assistance and favoring with rewards those who followed His way, while He prescribed misery and dispossession upon those who turned away from goodness, for "your Lord does not deal unjustly with His creatures" [41:46].

He commands us to be truthful and honest in our dealings, to practice candor and diligence in our production. He promises that the returns for such behavior will be blessed, "for we do not allow the reward for goodness to be lost" [18:30]. If we consider for a moment the dealings people have with each other in whatever circumstances, there are obviously differences involved that make for endless complications, since the prospects for advantage can change as interests overlap variously. As a result, every loss and gain, every shortcoming and excess, inevitably carries with it for the others some kind of impact, whether it be positive or negative.

We are speaking here of honesty on the part of a teacher in the process of education, of the sensitivity of a doctor toward a patient, of the competence demonstrated by an engineer or a worker. Let us look at the need for a professional to handle responsibly whatever matters are entrusted to him, at the truthfulness and moderation of a merchant, who should act with liberality in buying and selling, avoiding attempts to monopolize or to pad prices. We are concerned with the proper job performance of a government clerk, who should display genuine concern for the convenience of the public, without playing fast and loose with legalistic red tape. Likewise, the skill of a craftsman in forging the work of his hands begins with preparing a foundation, which requires cooperation in such matters as the settling of debts and the avoidance of chicanery and delays. All of these habits contribute to the spirit of mutual support and bolster the respect people have for one another as they make themselves worthy of God's mercy, winning His favor and His gifts.

The discipline shown by those who direct their lives along the course of God's law will allow them to follow an orderly path toward the desired goal of advancing civilization. But a lack of balanced judgment in these areas makes itself felt among the haves and the have-nots, and it cheats children as well. It unleashes enmity and hatred. It divides the ranks of a community and it unravels the bonds of unity. It thwarts mutual respect in a way that leaves us a people cast upon the mercy of God.

The Prophet, prayers and peace of God upon him, said: "Whoever shows no mercy, neither will mercy be shown to him." But the complaints of everyone against everyone else cannot provide the leverage needed to bring about a solution, since the remedy is given in these words: "Begin with yourself." With this attitude, the pillars of the world can be shaken to make people aware of the negligible effect of their complaining, since attempts to track down the motives behind evil schemes will surely continue until the Day of Judgment.

The promise of recompense for goodness has been made to all, while threats of punishment stand for cases of wickedness. Indeed, the Prophet declared his praise for any merchant who was trustworthy and faithful. He placed him in the ranks of the prophets and the righteous when he said: "The honest and faithful merchant stands with the prophets, the

righteous, and the martyrs." He also said: "Merchants will rise on the
Day of Resurrection as the merchants they were but with fear of the
Lord, in righteousness and in honesty."

He threatened the unscrupulous and greedy with the mighty fire,
saying: "Anyone who engages in sharp business practices among Muslims, such as raising prices unfairly, should know that God's law decrees
that he be dispatched to the mighty fire on the Day of Resurrection."
In another place the Prophet, prayers and peace of God upon him, spoke
thus: "He who sets unfair prices for food among Muslims, God will afflict
him with decisive ruin, whether the food is meant for humans or for
animals." This threat of his applies to all those who have any part in the
oppression and hardship of people, even those connected by circuitous
ways or in back rooms. Given that there is enough trouble and distress
in our world, the Prophet made it clear what was in store for those who
bring more when he said: "O God, may those who are the cause of misery
to my community be afflicted with misery themselves."

So fear God, you servants of God, and assist one another in goodness
and piety. Do not support each other in anything that causes offense
or hostility. Make smooth the ways that lead to the fulfillment of the
promises of cooperation and stability in our lives. This means helping
to shape public opinion about Islamic society, drawing upon its many
principles in order to protect its values and its norms. Its followers must
not approve of what is wrong and must not give in to what is forbidden.
Let them instead help to establish justice until the community is confirmed in that goodness which has as its precondition the bidding of what
is honorable and repudiation of what is dishonorable. For God says: "You
are the best community of those formed among humankind, calling for
what is good and refuting what is evil" [3:110].

For this reason, silly superstitions of all sorts are to be shunned lest
they inflict damage, because corruption introduced by any one member of
the body easily corrupts those others around it. For the noble Messenger,
prayers and peace of God upon him, was well aware of the foolishness
that may take possession of the hearts of so many among his people.
Hence, he cautioned them against such dangers when he related the

parable of a ship plowing through the high seas. There are many passengers on board, and some of them want to bore a hole in the hull. If they are left to do so, the whole ship would sink and everyone would be drowned. But if they hold back, the ship would be saved and the lives of all those on it would be safe as well. In the words of the Prophet, prayers and peace of God upon him: "Those upright and true in the ways of God can be compared to people sharing space aboard a ship, some of whom are quartered on the deck while others are below. Now, if those below find that water is dripping down on them from those who are above them, they might say, 'If we, for our part, were to bore a hole, we would get back at those afflicting us from above, for we have done them no wrong. But to act on this impulse will mean that everyone perishes, whereas if we show restraint we will save ourselves and all the others too.'" For he also said: "The one who repents his sin is beloved of the All Merciful."

Praise to God, the Most High, the Great, the Nourisher, the Judge. Praise Him and give Him thanks. Pray to Him for prosperity and forgiveness. I profess that there is no god but God, He who pardons, is kind, and is gracious. And I profess that Muhammad is the prophet called from among the Arabs who pleased God by his obedience, while God gave him the banner of praise and of advocacy. The prayers and peace of God be upon his family and his companions and upon those who follow his words until the Day of Judgment.

Now then, O community of Muslims, those who devote themselves to obedience are dear to God, for He exalts their works and He makes their memory to abide forever. He raises them to be strong in the midst of His people. They love God and He loves them. They abstain from sin and find solace in God, who will attend to their safety from the terrors on the Day of Resurrection. "For the friends of God need not fear, nor should they grieve" [10:62]. For every Muslim has the capacity to attain the status of friend of God, if he but devotes his will to God and then acts accordingly with full conviction. He need only turn his efforts to the path that pleases his Lord, excelling in obedience and in good works for the community.

So practice piety before God, you servants of God, and follow God in obedience. Dedicate yourselves to the improvement of society. Rejoice in what pleases your Lord, now and in the future. May you be well prepared for the Day of Reckoning. "Indeed, prepare your provisions, and the best of provisions is piety" [2:197].

Let prayers and peace abound upon the leader of those who are God-fearing, Muhammad, the trustworthy Prophet. I call upon you to be believers. O God, we implore you to strengthen Islam and to make Muslims prosper.

[Congregation responds:] Amen!

[Preacher:] And by Your grace, exalt the word of truth and religion.

[Congregation:] Amen!

[Preacher:] O God, show us plainly the fullness of truth and bless us that we may adhere to it.

[Congregation:] Amen!

[Preacher:] Show us clearly the error of falsehood and bless us that we may avoid it.

[Congregation:] Amen!

[Preacher:] Make us to have faith in our homelands.

[Congregation:] Amen!

[Preacher:] Allow no harm to afflict our belief.

[Congregation:] Amen!

[Preacher:] Let not great distress beset our world.

[Congregation:] Amen!

[Preacher:] Do not permit knowledge to be confounded.

[Congregation:] Amen!

[Preacher:] O God, make our lives abound with every good thing.

[Congregation:] Amen!

[Preacher:] At death give us repose from every evil.

[Congregation:] Amen!

[Preacher:] O God, grant pardon to all believers, those living and those who have died.

[Congregation:] Amen!

[Preacher:] O God, be pleased with the patron of this place.

[Congregation:] Amen!

[Preacher:] Servants of God, truly God summons us to justice and good deeds, to behave as relatives. He bids us to refrain from crime and forbidden acts and from all that is wrong. He appeals to you, that you might be mindful, so remember the goodness of God, that He may remember you. Call Him to mind that He may pardon you. Let us now rise for the prayer. [Salat follows.]

Figure 22. In this seventeenth-century Ottoman Turkish painting, Muhammad prays at the Kaʿba among pilgrims. Muhammad's Pilgrimage in 632 set the example for Islam's retaining much pre-Islamic ritual practice concerning the shrine in Mecca. At bottom, a pilgrim receives a drink from the well of Zamzam. Baltimore: The Walters Art Gallery, MS. W.679a.

3 Inspiration
Edification and Ethics

Religious and ethical inspiration are an integral part of every tradition of spirituality. Two broad categories of sources are the main veins running through Islam's mine of inspirational treasure. Poetic and anecdotal presentations of exemplary individuals speak of how spiritual strength more than makes up for human frailty. And several types of wisdom literature represent a further refinement of the example of the great models in the form of advice and encouragement along the path of virtue.

EXEMPLARY MODELS

Stories of religious heroes and heroines throughout Islamic history have offered Muslims a rich selection of ethical models. From pre-Islamic prophets such as Joseph (fig. 26) to Muhammad himself (fig. 22), his wives, and members of his extended family and successors (fig. 24); from early Companions of the Prophet to those personifications of holiness called Friends of God (fig. 25), exemplary Muslims have represented the highest virtue and religious commitment for emulation. Although traditional Islamic theology does not allow for mediating presences to close the infinite gap between the divine and the human, in practice millions of people believe that God has endowed these moral exemplars with extraordinary powers. The first section below includes examples of heroic poetry in honor of Muhammad, a modern reading of a classic life of Muhammad, and hagiographical accounts of several men and women renowned for their sanctity.

The Prophet: From Devotion to Edification

Poems in praise of Muhammad provide a natural transition from devotion to inspiration and highlight the often subtle differences between these two dimensions of Islamic religious experience. Here are two examples of the naʿt genre, one from Arabic and one from Urdu, that explore important facets of the Prophet's spiritual and ethical significance.

✳   Acrostic Poem in Praise of Muhammad

EARLE H. WAUGH

Muhammad's role in Islamic spirituality is as complex as it is pivotal. In the following poem, the Prophet remains a devotional focus, but in addition becomes the model of the seeker. Sufis have developed a genre of literature that is both useful for meditation and explicative of the mystical path, understanding the Prophet as the pioneer and pinnacle of spiritual maturity. The poetry that honors Muhammad as both supreme guide and intercessor is not only for the elite; rather, such writings and meditations proliferated for every taste and ability.

Sometimes these selections were put to music to make their memorization easier, or they took on the nature of a song of praise and proclamation such as could be performed in an evening of mystical devotion called a *sama'*. Often a shaykh would compose meditations to be memorized and repeated in *dhikr* rites (the word *dhikr* meaning "mentioning," "recalling" by means of verbal formulae). The poem rests on the premise that Muhammad is active as an intercessor in the world of the believer. Moreover, it uses the Arabic alphabet as a mnemonic device. The translation attempts to retain the sound of the original Arabic by beginning each sentence with an English word that sounds like the Arabic letter. Unfortunately, cadences and emphases cannot be similarly duplicated.[1]

IN PRAISE OF THE PROPHET MUHAMMAD

My brother: your relationship to evil has been for so long that your
    worst provision has been for the world to come.
Your sense departed and your concern lagged, so that you abandoned
    your ordinary reason.
Disobedience freely manipulated you, conveying you wherever it would;
    it found you easy to lead.
You have been summoned to leave, so listen. Deafen not yourself to the
    caller!
Surely sufficient warning to you is your white hair—that whiteness has
    now spread within!
Alif: Adoration have I for my intercessor in the hereafter.
    He who is that gentle morning sun, that moon of the cosmos,
    Muhammad.

Ba': Because he was chosen, strife and enmity have vanished;*

   the world is filled with purity, genuine affection and devotion, through
      Muhammad.

Ta': Truly the Exalted One, the supreme God in His greatness

   has adorned the heavens with the light of Muhammad.

Tha': Thanks to him, the sky is graced with a pair of moons,†

   for the cosmos is resplendent with the brilliance that is Muhammad.

Jim: Join the whole creation in witness:

   its warp and weft arise from the design and guidance‡ of Muhammad.

Ha': Having shielded true religion with his sword,

   the faith waxed triumphant by virtue of Muhammad.

Kha': Culminating as the seal of the prophets,§

   that seal has the exquisite fragrance of musk: Muhammad.

Dal: Distance was so minimal between him and Allah

   that he heard the greeting "O welcome Muhammad."‖

Dhal: That protection afforded by the Hashimi# is sufficient;

   it is precious and treasured by those seeking refuge with
      Muhammad.

Ra': Right pleasing is his presence: none among the prophets

   has the sublime character of Muhammad.

---

   * This refers to the general Muslim belief that the Arabs and, indeed, the world were in a state of chaos before Muhammad brought order and direction.

   † Ancient Arabian poetry speaks of individuals possessing such beauty and stature that they are as prominent as the moon in the clear night sky. The trope was applied to heroes and legendary figures, even to one's paramour. It has been taken over here and in Sufi literature to praise the Prophet.

   ‡ Some Sufis held that the "light" of Muhammad's goodness and dedication was so powerful that it was an eternal characteristic that informed and directed the creation of the universe.

   § The title "seal of the prophets" means that Muhammad is the last prophet God will send.

   ‖ No human was able to stand before God; but Muhammad came so close during his Ascension that he could hear the very voice of God.

The Prophet belonged to the Hashimi clan, one of the most important of the ruling Quraysh tribe. One's ancestral roots were very important in the development of Islam, and took on deeply religious meanings. Even now being related to the Prophet is critical for some rulers (those of Morocco, for example). Sufis have taken over the idea in the notion of being spiritually related to their shaykh and through him to the Prophet.

Za': Zoned sacred, his tomb offers atonement—it is obligatory,*

    O believer, to attend the resting place of Muhammad.

Sin: Sojourning on al-Buraq,† he rose to the highest heights

    enrapt in the very essence of aroma—Muhammad.

Shin: Surely an intercessor intercedes;

    glory be to Him who ascribed intercession to Muhammad.

Sad: Certain is this truth:

    woman has borne none like Muhammad.

Dad: Dazzled was humanity by his countenance.

    O God! How wondrous is the beauty of Muhammad!

Ta': Treading in the Hashimi's footsteps brings blessing;

    follow everlastingly the footprints of Muhammad.

Za': Zephyrous serenity flowed through the sky's vault with the arrival
of him who

    pleased God; acceptance was bestowed for the sake of Muhammad.

'Ayn: Above all that shines, joyous his light,

    happiness prevails everywhere through Muhammad.

Ghayn: Grand wealth accrues to the poor through their lauding of the
chosen one;

    Ah! victorious are those who exalt in praise Muhammad.

Fa': Far beyond all in sensitivity and grandeur,

    the Creator fashioned none like unto Muhammad.

Qaf: Qualities of righteousness reigned in his laws,

    while the people flourished through the patience of Muhammad.

Kaf: Keen in his generosity, perfected in his spirituality,

    beneficence is the being of Muhammad.

Lam: Languishing dry unto death, his sustaining rod sprouted;‡ the lizard

---

* Sufis developed the notion of the spiritual presence of a departed saint; it is best expressed in the concept of *baraka*, the power and authority manifest in the lives of the saints, mostly for the benefit of their devotees but sometimes to have an impact on the course of Islamic history and of creation.

† Buraq: the human-headed quadruped that carried Muhammad on his Night Journey and Ascension

‡ Legend says the Prophet had a cane or walking stick that, even though old and dry, sprouted because of Muhammad's spiritual presence.

proclaimed the good news of the coming of the dearly beloved
   Muhammad.

Mim: My love to him is as a sacred rite;
   Islam's rituals are the love of Muhammad.

Nun: Now commit I myself to attend the tomb
   of him who guides and intercedes for us, Muhammad.

Waw: Witness this by the truth of God: I yearn for you,
   The Zamzami* and the Hashimi, Muhammad.

Ha': How my love unfolds and my heart longs
   for that mausoleum's beacon in the darkness, Muhammad.

Lam Alif: Lacerate not,[†] O God,
   those who adulate the Hashimi, Muhammad.

Ya': Yes! Truly, I swear never to free myself from this vow;
   there, God will bind up our brokenness by Muhammad.

✳ *Na't* in Praise of Muhammad

ALI ASANI

In addition to Muhammad's role as a friend, helper, and beloved, his followers
have been grateful to him for conveying the message of Islam to the world.
Hence it is only natural that he is frequently conceived of as a guide and leader
to the truth. On the basis of various qur'anic verses, including one that declares
Muhammad a "mercy to the worlds" (21:107), many Muslims have come to
hold that a believer who trusts and loves him will be protected in the hereafter,
for the merciful Prophet will seek forgiveness of sins from God. Poems such as
the following example by the Indian Nazir Akbarabadi (d. 1831) often allude to
Muhammad's mystical or spiritual status, developing ideas inspired by accounts
of his mysterious Night Journey and Ascension to heaven (the *mi'raj;* see fig. 22).
This journey, the climax of which was a face-to-face meeting with God (often
interpreted metaphorically), provides for mystically minded Muslims the pro-
totype for the ascent of their own souls to higher spiritual realms. Although
Muslims do not ordinarily aspire to imitate Muhammad in this regard, his lofty
spiritual state is an integral part of his ability to inspire believers.[2]

---

   * Zamzami: associating Muhammad with the well of Zamzam.
   † A Sufi theme, from the romantic notion that the beloved tantalizes the lover
but always remains beyond his grasp, thus rending his soul and lacerating his spirit.

You are the ruler of this world and the next, O Muhammad the chosen.
You are the leader of the Muslims, O Muhammad the chosen.
You are the governor of the stable religion, O Muhammad the chosen.
You are the qibla of those with firm conviction, O Muhammad the
    chosen.

On the night of the mi'raj, you illuminated the heavens;
On account of your footsteps the highest heaven and divine throne
    became luminous and radiant;
The color and fragrance of the paradisiacal rose gardens increased
    markedly;
In a place yonder that is beyond the imagination of the angels
You are the reigning prince, O Muhammad the chosen.

O seal of the prophets, even God calls you His beloved,
And to you, with the [divine] revelation, comes Gabriel most respectfully.
Which prophet had attained such an [exalted] status as yours?
You belong to that ocean which is the most sacred ocean of prophethood.
You are a unique pearl, O Muhammad the chosen.

You are the emissary of the Righteous One and the best of mankind;
The master of each of the two worlds and the intercessor for the day of
    reckoning;
Your exalted essence is the fountain of kindness and generosity,
Not only for Nazir, but for all you are the asylum for assistance:
[Just] as here you are [with us]; there too you will be, O Muhammad the
    chosen.

✳   Taha Hussein
Interpreting Muhammad's Life in Modern Times
WILLIAM SHEPARD

Taha Hussein (1889–1973), though blind from childhood, managed to complete
his education at the mosque university of al-Azhar in Cairo and obtain a doc-
torate in France. He became one of the leading lights of the literary flowering
in Egypt following its independence in 1922, producing important works of both
literature and literary criticism. He was concerned that Egyptians, and Muslims

generally, be open to learn from the West, but also that they continue be inspired by their own tradition. His position was "secularist" in that he did not see in the Qur'an and the activities of the Prophet Muhammad prescriptive rules laid down for all time, but rather a heritage that should inspire later generations in a more flexible way. The following selection evidences that concern. It is the introduction to his three-volume work *On the Margin of the Sira*, published in 1933, in which he retells the story of the Prophet Muhammad. The word *sira* refers to a literary biography of the Prophet and in particular that of Ibn Ishaq (d. 767) as edited and expanded by Ibn Hisham (d. ca. 830). The distinction made toward the end of the passage between reason and emotion, and the assigning of these stories to the emotional side of life, are also typical of Hussein's thinking. Here are the reflections of one of the twentieth-century Arab world's most famous literary figures on the meaning of the life story of Muhammad. His prefatory remarks emphasize the function of the Prophet's sira as ethical paradigm.[3]

These pages have not been written for scholars [*'ulama'*] or historians, because my intention in them is not scholarship and my aim in them is not history. Rather, they are a picture that occurred to me during my reading of the *Sira* and which I recorded hastily; then I saw no harm in publishing them. Perhaps I saw some good in publishing them, since they will restore to people bits of the ancient literature that had slipped away from them and become inaccessible, being read only by those who have received a broad and deep education in ancient Arabic literature. Search for those who read what the ancients wrote about the *Sira* and the tales [*hadith*] of the Arabs before Islam and you will find hardly any.

Today people read only the modern literature that contemporaries write for them in their language or in one of the foreign languages that have spread through the Orient, and they find in reading it an ease and facility, an enjoyment and a pleasure that interest and entice them. As for the ancient literature, it is hard to read, harder to understand, and harder yet to enjoy. Where is the reader who will put up with reading lengthy *isnads* [chains of transmitters] and accounts that contain digressions and whose strange ancient language strays from the path of that easy understanding and appreciation that do not impose difficulty and trouble?

Moreover, the ancient literature was not produced in order to remain just as it is, fixed and settled, without changing or altering, and with people able to derive pleasure from its texts only by reading and reread-ing them, by memorizing them and devoting all their effort to doing so. No, truly fertile literature is that which pleases you when you read it because it satisfies both your reason and your feelings, because it reveals to you more than what is in it and inspires in you more than what its texts contain, because it gives you fertility from its fertility, wealth from its wealth, strength from its strength; because it speaks to you as it spoke to the ancients; because it does not settle into your heart until it takes on the form of your heart or makes your heart take on its form, and when you pass it on to people, you deliver it to them in a new shape adapted to the life they live, to the emotions that stir in their hearts, and to the thoughts that surge in their minds.

This is living literature. This is the literature that can resist the on-slaught of time and survive. As for that literature whose effect ends with the reading of it, it may have its value and it may have its use, but it is a temporary literature that dies when the age in which it appeared ends. If you look at the ancient and modern literatures, you will find a group of them that cannot be described as literatures of a particular age or a par-ticular environment or a particular generation, but they are literatures of all ages, all environments, and all generations, not only because they are admired by people of different ages, environments, and generations, but because they inspire people and reveal things [to them], and make of them poets, writers, and masters of diverse kinds of arts.

The immortality of the *Iliad* does not come merely from the fact that it creates enjoyment and stirs admiration in every time and every region. Rather, it comes both from this and from the fact that it has inspired and still inspires writers and poets to compose the most sublime marvels [*ayat*] of eloquence created by humans. Aeschylus, the father of Greek tragedy, used to say that he merely gleaned what dropped from the table of Homer, and the storytellers, playwrights, and composers (songwriters) of the West can still rightly say what Aeschylus used to say twenty-five centuries ago. And the stories of Aeschylus and the other Greek poets and playwrights are no less fertile than the *Iliad*. In fact, they have inspired ancient and modern poets and writers, are still able to inspire them today, and will be able to do so tomorrow. . . .

In our Arabic literature also, with its particular strength and the pleasure and enjoyment it affords people, there is a capacity for revelation and inspiration. Thus the tales and accounts of the pre-Islamic Arabs were not written just once and were not preserved in a particular form, but the narrators told them in diverse forms and the authors wrote them in various ways. And you can say the same thing about the *Sira* itself, for it, too, has inspired the poets and writers in most Islamic countries and ages. They have given it diverse forms that have varied in strength, weakness, and artistic beauty. You can say the same thing about the [stories of the Prophet's] wars and the [later] conquests, and about the civil wars and tribulations that befell the Arabs in different ages. Nor was inspiration limited to the great literary heritage of the writers and poets who composed poetry and ornate prose in the Classical Arabic language. Rather, it went beyond them to the band of popular storytellers who recounted to people in diverse forms and widely varying shapes the noble glory that their ancestors had achieved and the grim wars and the dark tribulations that had befallen them, and made known how they had withstood them and persevered through them.

There is no good in the life of the ancients if it does not inspire in the moderns sublime eloquence in poetry and prose. The ancients are not truly immortal if [their heritage] can be sought only in their own writings, if their descendants can come to know them only through the poems and literary collections that they left. The ancients are only truly alive and immortal when they and their deeds fill the hearts of later generations, however distant in time, when they are reflected in people's daily conversation, and when they form a treasury into which writers and poets delve to give life to their speech and poetry.

It was to this manner of giving life to the ancient literature and the memory of the early Arabs that I directed myself when I dictated the chapters in this book. I do not wish to deceive the readers concerning myself or concerning this book, for I did not give it a lot of thought and calculation, and I did not intend it to be a carefully written composition.

I was driven to it. I found myself reading the *Sira*, and it filled my soul, overflowed my heart, and flowed out of my tongue, and there I was dictating these chapters and other chapters, hoping they might be published after a time.

So this book does not represent a studied or self-conscious effort, it does not seek to excel and to avoid failure. It is just a simple, natural, and truthful picture of some of what I feel when I read these books that I put on a level above all other books, whatever they may be; that I never tire of reading and keeping companionship with; for which my love and admiration never ceases, nor my desire that people should read them. But unfortunately, people do not read them, either because they do not want to or because they cannot. So if this book can make young people love to read the books of the *Sira*, especially, and the books of ancient Arabic literature generally, and [get them to] seek artistic pleasure in their fertile pages, then I shall be truly blessed with success in the thing that is dearest to me and closest to my heart. . . .

And if this book can awaken in the souls of young people the realization that the old must not be forsaken just because it is old, and the new must not be sought just because it is new, but that the old is only to be forsaken if it is profitless and void of utility, while if it is useful and profitable, then people have no less need of it than they do of the new, I shall have been blessed with success in part of what I seek.

I know that a group of people will be uneasy with this book because they are modern people who glorify reason and put their trust and confidence in it alone. Therefore they will be uneasy with many of the tales and accounts that reason cannot stomach or accept. They complain and urge their complaint when they see the fondness of the people for these accounts, their earnestness in seeking them, and their desire to read them and listen to them, and they struggle to turn the people from these accounts and tales and to deliver them from their dangerous and intellec- tually corrupting sway. These people will be somewhat uneasy with this book because they will read in it a group of these accounts and tales that they have set themselves to war against and to obliterate from the souls of people. And I would like these people to know that reason isn't everything, and that people have other faculties that need to be satisfied and nourished no less than does reason.

If reason is not content with these accounts and tales, and if logic is not satisfied with them, and if they don't measure up to the canons of scientific thinking, still there is something in the hearts of people, in their feelings, their emotions, their imagination, their inclination toward the simple, their desire to seek refuge in it from the struggle and hardship of life, that makes them love and desire these accounts and that moves them to seek in them relaxation for their souls when life bears harshly upon them. There is a great difference between the person who relates these accounts to the intellect as scientifically established truths and acceptable bases for investigation, and the one who presents them to the heart and the feelings as something that will stir up good emotions, deflect evil impulses, and help them to pass the time and bear the burdens and demands of life.

I want people also to know that I have allowed myself the storyteller's liberty and inventiveness in relating these accounts and tales wherever I saw no harm in so doing, but not when the stories and accounts touch the person of the Prophet or any aspect of religion. At those points I gave myself neither freedom or latitude, but stuck strictly to that which is accepted by the ancient authorities on the *Sira* and hadith, the experts on the sources of transmission, and the scholars of religion.

Those who wish to look up the ancient sources from which I have taken the chapters of this book, which is old in its substance and basis but new in its shape and form, will have no great difficulty. For these sources are very few, hardly going beyond the *Sira* of Ibn Hisham, the [*Great Book of*] *Generations* [(*Kitab at-*)*Tabaqat (al-kabir)*] of Ibn Sa'd [d. 845], and the *History* of at-Tabari. There is no chapter or account in this book that does not revolve about an account or accounts appearing in one of these books. And when the account is related to the Prophet, I have given the reference so that anyone who wishes can look it up without any particular trouble, because I do not here follow any particular school of thought, but I freely elaborate in explanation and commentary, derive the moral of the story, and bring it home to people's hearts.

So may God ease the path of this book into people's souls and cause it to make good impression on their hearts.

Collections of Holy Lives

Ibn Hisham's refashioning of the *Sira* originally written by Ibn Ishaq was only the beginning of a tremendous legacy in Islamic hagiography. Numerous other writers down to modern times have recounted the lives of holy men and women. In some instances, as in the *Sira*, they focus on the story of only one individual. But another major genre, the bio-hagiographical anthology, has taken the lead of Ibn Sa'd's *Generations* (to which Taha Hussein refers) and developed into one of the most popular forms of inspirational literature. Here are several samples of brief stories, beginning with one from the eleventh century and moving through the early and later middle periods of Islamic history and into early modern times. Their subjects are from Spain, North Africa, Egypt, Syria, Iraq, and India.

✳ ## Asiya, an Exemplary Woman in Tha'labi's *Stories of the Prophets*
JOHN RENARD

Abu Ishaq Ahmad an-Nisaburi, also known as Tha'labi (d. 1036), wrote one of the most famous Arabic versions of *Stories of the Prophets* (*Qisas al-anbiya'*). His stories include those of several famous women as models of faith and virtue. Muhammad is reported to have observed that the four noblest women of all time were Asiya; Mary, the mother of Jesus; Muhammad's first wife, Khadija; and his daughter Fatima. Asiya was a believer in the true God who willingly suffered for her faith at the hands of her unbelieving husband, Pharaoh. Tradition has it that Asiya was the one who rescued the infant Moses from the river. Tha'labi's account is a fine example of midrashic narrative: the storyteller begins and ends with two halves of a relevant qur'anic verse and, in between, fills in details of a story suggested by the verse. The following anecdote highlights Asiya's fidelity no matter the cost.

THE MARTYRDOM OF ASIYA BINT MUZAHIM, WIFE OF PHARAOH

God Most High has said, "And God put forth as an example for those who believe the wife of Pharaoh" [66:11]. It is said that the wife of Pharaoh, Asiya, was one of the children of Israel. She was a sincere believer who worshipped God in secret, such that she would pretend to be seeing to her private needs but [actually] would go out to pray during the day disguised [lit., in her wraps] for fear of Pharaoh. She went on this way until Pharaoh murdered the wife of Hizqil.*

While Asiya was looking out a window in Pharaoh's palace she saw the handmaiden of Hizqil's wife being tortured and killed. And when the handmaiden died Asiya saw the angels taking her spirit heavenward, for God Most High so desired as a result of her high estate and willed the best for her. Then [Asiya's] certitude about God and her conviction increased. While she was in that state, Pharaoh entered and informed her about the handmaiden of Hizqil's wife and told her what he had done to her. So Asiya said to him, "Woe to you, O Pharaoh, for the retribution awaiting you from God Most High." He replied, "Perhaps you are afflicted by the [same] demons [or madness] that got hold of your companion." She replied, "The demons do not have me in their grip; on the contrary, I have put faith in God my Lord and your Lord, the Lord of the universe."

So Pharaoh called for her mother and said to her, "The demons that possessed the handmaiden have taken your daughter." Then he swore, "You will either taste death or forsake the God of Moses." When her mother was alone with her, she asked [Asiya] to comply with Pharaoh's wishes. She refused and said, "You [both] want me to forsake God; no, by God, I will never do that!" So Pharaoh ordered that she be stretched between four stakes and tortured to death, may God have mercy on her. And that is the meaning of God's words, "Pharaoh, the one with [or Lord of] the stakes" [38:11].

Ibn 'Abbas [the noted traditionist] said that Pharaoh took his wife Asiya and then began to torment her so that she would join his religion. Then Moses passed by her while he was tormenting her and she complained to him by a hand gesture, so Moses called out to God that he might alleviate her suffering. After that she suffered no more from

* Hizqil, Arabic for Ezekiel, is a name given in traditional lore to the anonymous "believer among Pharaoh's kin who had kept his faith secret" (40:28), who is said to have fashioned the floating cradle in which Asiya found baby Moses.

Pharaoh's torture until she died from it. And in the midst of the torture she said, "Lord, prepare me a home in your presence in the Garden and save me . . . " [66:11; the remainder of the verse reads "from Pharaoh and his deeds and rescue me from those who do evil"]. So God revealed to her [with the words] "Lift up your head." She did so and had a vision of a girl in the Garden of pearls and she laughed. Pharaoh said, "Observe the madness that is upon her: she laughs even as she is being tortured."

✳ Munawi's Life of Rabi'a al-'Adawiya

JOHN RENARD

Rabi'a al-'Adawiya remains the most famous and popular Sufi woman of Islamic history. By far the best-known hagiographical account of this Friend of God is found in Farid ad-Din 'Attar's Persian *Recollections of the Friends of God* (*Tadhkirat al-awliya*'). Another treatment, never before translated into English, is that of 'Abd a-Ra'uf al-Munawi in *Shining Stars*. Here is an excerpt from Munawi's notice, a good source for comparison with the Rabi'a of 'Attar's often anthologized work. Munawi's method, not unlike that of 'Attar, is to gather in additive fashion a series of vignettes about the holy woman's words and deeds. Some of his anecdotes appear in variant forms in 'Attar's work. 'Attar begins his account by anticipating his readers' questions about his including one of Rabi'a's gender in a collection about men; Munawi, in contrast, makes no explicit mention of her gender, perhaps because Rabi'a is one of nearly three dozen women in his anthology.[4]

Of the Qays [tribe], then of Basra,[5] chief among worshippers and foremost of the penitent and humble [or supplicants] who live in fear of infidelity, she lived during the time of al-Hasan al-Basri, God be pleased with him. Among the women outstanding in virtue and piety, such as Umm Ayyub al-Ansariya and Umm ad-Darda' and Mu'adha al-'Adawiya, she was noted for the depth of [her] asceticism, the abundance of [her] devotion, and the perfection of [her] integrity and self-denial. She used to perform a thousand ritual prostrations both day and night; so someone asked, "What is your goal in this?" She said, "I desire no reward for it; I do it so that the Messenger of God, may God bless him and give him peace, will delight in it on the day of Resurrection and say to the prophets, 'Take note of what a woman of my Community has accomplished.'". . . . [Here Munawi places an example of her prayer cited in part 2.]

Tradition has it that she used to perform the ritual prayer through the night; when dawn broke she rested quietly in her place of prayer for a while until dawn had passed, then she would rise energetically and say, "O soul, how long will you doze on and when will you bestir yourself? You are not far from sleeping a sleep from which there will be no revival until the call of the Day of Resurrection."

At a time when the daily income of his estate was eighty thousand dirhams, Muhammad Sulayman al-Hashimi wrote to the notables of Basra [in search of] a woman whom he might marry. They agreed unanimously on Rabi'a, God be pleased with her, so he wrote to her, "God has bestowed on me eighty thousand dirhams a day and I will give you that and that much more, so give me your answer." She wrote back to him, "Self-denial in this world is the body's rest, while craving for [this world] leaves a legacy of anxiety and sadness. So put your financial matters in order and prepare for your final destination. Make yourself your beneficiary rather than bequeathing your heritage to human beings. Let them divide among themselves the bequest of your dismissal of fortune and let death [be all that will] break your fasting. As for myself, had God granted me riches the like of yours and even more, it would not please me [enough] to make me distracted from the remembrance of God Most High for even the blinking of an eye. Peace."

Among the marvels she worked: A thief entered her apartment while she was sleeping. He took her clothes and went looking for the door; not finding it, he put [the clothes] down, and he found it. When he picked them up [again], [the door] again became invisible to him. This occurred many times; then a voice called to him: "Leave the clothes; we are looking after them and will not let you have them even if she is asleep." The mystic al-Buni said, "This is the underlying meaning in the word of the Most High, 'For every person there is a succession before and behind of beings who look after that person by God's command'" [13:11]. . . . [A second anecdote follows here.]

Someone asked her when the servant [of God] becomes satisfied. She said, "When trials give as much delight as blessings." She was a person of intense [spiritual] fear, so when she heard mention of the Fire she would pass out. She used to say, "Were the world the possession of a [single] man, it would not make him rich." "How so?" someone asked her. She replied, "Because it is passing away." They say she remained for forty years without lifting her head toward the heavens, out of modesty before God.

She used to say, "I never hear the call to prayer without being reminded that I am being called to the Day of Judgment. I never look upon the snow without being reminded of the final import of the pages [in the Book of Recorded Deeds]. And I never look at the locusts without being reminded of the Resurrection."

She said, "Our asking forgiveness requires [further] asking forgiveness for the lack of authenticity in [the request]."

Some people were disparaging this world in her presence, so she said, "The Messenger of God, God bless him and give him peace, said: 'One who loves something mentions it frequently.' Your mentioning this world is an indication of the falseness of your hearts; for if you were immersed in something other than this world you would not bring it up at all."

A man brought her forty dinars and said, "Ask me for help with the money to cover some of your needs." She wept, then lifted her head toward the heavens and said, "He knows that I am embarrassed to ask Him for things of this world, and He owns it! How could I accept such things from one who does not own them?"

When someone said to her, "Pray for me," she trembled and said, "Who am I? Obey your Lord and beseech Him and He will respond to the need."

Someone said to her, "Have you performed a deed you believe will be accepted from you?" She replied, "If there were such a deed, my fear is that it would return to me."

Sufyan ath-Thawri [d. 767], God be pleased with him, was with some of his brothers in religion and said, "Let's go to the educating woman with whom alone I find rest." And when he went in to her, Sufyan, God be pleased with him, raised his hands and said, "O God, I ask you for

peace." [To Rabi'a] he said, "Why are you crying?" She replied, "You
have moved me to tears. Are you not aware that peace in the midst of this
world means repudiating the things of this world? How can this happen
while you are immersed in and stained by those things?" [She said
further to Sufyan], "Besides, you are but a finite sum of days, so that
when a day passes, a part of you has gone; and when the part goes, the
whole cannot be far behind: know this and act accordingly."

Someone asked her: "What is the innermost reality of your faith?"
She replied, "I do not worship Him out of fear of His Fire, nor out of
desire for His Garden, as though I were a wicked mercenary. I worship
out of love for Him and desire for Him." Malik ibn Dinar [d. ca. 750] said,
"I visited her and she said, 'How many are the desires whose delights are
fleeting but whose consequences remain! O Lord, have you neither
penalty nor pedagogy apart from the Fire?" And among her personal
prayers: "My God, would you consume in the Fire a heart in love with
you?" Came the answer, "Do not think ill of Us." And she used to recite:

> Behold I have made You [God] the confidant of my deepest self [*fu'ad*];
> I make my outward form the property of any companion who wants it.
> For my outward form is familiar to the companion,
> While the Beloved of my heart is intimately acquainted with my inmost
> being.[6]

✳ Three Women of Iberia

R. W. J. AUSTIN

Ibn 'Arabi (d. 1240) was one of the most important religious and intellectual
figures of medieval Spain. Born in the town of Murcia along the coast south of
Barcelona, Ibn 'Arabi was part of a vast network of people linked to Sufi organizations. Two short biographical anthologies gather his recollections of the Sufis and spiritual guides he knew. Four of these spiritual guides were women. Here
are excerpts from Ibn 'Arabi's recollections of three of them.[7]

SHAMS, MOTHER OF THE POOR

She lived at Marchena of the Olives, where I visited her often. Among
people of our kind I have never met one like her with respect to the
control she had over her soul. In her spiritual activities and communica-

tions she was among the greatest. She had a strong and pure heart, a noble spiritual power, and a fine discrimination. She usually concealed her spiritual state, although she would often reveal something of it to me in secret because she knew of my own attainment, which gladdened me. She was endowed with many graces. I had considerable experience of her intuition and found her to be a master in this sphere. Her spiritual state was characterized chiefly by her fear of God and His good pleasure in her, the combination of the two at the same time in one person being extremely rare among us.[8]

NUNA BINT FATIMA BINT IBN AL-MUTHANNA

She came to the [Sufi] Way while still a young girl living in her father's house. I met her when she was already ninety-six years of age. . . . One day when I was with her a woman came to see her to complain of her husband who had gone away to Sidonia, two days' journey from Seville. She told us that her husband wanted to seek another wife in that place, which she found hard to accept. I asked Fatima whether she had heard the woman's plea and begged her to call upon God to restore her husband to her. She said, "I will make no supplication, but I will cause the chapter [of the Qur'an] 'The Opening' [Sura 1, al-Fatiha] to follow behind him and bring him back." Then I said, "In the name of God the Merciful, the Compassionate," and she recited the rest of the chapter. Then she said, "O chapter of 'The Opening,' go to Jerez de Sidonia to the husband of this woman and drive him back at once from wherever you find him and do not let him delay." She said this sometime between noon and the late afternoon.

On the third day the man arrived at his home. Then the woman came to inform us of his arrival and to thank us. I then told her to bring her husband to us. When he came we asked him what had brought him back. . . . He replied that he had left his house in the middle of the afternoon heading toward the municipal building for the marriage and that on the way he felt a constriction in his heart and everything suddenly seemed very dark to him. At this he became very anxious. Then he left that place and arrived in Triana before sunset, where he had found a boat for Seville. Thus he had sailed the day before and arrived in Seville that morning, having left all his baggage and effects behind in Jerez. He admitted that he still did not know why he had done it. I have seen various miracles performed by her.[9]

ZAYNAB AL-QAL'IYA

From the fortress of the Banu Jamad, she was of those devoted to the Book of God, the foremost ascetic of her day. Although she possessed both great beauty and considerable wealth, she freely abandoned the world and went to live in the region of Mecca. . . . I had contact with her both in Seville and at Mecca. . . . When she sat down to practice the Invocation [*dhikr*] she would rise into the air from the ground to a height of thirty cubits; when she had finished she would descend again. I accompanied her from Mecca to Jerusalem and I have never seen anyone more strict in observing the times of prayer than she. She was one of the most intelligent people of her time.[10]

✳ Holy Women of Morocco and Egypt
JOHN RENARD

Not long after Ibn 'Arabi had written his anthology, an Egyptian Sufi named Safi ad-Din ibn Abi 'l-Mansur ibn Zafir (1198–1283) wrote a similar work in Cairo. Safi ad-Din lived most of his life in Egypt and Syria. His work is a fascinating collection of sketches of more than 150 important Friends of God from all over Egypt, North Africa and Spain to the west, and Syria and the Hijaz (northwestern Arabian peninsula) to the east. Safi ad-Din is especially concerned with the spiritual qualities of his subjects, along with their lineages of initiation into the Sufi path. Here are his recollections of a Maghribi woman named Sitt al-Muluk and an Egyptian woman who lived near the pyramids of Giza.[11]

SITT AL-MULUK

I encountered a Maghribi woman of great [spiritual] estate, whom the Friends of God and religious scholars alike held in high regard, whose name was Sitt al-Muluk. She had come from the Maghrib [Morocco] in the company of Shaykh Abu Yusuf ad-Dahmani. She was visiting the Holy House [Jerusalem; see fig. 23] at the time when the great shaykh and Friend of God ʿAli ibn Ghalas al-Yamani was there. [Ibn Ghalas] recounted:

"I was in the Sacred Sanctuary when suddenly I witnessed a cord of light pointing toward one of the domes of the Sanctuary. So I walked toward that dome and found inside it this woman, Sitt al-Muluk, and the light that I had seen, in her place of prayer. I proposed marriage to her for [the sake of spiritual] companionship and she accepted."

And this woman said to me [the narrator]: "ʿAli ibn Ghalas entrusted to me an earthenware ewer and said to me, 'My sister, watch over it.' So I put it on a shelf in the house. One day while I was looking at it, it shattered suddenly into shards without moving at all and even though nothing had hit it. So I called on God and expressed my amazement at his command; I got up and collected [the pieces of] it, wrapped it in a cloth, and noted down the hour [of the occurrence]. A couple of days later word came that Shaykh ʿAli ibn Ghalas had died in Damascus at that very hour."

One day she said to me: "My son, I made out the sliver of crescent moon [whose appearance signals the beginning of the fast] of Ramadan, and at the moment of its appearance and my being sure of it, God Most High gave me insight into his Night of Power,* as to which night it was and how to recognize it with certainty. And when the appointed night came, the Night of Power, I ran from it as a debtor flees a creditor. But its lights probed me and flowed forth from my eyes, and, when the night was spent, I said, 'I swear by your might, O Lord, and your majesty, what need had I of your Night of Power when I was already with you?'" And the great Friends of God who have seen her attest to her sanctity, may God be pleased with her!

THE HOLY WOMAN OF GIZA

I encountered at Giza in Egypt a woman, one of God's fools [lit., one on the fringe of society], who for over three years had stood upright on her

---

* Tradition places the inaugural revelation to Muhammad on the twenty-seventh night of Ramadan, called the Night of Power.

Figure 23.   The Dome of the Rock in Jerusalem (692) is Islam's third holiest site, a reminder of Muhammad's exalted position of spiritual leadership, and the starting point of his Ascension to heaven after the Night Journey from Mecca on the twenty-seventh of Rajab.

feet in a spot of ground among the shoots of esparto grass. She sat down neither night nor day, neither winter nor summer; and she did not take shelter from the sun in summer nor from the rain in winter. The snakes took refuge around her; she ate what food was offered her, and she spoke with whomever addressed her. Hers was an amazing state.

✳ The Life of Sufi Badhni

BRUCE B. LAWRENCE

Shaykh 'Abd al-Haqq Muhaddith of Delhi (1551–1642) was a member of the Chishti Sufi *tariqa* (order) and author of *Chronicles of the Pious on the Secrets of the Righteous* (*Akhbar al-akhyar fi asrar al-abrar*). His works were part of the burgeoning literary output of Indian Sufis whose tradition of writing had been an important ingredient in Islam's spread in the subcontinent. The work from which come these recollections of Sufi Badhni represents the expanding popularity of a long-traditional Islamic genre, the hagiographical anthology.

Shaykh Nizam ad-Din* said that in Kaithal there was a saint whom
they call Sufi Badhni. He was so completely ascetical that he went about
totally naked. Shaykh Nizam ad-Din comments that according to Islamic
law, any person who abstains from that minimal amount of food and
water required to keep the body functioning, or who does not wear
enough clothing at least to cover the private parts . . . is committing a
punishable offense, but Sufi Badhni was a saint of such high character
that he was exempt from these restrictions. . . .

Sufi Badhni loved the life of prayer. He sat in the mosque in front of
the mihrab and had no other occupation but offering prayers day and
night. One day some ‘ulama’ came to see him, as many people used to
do. The shaykh queried the ‘ulama’: “Will there be prayer in paradise?”
They answered: “Paradise is the abode of reward, where no desire will
go unsatisfied, no need unfulfilled. Devotions are only necessary in
this world.” When Sufi Badhni heard that there would be no prayer in
paradise, he exclaimed: “I’ll have nothing to do with a heaven where there
is no prayer,” and then he added something in Hindi not fit to repeat.

Shaykh Nizam ad-Din continued to extol Sufi Badhni at some length.
He related the following anecdote. There was a person who used to visit
Sufi Badhni frequently. One day this friend, while climbing a mountain,
met a man from the Unseen. He inquired of the mysterious stranger,
“What sort of man is Sufi Badhni?” The stranger replied, “He is a great
man, but alas . . . ,” and said no more. Then he immediately began to ask
God for pardon, saying repeatedly, “God forgive me. God forgive me.”
The friend reported this conversation to Sufi Badhni. The latter quipped:
“If the stranger had said, ‘Sufi Badhni is a great man’ and not asked for
God’s forgiveness in the same breath, I would have thrown him down the
mountain so hard he would have broken his neck.”

Shaykh Nizam ad-Din related another anecdote: “When Sufi Badhni
was engaged in meditating on God, such a state would overcome him
that his head, hands, and feet seemed to separate from each other. If some
persons came to see him and chanced to find him in that condition, they

---

* Nizam ad-Din Awliya’ (d. 1325), himself a prominent Chishti shaykh, wrote
Morals for the Heart (*Fawa’id al-fu’ad*), a premier example of the *malfuz* genre.

would be terrified and run out of the mosque crying, 'Someone has murdered Sufi Badhni and cut him to pieces!' It is further reported that those who knew Sufi Badhni well would say, 'Don't worry—no one has been killed. This is just the manifestation of his special spiritual condition.' If the curious returned for a second look, they would find Sufi Badhni sitting peacefully before the mihrab."

Someone asked when Sufi Badhni lived, and Shaykh Nasir ad-Din* told them that he lived in the time of Shaykh Farid ad-Din.† They say that no one ever saw a crow sitting on the dome of the mosque when he prayed, or even flying over it. God alone knows the truth of the matter.

There is a famous story that one time he and Shaykh Qutb ad-Din Bakhtiyar Kaki [d. 1232] were taken prisoner by the Mongols of Genghis Khan. One day the prisoners had become desperately hungry and thirsty. By a miracle, Qutb Sahib produced bread from his sleeve, and Sufi Badhni a jug of water, which they distributed among the prisoners. This was how Khwaja Qutb ad-Din received the name "Kaki" (bread) and Shaykh Sufi came to be known as Badhni, which in Hindi means "water jug."[12]

✳ ## Jabarti's Account of 'Ali al-Bayyumi

WILLIAM SHEPARD

'Ali al-Bayyumi (1696–1769) was the founder of the Bayyumiya tariqa, one of the more popular Sufi orders in Egypt today. With his combination of scholarly ability and ecstatic behavior, 'Ali al-Bayyumi illustrated the kind of person a Sufi *wali* or Friend of God was expected to be in eighteenth- and nineteenth-century Egypt. This passage is taken from the early-nineteenth-century historical chronicle of Shaykh 'Abd ar-Rahman al-Jabarti (1753–1825) entitled *Historical and Biographical Marvels* (*'Aja'ib al-athar fi tarajim wa 'l-akhbar*).[13] Note the difference in tone from earlier hagiographical works.

There died [in the year 1183 H. (=1768–1769)] the Imam, the wali, the pious believer, the ecstatic [*majdhub*], the productive scholar [*'alim*]

---

* Nasir ad-Din Mahmud (d. 1356), called the "Lamp of Delhi," was a disciple of Nizam ad-Din and his successor as shaykh of the Chishti order.

† Farid ad-Din Ganj-i Shakar ("Sugar Treasure," d. 1265), was a Chishti shaykh known for his ascetical practices.

Shaykh 'Ali ibn Hijazi ibn Muhammad al-Bayyumi, a follower of the
Shafi'i school of religious law [*madhhab*] and of the Khalwatiya and later
the Ahmadiya [tariqas]. He was born about the year 1108 [=1695–1696
C.E.]. He memorized the Qur'an at an early age and became a scholar,
attending the lessons of the shaykhs [of his time] and studying Hadith
under 'Umar ibn 'Abd as-Salam at-Tatawani. He was initiated into
the Khalwatiya [tariqa] by Sayyid Husayn ad-Dimirdashi al-'Adili
and followed its practices for some time. Then he was initiated into the
Ahmadiya by several people. In time he experienced ecstasy [*jadhb*] and
hearts inclined to him, spirits were drawn to him, and people came to
believe in him greatly. Many followed his [Sufi] way [tariqa] and recited
his spiritual invocations [dhikr]. He attracted a large number of followers
and disciples. He lived in the Husayniya [quarter]* and held dhikrs in the
mosque of az-Zahir [just] outside the Husayniya, where he was to be
found regularly with his group, as it was near his house.

He was subject to [supernatural] experiences and strange states of
ecstasy [*ahwal*], and wrote a number of books, among them a commentary on *The Small Collection* [of hadith, by Suyuti; *Al-jami' as-saghir*],
a commentary on *The Aphorisms* [*Al-hikam*] by Ibn 'Ata' Allah al-
Iskandari [d. 1309],[14] a commentary on *The Perfect Person* [*Al-insan al-
kamil*] by al-Jili [d. ca. 1410], a work on the local Sufi orders,[15] especially
on the Khalwatiya Dimirdashiya, written in 1144 [=1730–1731 C.E.], a
commentary on the *Forty [Hadith]* [*Arba'in*, a brief popular collection]
of an-Nawawi, a treatise on the Shari'a punishments [*hudud*], and a
commentary on the prayer formula of the Ahmadiya and on talismanic
formulae. He spoke sublimely on Sufi practice [*tasawwuf*], and when
he spoke he was eloquent, clear, and dazzled his hearers.

He wore the same clothing in winter and summer, a white gown (or
shirt) and a white skullcap about which he wound a piece of red cloth as a
turban. He would leave his house only once a week to visit the Shrine of
Husayn, riding a mule with his followers going before him and following

* One of the "popular" quarters of Cairo, just north of the walls of the original
Fatimid city.

him, proclaiming the unity [of God] and invoking [His name]. Often he
would shut himself off for months meeting no one. He performed evident
miracles [*karamat*].

When he began to hold a dhikr every Tuesday in the courtyard of
the Shrine of Husayn that lasted until after dawn, bringing his people as
already mentioned, the *'ulama'* rose against him and objected to the way
they dirtied the mosque with their feet, since most of them went barefoot
and raised their voices very loudly. Working through some of the military chiefs, they almost managed to stop him, but Shaykh ash-Shubrawi,
who greatly loved the ecstatics, opposed them and helped him. He said
to the pasha and the chiefs, "This man is a great scholar and wali, and
you must not interfere with him." At that time the shaykh had him give
classes at the Azhar Mosque, and he lectured on the *Forty [Hadith]* of
an-Nawawi in the Tibarsiya [section of the mosque]. Most of the 'ulama'
attended and were so impressed [by his learning] that they calmed down
and the fire of discord was extinguished. . . . [Here he includes two first-
person accounts of visions, presented in part 7 below.]

Here are some of his miracles [*karamat*]: I have heard from trustworthy sources that he used to convert brigands from their criminal ways so
that they became his disciples and some even fully initiated Sufis.[16]
Sometimes he would chain them with a heavy iron chain to the pillars
of the Zahir Mosque, and sometimes he would put a collar around their
necks and discipline them as he saw fit. When he went riding they would
follow him with weapons and staves. He had an awesome regal presence.
When he took part in the dhikr at the Shrine of Husayn he would reach
a state of excitement in which he would become as strong as a fierce
wild beast, but when he sat down after the dhikr he would be extremely
weak. Sometimes his face would appear to those present like that of a
wild animal, sometimes like that of a calf and sometimes like that of a
gazelle.

Mustafa Pasha [the Ottoman governor], when he was in Egypt,
believed in him and favored him, and once when he visited him [Shaykh
Bayyumi] said to him: "You will be called to the position of Grand Vizier
at such-and-such a time," and it happened as he said. When he became

grand vizier he sent orders to Egypt and had Amir 'Uthman Agha, the representative of the Sublime Porte,* build for the shaykh the mosque that bears his name in the Husayniya [quarter], as well as a fountain, a primary school [*kuttab*], and a domed mausoleum. When he died the prayers were said for him at the Azhar and there was a great funeral procession. He was buried in the tomb built for him in the domed shrine in the above-mentioned mosque.

WISDOM LITERATURE

One can trace the origins of Islamic wisdom literature back to the Qur'an and, in particular, to the sura named after the sage Luqman. After a complete, annotated translation of that sura, samples of the genre known as the aphorism from both Arabic and Persian sources exemplify the wide reach of popular wisdom literature in the form of moral advice.

✳   ### The Qur'anic Paradigm of Wisdom
Surat Luqman

MUSTANSIR MIR

Luqman is a Meccan sura. It is said to be fifty-seventh in the order of revelation, which suggests that it was revealed fairly late in the Meccan period. The sura's principal themes are monotheism (dealt with in section 3, which speaks against idolatry) and the Last Day (section 4, which in presenting its arguments implicitly maintains that life in this world is not the only life there is).

The sura makes a direct appeal to young people. It was revealed at a time when the Islamic message had begun to draw the attention of independently minded Meccans—especially youths, who were relatively free from the pull of the tradition of idol worship and who were experiencing increasing pressure from their parents and the city elders to stay within the fold of the received, ancestral religion. The Qur'an is, on the one hand, encouraging Meccan youths to think for themselves and, on the other, warning the parents and elders who were trying to stop them from converting to Islam (see verse 33).

Finally, the sura is a type of wisdom literature to the extent that it highlights the relation between reason and revelation. While some Muslim scholars are of the view that Luqman was a prophet, the majority hold that he was not a prophet

* Sublime Porte: the court of the Ottoman sultan, Topkapi Palace, Istanbul.

but a wise man. The Prophet Muhammad is said to have remarked: "Luqman was not a prophet, but rather a servant of God who was given to reflection and had strong faith. He loved God, and in turn God loved him, bestowing wisdom upon him." The fact that prophecy is not one of the main themes of this sura is significant. The sura seems to be arguing (verses 12ff.) that Luqman's wisdom (*hikma*) led him to discover insights essentially similar to some of those furnished by prophetic revelation. In other words, reason, if used properly, brings one to the threshold of revelation and points to the same broad conclusions that revelation presents and confirms.

[I: QUR'AN GUIDES THE RIGHTEOUS (1–11)]

[1]Alif Lam Mim.* [2]These are the verses of the Wise Book, [3]a guidance and a mercy for the doers of good deeds, those who establish salat and pay zakat. [4]It is these people who are truly convinced of the hereafter. [5]They are upon a[n excellent] guidance from their Lord, and it is they who are going to meet with success.

[6]There are some people, however, who opt for frivolous talk, so that, lacking all knowledge as they do, they might lead people astray from the Path of God, and so that they might make fun of them.† They have a humiliating punishment in store for them. [7]When our verses are recited to them, they turn away arrogantly, as if they did not hear them—as if they were hard of hearing! Give them the good news of a tormenting punishment!

[8]Those who have believed and done good deeds, there are gardens of bliss for them; [9]they shall live in them for ever—a true promise of God! He is the Almighty, the Wise. [10]He created the heavens without any pillars you could see: He cast mountains in the earth, lest it should go into a lurch, taking you along; and He spread in it all kinds of animals. And We sent down from the sky water, by means of which We grew in it all kinds of useful plants. [11]This is the creation of God! Now show me

* Alif Lam Mim: such "broken" letters occur at the beginning of many suras, as in that of Joseph in part 1 above. Nothing can be said with certainty about their meaning. Many scholars simply regard them as the names of the suras in which they occur.
† Them: the object pronoun in Arabic refers to the verses of the Qur'an (verse 2, above). Alternatively, it could refer to the "Path of God" (verse 6), in which case "it" would replace "them" in translation.

what has been created by those other than Him? The fact is that the wrongdoers are in plain error.

[II: LUQMAN'S ADVICE TO HIS SON (12–19)]

[12]We gave Luqman wisdom—"Be grateful to God!"* And he who shows gratitude does so for his own good. But he who disbelieves—God is Self-Sufficient, Praised.

[13]And when Luqman said to his son—he was giving him advice— "My son, do not associate anything with God; association is a great wrong indeed."

[14]† And We advised man concerning his parents—his mother bore him, suffering one debility after another, his weaning taking two years: "Be grateful to Me and to your parents; to Me is the return." [15]But if they should put pressure on you to associate with Me something you have no knowledge of, do not listen to them. Associate nicely with them in the world, though, and follow the path of those who turn to Me. Then you will come back to Me, and I shall apprise you of what you used to do.

[16]"My son, if there be something of the weight of a mustard seed, be it in a rock, in the heavens, or inside the earth, God will bring it forth; God is Subtle, Aware. [17]My dear son, establish salat, enjoin good and forbid evil, and be steadfast in any adversity you might face; this,‡ indeed, is one of the acts of resolution. [18]Do not be wry-faced with people, and

---

* "Be grateful to God!": that is, wisdom begins with the recognition that one must be grateful to God. Herein lies the essence of the wisdom Luqman received from God.

† The whole of verses 14–15 is parenthetical. The theme of monotheism, which is a right of God over human beings, and the theme of kindness toward parents, a duty of human beings in relation to one another, go together in the Qur'an. As a modern Qur'an commentator has noted, Luqman talks about the first right but, since he is advising his own son, omits, out of modesty, mention of his own right as a parent. God, however, supplies the omission in the form of a parenthetic remark, hence the shift of person (in verses 12–14) from "he" (Luqman) to "We" (God).

‡ This: The demonstrative could refer exclusively to the act of remaining steadfast in the face of a difficulty, or it could be a compact reference to the several acts of establishing prayer, enjoining good and forbidding evil, and persevering in the face of difficulties.

do not walk on the ground with a swagger; God does not like anyone who is vain, conceited. [19]Be modest of carriage, and keep your voice low; the most disgusting voice, indeed, is that of a donkey."

[III: MONOTHEISM—ARGUMENT
AGAINST IDOLATRY (20–27)]

[20]Have you not seen that God has pressed into your service what is in the heavens and what is in the earth, and has so amply bestowed on you His blessings, both obvious and hidden? And yet there are some people who would wrangle about God—without knowledge, guidance, or a book that would shed light! [21]When it is said to them, "Follow that which God has sent down," they say, "Rather, we shall follow what we have found our forefathers practicing." Even if Satan were inviting them* to the punishment of flames?

[22]One who turns his face to God in submission, being a doer of good deeds, surely holds on to the Firm Loop.† And with God rests the conclusion of all matters.‡ [23]But he who disbelieves, let not his disbelief grieve you. To Us is their return, and then We shall apprise them of what they have done; God is aware of the secrets of the hearts. [24]We shall give them a meager provision [in this world], and shall then drag them over to a harsh punishment [in the next].

[25]If you should ask them, "Who created the heavens and the earth?" they would surely say, "God!" Say, "Praise be to God!" Most of them do not know, however.

[26]To God belongs what is in the heavens and the earth: God alone is the Self-Sufficient, Praised One. [27]Even if all the trees of the earth were to become pens, and the ocean were to be augmented after that by seven

---

* Them: The object pronoun could refer to those being addressed by the Qur'an or, preferably, to their forefathers, in which case their present-day followers would also be included by implication.

† Loop: The image is that of someone grasping the loop at the end of a rope and is thus saved from tripping, falling, or drowning.

‡ And . . . matters: more literally: "And to God is [to be referred] the conclusion of all matters."

more oceans,* the Words of God† would not be exhausted: God is Powerful, Wise.

[IV: THE LAST DAY—SUPPORTING ARGUMENT (28–34)]

[28]Neither creating you nor raising you up is any different than a single individual:‡ God is One Hearing, Watching. [29]Have you not seen that God injects night into day and injects day into night, and holds the sun and the moon in subjection—each coursing along up to a designated time—and that God is aware of what you do? [30]This is so because God alone is the true deity and those other than God they call upon are the false ones; and He alone is the Exalted One, the Great.

[31]Have you not seen that ships sail in the ocean by the grace of God, in order that He might show you some of His signs? In [all of] this, indeed, there are signs for all those who are truly steadfast and grateful.

[32]And when they are enveloped by waves that are like canopies, they call upon God, making submission to Him exclusively. But when He conveys them safely to the land, some among them keep to the straight path.§ The only people who stubbornly reject Our verses are those who are perfidious, ungrateful.

[33]O people, fear your Lord and dread a day when a father shall be of no avail to his child, nor is a child going to be of any avail whatsoever to his father. God's promise is true, so life in this world must not lead you into deception. Neither must the Deceiver [Satan] lead you into deception about God.

[34]Knowledge of the [Last] Hour rests with God only. He [alone] sends down the rain, and He [alone] knows what is in the wombs. No

---

* The ocean . . . more oceans: that is, if the ocean were to become ink and, after its depletion, were to be replenished by seven more oceans of ink.

† Words of God: The Arabic phrase *kalimat Allah* refers to descriptions of the praiseworthy attributes and marvelous acts of God.

‡ Neither . . . individual: that is, creating all of you or raising all of you from the dead is no more difficult for Him than creating or raising up from the dead a single individual.

§ Some . . . path: The implication is that only some keep to the straight path, whereas the rest forget the commitment they made at the time of crisis.

individual knows how he is going to perform tomorrow, and no individual knows in what land he will die. God is Knowledgeable, Aware.

Morals for the Masses

Here are two examples of the form called the aphorism. The first is a selection from an Arabic collection attributed to ʿAli, cousin and son-in-law of Muhammad and fourth of the Rightly Guided Caliphs regarded as paragons of virtue (fig. 24). The second is from a Persian source, and the sayings are attributed to a thirteenth-century Indian Sufi.

✳ Aphorisms of ʿAli

PETER HEATH

Collections of moral maxims and proverblike utterances have often been attributed to central religious figures. Here is an abridged version of such a collection, called the "Aphorisms of ʿAli" ("Amthal ʿAli"). A noteworthy feature of the text is its acrostic structure: sayings are grouped not according to thematic content but according to the alphabetical order of the Arabic letter with which each begins. This anonymous, undated compendium is taken from an anthology of short collections of wise sayings and literary and moral prose treatises.[17] As is often the case with proverbs, these sayings are religious and "Islamic" largely by virtue of their association with an important religious figure.

THE APHORISMS OF OUR LORD ʿALI
(MAY GOD HONOR HIS COUNTENANCE)
ACCORDING TO THE NUMBER OF LETTERS IN THE ALPHABET

In the Name of God the Merciful and the Compassionate

Praise be to God, Lord of the Worlds, and Blessings on our Lord Muhammad and on all of his Family and Companions.

Now then: These words are from among the sayings of the Leader of the Pious, the Heir to the Apostle of the Lord of the Worlds, the Commander of the Faithful, ʿAli ibn Abi Talib (May God honor his countenance), according to the letters of the alphabet. There is a symbolic hint in the meaning of each of these letters. Each saying is arranged according to the twenty-nine letters [of the Arabic alphabet],

Figure 24.   Names of Muslim leaders cover this seventeenth-century Syrian decorative tile panel symbolizing the Gateway to Paradise, representing the symbolic presence of exemplary figures: across the top from right to left are Allah, Muhammad, Abu Bakr, ʿUmar (the first and second caliphs); at lower right, ʿUthman (third caliph), and lower left, ʿAli (fourth caliph). The panel in the center says "Glory to God." Note the lamps hanging in the three arches, recalling the imagery of the prayer rug and mihrab panels. New York: Metropolitan Museum of Art, Gift of Mrs. Frederick F. Thompson, 1915 (15.76.3).

according to the saying's beginning. Peace be on whomever follows the Mahdi.

The Letter Alif

Whoever consoles you in distress is your brother.
Act well toward whoever seeks you harm, so that you guide him.
The soul finds rest through renunciation.

The Letter Ba'

Cheer your soul with the news that success follows steadfastness.
Sell this world for the next and you will profit.
A person weeping out of fear of God is a delight to the eye.

The Letter Ta'

Delaying misdeeds is part of drawing near [to God].
At life's end you perceive what escaped you at its beginning.
Slackness in prayer is a sign of feeble faith.

The Letter Tha'

Three deadly perils are greed, lust, and naivete.
A third of faith is modesty, a third intelligence, and a third generosity.
The spirit is maintained through food, the soul is maintained through
     mystical ecstasy [*fana'*].

The Letter Jim

A person's beauty lies in wisdom.
The promenade of vanity lasts an hour.
The promenade of truth lasts forever.

The Letter Ha'

A person's wisdom is his succor.
A person's modesty is his shield.
A person's wrath can destroy him.

The Letter Kha'

Fear God and you will be safe from everyone else.
The best of friends is one who guides you toward virtue.
An empty heart is better than a full purse.

The Letter Dal

The proof of one's intelligence is speech; the proof of one's upbringing,
     deeds.

Government of the vile is an affliction for humanity.
The coin of the miser is a stone.

The Letter Dhal

Remembrance of saints makes Divine Compassion descend.
The humiliation of poverty is dear to God.
Remembrance of death purifies the heart.

The Letter Ra'

Your sustenance will seek you out, so be at ease.
The messenger of death is birth.
Relating prophetic traditions relates one to the Prophet (May God bless
    and keep him).

The Letter Zay

The passing away of knowledge is easier than the death of scholars.
The asceticism of commoners can lead one astray.
The corners of this world are weighed down with calamities.

The Letter Sin

Thinking the worst is part of prudence.
Immorality is a desolation from which there is no salvation.
The leaders of the community are the religious jurisprudents.

The Letter Shin

The disgrace of knowledge is boastfulness.
A pinch of knowledge is better than a pound of work.
A cure for madness is reading the Qur'an.

The Letter Sad

The health of the body is in fasting.
The prayers of the night are the splendor of the day.
The ignoramus's health is his only shelter.

The Letter Dad

The tongue's lash is harsher than the teeth's bite.
The heart's destitution is more severe than the hand's.
The world is narrow for those who hate one another.

The Letter Ta'

A long, pious life is one of the bounties of the prophets.
One whose hopes are short lives long.
Blessed is the one who has no family.

The Letter Za'

The oppression of kings is better than the guidance of the people.
The shadow of the sultan is like the shadow of God.
The crooked person remains crooked.

The Letter 'Ayn

The defect of speech is prolixity.
An intelligent enemy is better than an ignorant friend.
Memorize books without condensing them.

The Letter Ghayn

The price of those who trust in God has increased [because of their
      scarcity].
An intelligent youth is better than an ignorant elder.
One who has enraged you over nothing has cheated you.

The Letter Fa'

One who is safe from his own evil has triumphed.
A person's redemption lies in veracity.
Every heart has a preoccupation.

The Letter Qaf

Accepting the truth is part of religion.

Strength of heart is part of correct faith.

Consider your actions and you will be saved from mistakes.

The Letter Kaf

A generous infidel is preferable to a stingy Muslim.

Being ungrateful for a blessing eliminates it.

May white hair suffice as an illness.

The Letter Lam

Fame does not come from frivolity.

Every enmity can be reconciled except the enmity of envy.

If the believer saw death and its bitterness, he would not despise hope and
   its illusions.

The Letter Mim

The drinking trough of pleasure is crowded.

The meeting place of learning is a garden.

The meeting place of the noble is the citadel of speech.

The Letter Nun

The light of the believer is nightfall.

Forgetting death is the heart's rust.

Sleep in good faith and you will lie in the softest bed.

The Letter Ha'

Fleeing from yourself is more beneficial than fleeing from a lion.

Making a stew is not the same as eating it.

The greedy person has perished without even knowing it.

The Letter Waw

The responsibility of giving alms generously is greater than merely being
   rewarded for it.

The governance of the idiot soon passes.

Solitude is better than an evil companion.

The Letter Lam Alif

A person without honor is without religion.
The envier never finds rest.
The corrupt person is never esteemed.

The Letter Ya'

A fearful person finds safety when he faces what he fears.
A person enters the abodes of the great through trustworthiness.
The heart's despair is the soul's repose.

This completes the Aphorisms of 'Ali (May God honor his countenance).

✳ Sayings Attributed to Mu'in ad-Din Chishti

BRUCE B. LAWRENCE

Treating an enormous range of everyday matters of conduct, the Aphorisms of 'Ali are directed to a very broad public. Some collections of wise sayings, such as those attributed to the Indian city of Ajmer's premier Friend of God, Shaykh Mu'in ad-Din Chishti (d. 1236; see fig. 25), have a slightly narrower public in mind. Although they also include counsel of a more general sort, these aphorisms focus on the demanding aspects of interior demeanor expected of individuals intent on a life of spiritual seeking. Employing a literary conceit that claims the authority of a great teacher, the text begins by explaining the alleged origin of the sayings in the conversations the shaykh had with his disciples.[18]

Among the holy, celestial dicta of Mu'in ad-Din in *Guidance of the Mystics* [*Dalil al-'arifin*] that Khwaja Qutb ad-Din Bakhtiyar Oushi [d. 1235] compiled from the conversations of his master—may God sanctify his secret—are the following:
   The heart of the lover is set ablaze with love. Everyone who enters the domain of love is scorched. It should not be avoided, since there is no loftier fire than the fire of love!
   Listen to the voice from the incoming waves; it is loud. But when the tide goes out, the voice becomes silent.

Figure 25.   The tomb of the influential thirteenth-century Indian religious leader Mu'in ad-Din Chishti (d. 1236) in Ajmer, India, shown here on a calendar poster, is an important place of pilgrimage. Courtesy of Carl Ernst.

I heard from the tongue of Khwaja 'Uthman Haruni—may God sanctify his secret—that those who befriend God Almighty, even though for a time they become veiled from Him in this world, will not remain veiled.

I have heard from the tongue of Khwaja 'Uthman Haruni that everyone in whom these three qualities are to be found—it is certain that God Almighty has befriended him. First, generosity like the generosity of the ocean. Second, compassion like the compassion of the sun. Third, humility like the humility of the earth.

The company of the righteous is better than a righteous deed, just as the company of the evil is worse than an evil deed.

That disciple is firm in his resolve to repent when the angel on his left side records no sin for him during a period of twenty years! (The recorder of these lines attests that some of the early saints also spoke such words and the truth of the meaning of these words is such that some of the latterday scholarly Sufis have said:) Repentance and seeking forgiveness are indispensable for the spiritual development of the disciple, and the recording of sins, once repentance and seeking forgiveness are evident, is impossible since by nature such a person can commit no sin. And for this reason they have made it incumbent [on disciples] to recite the prayer seeking forgiveness just before going to sleep, in order that the recording of sins from the previous day, having been suspended due to the mercy of God Almighty, will not become manifest.

From the blessed tongue of Khwaja ʿUthman Haruni I have heard the question, "Who is the one who has attained [spiritual] poverty? It is the one for whom in the world of annihilation [*fani*] nothing remains [*baqi*]."

The sign of love is that you obey [unconditionally], and not out of fear that the Friend is near.

There is this rank for the mystics that when they reach it, they see the entire world and all that is in it between two of their fingers.

The mystic is one who whatever he wants he acquires, and whatever he asks he obtains an answer from God.

The lowest stage and degree of the mystic, with respect to love, is that the divine attributes appear in him. The highest degree for the mystic, with respect to love, is that if someone requests something of him, he provides it through the power of saintly miracles.

For years we are engaged in this work, and in the end we obtain nothing but awe [*haybat*] [at God's power].

Your sin serves no function except to bring despair and distress to your fellow Muslim.

For the people of intimate knowledge [*maʿrifa*] worship takes precedence over [the desires of] their lower selves.

The sign of having recognized God Almighty is that you flee from people and remain silent in [your] intimate knowledge.

The mystic does not achieve intimate knowledge till he forgets the signposts of intimate knowledge.

The mystic is someone who banishes from his heart whatever is without God, so that he remains alone and apart, just as the Friend is alone and apart [from all others].

The sign of perversity is that someone sins and still hopes that I will accept [him as a disciple].

The sign of a mystic is that he remains silent and sad.

Whoever finds grace discovers [the meaning of] generosity.

The dervish is every servant [of God] who chances on someone in need and does not leave him wanting.

The mystic on the path of love is someone who has freed his heart from both worlds.

The most precious of things in this world is that dervishes sit with other dervishes, and the worst of things is that dervishes remain separated from other dervishes, especially when there is no cause for their separation.

Someone trusts in God who flees from the affliction and distress of people, and also listens to no complaint from another, nor tells any story about another.

The foremost of the mystics are those who are most agitated.

The sign of the mystic is that he befriends death, forgoes comfort, and eschews intimacy, [because he is immersed] in remembrance [*dhikr*] of his Lord.

When God Almighty revives the lovers, He grants them the vision [of their revival] through His own lights.

The people of love are those who, without the mediation of a teacher, hear the speech of the Friend.

The mystic is someone who, when rising in the morning, has no recollection of the previous evening.

The best of times are those unsullied by the whispers of the tempter.

Knowledge is a vast ocean, intimate knowledge but a wave of that ocean. Where then is God, where His servant? Knowledge is God's domain; intimate knowledge, His servant's.

Mystics are suns, suns that shine over the entire world, and the effulgence of the world, all of it, is due to their lights.

A person should not go from one halting place to the next until he takes leave [of his host] at the end of prayer; for the "ascent of the [ordinary] believer is his very prayer"!

ENCOUNTERING THE EXEMPLARY PERSONS

Storytelling as Entertainment

Many millions of Muslims over the centuries have received the bulk of their religious education as part of their family entertainment. Storytelling, now an all but lost art in many parts of the world, has been one of the most important vehicles for spreading values, and it continues to do so in traditional societies. Here we have selections of stories that have come to us in two very different ways. The first is a traditional Afghan tale handed down orally and recorded by anthropologist David Edwards. The second group of anecdotes were written down much nearer to their point of origin and collected in a literary anthology.

✳ ### Telling Tales
A Miracle of Mulla Hadda

DAVID EDWARDS

Najmuddin Akhundzada, who is usually referred to as the Mulla of Hadda or Hadda Sahib, was one of the most important Muslim figures in Afghanistan in the latter half of the nineteenth century. A disciple of the Akhund of Swat, Najmuddin spent most of his adult life at the *khanaqa* (Sufi residence) that he founded in Hadda, outside of Jalalabad, but he also lived a number of years with the Shinwari and Mohmand tribes. Most of Najmuddin's life was spent engaged in the practice of *tasawwuf*, or Sufism; indeed, he was the most important Sufi figure on the Afghan side of the Afghan/Indian frontier during this time. He also gained considerable renown as an opponent of the great Afghan king Abdur Rahman Khan, who ruled from 1880 to 1901.

Although various documentary sources refer to Najmuddin, he is best remembered in Afghanistan through countless miracle stories about him and his disciples. The following story concerns a journey purportedly made by Najmuddin to Mount Qaf (Koh-i Qaf)* and was told to me by the descendant of one of Najmuddin's closest disciples. This is one of the most fabulous stories

---

* The mountain range that encircles the entire earth, the goal of all mystic journeys.

told about Najmuddin, the majority of tales being content to describe the saint's magical production of an endless supply of rice from a simple pot or his transformation of a sack of corn into a sack of gold. Few stories that are told these days speak of places like Koh-i Qaf, and to the degree that this one does it can be taken as unrepresentative of Afghan miracle stories. At the same time, the story is no less interesting for being unrepresentative, and illustrates the continuing link of present stories to much older traditions.[19] The account begins:

There are many miracles of Hadda Sahib. Mawlana Abdul Baqi, who was Hadda Sahib's servant and lived his entire life in the same room with Hadda Sahib, told the following story:

After the evening prayers, Hadda Sahib would come back to his room, perform three hundred prayers, and recite fifteen verses of the Qur'an.

One night, Hadda Sahib was sitting on his prayer carpet with the door closed. I was wrapped in my blanket but still awake. All of a sudden I heard someone say, "Salam 'alaykum," and Hadda Sahib replied, "Wa 'alaykum as-salam."

I looked out from under my blanket to see who it was. I hadn't seen the door open, and no one could fit through the small opening in the ceiling. How could anyone have entered? Then I saw that it was a snake, and his head was on Hadda Sahib's prayer carpet.

Hadda Sahib said, "What do you want?" The snake said, "Dear sir, I have come from Koh-i Qaf."

He said, "Why have you come?"

The snake said, "I have come from Peristan [the Land of the Fairies]. I want to marry a man's daughter, but she is from a noble family. Her father will not allow me to marry her. I know that she is devoted to you and that she has received *tariqat* [mystical teaching] from you, so I am asking you to go with me to Bagh-i Haram [the Forbidden Garden]."

Hadda Sahib said, "Where is Hadda and where is the Forbidden Garden?"

The snake said, "Dear sir, you ride on my shoulder, and in the blink of an eye I will deliver you there."

Hadda Sahib said, "I will give you a letter, and your problems will be over."

"But if you don't go yourself," the snake replied, "there will be no solution."

(For this reason, Hadda Sahib felt obliged to go with him. Abdul Baqi said that) at this moment, when I realized that Hadda Sahib was ready to go with him, I threw off my blanket and sat up in my bed. Hadda Sahib said to me in Afghani [Pakhtu],

"There is much time left before morning prayers. Go back to sleep."

I said, "Dear sir, I can't sleep anymore if you're going. I don't want to sleep if you're going to leave me behind."

He said, "Where are you and where is the Forbidden Garden?"

"I don't want to stay if you're going," I replied, and then he told me, "Okay, if you accept my advice. Perform your ablutions and say two sets of prayers."

He permitted me to say my prayers on his prayer carpet, and when I had finished, the snake placed his head on the carpet. He turned himself into his original shape [that of a dragon] and made himself ready for Hadda Sahib to sit on his wing. But Hadda Sahib said, "God has not made me so useless that I must go on your back. Put Abdul Baqi on your shoulder and come along."

(Abdul Baqi swore by God that when they reached the Forbidden Garden all of the people—even the king of the place—were standing to receive Hadda Sahib, even though it was the middle of the night. His spiritual quality [*ruhaniyat*] was so extraordinary that even the king of those people was present to welcome Hadda Sahib.)

When we reached there and had sat down, we saw that they had prepared all sorts of different fruits from the garden. I said to myself, "Who will believe me when I go back to Hadda?" Then I took a sample of every unfamiliar fruit I could find, and I tied them in my handkerchief so that I could bring some memento back with us.

In one night, Hadda Sahib performed seventy wedding ceremonies. When all those people who were engaged to the daughters of rich men heard the news that Hadda Sahib was there, they came to him, and he performed seventy marriages. When these weddings were finished, Hadda Sahib said that he would go back. They strongly insisted that he stay with them, but Hadda Sahib said that he wouldn't be delayed any further.

In short, I took my handkerchief. The dragon put me back on his shoulder. The dragon was the prince of Peristan. Soon we were back in Hadda, and the roof and ceiling of our room rose up so that no one would know [we had been gone]. When Hadda Sahib and I were sitting back in the room, the roof and ceiling returned to their place. The mulla was reciting the morning call to prayer.

I was in a hurry to tell the others that we had gone to the Forbidden Garden, but as we left for the mosque Hadda Sahib said, "Be careful not to tell anyone what we did."

My next thought was to open the handkerchief in front of the others so that they would ask about the fruit. When I opened the handkerchief, however, I was amazed that all of the fruit had turned into the same kind of fruit we have in our own land. Even if I swore, no one would believe me. This was one of his extraordinary actions.

✳ Edifying Anecdotes
Ziya' ad-Din Nakhshabi
BRUCE B. LAWRENCE

Ziya' ad-Din Nakhshabi (d. 1350) is perhaps best known for his delightful fifty-two-"night" narrative cycle *Tales of a Parrot* (*Tuti nama*),[20] but he also penned a number of other works, including *The Path of the Devotees* (*Silk as-suluk*), a collection of miscellaneous sayings and anecdotes of individuals known for their piety. The author was born in central Asia (in present-day Uzbekistan); he moved to India sometime in the first quarter of the fourteenth century and joined a Sufi group headed by Shaykh Hamid ad-Din Nagauri (d. 1276), centered in Badaon not far from Delhi. Nakhshabi's anecdotal style is part of an ancient heritage of moralizing vignettes featuring famous religious figures. He does not shrink from the occasional caustic observation, but his overriding purpose is to provide a blend of entertainment and morally uplifting reflection. His call to "Listen, listen!" is a characteristic of the raconteur's insistent and enthusiastic style.[21] Note the role of prophets (fig. 26) and Friends of God as exemplars in Nakhshabi's anecdotes.

Listen, listen: One time Moses—may peace be upon him—was given a divine order: "Select the righteous ones from among your people." Moses gave the call, and many came forward. Then he was ordered to go back

Figure 26.   In this Iranian miniature painting from a manuscript of Jami's *Haft Awrang* (Iran, 1556–1565), the prophet Joseph is enthroned with his bride Zulaykha after their mystical marriage, a story told by a number of famous Muslim poets. Washington, DC: Freer Gallery of Art, Smithsonian Institution, 46.12.188.

and select the most righteous of them, and Moses chose seventy. Again he was ordered to go back and select the most righteous of these, and he chose seven. Then God told him to go back still another time, and from the seven, Moses chose three. "These three," thundered the voice of God, "these three are the most odious of all in My eyes because, when they heard the call for the righteous, they counted themselves."

O my dear friend, this is such a Way that one is better off if he disobeys than if he obeys. In the realm of law, it is the defendant who is put behind bars, but in the Way, the prosecutor is imprisoned.

> Nakhshabi, until you look to yourself,
>> No other Sufi will do this work for you.
> Everyone must examine himself—
>> No one else can do this work for him.

My dear friend, they call those people who neglect their sins the living dead. Before this time there were people who, on hearing of the sins of others, got heated up . . . and yet you do not become agitated even on account of your own sins. It is an ancient custom that at the time the roses bloom, people divert themselves with various kinds of frivolities. Every year, as the time of the blooming of roses drew near, Ma'ruf Karkhi,* who is an example for every age, became upset and would exclaim: "The time of the rose has come; once again, people will engage in foolishness."

One evening, a dervish who was a beginner in the Way was saying his prayers in a mosque. He began to cry aloud, but his heart was back in the peace and quiet of his cell. From a corner he heard a voice saying, "Dervish, your prayer does not find favor with me. Hour after hour you are sending messages of contentment to your cell, while to me you are giving everything that is sordid."

They gave Adam the seven heavens; and he fled from them all in one day—but they made a particle of love to appear in him, and the eternity of heaven remained fixed in him. Alas! The fall of Adam was due to his preoccupation with love, and the sin of Iblis [the Devil] was due to his self-contentment.

---

* An early Sufi of Baghdad, d. 815.

Nakhshabi is without heart's ease—
For the pain of the heart is none other than the light of the heart.
The contented heart is a sign of idleness:
For the lovers there is no contentment of heart.

People asked Rabiʿa of Basra, "Do you hate Iblis?" "No," she replied. "How can this be?" they asked. "I have so much love for the Friend," she declared, "that I take no notice of enemies."

One saint was asked: "What is this world like?" "This world," he replied, "is so insignificant that there is nothing like it."

One man came to a dervish and said: "I would like to stay with you for some time." "When I am no more," queried the dervish, "with whom will you stay?" "I will remain with God," answered the man. "In that case," said the dervish, "consider me gone, and from this moment on, remain with God."

One time a worldly man asked for a drink at the house of a dervish. He was given water that was neither cool nor clean. "This water," he complained, "is very warm and dirty." "Aye, sir," replied the dervish, "we are prisoners, and prisoners never drink good water."

After his death, Yahya Muʿadh* appeared in a dream. He was asked: "How is it with you?" "When I arrived," he explained, "they asked me, 'What have you brought with you from the world?' I replied: 'I am coming from a prison—and what can one bring from there? If I had anything, after seventy years in prison it would certainly have been used up.'"

One time a group of disciples asked a master: "Which way should we take to reach God?" "What way have you been traveling on that the Way is not known to you?" answered the master.

What man is so courageous that he is not irritated by the cowardly?

When the virtuous die, a treasure goes out of the world. One of the masters of the Way said, "For a decade I shed tears of water; another, tears of blood; and for the last ten years I have been laughing."

They saw Shibli after his death in a dream (see note page 63). They

---

* Yahya ibn Muʿadh ar-Razi (d. ca. 871) was a Sufi from Rayy, near Tehran in Iran, noted for his preaching.

asked him: "How did you acquit yourself before Munkar and Nakir?"*
He replied: "If you had been there, you would have seen how they left
me in the end. They queried me: "Who is your God—tell us!" I replied:
"My God is the One who commanded you and your brothers to prostrate
yourselves before my father [i.e., Adam; cf. 2:34], and I, together with all
my brothers who were still in his loins, saw you. "We'd better be going,"
said the angels; "we asked him about himself, and he replied on behalf of
all the descendants of Adam."

Listen! Listen! One time a poor grocer who thought the heavenly
scales had a counterweight like his own saw a man who was riding a lion
and using a snake for a whip. "All this is very easy," said the stranger;
"the real task is to sit on both sides of the scales and do the work of God."

Ibrahim ibn Adham†—may peace be upon him—often said: "We go
out in search of poverty, and at every turn wealth appears before us."
One time a man said to him: "I know the world is corrupt, and since it is
full of people, in the end someone is sure to prevent me from doing my
work." "And what is that work?" asked the saint. "My work," he replied,
"is to fill the world with people of religion—for now that people of
religion have become few, the world has become corrupt."

Khwaja Junayd‡ appeared to people in a dream, and they asked him:
"How far have you progressed in your work?" "The work of the upper
world," he replied, "is more difficult than we imagined [when we were]
in the world below."

Listen! Listen! A saint wished to go to the bazaar to make some
purchases, but the coin he had weighed first in his house was found to
weigh less in the bazaar, and he began to cry. When people asked the
reason for his weeping, he answered: "When what is right in the house
today is found wanting in the bazaar, how can the reckoning of this world
be correct tomorrow in the world beyond?"

---

* Munkar and Nakir are the two angels who interrogate the dead in the grave.
† Ibrahim (d. ca. 790) was an early Sufi from Balkh in central Asia legendary for
his asceticism.
‡ Junayd (d. 910) of Baghdad is traditionally held to be the founding father of
"sober" mysticism.

Figure 27.   A sixteenth-century Persian manuscript frontispiece illumination, typical of the adornment of elaborately illuminated and illustrated texts of poetry, is a fine example of the infinitely repeatable floral and geometric patterning known as arabesque. St. Louis: St. Louis Art Museum, 387:52.

4 Aesthetics
From Allegory to Arabesque

Muslims have communicated religious values and experience eloquently in both the literary and visual arts. Part 4 features sources that discuss and exemplify a variety of themes and artistic forms. In the first section, a poet describes his motivations for incorporating religious imagery into his work; a commentator explores the hidden meanings beneath a poet's highly charged imagery; and a major medieval Persian author presents an allegorical interpretation of the story of Joseph. The second section then offers samples of didactic and lyric poetry from three languages: Arabic, Persian, and Urdu. Visual themes are four major architectural styles: the Mamluk (Egypt; figs. 28, 29), the Timurid (Iran and central Asia; figs. 30, 31), the Mughal (India; figs. 32, 33), and the Ottoman (Turkey; figs. 34, 35).

LITERATURE AND SPIRITUALITY

Part of what makes great literature great is the depth of its imagery. Literal meanings cloak layers of other, more tantalizing meanings, drawing the reader gradually toward some still mysterious but eagerly awaited revelation at the heart of the work. Sometimes the literary artists themselves preface their creations with suggestions as to how one ought to read them, as in the first selection, from Mir 'Ali-Shir Nawa'i. More often the task of interpretation is left to a later commentator, as in the selection by Lahiji. In the case of the allegory on Joseph, by Suhrawardi, the author presumes that the reader's familiarity with the scriptural text will supply the necessary interpretive key.

Interpreting Religious Poetry

✳ Mir ʿAli-Shir Nawaʾi
A Poet's Intentions

WHEELER M. THACKSTON

The central Asian poet Mir ʿAli-Shir Nawaʾi (d. 1502) composed several collections of poetry, called *divans*, in both Persian and Turkish. The preface to his first Chaghatay Turkish divan, *Novelties of Youth* (*Gharayib as-sighar*), suggests the importance not only of expressly religious intent and imagery, but of the role of the princely patron as well. The term for "preface," *debacha*, means "brocade"—an important clue to the kind of ornate literary tour de force that awaits the reader. (For the visual equivalent, see fig. 27.) After explaining that he has arranged the *ghazals*, short monorhyming lyric poems of around ten to twenty verses, in groups whose initial words begin with successive letters of the alphabet, the poet describes how he has taken care to weave deep spiritual meanings into his verse, so that they are not merely generic metaphors of the beautiful. He begins with a section in verse, then continues alternating verse with prose:[1]

> Although God's word is, from beginning to end, eternal speech,
>> See how at the beginning of every chapter [of the Qurʾan] is,
> "In the name of God the Compassionate, the Merciful."
>> The hadith is a witness to the fact that "everything has a purpose."
> The Apostle [Muhammad] realized and said that "in
>> everything God made is an indication of Him."

In order that this be remembered, the first ghazal of each letter begins with praise of God, laud to the Prophet, or an exhortation that indicates one of the two. It seems that when some people put their poetry together and make divans, no purpose, other than to describe metaphorical beauty* and to extol external beauty marks, can be discerned. There are divans in which not one homiletic line can be found: such a divan is a total waste of effort. For this reason, in this divan, aside from praise of God and laud of the Prophet, in every passionate ghazal, the hearing of which causes moon-faced beauties to be refractory and the grief stricken to be confused, one or two homiletic lines of good advice have been inserted, so that, through the lightning of chastity, the brilliance of their cheeks not shine

---

* That is, physical beauty, rather than "real" or divine beauty.

so, and so that the harvest of their existence not be completely destroyed by the conflagration of that lightning bolt. If the gazelles of these ghazals should begin to flirt or act immodestly, the homiletic advice of those lines will hold them in restraint.

> If the rosy-cheeked beauties should flirt and begin to plunder reason and
>> religion,
>> If they make eyes and wink, if they act immodestly and saucily,
> If, with the glow of their cheeks, they make the world burn with desire,
>> This wise advice, a million pieces of good advice, will constantly
>>> prevent them
> so that the world may obtain relief from sedition.

Another thing is that in other divans they bypass the conventional ghazal style and do not bedeck the bride of speech in her special typology, and if sometimes the first line is in a particular mode, they do not finish dressing her in her garments in accordance with the contents of the first line. All too often, if the contents of one line sprout roses during the spring-time of union, the next line looks like the thorns of the autumn separation: such form is considered outside of and beyond consistency and harmonious-ness. For this reason I have endeavored that the contents should be agree-able in form and comfortable in meaning from the first line to the last. . . .

The purport of this preface, what was written for the face of this beauty, the object of this introduction, which was written for the cheek of this lovely, is that, when any ruler builds a building impregnable or raises a portico high, he has his own name and titles inscribed on the arch in order that, as long as the arch remains, his name may remain therein.

> Whoever builds a structure that is destined [to remain],
>> When [his] name is inscribed therein,
> For as long as the structure lasts, that name will be on the lips of people.

Since the architect that is His Majesty's delicate nature has constructed an exalted castle that is like the celestial dome, and since the gardener that is His Highness's noble imagination has designed a world-adorning garden that is like heavenly paradise, what wonder is it if his regal titles are inscribed on the foundation arch of this castle or on the arcade of this garden palace?

The goal was this exalted palace—O Lord, may it never pass away.
It is a structure founded by the king, made as flourishing
as the castle of time. The king had it built with his patronage.
Consider me not the architect, but rather a laborer.
Whether laborer or expert architect, when a thousand wages were paid,
when the king's gilded palace is finished, what have they to do with the
      palace?
If Abraham made the Ka'ba flourish, is it known for certain what master
      built it?
The dam that Alexander made famous, who can say who labored upon it?
In the effort of construction, the building will
be known by the name of whoever pays the gold.
[People] will call the building by the name of the person who has had it built.
However, it is the rule among people for the builder's name to be inscribed.
When I realized this, I inscribed the king's name on the portico of this palace,
so that as long as this celestial palace remains this name may show on
      the portico.
As long as the palace of the heavenly sphere travels,
may the stars spin about the portico.
Like the king's portico, may the foundation of
his life be as stable as the foundation of the heavens.
May destiny every moment grant his every wish from this divan. Amen. . . .

[The poet concludes with this prayer:]

O Lord, many sins have been registered
against me, and I have blackened my book and wasted my life.
If You do not wash that book with the
water of mercy, alas! on doomsday what will I do with my black book?
O Lord, give Nawa'i his wish for [spiritual] annihilation,
since he has passed away in your path, O Lord.
Graciously grant him eternal life, O Lord, but,
whatever you do, O Lord, do not disown him!

✳   Shams ad-Din Lahiji
Commentary on Shabistari's Garden of Mystery

LEONARD LEWISOHN

Shams ad-Din Muhammad Lahiji's (d. 1507) commentary on Mahmud Shabistari's (d. ca. 1340) *Garden of Mystery* (*Gulshan-i raz*) is a fine example of a religio-aesthetic interpretation of a classic of spiritual poetry. Shabistari was an important Sufi leader in the northwestern Iranian city of Tabriz (see map) during the reign of the Il-Khanid dynasty. Lahiji investigates here the challenging subject of the relationship between aesthetics and hermeneutics. His views are heavily influenced by the thought of Ibn 'Arabi (d. 1240). In this excerpt, Lahiji delves into the many layers of meaning suggested by the poet's use of the imagery of "idol" (*but*) and "idolatry." He takes a daring approach to a very vexing issue.[2]

ON THE SYMBOLIC MEANING OF THE IDOL

The question raised here concerns a few of the statements expressed by the Perfect Masters, statements to which they hold themselves accountable, even if discussion of these matters is, in appearance, incompatible with their spiritual state—which is, in fact, the very issue raised by the questioner himself in his couplet which demands . . . "On this Path followed by lords of mystical states and perfectly realized masters, are not idols, cinctures, and Christianity all heresy [*kufr*]? If not heresy, then please elucidate the meaning and purport of such expressions."

The master's reply is in accord with the theosophical doctrine [*mashrab*] of unitarian Sufis who believe God to be the sole existing Being in creation. Hence, as the poet asserts in the first couplet of his reply:

> On Love's Path idols are all signs and emblems
> which theophanically betoken Unity and Love;
> the cincture's symbol is your fealty to serve mankind. . . .

Since everything that is created and has life is itself the truth, as in the verse "O God, you did not create all this in vain" [3:191], the author declares:

> Beheld from Being's range and scope, the idol is
> all truth. Think deep, oh savant: falsity
> there does not adhere.

Following the precept enjoined by the verse "And they meditate upon the creation of the heaven and the earth . . . " [3:191], the author encourages the learned and discerning reader to consider if it is possible that an idol, whose very being and existence is a physical receptacle of divine manifestation, can seriously be regarded as having been created in vain.

Since from God, the omniscient and absolute Being, nothing futile ever emanates (as the verse attests: "We have not created these two [heaven and earth] but in the Truth" [44:39]), insofar as myriad utilities and wise virtues are harbored in the creation and production of each living being therefore, simply because someone finds it impossible to comprehend the ways in which God manifests His wisdom, such wisdom cannot be abrogated or denied thereby. [As Rumi says,] "The Omniscient makes no errors in his deeds; the acts of Truth are not blunders, my meek man. All you see is good, is wisdom absolute, whether from it you are hurt or you are happy."

Since nothing evil or futile proceeds from God, the master pronounces:

> Since God Almighty
> has fashioned it and He's a perfect architect,
> so from the Good, all that emanates
> know it proceeds beatifically.

That is to say, God Almighty is the Creator of all things and everything which He creates is good, for from Good evil never issues. "Evil" relates solely to us, whereas vis-à-vis God this same "evil" is pure good and absolute wisdom. [As the Shaykh (Shabistari) says in the *Book of Felicity* (*Saʿadat nama*), verses 1176–1178,] "As long as you are possessed by egotism, you are a foe to God. As long as you perceive God's action from your own finite perspective, good will appear to you as evil. No one who is conceited [lit., who "beholds himself"] can see the good in the world: here ends all debate on this issue."

Since it has been resolved [from the foregoing discussion] that existence is a highest good, he declares:

> For Being is highest good, total good, everywhere
> you look: the source of bad and woe that's there
> exists elsewhere in nullity.

That is to say, existence or being, wherever it is, and in whatever form it is found, is sheer and absolute good. If an evil appears to be manifested in

Being, that evil is from elsewhere [*ghayr*],[3] which is [ultimately] nonexistence or nullity. According to the Sufi sages and theosophers who verify the truth of things, it should be understood that this problem has been resolved in the following fashion:

Since Being is sheer good, any "evil" that appears manifested therein arises from nonexistence. The following example illustrates this point.

Imagine that Zayd slays ʿAmr by striking off his head with a sword. Insofar as Zayd possesses the ability to take away life, this circumstance should be considered good. The keenness of Zayd's saber is also good, and from the point of view that the limbs of ʿAmr were receptible to such an act, it is good as well. The sole evil involved here concerns the concurrent "privation of life" or, in other words, "nonexistence" required by this act. Hence, considered from this [ontological] standpoint, "evil" and "bad" are merely a retrogression to nonexistence, while Existence remains, wherever it is, the highest good.

Viewed from the cosmic perspective of [the innate goodness of] Being and Existence, the idol cannot therefore be said to be in essence "evil." [The Shaykh elucidates this principle in the *Garden of Felicity*, verses 924 and 932, as follows:] "'Good' and 'Evil,' the former is existence and the latter, nonexistence; put this truth into practice, don't just preach it! Nothing evil ever proceeds from the omniscient being; whatever God does is just and right."

Since behind the veil of the determined form of each atom of existence the sun of divine unity is latent and concealed, he remarks:

> If Muslims knew what idols were, they'd cry
> that faith itself is in idolatry.

This means that if the [formalist] Muslim who professes divine unity and disavows the idol was to become aware and conscious of what the idol is in reality, and of whom it is a manifestation, and of what person it is who appears in the idol's form, he would certainly comprehend that the religion of the Truth lies in idolatry. Since the idol is a theophany of the absolute being Who is God, therefore *in respect to its essential reality, the idol is God*. Now, considering that the religion and rite of Muslims is Truth-worship and [as has been explained above] idolatry and Truth-worship are now seen to be one and the same thing, therefore true religion is in idolatry!

Since the so-called blasphemy of the idolaters arises from their ignorance of the idol's inner reality, he adds:

> And if polytheists could just become aware
> of what the idols are they'd have no cause to err in their faith.

That is to say, if the polytheist who adores idols were to become aware of the idol and its reality, and were to understand that the idol is actually a theophany of God, and that through its form God manifests Himself, and thus he actually prostrates, adores, and is devoted to the one supreme Being, then where in his religion and faith should he have gone astray and have been in error? This couplet contains a positive interrogation with a negative sense, implying that the polytheists never would have erred in their faith, but would all have become unitarians worshipping the Truth, and not have rejected the religion of Islam. And since the "heresy" of the idol worshipper consists solely in his attitude and attention, which is focused in the wrong direction toward the outer form of the idol, the writer observes:

> The graven image they have seen
> is but external handiwork and form.
> And so by Holy Writ their name is "infidel."

The implication here is that the so-called idolater's vision and perception were limited to the outer form of the idol, and it is this limited vision that makes an "infidel" or "heretic" in the legal sense of the Prophetic commentary [*sharh*]. However, should the attention of the idolater have been directed toward its reality where the idol is revealed as a divine theophany, he certainly should not have been considered a heretic in the Scripture, and would be considered a Muslim. Since he has stated that the cause of the idolater's blasphemy consisted in this attention to the illusory external created form of the idol, he furthermore declares:

> No one will call you "Muslim," thus, by the word of Law

> if you cannot perceive the Truth concealed therein,
> see the God within an idol hid.

The reason for the idolater's heresy according to the Canon Law of Islam was shortsightedness and his [mis]perception of the external created form of the idol. Likewise, if you who make claims to Islam and orthodoxy perceive naught but the idol's visible form and do not envision God hidden behind the veils of its determined form—and it is this particular form which is a corporeal receptacle for God's theophany—you properly and legally also cannot be called a Muslim! In fact, you are an infidel because you have veiled God's theophany appearing in the idol! [As Rumi says:]

> Give not your hand to anyone who cannot tell
> the difference between the beloved's visage and her veil:
> I swear by Canon Law, he is an infidel.

Since the last couplet, affirming that anyone who cannot see behind the scenes to perceive God's theophany manifest through an idol's form is therefore not a Muslim, will cause a person to feel an aversion to Islam, he comments that

> Whoever sees unveiled the real infidelity
> and face to face perceives the truth-of-heresy
> detests all rites, all forms of fake "Islamic" falsity.[4]

This couplet addresses the question first posed [by Mir Husayni Harawi] at the beginning of the chapter. The very thesis of this question relates to certain assumptions entertained by some people concerning Islam and, in particular, the belief that the existence of possible things is separate and independent from the necessary being, so that each possible entity is held to be completely separate and independent from God. Such a person may wonder if the statement affirming that no one is an orthodox Muslim according to the *shari'a* if he cannot contemplate God's theophany in an idol isn't heretical and contrary to Islam. The author answers such a person by affirming that the idea that the necessary and possible being are absolutely separate from each other is merely a sort of "metaphorical" or unreal Islam, not true Islam.

When a mystic realizes "real infidelity"—which connotes the covering up of the determined forms of multiplicity and existential diversity in the one true existence—he becomes disillusioned with "false metaphorical Islam," based on the premise that possible being is absolutely distinct and separate from necessary being, God. He will then perceive that it is, in fact, necessary being that reveals itself through the forms of possible beings and there is no other being besides this one single existence. If to all appearances this person seems to be an infidel and heretic, in actual reality he has attained the essence and the loftiest degree of Islam. Such "heresy" is the zenith of Islamic practice [as Rumi says]:

> Muslims, Muslims, preserve your faith!
> Shams-i Tabriz,* be warned, was once
> a Muslim, but turned an infidel!

Since God's existence is concealed behind the veil of the phenomenally determined forms of things, he states:

> All infidelity has faith inside;
> within each idol's heart a soul resides,
> and every heresy has hymns and litanies.

This means that within every idol, form, or beloved object that you may see lies a hidden soul, spirit, and reality; and beneath the determined form of every infidelity exists a secret faith. That hidden soul within the idol and that faith within infidelity [and inside anything else that one may imagine] are actually the necessary being that is manifested through its form but veiled and disguised by and in the specific determination of that form.

. . . Since all beings in their essences are continually engaged in the invocation of God according to the verse "The seven heavens and the earth and all that is therein praise Him, and there is not a thing but hymns His praise; but you understand not their praise" (17:44), he declares:

> And daily, infidelity recites the rosary.
> Verily, all that is, does hymn his praise.

* Shams was the inspiration for much of Rumi's own poetry.

It should be understood that all living beings manifest the divine form in their secret selves and that God is the Spirit of all things. Now, the form of every human being is constantly occupied in praising and invoking blessings upon its own spirit, which in turn manages and controls this form. The bodily limbs, being only corporeal, would be deprived of every practical and intellectual virtue and lack all motion and understanding were it not for the agency of the spirit. In any case, it has been established that the divine form of each human being is constantly occupied in praising and invoking blessings upon its own spirit. By medium of this beatific invocation, God operates and controls the forms of the world [of which human beings are one], which in turn glorify and magnify God. It is based upon this magnification of God on the part of these forms that all types of imperfection [that is, the Contraries within the divine Plenitude] are annulled and distanced from the spiritual realm [which is God]. This relationship is also reciprocal, for it is through the theophany and appearance of these forms that the world of the divine virtues and perfections [which is, in turn, but an emanation of those forms] can glorify God. In any case, all the entities of living beings glorify and magnify God, although as the Scripture states, "but you do not understand their praise," since we do not fathom the language they speak, just as Turks cannot speak Hindi.

With this introduction, we may now understand the logic behind the master's statement that "and daily, infidelity recites the rosary." He means that insofar as infidelity is an existent entity, it also constantly glorifies God and affirms the divine transcendence and distance from all imperfection standing in opposition to the plenitude of divine virtues. Infidelity itself is a theophanic exposition of these virtues, and so it also glorifies God. Since God declares in the Qur'an, "and there is not a thing but hymns His praise" (17:44), the interpretation is that everything without exception engages in the glorification and magnification of God, so how can anyone object to or be piqued with my statement that "daily, infidelity recites the rosary," since infidelity is, after all, also some "thing."

Figure 28.   Mamluk style: the funerary complexes of Sultan Inal (*right*, 1451–1456) and of Qurqumas (*left*, 1506–1507) in the northern cemetery of Cairo, as seen from a minaret of the *khanqah* of Faraj ibn Barquq (SD fig. 29). Note the typically Mamluk stepped exterior of the "zone of transition" beneath the carved stone domes, and the elaborately carved multistaged cylindrical and polygonal minarets.

Allegory

✳   Yahya Suhrawardi Maqtul
Allegory of Beauty and Love
LEONARD LEWISOHN

Shihab ad-Din Yahya Suhrawardi Maqtul (d. 1191), known as the shaykh of (the school of) Illumination (*Ishraq*), wrote a number of remarkable and challenging works. Among them are several imaginative allegorical "treatises" in which the author explores various dimensions of Islam's spiritual tradition. In the *Treatise on the Reality of Love* (*Risala fi haqiqat al-ʿishq*), Suhrawardi uses the story of the prophet Joseph to elaborate on the relationships among the attributes of Intellect, namely, Beauty, Love, and Grief:

Know that the first thing created by God, the glorious and exalted, was a brilliant substance, which he named the Intellect. Because [according to a

Figure 29. Mamluk style: the Cairo mosque-mausoleum complex of Amir
Khayrbak (1520–1521), first Ottoman governor of Egypt. The minaret was
originally topped by an octagonal columned pavilion similar to that of the
mosque of Aqsunqur (1346–1347) in the background. The dome's carved
decoration, a Mamluk signature item, is among the most ornate of its kind.
(See also SD figs. 7, 22.)

Tradition of the Prophet], "the first thing God created was the Intellect."
And upon this substance, He bestowed three attributes. One was the
cognition of God. One was the cognition of itself. And one was the
cognition of "what was not, then was."

From that attribute relative to the cognition of God, Beauty came into
being, which is called the Good. From that attribute relative to the
cognition of itself, Love arose, which they called kindness. And from that
attribute relative to that which "was not, then was," Grief arose, and this
they called deep sorrow.

All these three originated from a single fountainhead, being brothers
of one another. Beauty, the eldest brother, contemplated himself and saw
himself as exalted and good. He became mirthful. He smiled. From this
smile, many thousand of the most proximate archangels came into
existence. Love, the brother between, had a deep attachment to Beauty.
He could not refrain from his contemplation, being devotedly in his
attendance. When Beauty's smile shone, a frenzy struck him. Deeply
disturbed, he wished to move. Then Grief, the younger brother, took hold
of him. Out of their struggle heaven and earth were created. . . .

Suhrawardi next describes how Beauty, Love, and Grief entered the world of
human experience: After God created Adam, Beauty, king of the angelic realm,
set forth into the world and possessed Adam completely. Love fainted at Beauty's
departure. Comforted by Grief, Love led all the angels earthward; smitten by
the Beauty in Adam, they prostrated themselves (in obedience to God's command, cf. 15:30, 38:73). After Adam's day, Beauty returned to the angelic realm,
awaiting an appropriate time to return to earth. At the birth of Joseph Beauty
again headed for earth, followed again by Love and Grief. Beauty, now indis-
tinguishable from Joseph, can see no future in a relationship with Love. Grief
and Love decide they must separate in a journey of penance in quest of a spiritual guide. Arriving in Canaan, Grief discovers Jacob mourning the loss of his
son Joseph and becomes Jacob's pupil. Love goes to Egypt, where he meets the
wife of Pharaoh's minister, Zulaykha, who asks Love to tell her his story. He
recounts the events that have brought him to Egypt.

Zulaykha, upon hearing all this, surrendered her house to Love, holding
Love dearer to herself than her own soul; that is, until Joseph appeared in

Egypt. The people of Egypt all assembled in agitation. The news reached Zulaykha, and she immediately told Love. Love seized Zulaykha by the collar and both of them set out to view Joseph. Zulaykha wanted to move forward as soon as she beheld the face of Joseph, yet the foot of her heart tripped upon a boulder of wonder, and slipped from the orbit of restraint. She stretched out the hand of blame, and rending the veil of security from herself, became instantaneously enraptured. Then the people of Egypt began to slander her, while she, selflessly, repeated these few lines:

> She's not guilty, not guilty, the person who reveals the secret
> (And in my case, too, because there was no way I could hide it,
>   anyway),
>
> They claimed, and they claimed that "I" loved "You,"
> But *my* Love transcended all "their" claims!

After Joseph became the Beloved of Egypt, the news reached Canaan. Jacob was smitten with yearning, and he told Grief of his condition. Grief advised him to take his sons and go toward Egypt. Submitting to Grief, he set out for Egypt with all his sons. When he arrived there, he entered the court of the Beloved of Egypt. Suddenly he saw Joseph, together with Zulaykha, seated upon the imperial throne. Out of the corner of his eye, he beckoned to Grief. Grief, seeing Love, fell on his knees in prostration to Beauty and placed his face on the ground. Jacob and his sons, in conformity with Grief, all placed their foreheads on the ground. It was then that Joseph turned to Jacob and said, "O father, this then is the interpretation of that dream I once related to you:

> . . . O my father I did see seven stars and the sun and the moon,
> I saw them prostrate themselves to me!" [12:4]

Know that from all the names of Beauty, one is Splendor and one is Perfection, and there is a holy prophetic tradition that goes: "Truly, God is beautiful, and loves beauty"; and all that exists, whether spiritual or physical, is in search of perfection, and furthermore you will never see anyone without some sort of inclination toward Splendor. Then if you meditate well on this, you will realize that everyone is in search of Beauty, and all are constantly struggling to attain Beauty. But attainment of Beauty, the Sought-after of All, is extremely difficult, for union with Beauty occurs only by way of the mediation of Love, and Love does not admit to himself just anyone, does not make just anywhere his residence, and does not show his face to every eye. And even if somewhere, sometime, he were to find a sign of someone who truly merited that grace, he first would send Grief, the guardian of his gate, to purify the house and prevent the entry of anyone "else" and to inform everyone of the arrival of the Solomon of Love, with the proclamation:

> O ye ants, get into your habitations,
>   Lest Solomon and his host crush you [27:18]

—so that the ants of the external and internal senses, each will entrench itself in its own position, remaining secure from the onslaught of Love's army, and no derangement penetrate the brain.

Then it is that Love must encircle the house and review all and, entering into the chambers of the heart, destroy some, rebuild some, totally reorienting its previous work, and remain occupied with this work for a few days, then set out for the court of Beauty.

And since now it is obvious that it is Love that enables the seeker to attain the Sought-after, you must struggle to make yourself suitable and worthy, to understand Love, the degrees and the stations of the Lovers and, then, surrender yourself to Love, and then—then—you will see miracles.

> Empty the empty noise out of your head,
>   Cease flirtation and being attractive—increase spiritual need.

> Love itself is your Beloved, and when you attain it
>   It will tell you what to do.

PRINCIPAL POETIC FORMS

Two broad categories of poetry, each encompassing several distinct genres, are the didactic and the lyric. Didactic poetry is primarily concerned with communicating fundamental religious teachings and insight into the meanings and conditions of belief and practice. Two examples, one from a thirteenth-century Persian poem and one from a more recent Indonesian poem in the Gayo language, treat two very different topics. Lyric poetry probes more dangerously into the heart and psyche, drawing upon depths of feeling and personal commitment. In what follows, six poets speak in three tongues and four genres.

Didactic Poetry

✳ Sana'i of Ghazna
Two Teaching Parables

JOHN RENARD

Abu 'l-Majd Sana'i (d. 1131) was one of the earliest masters of the Persian didactic genre called the *mathnawi*. His *Enclosed Garden of Ultimate Reality* (*Hadiqat al-haqiqa*) incorporates numerous parables (*tamathil*) designed to teach truths both ordinary and arcane. The following "parable sandwich" encloses one parable within the two halves of another. The parables are doubly didactic: they set out to teach a lesson; in this case the lesson is about how human beings learn, or refuse to learn, and about God's pedagogical methods. Note how Sana'i puns on the meanings of straight and crooked, single and double.[5]

THE PARABLE OF THE HEEDLESS ONE

A simpleton spied a camel at pasture
   and said, "Your shape is all crooked—why?"
Replied the camel, "With this estimation
   you heap insult on the sculptor—wise up!
On my crookedness do not look reproachfully,
   and depart from me by the straight road if you please!
My shape has come to be so for good purpose,
   as the rightness [lit., straightness] of a bow comes from its bend.
Take your meddlesome ways away from me.
   The ear of an ass fits best on the head of an ass!"*
Though you may find it less than pleasing, a fitting
   arch is the eyebrow for the curve of the eye.
The eye can look toward the sun, thanks to the brow,
   and the face like [nature] in springtime gains character.

---

* "Head of an ass" is also an idiom for meddler.

Evil and good, as the wise view them,
    are [both] very good; from Him no evil comes.
Far better if all things you would see [as coming] from Him,
    even if [apparently] evil, you regard them as good.
Body gets its share of both rest and suffering;
    for spirit, rest is like a treasure.
But a coiled serpent is above it,
    the hand and foot of wisdom by its side.

THE PARABLE OF THE CROSS-EYED ONE

A cross-eyed son asked his father,
    "You whose speech is like a key to what is locked,
how is it you said a cross-eyed person sees double?
    I see no more than what is there.
If a cross-eyed person really counted crookedly,
    heaven's two moons would look like four!"
Of course, the one who said that missed the point;
    for when a cross-eyed person looks at a cupola it doubles.
I am afraid that on religion's prescribed [*shari'*] path
    you are like the cross-eyed one whose vision is crooked,
or like the simpleton who criticized the camel
    absurdly because of what the Creator had done.
The qibla of intellect is His perfect creation,
    the Ka'ba of desire His immutable essence.
He ennobles the spirit with wisdom,
    on [our] sins He feeds His forgiveness.*
God is well aware of your repentance;
    His wisdom causes him to delay a response:
even if he listens to a request for dung,
    a physician does not give mud to a mud-eater. . . .
[Skipping two verses]

* Perhaps playing on the alternative meaning: gives his forgiveness fodder for good pasture.

So numerous are those who have drunk
  the cup of undiluted poison and have not died from it.
On the contrary, it is life-sustaining to the one
  who as a result of protracted illness has become like a straw [reed].
To all on the way of His wisdom and justice
  that which is needed—and more than that—He gives.
Should a gnat chomp into an elephant's hide,
  say "Wave your ear—it's made to banish gnats!"
If a louse [bothers you], use your fingernail;
  when a flea jumps on you, rebuke it.
If the mountain is full of snakes, don't worry:
  stone and antidote are also on the mountain.
And if your heart is distressed because of the scorpion,
  you have shoe and sandal to deal with it.
If there is abundant suffering in the world,
  everyone has a thousand cures. . . .
[Skipping four verses]
Spiritual sovereignty and [temporal] kingship [alike] exist in the world.
  Above the throne there is light; below it, darkness.
These two elements He gave as gift in His creation,
  when He cast His shadow across His handiwork.
A physical world in largess He bestowed on [bodily] life,
  the spiritual realm out of generosity He gave to the spirit,
so that both inner and outer [person] gain sustenance:
  the body from the powers of this world, the soul from the Lord of the
    spiritual realm.
For the benefit of the noble soul God has
  maintained through all his handiwork grace upon graciousness.
One who reflects deeply knows that
  whatever He does is for the best.
You are the source of the labels "evil" and "good,"
  otherwise everything that is from Him is pure beneficence.
Evil does not come into being from Him;
  how could evil exist in divinity?

Witless and foolish people alone work evil;
    He, the creator of good, does no evil.
Consider as antidote whatever poison He offers;
    consider as graciousness whatever punishment he imposes.
For both the cupping glass our mothers use on us
    and the dates [they give us] are good.

RETURNING TO THE PARABLE OF THE HEEDLESS PERSONS

Have you not observed how a child's nanny,
    when the babe is still in infancy
sometimes confines [the child] to the cradle,
    and sometimes holds the child for long periods on her breast;
sometimes disciplines the child, and sometimes comforts,
    and at other times keeps the child at a distance;
now tenderly kissing its cheeks,
    now caressing and taking on the child's pain?
When a stranger sees all this,
    the [outsider] becomes angry with the nanny and sighs [in
        frustration].
The stranger says, "The nanny has no compassion,
    and the child does not matter to her."
How do you know that the nanny knows best?
    [Because] these are the set terms of her employment.
With the servant [i.e., human beings] the Creator, too, according to
        contract,
    fulfills His obligations to the fullest.
Whatever is appropriate He gives every day:
    sometimes it is frustration, sometimes victory.
At times He sets a jeweled crown on [the servant's] head,
    at times He leaves him penniless and needy.
Either be satisfied with God's choices
    or complain loudly and take [your case] before the judge,
to see if he will set you free from His decree:
    One who reasons this way is a fool.

Whatever is the case, whether hardship or success,
  it is utterly beneficial and its dark side [only] temporary.
He who brought the world [into being] with "Be, and it was,"
  how could He bring evil upon His creation? How?
Good and evil do not exist in the realm of [God's] speech;
  the terms "good" and "bad" are yours and mine.
When God created the earthly climes,
  He created no unbounded evil.
Death for this one is destruction and for that one revival,
  poison is this one's food and that one's death.
If the face of the mirror were black like its backside,
  no one would look at it.
A mirror's utility is in its face,
  even if its back is encrusted with gems.
The sun's mirror-bright face is excellent
  whether its back is black or white.
If the peacock's foot were like its feathers,
  night and day its splendor would shine.*

✳ ## Mude Kala
Gayo Didactic Religious Poetry
JOHN R. BOWEN

During the first three decades of the twentieth century, a growing number of scholars and students returned to the Dutch East Indies from Egypt and Arabia, where they had become excited by the teachings of modernist scholars, in particular the followers of Muhammad 'Abduh. These scholars established schools throughout the archipelago where they taught Arabic and English, history and geography, but especially modernist teachings about ritual, faith, and social life. They urged the graduates of these schools to return to their homelands and encourage their own people to become better, modern Muslims.

The Gayo people of highland Sumatra, in the province of Acheh, had been Muslim since at least the sixteenth century. In the 1920s, Gayo men left the

---

* That is, all created things are limited both in their apparent goodness and in their apparent evil.

Figure 30. Timurid style: the Gur-i Mir in Samarkand (ca. 1400–1404). Inscriptions on the drum of the hundred-foot-high dome read, "To God [belongs] survival"—a stark contrast to the human mortality enshrined in a mausoleum. Notably Timurid features include the dome's "rolled and pleated" surface treatment, its slightly bulbous contours, and a very high drum (the cylindrical form just beneath the dome itself). On the walls are the names Allah and Muhammad in squared Kufic script. (See also figs. 38, 39.)

Figure 31.   Timurid style: the Congregational Mosque of Isfahan, whose construction history spans more than eight centuries (8th–17th). Typical features are the inward-facing vaulted halls (*iwan*s) fronted by large decorative facades (*pishtaq*s), and the two-tiered arcade around the central courtyard.

area to study in these new schools, and when they returned they began to urge others to purify their religious activities of non-Islamic elements and associated themselves with the general Indies-wide movement for religious reform called the "young group" (*kaum muda*). Finding most villagers little interested in listening to extensive theological debates, and often repelled by the arid quality of the reformers' ideas, the teachers searched for new ways to spread their message. About 1935 Tengku Yahye began to write short verse works in which he translated passages from the Qur'an and Hadith. He thus invented the genre of popular religious poetry called *saèr*, from Malay/Arabic *sha'ir*, featuring one or more lines of Arabic scripture, followed by an elaboration of the scriptural message in Gayo verse. As sung by local poets the form became a highly popular performance genre. A collection of ninety of Tengku Yahye's poems called *Gayo Scriptural Commentary* (*Tafsir al-Gayo*) was published in Cairo in 1938.

A scholar-poet called Tengku Mude Kala developed the form further during the 1940s. Poem 45 from Mude Kala's 1950 collection (unpublished) is one of several that makes the specific claim that those who engage in worship (*salat*) without the proper intent are toying with God, and will not enjoy the benefits of their worship. The poem begins with a hadith reported by at-Tarmazi:* "Be informed that God does not respond to a prayer from an inadvertent and oblivious heart." Mude Kala then contrasts the unthinking way that most people just run through their worship with the earnest yet ridiculous way in which they recite spells.

Said the prophet Muhammad, explaining to his people,
about prayers that are not received:
Do you know, all of you,
about prayers that are not effective?

God does not accept people's prayers
if prayers are simply memorized.
The mouth prays; the heart is lazy,
as if weak; thoughts wander.

Asking for blessings is not done earnestly,
as long as you pray, you don't have to mean it.
When the heart is roaming,
even though worship has already begun,

the mouth is reciting, the heart is figuring,
all sorts of matters arise and fall.
In the middle of worship, thoughts are flying
like a kite no longer held down.

The heart is far off:
"There are the hills, the knoll is in view.
There is the field's edge, with every little row;
there is the corner, the stream now's in view."

Who knows where's the *takbir* or the *wajah*,
al-Fatiha or the *atahyatul*.†
He doesn't know the sense of what he recites;
whatever the meaning, he says it's deep.

---

* Abu 'Isa Muhammad at-Tirmidhi (824–892), whose name is pronounced Tarmazi in southeast Asia, compiled one of the six authoritative collections of hadith.
† *Takbir, wajah, atahyatul*: Arabic-based names of fixed recitations spoken during worship.

He knows which is the end, which the beginning,
turning all around, all confused.
Think it through yourself:
can a dull knife cut sharply?

But an invulnerability spell—it would work
because, with feeling, he shakes his head back and forth.
Because he feels there is a benefit:
when he fights, knives won't cut him.

Spells to unnerve or create confusion,
spells to make tough and strong;
but from the takbir all the way to the *salam* [ending salat],
his heart is off soaring and shaking.

After worshipping, he sets in to pray,
closing his eyes like someone meditating.
The drum's sounding* is over, now he shakes;
the fish are gone, now he sets the net.

If worship is done in that way,
said the Prophet: how can it be effective?
We make requests not to a little guy;
we speak with a big guy.

The worshipper ridiculed in the poem has memorized the verses, but loses track
of them while engaged in worship. His heart wanders all over the terrain, pic-
turing his rice fields. But after worship he starts in to recite petitionary prayers,
shaking his head as if to make them more efficacious. Only then, after the main
work of worship has concluded, does this Muslim focus on his actions. But he
has missed the boat, set his net after the fish have come and gone.

These poems had a wide appeal until the mid-1950s, when the outbreak of
rebellion against Jakarta turned Gayo attention away from internal religious
disputes and toward issues of political autonomy, national pluralism, and sheer
survival. But they are still sung by older people, revived from time to time, and
collected for publication as small pamphlets.

* Drums were once used to call people to worship.

Lyric Poetry

In the generally briefer genres called *ruba'iyat* (quatrain) and *ghazal*, and the often longer forms called *qasida* and *na't*, Muslim lyricists have poured out their souls in well over a dozen major languages. Here are examples of those genres originally written in three languages: Arabic, Persian, and Urdu. This section spotlights Ibn al-Farid, featuring several of his works as well as a literary hagiography about him.

✳ Ibn al-Farid
Ruba'iyat, Ghazal, Qasida
TH. EMIL HOMERIN

'Umar ibn al-Farid is the unrivaled Arab poet of mystical Islam. He was born in 1181 in Cairo, where, under his father's guidance, he memorized hadith and studied Islamic mysticism and Arabic literature. Ibn al-Farid went on pilgrimage to Mecca and stayed there for some years before returning to Cairo. Then he took up residence at the Azhar mosque, teaching hadith and poetry until his death in 1235. Ibn al-Farid was a master of the Arabic poetic tradition, composing poems in a number of forms including ruba'iyat, the ghazal, and the qasida. Whether highly lyrical or occasionally didactic, Ibn al-Farid's verse takes up a number of religious themes revolving around the love between the human being and God. Generally, Ibn al-Farid embraces a mystical view of existence in which creation is intimately involved with its divine creator such that life, when seen aright, reveals a ray of primordial light. This view is mirrored in the beauty and moving power of his verse, which has influenced generations of poets and earned Ibn al-Farid the lasting reputation as *sultan al-'ashshiqin*, "the sultan of lovers."[6]

In the spirit of the Persian master 'Umar Khayyam, Ibn al-Farid composed ruba'iyat to make pointed observations on life and destiny. In several of his more than thirty quatrains, the poet prays for God's forgiveness and acceptance of him on the Judgment Day:

My spirit longed to meet you, oh my love,
    while the earth—like my deceit—pressed down upon me.

Though my soul melted from passion and pain,
    it was unfit for love next to your acceptance.

More often, however, Ibn al-Farid's quatrains focus on particular aspects of love. In the following quatrain, the lover swears his undying fealty to the beloved, whose sharp, arrowlike glances have left him mortally wounded:

If I die and the one I love visits my grave,
  I'll whisper out loud "I'm here to serve [*labbayka*]!"

But secretly within I'll say, though without complaint:
  "What do you think of what your glances made of me?"

While Ibn al-Farid highlights individual love images and motifs in his quatrains, he presents a fully developed repertoire of love in his qasidas and ghazals. Ibn al-Farid was heir to a long ghazal tradition originally ascribed to the 'Udhra clan of seventh- and eighth-century Arabia. Feelings of loss and despair pervade these poems as the lover pines away in abject humility, accepting and even relishing the cruelties of unrequited love. Unable to attain the object of his desire in the material world, he dies love's martyr, longing for a union of spirits in eternity.

In the following ghazal, Ibn al-Farid compares the memory of lost love to a wine that intoxicates and consoles the lover in the beloved's absence. The lover claims to have traded his selfish life for one of selfless love; he is oblivious to those who blame him for excessive passion. Though emaciated by love, he remains true to his memory of the beloved. In fact, his will and desires have been so purged that he becomes the archetypal lover encompassing within himself all passion and every heart slain by love. Nothing remains of the lover's selfish will, so when the beloved appears at last, there can be no gross physical contact as the lover passes away in a rarefied moment beyond time and space.

Ibn al-Farid reinforces the spiritual nature of this love by allusions to God, Muhammad, the Qur'an, and especially Sufi doctrine and practice. In the opening verse of this poem, he refers to the intoxicating effects of "recollecting" (*dhikr*) the beloved, thereby suggesting the ecstatic mystical trance produced by Sufi dhikr ceremonies. In addition, the phrase "tales of the beloved" (*ahadith al-habibi*) is a clear reference to the traditions (*ahadith*) of the prophet Muhammad, "the beloved" (*habib*) of God.

Ibn al-Farid also uses a number of terms standard to the Sufi lexicon of his time to describe the lover's purified heart (*qalb*) and subtle essence (*ma'na*); in the station (*maqam*) of rapture (*wajd*), the lover passes away from self-will to abide (*baqa', yabqa, yubqi*) with the beloved. To these terms the poet adds several references to the beloved as the object of the lover's prayers and pilgrimage; when taken together, these multiple allusions leave the lasting impression that this and other ghazals by Ibn al-Farid are hymns of love for God and His prophet Muhammad.

Pass round remembrance of one I desire, though that be to blame me,   1
    for tales of the beloved are my wine.

Let my ear witness the one I love, though she be far away,
    in blame's fantasy not the phantom dream of sleep.

For her memory is sweet to me in whatever form,
    even if those rebuking me mix it with bitter grief,

as if my blamer brought good news of union,
    though I hadn't hoped for even "Peace!" in reply.

My spirit be her ransom, in loving her I've lost it;   5
    my fate was at hand before my day of death.

But because of her, my disgrace is good, and savory still
    is being thrown and broken down from my high station [*maqam*];

for her sake, my open shame is sweet,
    so too my wanton ways and ride for sin, not my righteous path of old.

I pray and chant when I recite, in memory of her,
    and I delight in the prayer niche where she leads my prayers before
        me;

on pilgrimage, purified I cry in her name: "I'm here to serve [*labbayka*]!"
    and I see my holding back from her to be like the breaking of my fast.

Yet my affair makes my tears flow running fast over what has
        passed,   10
    while my sobbing speaks true of my love thirst.

On the edge of night, my heart [*qalb*] is parched for passion,
    while in morning light my anguished eyes shed tears.

My heart and my eye: one is snared by her beauty's subtle sense [*ma'na*];
    the other lured by her soft, supple stature.

So my sleep is lost, to morning I have bid farewell,
    for sleeplessness I have found as my desire grows,

and my bond and pact are neither loosed nor withdrawn,
    with rapture [*wajd*] my joy, burning passion my affliction

as sickness wears my body out so that secrets show through,   15
    my bones wasted there to bare essence [*ma'na*],

thrown down by love's passion, ribs pierced,
    eyelids wounded by endless bloody tears,

passion so pure that my ethereality
    raced with dawn's breeze, the zephyr's breaths my companions.

Sound yet sick, so seek me from the east wind
    where wasting willed my station [*maqam*].

I was hidden, consumed, concealed even from consumption
    and, too, from my diseases' cure and the cooling of my burning thirst,

and I knew no one save passion who knew my place,   20
    and my keeping the secrets to guard my honor.

All that love left of me [*yubqi*] was a heart broken
    by grief, affliction, and boundless disorders.

As for my burning desire, my patience, and consolation,
    nothing remains [*yabqa*] with me but their names.

Let one free of my passion safely save his own soul;
    as for you, my soul, leave me in peace.

"Forget her!" said my accuser, burning to blame me on her account;
    "Forget blaming me!" I countered.

Could I seek solace instead, who would be my lead in love then,   25
    since every love guide follows me.

For in my every member is every passion rushing to her,
    desire tugging at my reins.

She swayed as she walked, so we thought her quivering sides
    to be branches on a dune beneath a full moon.

So in my every limb was every heart
    hit by every arrow whenever she gazed with pleasure.

Had she unrolled my body, she would have seen in every essence
    every heart holding, every burning passion.

In union with her, a year is but a moment to me,   30
    while exile's hour is like a year to bear.

When we met in the evening, joined by two straight paths,
    one from her tent, the other from mine,

we swerved a little from the tribe
    to a place without a spy or slanderer with lies,

And I rubbed my cheek in the dust for her to step on,
    so she said: "Good news for you, kiss my veil!"

But my soul would not have it, guarding me jealously
    to keep my longing pure.

So we passed the night together as my command willed over
        desires: 35
    I saw kingship my kingdom and time my slave.

The tones, moods, and themes of Ibn al-Farid's ghazals permeate his qasidas as well, though the qasida contains other sections and subjects, most notably those of the *rahil* or "journey." Ibn al-Farid invokes them to meditate on a past encounter with the beloved and the quest for reunion, as in the following ode, which opens with a lover's precious memory of a night in the Najd, the 'Udhri Arcadia. Ibn al-Farid compares the beloved to Layla al-'Amiriya, a legendary beauty of the 'Udhra clan; the beloved's ability to change dusk to dawn further suggests her extraordinary character. The lover imagines the route to be taken to his beloved's camp, naming the stops along the way, which correspond to actual sites in Arabia lying on the Cairo-to-Mecca pilgrimage route. The goal, then, is clearly situated in the sacred precincts near Mecca, for the messenger rides from Na'man al-Arak ("Na'man of the Arak trees"), a valley two leagues from Mt. 'Arafat, to al-'Alaman ("The Two Markers"), which lies on the pilgrims' path between 'Arafat and Mina. Significantly, Mina is where the pilgrims camp and celebrate the end of the hajj; this suggests, therefore, that the time and place of the lover's prior meeting with his beloved occurred during the pilgrimage, a popular occasion for rendezvous in classical Arabic love poetry. In this light, the courtyard (verse 7: *janab*) is most likely the area immediately adjacent to the Ka'ba, with the place known as Abraham's station and the well of Zamzam nearby (verse 25).

With such an exact and detailed itinerary, Ibn al-Farid consciously links his residence in Cairo with Mecca, his spiritual home. In addition, the Najd of Arab nostalgia and love lore is joined to the sacred rites of the Muslim pilgrimage, suggesting the holy nature of both this love and the beloved. Ibn al-Farid's qasidas, then, may be read as devoted memories of the hajj, loving recollections that, like the Sufi dhikr, invigorate the lover and revive his spirit with a momentary flash of the divine presence.

Did lightning flash at dearest Abraq,   1
    or do I see a lantern in the hills of Najd?

Or did Layla al-ʿAmiriya unveil her face at night
    and so turn dusk to dawn?

Oh rider of the sturdy she-camel—may you be protected from ruin—
    if you cross the rugged hard ground or roll up the wide-spread torrent
        beds

traveling by Naʿman al-Arak, turn aside there
    to a wide valley, which I knew well.

Then to the right of ʿAlaman, east of Naʿman,   5
    halt and head for its fragrant *arin* blossoms.

When you reach the dune's winding folds, sing out to a heart
    that wandered away in that dear torrent bed,

and greet with "Peace!" on my behalf its dear folk and say:
    "I left him thirsting for your courtyard!

Dwellers of Najd, is there no mercy
    for one bound to a love but who doesn't want release?

Why haven't you sent glad tidings of long life
    spirited within evening's pure winds to one filled with longing

with which he might live, this one who reckoned your forsaking him   10
    a joke, while holding jest to be out of place?"

You, blaming one consumed by longing,
    ignorant of what he endured so long, may you never succeed.

You've tired yourself out advising one who believes
    that he will never see success or prosperity.

Cut short your blame; I'm done with you! Cast aside one whose heart
   was slashed and slaughtered by wide wounding eyes.

You were a true friend before your advice to one burning with passion;
   have you ever seen a young lover fond of sage counsels?

If you're eager to reform me, well, I never wanted   15
   to save my heart depraved in passion.

What do the blamers hope to gain from blaming one robed in a life
   stripped of all restraint, one of rest and relaxation?

You, my love's worthy ones, can one hoping for union with you
   ever attain his desire that his mind might be free and easy?

Since you vanished from my sight my moaning has filled
   the quarters of Egypt's land with lamentation;

when I remember you, I stagger as if I'd drunk wine
   from the sweet scent of your memory [*dhikr*],

and if I'm called to forget my covenant with you,   20
   I find my heart won't give in.

May those days be fresh forever that were passed with close neighbors
   who turned our nights into feasts of joy and great delight,

where the sacred precinct was my homeland, and the people of Najd my
      peace,
   where my going to water there was declared right and clear;

its dear folk were my aim, the shade of its palms my trembling joy,
   and the sand of its two valleys was my place of repose.

Oh for that time and its sweetness,
   days when I found rest from weariness.

I swear by the Zamzam well, by Abraham's station, and the pilgrim   25
   coming to the holy house crying out: "I'm here to serve [*Labbayka*]!"

Whenever the east wind sways the fragrant wormwoods in the hills,
   it brings the breath of life from you.

Figure 32. Mughal style: the monumental gate to the tomb of Akbar in Sikandra, India (1605–1613), with its polychrome cut marble and other stone mosaic panels set into red sandstone. The *pishtaq* and the two-tiered arcade show Iranian influence. (See also fig. 31; and SD figs. 23, 26.)

Figure 33.   Mughal style: the Congregational Mosque in Delhi (1644–1658), built by Shah Jahan (who also built the Taj Mahal); it uses red sandstone as its basic building material and white marble as its principal ornamental medium. The triple ogival domes over the prayer hall and the small roof and minaret pavilions (*chattris*) became hallmarks of Mughal mosque architecture. (See also fig. 15; and SD figs. 24, 31.)

✳ Munawi's Literary Hagiography of Ibn al-Farid

TH. EMIL HOMERIN

'Umar ibn al-Farid's beautiful Arabic verse inspired generations of Muslims to venerate him as a saint. Belief in him as the unsurpassed poet of divine love was promoted further by accounts of his life composed by his devotees, including this extensive one by Muhammad 'Abd ar-Ra'uf al-Munawi. Munawi knew many of the anecdotes and stories involving the poet, and he carefully edited and arranged them to render a reverential portrayal and spirited defense of Ibn al-Farid's mystical life, verse, and miracles. Here the biographer weaves together an appreciation of Ibn al-Farid's poetry with the story of his life.[7]

'Umar ibn Abi al-Hasan 'Ali ibn Murshid ibn 'Ali, of Hama by origin, Egyptian by birth, residence, and death, Abu Hafs and, it has been said,

Abu al-Qasim, known as Ibn al-Farid . . . was given the title "Sultan of
Friends and Lovers," and both his supporters and detractors have characterized him as the absolute master-poet of his age.

His father came from Hama to Egypt, where he lived and began to
substantiate claims by women against men in arbitration. Then he was
entrusted with the position of assistant arbitrator, and so he came to be
called by the name "al-Farid" ["the woman's advocate"]. Then ['Umar]
was born to him in Egypt in the month of Dhu al-Qa'da in the year
566/1171 [sic]. He was raised under his father's protection in virtuous-
ness and security, in worship and religiosity, even in asceticism, temper-
ance, and piety, which enfolded him. So that when he became a young
man and reached the prime of life, he occupied himself with Shafi'i
jurisprudence, and studied Hadith under al-Hafiz ibn 'Asakir [d. ca. 1203];
subsequently, al-Hafiz al-Mundhiri [d. 1258] studied under [Ibn al-Farid].

Then solitude and entering the Sufi path became dear to him, so that
he devoted himself to asceticism and seclusion. He would ask permission
of his father to be a wandering ascetic, then he would wander on the
second mountain of Muqattam [just east of Cairo]. At times, he would
retire to a certain valley there and, at other times, to a certain forsaken
mosque among the ruins of the Qarafa cemetery. Then he would return
to his father and stay with him for a while until he again longed for
solitude and so returned to the mountain. Thus, he became intimate with
loneliness while the wild animals became intimate with him, such that
they would not shy away from him.

Nevertheless, he was not spiritually inspired until [the shaykh 'Ali
Abu al-Hasan] al-Baqqal informed him that he would be enlightened
only in Mecca. So [Ibn al-Farid] set out at once, though it was not the
month for pilgrimage to Mecca. But [a vision of] the Ka'ba remained
before him until he entered [Mecca]. Then he withdrew to an oasis
ten nights' journey from Mecca. Every day, accompanied by a ferocious
lion, he would go from that oasis to Mecca in order to pray the five daily
prayers there, and then he would return to his residence the same day. He
produced the majority of his poetry under these conditions. The lion used
to speak to him, requesting that he ride on it, but he refused.

He lived thus for about fifteen years, then he returned to Egypt and took up residence in the Hall of the Friday Sermon at the Azhar congregational mosque. Learned scholars devoted themselves to him, and he became an object of pilgrimage for the nobles and the common people, to the extent that [the Ayyubid sultan] al-Malik al-Kamil [r. 1218–1238] came to visit him. [The sultan] asked if he could make a tomb for him next to his own grave to be under the dome that he had built over the tomb of the Imam ash-Shafiʿi, but [Ibn al-Farid] refused.

[Ibn al-Farid] was handsome and noble, of excellent form and dress, of good companionship and company, of refined nature, a sweet pool and spring, eloquent in expressions, delicate with allusions, amenable, creative when making statements and quotations, generous and magnanimous. Once he turned to go to the mosque of ʿAmr [Ibn al-ʿAs in nearby Fustat]. A certain donkey driver said to him, "Ride with me on the basis of alms." So he was riding when a certain amir passed by and gave [Ibn al-Farid] one hundred dinars, which he, in turn, gave to the donkey driver.

When the Nile was high, [Ibn al-Farid] used to visit the mosque known as al-Mushtaha on [the island of] Roda, desiring to see the river in the evening. One day, he was on his way there when he heard a bleacher who was saying while bleaching:

> This piece of cloth has torn my heart,
> but it's not clean till it's shredded!

[Ibn al-Farid] yelled and fell down in a swoon; then he came to, repeated that verse, became agitated, and swooned again; and so on.

While [Ibn al-Farid] was keeping a forty-day fast, he craved a dish of meat and barley [*harisa*]. So he procured it, and raised a piece of it to his mouth, when a wall burst open and a handsome youth emerged and said: "Shame on you!" To which [Ibn al-Farid] replied: "Only if I eat it!" He threw it away and disciplined himself with an extra ten nights' fasting.

In a dream, [Ibn al-Farid] saw the Chosen Prophet [Muhammad]— God's blessing and peace be upon him—who said: "To whom do you trace your lineage?" He replied: "Oh Messenger of God, to the Bani Saʿd, the tribe of Halima [Muhammad's wet nurse]." Then [the Prophet] said: "No, your lineage is connected to me!" meaning a lineage based on love and following [his way]. . . .

Among [Ibn al-Farid's] wondrous miracles and strange states is that he saw a water carrier's camel and fell madly in love with it. He would come every day to see it, drinking a great deal from its load. He also used to fix his stare at a pole or a column for some days—a week, or more—never closing his eyes. Other events like these happened to him, but this will suffice.

How remarkable is his collection of poetry, his *Divan*, whose beauty is acknowledged by both his supporters and detractors, and this is especially true of his "Ta'iya" ["Ode Rhyming in T-Major"]! A group of eminent scholars . . . who were not fault-finders, and who ignore statements made by those envious people who characterized his poetry as "monism," have taken pains to compose a number of commentaries on it, and on his "Khamriya" ["Wine Ode"], and other poems.

A reliable source mentioned that a literalist . . . once wrote a commentary on the "Ta'iya," which he sent to one of the eminent Sufis of the time for his approval and support. [The Sufi] studied it for a while, and then when he sent it back, he wrote on it:

> She set out west; you went east—what a distance between
>   where the sun rises and where it sets!

[The Sufi master] was asked about this, so he replied: "The honorable commentator took great pains to trace the pronouns, subjects, and predicates, the wordplays and metaphors, as well as matters of language and style, but the intent of the poet was beyond all that!"

Even those who have disapproved of [Ibn al-Farid's] religious belief have praised his *Divan*, including Ibn Abi Hajala [d. 1375] who said:

> [Ibn al-Farid's *Divan*] is among the most refined collections of poetry and among the most precious pearls of land or sea. It is among the quickest to wound hearts, and absolutely one of the best in lamentation, since it was drawn from the outpourings of heartache, from a forsaken lover and a heart broken by the fever of separation. The people are fond of its rhymes and its intensity. He has become so popular that few are those who have not seen his *Divan*, or have not had his resounding odes ringing in their ears . . .

Al-Kamal al-Udfuwi [d. 1347] said:
The most beautiful [parts of the *Divan*] are the "Ode Rhyming in F,"
which begins:

My heart tells me you will end my life . . .

And his "Ode Rhyming in L," which begins:

It's love, so guard your heart, passion is not so simple . . .

And his "Ode Rhyming in K," which begins:

Be proud of your teasing signs, which you have a right to make. . . .

As for his "Ode Rhyming in T-Major," in the opinion of the people of
religious knowledge—he means the literalists—it is unacceptable, as it
alludes to wicked affairs.

['Abd al-Ghaffar] al-Qusi [d. 1309] mentioned in his book *The Divine
Unity [At-tawhid]* that the shaykh [Ibn al-Farid] owned slave girls in the
town of al-Bahnasa. He would go to them, and they would sing to him
accompanied by tambourine and reed flute while he danced and went into
ecstasy. Every folk has a source of inspiration, and every group a quest.
But the audition [*sama'*] of depraved people is not like that of the Sultan
of Lovers, for he stayed in that state, ascending to his perfection, until he
was at the point of death. Then he requested of God that a group of saints
be present with him at that dreadful event, so a group was with him, and
among them was al-Burhan [Ibrahim] al-Ja'bari [d. 1288]. As reported by
Ibn al-Farid's grandson ['Ali], al-Ja'bari said:

I saw the Garden displayed to him, so he cried and changed color and said:

If my resting place in love near you
    is what I've seen, then I wasted my days!

So I said to him: "Oh master, this is a great station!" But he replied:
"Oh Ibrahim, Rabi'a [al-'Adawiya]—and she was a woman—has said: 'By
Your might, I did not worship You in desire of Your Garden, but only for
Your Love!' I have not spent my life seeking [Paradise]!"
Then I heard a voice say to him: "What do you desire?" To which he
responded:

I desire—though time has passed—one glance from you!

His face glowed; his lamentation ceased, and so I believe that his wish was
granted.

But [Ibn al-Farid's] critics have condemned him with that [verse], for one of them has said: "When the veil was torn away and it was clear that he was not God, and that there was neither an incarnation nor a union, he recited that verse." Another of them has said: "He said this [verse] when the Angel of Death came to him."

How awful! Let him ask forgiveness from God—may You be glorified—for this is a great lie! Hasn't this forsaken critic heard the statement of the Chosen Prophet—God's blessing and peace be upon him—that "God is near the tongue of every speaking worshipper." How can the critic claim such a thing? Is he so certain regarding the reason for [Ibn al-Farid's] statement, as if he had been there as an eyewitness instead of al-Burhan [al-Ja'bari]? The literalists have no way for witnessing such secrets, so how can they know that [Ibn al-Farid] saw the Angel of Death? As for al-Burhan, he is among the eminent ones of the worthy folk of spiritual illumination and insight, and he has reported that [account] based on his observation of it. So what is all this bigotry taking place in the imagination of the feeble-minded and leading to unhealthy strife? . . .

In fact, a group of great men have taken back their censure [of Ibn al-Farid]. It is related regarding al-Shams ibn 'Imara al-Maliki [d. 1440] that he used to censure him. He went to visit the [tomb] of Joseph's brothers when thirst overcame him, but he could not find any water save a little upon the grave of Ibn al-Farid. So he recanted.

Al-'Izz ibn al-Jama'a [d. 1416] used to censure him but, in his sleep, he saw a group that had been made to stand in front of the shaykh [Ibn al-Farid] to whom it was said: "These are the deniers!" Then [Ibn al-Farid] cut out their tongues. [Ibn Jama'a] awoke terrified, recanted his censure, and believed in him. . . . Accounts like these are many.

[Ibn al-Farid] died in the year 632 [1235], and he was buried in the Qarafa cemetery. He was seen in a dream, and was asked: "Why didn't you praise the Chosen Prophet in your *Divan?*" So he said:

> I think all praise of the Prophet falls short,
>   though one exalts him to great heights.

> When God exalts the worthy one,
>   what mortals praise is worthless!

When some people hear [Ibn al-Farid's] verse, they believe that the inner meaning of all his words praise the Prophet—upon whom be peace. But most of his words do not support this as his intention.

✳ Jalal ad-Din Rumi
Ghazal

FATEMEH KESHAVARZ

From just across the Mediterranean comes a lyric poem from a younger contemporary of Ibn al-Farid, Jalal ad-Din Rumi (1207–1273). Few people have impacted the modern Western understanding of Islamic mysticism as Rumi has. He is best known for his mystical epic *The Spiritual Couplets* (*Mathnavi-i ma'navi*), but it is his unconventional, dramatic, and vibrant *Divan-i Shams*, a collection of over 35,000 lyric verses, that bears the mark of Rumi the poet more than any other work.[8] In the following ghazal, Rumi likens the blue of the sky to the ihram, the seamless clothing worn by Muslim pilgrims to Mecca. Developing the "scientific" notion that the sky revolved around the sun, Rumi envisions the ihram-wearing sky engaged in the pious act of circumambulating the Ka'ba. Recasting the natural phenomenon in its new role, however, Rumi concludes that all parables ultimately fail to contain love in their descriptive net and that meaningful verbal expression has only one natural culmination: intentional silence. The sky's endless allegorical pilgrimage fails to lead the seeker to the "house of God" because in truth God has only one house: indescribable love itself. The following ghazal, therefore, attempts to convey something of the magnitude of this house in its tribute to silence:

O sky that turns above our head!
    In love of the sun, you share the same mantle with me.
By God you are in love—and I shall tell what reveals your secret:
    Inside and out you are radiant and lush.
You do not get soaked in the sea, you are not bound to the earth;
    You do not burn in fire, and are not disturbed by the wind.
O millstone! what is the water that makes you turn?
    Tell me! perhaps you are a wheel made of iron.
You turn one way and make the earth green [with raindrops] like
        paradise;
    Then you turn the other way and uproot the trees [in a storm].

The sun is a candle and you a moth in action;

    Weaving your web around this candle.

You are a pilgrim wearing an ihram turquoise in color;

    Like pilgrims you are in circumambulation of the Ka'ba.

God said: "Whoever performed the hajj is safe";

    O dutiful wheel [of the sky]! you are safe from harm.*

Everything is pretext, there is love and nothing besides love;

    Love is the house of God and you are living in that house.

I will say no more, for it is not possible to say;

    God knows how much more is in me crying out to be told.

✳ ## Muhammad Shirin Maghribi
Ghazal

LEONARD LEWISOHN

Muhammad Shirin Maghribi (d. ca. 1408) was born in the northwestern Iranian village of Ammand. He wrote over a thousand lines of Arabic poetry as well as more than 200 Persian poems of several genres. He belonged intellectually to the tradition of Mahmud Shabistari (the subject of Lahiji's commentary earlier in this part).[9]

THE RELIGION OF LOVE

Our theme is kept beyond the aim and quest every seeker has.

    Our sensibility and feeling are above the tastes aesthetes-of-taste

        appreciate.

As yet no one to soul's delight has drunk a cup-drop or draught

    Of that wine our lips constantly drink.

Our heaven's star revolves outside all heavens: the Essence Divine and

    Sacrosanct itself

    Acts the heavenly sphere of our star.

Oh many the horses that hearts have spurred on and on . . . As yet no

    rider has sped

    And reached the dust our thoroughbred has left.

---

* A reference to Q 3:97 concerning the Ka'ba: "In it there are veritable signs at the spot where Abraham stood. Whoever enters it is safe."

Figure 34.   Ottoman style: the Mosque of Bayezid II (1484) in Edirne, Turkey, not far from the Bulgarian border. This is an early example of the central dome plan, prior to the use of flanking half-domes to increase both dome height and lateral interior space. Like other imperial mosques, it is part of a large complex, including a hospital and medical school, and residential facilities for dervishes flanking the prayer hall. (See also figs. 40, 43, 44.)

Figure 35. Ottoman style: the Selimiye Mosque in Edirne (1569–1575), built for Suleyman the Magnificent's son Selim II, the culmination of a century of experimentation with the central dome plan. Sinan's final masterpiece uses a single dome set on an octagon, without flanking half-domes (such as those visible in fig. 41). Along with the massive central domes, slim cylindrical minarets, varying in number from one to six, with conical caps and from one to three galleries, are characteristic of Ottoman religious architecture. (See also fig. 11; and SD fig. 19.)

When day and night as yet were not, when both in the universe were
    un-create,
  Her face our day, her tress our night was all there was—thus for us it
     was.
For one who gives up soul and world and buys instead her love will know
  Alone our gain and loss, and know the sort of business that love is.
Our sighs and cries "Oh lord" and tears no one does know, except if he
    inside
  Be burnt like us, his heart be scorched with sighs: *our* cries, *our* tears
    and prayers.
You should embrace our creed and faith in all respects: principles and parts,

Articles and essentials, since Truth itself is our faith—our religion,
   God's own.
But first erase, like Maghribi—if you'd apply to our university,
   All taint and mark the world upon your heart's slate has writ.

✳   Nuri and Shad
      Naʿts

ALI ASANI

The two poems translated here are from Urdu, a language commonly associated with Islamic civilization in South Asia. In this language poems in praise of the Prophet Muhammad are called *naʿts*. Naʿts constitute such a significant literary genre that every Urdu poet, no matter how minor he or she may be, has composed at least one. By poetic convention, the last verse of each naʿt, its form notwithstanding, contains the poet's pen-name or *takhallus*. Over the course of time, the composition of poetry in praise of Muhammad has become such a significant literary activity that even Hindu poets writing in Urdu, influenced by the Islamic environment in which they live, have been inspired to write naʿts. Some of these naʿts are indeed so fervent in their expression of devotion that one cannot tell that they were written by non-Muslims. Nuri is the pen-name of a mid-twentieth-century poetess named Sayyida Musarrat Jahan Begum Shafiq.

NAʿT BY NURI

There has come a sign from the unseen that I should praise Ahmad
      [Muhammad];
   Friends, in neither my pen nor tongue is there the ability or capacity
      for this.
My mind and speech are perplexed: if I am to recite, what should I recite?
   How can I praise him who is loved by God Himself?
This pride, my dignity, they rely on your being,
   The outcome of my life is but a spark of your love.
He is the Prophet, entirely mercy, consoler of the community;
   He has been so kind to us that [out of embarrassment] we can hardly
      raise our heads.

No one in this world shares in pain and sorrow like him;

O soul, after God, refuge lies in his being.

May my naʿt be accepted and I be allowed to enter his presence:

Whether it be a revelation of the holy door or a vision or a glance.

I would sacrifice heart and soul if I have the good fortune of his presence;

My soul would be in ecstasy, the sign of [true] desire.

My prayer is that on the day of resurrection, my master should say to me:

"Nuri, why are you fearful? Surely you are not unprotected!"[10]

NAʿT BY THE HINDU POET SHAD

Shad is the pen-name of Kishan Prasad (d. 1943), former prime minister of the Indian state of Hyderabad. He writes:

The splendor present in the two worlds is on account of the king of nations;

Everything is manifest through his existence.*

We are supplicants at your door, indeed, we are your slaves;

Our desire is neither paradise nor its gardens.

If granted your grace, this unhappy one would rejoice;

My aggrieved heart of sorrow is prostrate with pain.

"Do not despair" provides comfort for me;†

I hope only for your grace and bounty.

He will not know the secret of annihilation and eternity

Who thinks the purpose of humankind is existence and nonexistence.

My desire is to remain constantly at your door;

I have no desire for wealth, worldly rank, or pomp.

---

* A reference to a sacred hadith in which God says to the Prophet: *Lawlaka ma khalaqtu 'l-aflaka*, "But for your sake I would not have created the spheres."

† A reference to Q 39:53: "Do not despair of God's mercy. Surely God forgives sins altogether. He is indeed the Forgiving, the Merciful."

O Shad, in your na't you have made roses blossom well;
      This branch has flourished and blossomed on account of your pen![11]

✳   Bibi Hayati
      Ghazal

LEONARD LEWISOHN

Bibi Hayati was born in the early nineteenth century to a Sufi family of the Iranian city of Kerman. Her brother was the spiritual guide (shaykh) of a leader of the Ni'matullahi order named Nur 'Ali Shah. After long acquaintance with the order and its practices, Bibi Hayati was initiated as a member and eventually married Nur 'Ali Shah, who encouraged his wife's poetic talents. The following ghazal, addressed to the Beloved, offers a small sample of this Sufi woman's literary art.[12]

His visage like tulips,
      His temper fiery, his faith wine.
Sprightly, a wild juniper in grace,
      Reckless in his gallantry,
Drunken in this ecstasy.
      His ruby lips devoted to wine,
His curls kinks of hyacinth,
      A seductive violence in his narcissus eyes,
His approach: bloodthirsty coquetry.
      Then, teeth clenched, and lips locked,
His blood throbbing, his heart pounding,
      He arrived at my bedside one midnight . . .
His lips parted then,
      Like rosebuds opening to speak:
"Oh you, who are in ecstasy unconscious,
      Drunk on the Cup of my human display—
Whoever has lost eyes to Love,
      What dream of sleep, what mind for food
Can his bosom still sustain?

How happy the lover
Who never stoops down, on the first step,
    To food or sleep . . . "
From the consorts of paradise,
    Who shall seize Heaven's wine?
Whoever like Hayati was intoxicated with God
    Before the beginning of time.

Figure 36.   Main *iwan* of Madar-i Shah Madrasa in Isfahan
(1706–1715), viewed from the main entry arch. Madrasas
have been important the world over as cornerstone community institutions. (See also figs. 48, 51–53.)

5 Community
Society, Institutions, and Patronage

Since the time of Muhammad, Muslims have considered the growing and now global collectivity of believers one united community, an *umma*. Global unity has always been a lofty ideal, though sheer numbers and diversity long ago rendered the ideal abstract. Even so, the idea of an Umma has informed the genesis and functioning of communities on a smaller scale. Muslim communities have developed and thrived within every imaginable kind of political, economic, and cultural context. The texts and illustrations featured in part 5 offer a view of three broad facets of Islamic community. We begin with the story of one man from a traditional Middle Eastern village. A series of texts then exemplifies several major types of documentation about the shaping of public and private religious institutions. A look at patronage and economic realities from several perspectives completes the picture.

SOCIAL AND HISTORICAL CONTEXTS
Religion, Society, and Culture

Community presupposes a variety of complex interrelationships among the individual, the family, the town or village, and the Islamic educational and religious institutions around which they revolve. The following story of a village preacher in Jordan, as told to anthropologist Richard Antoun, gives all of those relationships concrete shape and character. Shaykh Luqman's life story puts a human face on some aspects of a religious and spiritual tradition that might otherwise remain cold and impersonal. Luqman's story, like those of hundreds of millions of other "ordinary" Muslims, exists not as a text, but as a living narrative. Note especially how social forces, traditional Islamic institutions and pedagogy, and personal conviction shape Luqman's choices. His story makes an interesting contrast with that of Ibn Marzuq (related below), who was also a preacher, but who functioned within a very different set of institutional circumstances.

❋ ## Shaykh Luqman
A Contemporary Life in a Traditional Context

RICHARD ANTOUN

Shaykh Luqman (a pseudonym) is the second son of Hajj Muhammad, a fairly large landowner and the head of a large polygynous family composed of two wives, six sons, two daughters, and numerous grandchildren. He is a member of the largest clan in the village of Kufr al-Ma and a member of one of the village's two most influential patrilineages, which included one of the two village mayors, a prominent local bureaucrat, and a number of prominent elders. However, this clan and lineage also numbered some of the poorest community members. Luqman was born in 1928. From age eight to age eleven he studied and completed the Qur'an with two teachers, one a local resident (with whom he was later to compete for the preachership of the village) and the other a peripatetic teacher.

In 1939 he entered the primary school in the next village (there was none in Kufr al-Ma at the time), where religion was one of the regular subjects. At the end of the third grade his father told him that it was time for him to join his elder brother behind the plough. Without his father's knowledge, Luqman went by himself on the first day of school and registered for the fourth grade. His father found out and went to the school and told the teacher that he needed Luqman to work the land, since he already had two younger sons in school. The schoolmaster replied, "No, you cannot have him. He is our son now."

Luqman remained in school for three more years, finishing his primary education in 1945 at the age of sixteen. He asked his father to allow him to continue his schooling—he was first in his class in all subjects—but his father refused. For the next three years Luqman took every opportunity to absent himself from (or sneak out of) the village to study with the preacher and marriage officer in the next village, which was also the subdistrict center. This preacher, Shaykh Ahmad, had pursued Islamic studies for six years in Damascus. When the month of fasting, Ramadan, arrived Luqman was always the first in the mosque, preceding Shaykh Ahmad.

Finally in 1948, after three years of friction between father and son, Shaykh Ahmad came to Luqman's father and asked permission to hire Luqman as assistant instructor and drill-master [in school lessons] in exchange for three and one half sacks of wheat a year. Every student used to give Ahmad two measures of grain as payment, and Ahmad gave them private lessons in history, geography, and religious studies in the subdistrict center. The Hajj, Luqman's father, agreed provided that his son continued to work every harvest time.

For the next three years Luqman taught students for Shaykh Ahmad and at the same time pursued religious studies with him. Often when he was sitting in his father's guest house—all village men were expected to attend a guest house, converse, and drink coffee in the evening—and someone addressed him, he did not reply, being sunk in silent recitation of the Qur'an or meditation or study of the books he had brought back from Ahmad's. His father became angry at this breach of guest house etiquette and told Ahmad that if Luqman brought any more books into the house he would burn them, and he forbade Ahmad to continue to instruct his son. Luqman's father thought that his son was on the verge of insanity. Thereafter, Luqman never brought any books back home, but he spent whole nights reading at Shaykh Ahmad's.

At this point in his quest for religious knowledge Luqman's behavior became decidedly mystical. He recounted to Ahmad that often when he slept in the summer and awoke, he thought he was covered by a tent, white like the sun. Ahmad replied that knowledge was like that.

When Ahmad declined to teach him further, following the promise he had given to his father, Luqman threatened to cease forthwith teaching his students. Ahmad therefore continued teaching the young man without the knowledge of his father. Luqman's final breach with his father occurred in the summer of 1949. The Hajj demanded that Luqman go down to the Jordan Valley and harvest along with his brothers. Luqman declined because that year the harvest coincided with Ramadan and Luqman had vowed to fast. The Hajj charged Ahmad with discouraging Luqman from fulfilling his harvesting obligation. Ahmad prevailed on Luqman to join his brothers in the Jordan Valley for the harvest. Luqman went, but he continued to fast during the harvest. His brothers excused him and told him they could get along without him.

On Fridays during the month he returned to the village to attend the Friday congregational prayer. On one occasion he was late getting back to the threshing grounds. His father grew angry and raised his arm to hit him. For a week Luqman did not see or talk to his father, sleeping in the mosque by night and working on the threshing ground by day, all the while fasting. He and his father were temporarily reconciled by a relative and village elder—for Ramadan is the time when all estranged believers should be reconciled. But Hajj Muhammad's patience had been exhausted. He told Luqman that as soon as the harvest was over he was to move his belongings out of the house. On hearing this Luqman's mother said, "If he goes, I go too."

In the summer of 1949 at the age of twenty-one Luqman, his mother, and his full brother moved out of the Hajj's house. The Hajj gave Luqman's mother and brother their fair share of the harvest but gave Luqman nothing. Luqman's full brother started plowing as a sharecropper and Luqman continued his studies, now as a full-time teaching assistant to Ahmad; they split all proceeds on a 50–50 basis. These were hard years, but the matricentral cell (mother and two sons) from what had been a single polygynous household at first rented a house from a relative and then, in 1951, managed to buy a small two-room house in the village. As if to add insult to injury, Luqman's father used the proceeds of the harvest to obtain a wife for Luqman's younger half-brother, a violation of village norms, which respect the birth order among siblings in marriage. The same year Luqman suffered another blow when his mentor, teacher, and friend, Shaykh Ahmad, moved to a village in another area, ending their four-year working relationship.

In the meantime, in 1951, the preachership of the mosque in Kufr al-Ma became vacant. It had always been occupied by a series of peripatetic preachers who stayed a year or more and then moved on. A preacher from Syria who passed through the village was hired as village preacher, and Luqman became the prayer leader, *imam*, at the mosque. At this time another itinerant preacher came to stay in the village. He was an Egyptian and had had some training at the famous religious university of al-Azhar in Egypt. He was sustained by the community and in return he taught the Qur'an and gave occasional Friday sermons. In addition, for a year he gave Luqman intensive training in Arabic and in religious studies. After this shaykh left, the village was without a preacher for four months. Mustafa Basboos, an elderly villager and self-styled preacher (he wore the white turban of the learned man) with a smattering of religious learning picked up in Egypt where he had been interned during World War I as a prisoner in the Ottoman army, began delivering the Friday sermon. Luqman thought he was better qualified, but most considered him too young.

One Friday morning, against the advice of many of his friends and to the amazement of the assembled worshippers, Luqman strode up to the pulpit from one side and Mustafa Basboos strode up from the other and both proceeded to deliver the sermon at once. With his evangelical delivery and surer sense of learning, Luqman apparently drowned out his rival and proceeded to give a sermon on "hypocrisy." After the sermon those who had opposed him, now recognizing his talent, congratulated him. For two months he continued to deliver the Friday sermon but without remuneration or any formal designation by the village. He finally said to several elders, "I have been offered the preachership at Tibne," a smaller and more remote village in the vicinity; "if you want me you must hire me as imam." The elders said, "Go write up a contract; we will hire both you and Mustafa Basboos at ten sacks of grain [annually] each." Luqman agreed and drew up a contract.

Now, at this time there were two village mayors (*mukhtars*) from the two largest clans, Beni Yasin and Beni Dumi. Luqman was a member of Yasin and Mustafa Basboos was a member of Dumi, and so the arrangement seemed acceptable all around. But when presented with the contract, the mayor of Dumi said, "No, we want only Luqman. Mustafa Basboos can't perform the duties. He's a dunderhead. Draw up another contract for yourself, and all of Beni Dumi will sign it." In August 1952, at the age of twenty-four, therefore, Luqman was hired as imam of the village at a salary of twenty sacks of wheat to be paid in proportion by each household at harvest time. A year later Luqman married a woman from his own clan.

That same year he applied to become marriage officer (*ma'dhun*), but no vacancy was available. In 1956, after passing an examination administered by the religious court system, he was given a certificate (*ijaza*) and was officially appointed imam by the central government. This appointment carried with it a stipend of nine dollars a month. Perhaps more important, after passing this examination Luqman began wearing the red fez and white turban, the symbols of certified religious knowledge. In 1961 he received an appointment as ma'dhun for a number of villages in the subdistrict; and in 1971 he was appointed guide (*murshid*) for Jordanian pilgrims going to Mecca. In 1971, at the age of forty-one, Luqman was a successful village preacher. He had a growing library, an increasing income, and a cumulative occupational role inventory.[1] Moreover, in 1971 the large green dome for the central village mosque had just been completed under his tutelage; and in 1977 he opened a Qur'an school. Thanks in large part to such institutional developments, Kufr al-Ma was no longer merely a village.

By 1986 Luqman had vicariously realized his own career goals through his son, who had recently been employed in the university; he was in the process of marrying off the second of his sons; he had overseen the building of a second mosque in the village, in which he now preached; he sometimes entertained the area's fundamentalist elite in his home; and he had just purchased a new bus to run to the next village and back. But it was his status as a man of knowledge, rather than as a ritual specialist, marriage officer, or pilgrim guide, that was most important to Luqman. And it was the role of preacher that allowed him to elaborate that status in the fullest and most satisfactory manner.

Luqman was an unusually sensitive and reflective individual, particularly about his own life. He regarded his life as eventful and problematic—involving struggle against his own father and the community. His personal growth involved his forsaking the relative prestige of a land-owning family for a vocation of low status. A village preacher had to perform many demeaning tasks, such as the ritual washing of the dead, and was often reduced virtually to begging, a condition suggested by a proverb: "There are three things unseen to the eye—the legs of the snake, the eyes of the scorpion, and the bread of the preacher." In order to follow his lights, therefore, Luqman was going against the social grain in many ways.

An important factor to be considered in evaluating the careers of village preachers is that Muslim religious organization in Jordan and many other Muslim countries is congregational rather than episcopal. Although a village mosque, or any other mosque, does not constitute a "parish" in the sense of a formally defined discrete corporate religious unit, it is the village community and not some other social unit that sets the terms of the preacher's service, and that contract is open to renegotiation on an annual basis. Both the preacher and the village are free to terminate the contract at the end of each harvest season. It was precisely the local and achieved character of his status as preacher that allowed Luqman to struggle for and win the position.

Several dimensions of the "life history" approach—the cultural, the social, and the psychosocial—are useful in understanding Luqman's story.[2]

The cultural dimension refers to "the mutual understandings, expectations and behavior patterns held by a people among whom a person grows up."[3] Luqman championed Islamic norms to a greater degree than most of the village's population. He preached against inequality in polygynous marriage, perhaps because his father had taken two wives, as had his brother-in-law, and he felt his mother and sister to be neglected. He also preached against the unequal treatment of siblings by fathers and advanced a reformist interpretation of religious obligation on the occasion of death: it was, he said, a general obligation of an adult Muslim to wash the body after death and to read the burial prayer at the cemetery, and not specifically the duty of the preacher.

On the other hand, Luqman violated a number of family and village norms. Each son was expected to contribute his labor to earn both his own and his brothers' marriage payment and to play the role of breadwinner. Luqman also persistently disobeyed his father, preferring reading or meditating to engaging in all-male guest house conversation. His championing of Islamic norms along with the persistent violation of family and village norms produces an engaging tension in Luqman's life history.

The social dimension focuses on "common ways of working out recurrent conflicts" and on the "emotional experiences of reward and penalty."[4] Luqman's continuing abrasive relations with his father and his career ambitions for his own son are closely related. The father never understood the son's desire for religious education as an essential component of his evolving identity. Luqman, in turn, was disappointed in his aspirations and, as a result, never became more than a village preacher, though at that level a highly successful one. Luqman's oldest son became a vicarious realization of these yearnings, since he was sent for higher religious education to the Islamic university at Medina in Saudi Arabia; he returned with diplomas in hand and subsequently attained a research position at Yarmouk University in Jordan. By contrast with Luqman's abrasive relationship with his father, his mother had stood fast with him; Luqman gave one of his most powerful sermons on the topic of *rahm*: "womb," "kinship," and "compassion."

Finally, the psychosocial dimension "focuses on the individual's subjective world, his general feelings and attitudes," as well as on his models for behavior and self-images.[5] Luqman's models were drawn from outside the village. Besides his mentor, Shaykh Ahmad, the series of religious judges who were posted to the nearby subdistrict center and who supervised the preachers of the area were the figures Luqman respected and admired for their erudition, their goodness, and their kindness. His convictions about individuality and the right to have one's own thoughts and views took him beyond the accepted ways of thinking of his fellow villagers, but despite such intellectual independence Luqman was very much a son of the village, which constituted for him a security blanket and restricted his career mobility.

INSTITUTIONAL TEXTS

Against the backdrop of this very personal story of a specific individual it is easier to understand the major dimensions of institutional development and the role of patronage in shaping Islamic communities. We look here at institutions both from the outside and from the inside. Much of our information on the nature of public support for the development of community comes in the form of historical epigraphy and foundational (*waqf*) documents. Texts about how Muslims have regulated and structured their religious organizations treat matters of private discipline.

Public Support

✳ ## Historical Epigraphy of Mamluk Sultan Faraj ibn Barquq

JOHN RENARD

Religious sentiments expressed on the facades and doorways of monuments offer important insights into the rulers for whom religious legitimation was also a significant political concern. Earlier sections have discussed several examples of how epigraphic texts help us interpret objects and buildings alike. Here are several inscriptions from the early-fifteenth-century *khanqah* (Sufi residence; see also SD fig. 29) and mausoleum complex of the twenty-sixth Mamluk ruler, Faraj ibn Barquq (r. 1389–1412), in Cairo's northern cemetery. Note how the choice of qur'anic texts reflects the purposes of the funerary sections of the building, and how the dates on the three texts suggest that the whole structure was completed only several years after the sultan was buried. On a molding on the west wall of the mausoleum is written:

In the name of God the Gracious and Merciful. By the bounteous leave of the beneficent God and His infinite largess, the sultan, al-Malik al-Mansur, the sultan of Islam and of the Muslims, who strikes the unbelievers and the polytheists, reviver of justice in the two worlds, deliverer of those who have suffered from injustice, father of the poor and weak, refuge of the widows and the marginalized, al-Malik al-Mansur 'Abd al-'Aziz, son of the deceased Sultan Barquq, may God shelter him with mercy and approval, ordered the completion of this blessed and felicitous mausoleum. "In the name of God the Gracious and Merciful. And she [Mary] was given into Zakariya's care. Whenever Zakariya went into her room he discovered that she had provisions; he said, O Mary, from where did this come to you? It is from God, she replied; God provides unstintingly for whom he chooses [3:37; see also fig. 8]. Those to whom We have given the Book know this as well as they know their own children, but among them are some who cover over the truth even though they are aware of it. The truth is from your Lord, so do not be among those who doubt. He orients each one in a direction; therefore vie with each other in good deeds. Wherever you are, God will unite you, for over all things God is powerful" [2:146–148]. God the Almighty has spoken truly, as has his noble messenger, and may God bless and grant peace to our master Muhammad on this date, the 2d of Jumada II, the 808th year of the Hijra [November 25, 1405]. Thanks be to God.[6]

An inscription on the walls of the burial chamber of the father of the complex's founder incorporates another text of Scripture appropriate to a funerary monument:

"In the name of God the Gracious and Merciful. Factions among them were at odds with each other, so grief will come upon those who do injustice in the punishment of a fearsome day. Are they but idling away until the Hour, so that it will happen upon them suddenly when they are least aware? On that day friends will become enemies one to another, except for those who are God-fearing. O my servants, you shall have no fear on the Day, neither shall you be sad. You who have put faith in our signs and have surrendered [to God; lit., "been muslims"], enter the Garden along with your spouses, rejoicing. Among them will be passed trays and cups of gold, containing every soul's desire and eye's delight; and there will you remain" [43:65–71]. God the Almighty has spoken truly. The construction of this blessed mausoleum of our master the late Sultan al-Malik az-Zahir Abu Saʿid Barquq—may God shelter him with his mercy and bring him by his grace and bounty to dwell in his ample Garden—was ordered in the days of his son our master the Sultan al-Malik an-Nasir Abu 's-Saʿadat Faraj—may God fortify his support and redouble his might through Muhammad and his Family. And that [occurred] in the months of the year 803 of the Prophet's Hijra [1400–1401], blessing and peace be upon them.[7]

And on the tomb itself is a text that tells more about the feelings and wishes of the deceased ruler's survivors:

"In the name of God the Gracious and Merciful. All things upon [earth] are passing away, while the face of your Lord abides forever, majestic and honored" [55:26–27]. This is the burial place of the servant needy of God Most High, the late happy al-Malik az-Zahir Abu Saʿid Barquq—may God sanctify his spirit and illumine his grave through Muhammad and his Family. His last will commanded it. He was taken to the mercy of God Most High before the call to the dawn prayer on Friday the 15th of Shawwal in the 801st year of the Hijra [June 20, 1399]—may God bring the year to an auspicious close through Muhammad and his Family—and he was buried after the congregational prayer [just after noon] on the same day amid a numerous crowd of Muslims and their Imams. It was a memorable day of public celebration. May God transform his grave into one of the gardens of Paradise through Muhammad and his Family, Amen, and may God bless our master Muhammad and his Family, his companions, his descendants, and his followers until the Day of Judgment and give them peace. Amen.[8]

Two *Waqf* Documents: Sultan Barquq and Khwaja Ahrar

✱ Mamluk Sultan Barquq's *Waqf*

JOHN RENARD

From Faraj ibn Barquq's historical inscriptions we move to another type of documentation that offers information about that sultan's own father, Barquq, who is buried in the building complex just discussed. The foundational document (*hujjat waqf*) governing the late-fourteenth-century complex of the Mamluk sultan Barquq (1336–1399) in Cairo provides a wealth of information about how this major religious and social institution shaped Muslim life. An example of royal patronage, the text begins with a detailed description of the building, leading the reader virtually room by room from one section to another, pointing out important formal and functional features. Then it describes the qualifications and duties expected of principal staff, and gives details about salary and other material benefits attached to each position. Note that the building included four vaulted halls, called *iwans*, each for the use of one of the four Sunni schools of religious law, with the largest iwan given to the dominant school in Mamluk Egypt, the Hanafi school. Here are the waqf document's descriptions of some of those critical posts:[9]

The overseer and administrator of this endowment must make advantageous use of its revenues [from attached shops] according to the principles of shari'a. That begins with the structure of this *madrasa* [college of religious studies and law] and the other endowed facilities, with their repair and improvement, with whatever assures its permanence and secures lasting advantage for it, even if he should spend all its income on that. He will therefore pay the owner of the property the real estate rent due as prescribed by shari'a. What is left over he will spend as follows:

The Hanafi shaykh-professor: [The administrator] will hire a good, religious, devout, upstanding man, an excellent jurist of the Hanafi school who is learned in the principles of the religion, in qur'anic exegesis, in the Prophetic hadith, in the jurisprudence of his legal school and its positive law, in both its difficult and subtle aspects. He is appointed this madrasa's chief professor of the study of the advanced learning of his law school and the shaykh of [the madrasa's] Sufis, who will be described below. Each month of the lunar year [will be issued] 500 newly minted silver dirhams, or its equivalent in currency if that is not possible—300 silver dirhams for the professorship and 200 for his duties as shaykh—along with two measures of sweets, and 100 silver dirhams annually for clothing. In addition, he will appoint forty Hanafi scholars occupied as specialists in the method of the great Imam Abu Hanifa—may God be pleased with him and make him content—and in other shari'a-related sciences. It is stipulated that every day of the week except Tuesday and Friday this shaykh will hold session with his students in the qibla iwan; every student will busy himself with whatever the shaykh chooses, from the legal school's law and jurisprudence, to exegesis and grammar, to doctrine and other matters. The shaykh must clarify for them whatever difficulties they might find in obscure or recondite questions, and accompany them on the road of learning and benefit as is customary in such matters. Their sessions will occupy them for three and a half hours beginning at sunrise.

The Shafi'i professor: In addition, the administrator will appoint a religious and righteous man, a fine jurist of the Shafi'i school learned in the method of his legal school and its jurisprudence, as professor in this madrasa. And he will appoint along with [the professor] twenty legal scholars occupied with the Shafi'i school of the great Imam Muhammad ibn Idris ash-Shafi'i—may God be pleased with him and grant him contentment—and with other shari'a-related sciences. It is stipulated that every working day of every week this shaykh and these students of his will gather in the Bahri iwan [opposite the qibla iwan] in this madrasa and proceed as is customary for Hanafi students. And their session should extend from noon until the time of the afternoon [ritual prayer]. This shaykh's portion each month of the lunar year will be 300 silver dirhams and two measures of sweets, and annually 100 silver dirhams for clothing.

The Maliki professor: Similarly, the administrator will appoint a good, religious man who is of superb learning and experience in the law and jurisprudence of the Maliki school and a master of its interpretation and transmission as professor in this madrasa. To him will be allotted a monthly payment of 300 newly minted silver dirhams and two measures of sweets, and 100 silver dirhams annually for clothing. He will be assigned twenty students dedicated to the lofty Maliki science in the school of the Imam Malik ibn Anas, Imam of Medina [lit., the abode of the Hijra]—may God be pleased with him and grant him contentment— with the understanding that this shaykh will gather with these students every working day of every week in the eastern iwan [to the left of the qibla iwan] in this madrasa, from noon until the time of the afternoon [ritual prayer], and that they will conduct themselves as is incumbent on the Hanafi and Shafi'i groups, as has been explained.

The Hanbali professor: The administrator will appoint also a good, devout man, an excellent scholar knowledgeable in the law of the Hanbali school and in its jurisprudence, a competent exponent and practitioner, as professor in this madrasa. He will appoint along with the shaykh twenty Hanbali legal scholars engaged in the legal method of the Imam al-Kirmani Ahmad ibn Hanbal ash-Shaybani—may God be pleased with him and grant him contentment—and in other shari'a-related sciences. It is under- stood that this shaykh will gather these students every working day of each week in the western iwan [to the right of the qibla] of this madrasa. They will conduct themselves in the manner that has been described in the case of the other three legal schools. Their sessions will run from noon until the time of the afternoon [ritual prayer], as already described. [Compensation equal to that of the Shafi'i and Maliki professors.]

The shaykh of Hadith: In addition, the administrator will appoint a good, devout man of outstanding erudition in linguistic science, who knows the Qur'an by heart, a Hadith scholar familiar with and steeped in the sayings of the Prophet—may the choicest blessings and peace be upon their speaker—and whose credibility is well founded. The administrator will appoint him as professor in this madrasa, and will compensate him with a monthly payment of 150 newly minted silver dirhams, one measure of sweets, two Egyptian measures of soap, two measures of oil, three Egyptian measures of bread daily, and for his clothing 80 silver dirhams a year. Assigned to the shaykh will be fifteen students of the lofty science dedicated to knowledge of Prophetic hadith—may the choicest blessings and peace and mercy be upon the one who uttered them. It is stipulated that this shaykh and these students will gather every work day of each week in the place which the administrator designates for them in this madrasa, and these students will occupy themselves there with the noble sayings of the Prophet. The shaykh will analyze for them what they find difficult, and clarify for them what needs further explanation, as is customary in such matters. Their sessions will run from noon until the afternoon [ritual prayer].

The shaykh of the seven Qur'an readings [*qira'at*]: The administrator will also appoint a good, devout, upright man who knows by heart the beloved Book of God and who has mastered the seven ways of reading Qur'an,* one who fulfills the requisite conditions for one devoted to the seven readings, as professor in this madrasa. He will be paid a monthly sum of 100 silver dirhams, one measure of sweets, two Egyptian measures of oil, two Egyptian measures of soap, 50 silver dirhams annually for clothing, and three Egyptian measures of bread daily. Ten Qur'an reciters who have memorized the Book of God Most High will be assigned to him and dedicated to the science of the readings of Qur'an, with the understanding that this shaykh will hold sessions every working day of each week in the place the administrator appoints for them in this madrasa. The shaykh will have these students recite the exalted Qur'an in the seven modes of recitation, and will instruct them as needed in those skills. And if someone approaches this shaykh for [instruction in] recitation in the manner of these students, he shall teach them to recite in the same way, so that no one will be turned away from [learning to] recite.

The students of the four law schools and the students of Hadith and of the readings of Qur'an: To each of these students of the four law schools and traditionists and reciters of the seven Qur'an readings the adminis-

---

* Seven slightly different versions, distinguished by only minor variations in voweling or phrasing, were agreed on in the eleventh century. Sufis often interpret the seven readings as levels of meaning.

trator will allot a monthly stipend of 20 silver dirhams, one measure of sweets, two measures of good oil, and two Egyptian measures of soap, along with 30 silver dirhams annually for clothing, and three Egyptian measures of bread daily.

The Sufis: The administrator will also appoint sixty good and upright Muslims, Sufis, on the understanding that they will gather in this madrasa and act according to the requirements of this document. Each of them will receive, in view of their Sufi assignments, a monthly allotment of 10 silver dirhams, two measures of oil, two measures of soap, one measure of sweets, three Egyptian measures of bread daily, and 30 silver dirhams annually for clothing.

Our master the sultan, founder of this endowment—may God make his reign eternal—has stipulated that the shaykh of this khanqah, of the Hanafi school, who has already been mentioned, along with the students of the four law schools mentioned above, the shaykh of Hadith and his students, the shaykh of the seven Qur'an readings and his students, and the Sufis just mentioned, numbering 187 persons in all, shall gather daily to perform the afternoon prayer in this madrasa-khanqah. The above-mentioned shaykh will take his seat in the qibla iwan surrounded by this assembly. Everyone will recite two full sections [*ahzab*] from the sixty [total] sections of the exalted Qur'an either from memory or from revered texts [lit., "quarters," one of the designations of segments into which Qur'an is traditionally divided] circulated among them in sections, and they will proceed as described earlier.

The imams: The administrator will appoint two individuals from among the sixty Hanafi Sufis already mentioned. One of them, an excellent jurist steeped in the seven qur'anic readings, will lead the Muslims, in the qibla iwan at the front of which is the mihrab, in the five prescribed ritual prayers and for the opening of the month of Rama-dan and the times of assembly prescribed in shari'a. His compensation will be 70 silver dirhams a month, 50 silver dirhams for clothing annu-ally, in addition to what is allotted him from the Sufi activities described earlier. A second man will lead the Muslims in the five [prayers], as is customary, in the mausoleum [*qubba*] in this madrasa. He will be paid 30 silver dirhams monthly, and 20 silver dirhams annually for clothing, in addition to what is set aside for him from his Sufi duties already mentioned.

The muezzins: The administrator will also appoint six of these Sufis with beautiful voices who will intone the call to prayer and the exclamation of praise to God [*tasbih*], and magnification of God at times of fasting and the beginning of ritual prayer, and the enunciation "God is supreme" [*takbir*] behind the imam, and the invocation of peace [*taslim*] upon the Prophet, "may God bless him and give him peace," on Friday nights and at times of fasting. They will do that by turns as designated by the administrator in this waqf. Each of them will be paid 15 silver dirhams a month in addition to what is allotted them from Sufi activities.

✳ ## A Central Asian *Waqf* of Naqshbandi Sufi Master Khwaja Ahrar
JO-ANN GROSS

From a little less than a century later and a thousand miles to the northeast comes a Persian waqf text that offers detailed information about community concerns associated with a major Sufi architectural complex. Whereas the Mamluk texts exemplified several facets of royal patronage, the foundational document of Khwaja ʿUbayd Allah Ahrar (1404–1490) represents patronage of a different sort, that of a leader of an influential Sufi tariqa. Khwaja Ahrar was the spiritual master of the Naqshbandi Sufi order in Central Asia.

Although much of Ahrar's prestige rested on his spirituality as well as on his place in the Naqshbandi *silsila* (Sufi lineage; lit., "chain") as the successor to Mawlana Yaʿqub Charkhi, waqf documents, purchase deeds, narrative stories related in his hagiographies, and correspondence all reveal Ahrar as a major player in the local economy of central Asia, particularly in the regions of Samarkand, Tashkent, and Bukhara. Between 1470 and the year of Ahrar's death in 1490, three trust deeds were established that enumerate his endowments and their beneficiaries, who were Ahrar's male heirs: a madrasa in Samarkand; a mosque and madrasa in Tashkent; and the shrine complex on the outskirts of Samarkand where Ahrar was buried. These endowments encompassed a broad base of economic interests, including cultivable land, mills, gardens, orchards, shops, baths, and houses.

The following text is from is a waqf dated January 25, 1470, for the benefit of Khwaja Ahrar's madrasa at the Suzangaran Gate in Samarkand;[10] it is one of twelve known waqf documents drafted during Ahrar's lifetime.[11] The document illustrates the process by which a founder such as Khwaja Ahrar might establish a family waqf (*waqf ahli*) for the dual benefit of public institutions as well as his own family fortune, since through this and other endowments Khwaja Ahrar was able to establish the future control of the administration and collection of revenues of the endowment for himself and his heirs.

This text is included here as a concrete example of the concern for detail that attended this aspect of Islamic community development set forth in a legally binding document. Note especially the mention of the various major institutions (mosques, madrasas, and khanqahs) that would benefit from revenues dedicated by the endowment. After designating the village of Dayj within the Timurid city of Samarkand as the property in question, the text goes on to delineate in precise detail the boundaries of the waqf property. It specifies well over a dozen parcels of land and holdings of various kinds that are exempted from the terms of the waqf, and then continues:

In such a way the great founder of the waqf [Khwaja Ahrar] made these properties with all rights thereof, their use and subsidiaries into waqf, in all correctness, truthfully, and without fail, during his life and after death, eternal, permanent, may it not be sold, transferred under inheritance or misappropriated. [This waqf is made for the benefit] of a leader in prayer [*imam*], teacher [*mudarris*], and prayer caller [muezzin] of the specified mosque, the building of which is found in the southeast corner of the madrasa.[12] This mosque and madrasa were built by the great founder of the waqf in the protected city of Samarkand, may God safeguard it from harm, in the quarter and neighborhood of the Suzangaran Gate, with the following boundaries.

On the east they adjoin with the public lane through which flows the canal, and from there, the water. The northern boundary of them adjoins the grounds of . . . Amir Yahya, . . . which at the present time is under the control of his heirs. The western and southern boundaries adjoin the *'arsa*, which is the private land of the founder of the waqf [Khwaja Ahrar] with a house of the above-mentioned Khwaja Yahya, and adjoins the public lane and then veers off, turns north, and adjoins with a dead-end lane. Then running diagonally, it turns west and adjoins with the garden and houses of Khwaja Hamid ibn Amirak Qadi. It also adjoins the grounds of Amir Shah Vali ibn Sultan-Vays Barlas. The southern boundary partly [adjoins] with the houses of Mawlana 'Ali Qushchi,* partly with the houses of Ustad Urus . . . and partly with the houses of Mawlana Ahmad 'Ali Khwarazmi, which is at the present time found in the hands of his heirs. Also one other part of that boundary adjoins in this part with the houses of Ustad Baha ad-Din, . . . and partly with the shop that is waqf for use by the mosque of this neighborhood, which is called the mosque of Sayyidzada. It is established that the waqf administrator and supervisor of these waqf properties will be, while alive, the founder of the waqf himself. He will expend whatever God provides him from the income, after payment of royal and state dues and taxes first of all, on the necessary building and repair of the waqf property, and second, for the perpetual repair and fixing of this mosque. What remains from this [let him spend] on the maintenance of a prayer leader, teacher, and prayer caller, whose needs and remuneration shall be determined. Then after, to be used for the benefit of whatever is the wish of the founder of the waqf in the manner he decides, and in the amount he wishes.

To this founder of the waqf, therefore, belong the responsibilities of assigning to the waqf whomever he wants. And if he sees it advisable to change the custodian or change some items and replace others, it is his prerogative. When he hears the call [of death], "Oh, you soul, come back to your Lord" [89:27–28], then the waqf administrator and manager of this [waqf] will be the eldest of the male heirs who is descended from [Ahrar] in the male line, from generation to generation, what comes into being [i.e., who is born] and propagates itself, right up to the Day of Judgment.

It is settled that what incomes remain from these waqf properties after royal and state dues and taxes, let them be divided into sixty portions. Twelve portions will be used, after the evaluation of his needs, to provide for a teacher to be present continually [in the madrasa] under the condition that he be able to recite the Qur'an. Six portions [let be used] for the maintenance of a prayer leader, after evaluating his needs. Three

---

* 'Ala' ad-Din 'Ali Qushchi is the famous astrologer and collaborative worker of the Timurid prince Ulugh Beg.

portions let be spent for the prayer caller under the condition that he renders janitorial services such as shoveling the snow off the mosque's roof, lighting candles, and sweeping the mosque. Let two portions be used for mats and candles for the mosque.

Ten portions [let be used] for the descendants of the manager [of the waqf] for his own expenditures. Nine portions [let be used] for three Qur'an memorizers who should study the Qur'an under the direction of this teacher, on condition that they live in this madrasa. Give to each of these three Qur'an memorizers three portions [of income], for three years. After those three years pass, let them be discharged and, in place of them, assign another three Qur'an memorizers in the described manner, as long as the mosque and waqf properties remain functioning. The remaining eighteen portions should be kept for the time when the mosque and the waqf properties may need construction and repairs, and if repairs are not necessary, then let him buy immovable properties [as-bab] adjoining this waqf [and place them] under the same arrangements. And this descendant also, if he wants to manage the custodial affairs [of the waqf] himself, and if he desires, let him be entrusted with this by the proper person and choose [for himself] compensation from that ten portions . . . set aside for that [purpose], as he sees fit. And order [him] to spend the incomes [of the waqf properties] on the needs of the prayer leader, teacher, and prayer caller under the same arrangements.

And if that mosque is destroyed or emptied of the functionaries in a manner that it cannot return to the previous state, may God prevent that, then [let] him spend the proceeds on the children and the children of the children of the founder of the waqf. And if the heirs cease, may God forbid, and one cannot find any heirs, then let the incomes be shared by the pious poor, as long as the heavens and earth exist. One of the conditions is that he make use of this waqf property in the best way that conforms to the time, and that he does not ever cut them short from whomever takes possession of those lands adjacent with them on an illegal basis and [calls] to change [their fortune]. And so it was, they preserved from a deceptive ruler who disposes himself against the terms [of the waqf]. And if he stands to take charge, then he is the usurper and his repossession [of the waqf] is null and void.

But if someday this waqf has left [the control] of the undertakers and managers which is provided from among the said heirs, may God prevent that from happening, then at that time the *qadi* [judge] of the Muslims will decide, according to the law, to choose a just, modest, pious, and devout [person] to preserve the property. Let him give to him the business of managing [the *awqaf* (=pl. of *waqf*)]. And the measuring of the salary will be in comparison to that set [by the founder]. Whoever changes anything from these conditions will be liable to the wrath of the Creator, suffering terrible torment, and together with Pharaoh and Haman will be plunged into hell. Damnation and abuse will fall to his lot. On the earth may he be lowly and abandoned in tears, remorseful and ashamed by God and people [Q 2:177], and whoever betrays that after that, as he heard, will have sinned. Indeed, "God is all all-hearing and all-knowing" [2:81].

The witnesses of this event [testify that] on Friday, the 22d of the esteemed month of Rajab, may God increase its honor, of the year 874 [=1469] from the Hijra of the Prophet, I ruled on the aforementioned waqf as correct and binding on all those who oversee it under the said condition and clear specification, upon the legitimate and open litigation that came before me by the present litigant [and I] legally grant [in favor of] him in a lawful decision [applicable] in all proceedings. I, reliant upon His forgiveness and taking refuge in the one and only everlasting [God], this lowly one, Abu Mansur Muhammad ibn Muhammad, thank God and pray [to God]. [The document concludes with a list of signatories, witnesses, and eyewitnesses to the document.]

Private Discipline

✳ Shihab ad-Din 'Umar Suhrawardi
Treatises on Sufi Chivalry
LEONARD LEWISOHN

During the twelfth and thirteenth centuries, fraternities of chivalry (*futuwwat*) with their own institutional structure became prevalent throughout Anatolia and Persia. When the Abbasid caliph an-Nasir (1181–1223) attempted to establish a "pan-Islamic *futuwwa*" throughout the entire Muslim East, he had help from an influential ally. Shihab ad-Din Abu Hafs 'Umar Suhrawardi (d. 1234), author of a famous manual of Sufi discipline entitled *The Conduct of Seekers* (*Adab al-muridin*), had also composed two *Treatises on Chivalry* in Persian.[13] In these treatises Suhrawardi incorporated the ethics of Sufism into those of chivalry, thus becoming "the first of a series of writers in Persian to inaugurate a literary category which, in Irano-Turkish territories (and also in Egypt during the Ottoman period) was to continue until the beginning of modern times."[14] The caliph's invitation to neighboring princedoms in the Middle East to join his futuwwat organization gave it the stamp of official state recognition and has, in fact, been termed "the most important historical event in Islamic chivalry. The most important by-product of this political movement was the tradition of Sufi chivalry (*futuwwat-i sufiya*)" espoused by Suhrawardi.[15] By the caliph's patronage, the futuwwat tradition was not totally crushed by the Mongol invasion but continued and underwent a revival in Saljuqid Anatolia, leaving behind an extensive literary legacy on the subject.

Suhrawardi considered chivalry to be the substructure of Sufism. According to his own simile, chivalry was part of the mystic's uniform, the "undershirt" worn below the traditional Sufi "mantle [*khirqa*]."[16] Chivalry and Sufism were considered completely interdependent;[17] the respective institutions of both movements, the "House of Chivalry" (*futuwwat-khana*) and the *khanqah* (see also fig. 37 on a parallel institution, the *tekke*), are held to be closely connected as well.

The House of Chivalry [*futuwwat-khana*] resembles the Khanqah. The master of Chivalry earns his living by his hand, whereas the Khanqah is erected by other people [besides the Sufis], such as princes, kings, and chieftains who enjoy spending their gold in building Khanqahs. . . . The master of Chivalry is also a founder of Khanqahs. The shaykhs and the others who live therein are all his protégés indebted to his services.

All those who enter or leave the Khanqah must benefit from the visit of a master of Chivalry, whether this advantage be food, drink, clothing, alms or knowledge, words of wisdom, instruction in virtue, esoteric lore, or courtesy [*adab*]. The door of both the Khanqah and the House of Chivalry should always be open to guests, who include the poor, foreigners, and traveling students; these should never come to its door and find it closed, for then they would gain no advantage and might depart offended, lacking all benefit from the good things therein. What, then, would be the difference between a ruined building and a Khanqah or a House of Chivalry?[18]

The relationship between Sufism and chivalry is revealed further on in this treatise in Suhrawardi's definition of chivalry where he draws attention to the Sufi contemplative disciplines undergirding the "Way of the Chevalier":

Futuwwat is to make purity of character a way of life, to gird your loins in obedience to the commands of God, not to step aside from the way of the *Shari'at, Tariqat* [Sufi Path], and *Haqiqat* [ultimate reality] . . . to perform the five ritual prayers at their ordained times, and to engage in works of supererogation, night prayers, and fasting. It is to make one's living by the labor of one's own hands, giving a portion of it to one's spouse and another portion to the dervishes and the poor. It is to shut one's eyes to the faults of one's Muslim brothers, lowering one's own head into the bosom of contemplation, beholding reflected in one's own works the events of the age taking place as if looking in a mirror. *Between the man of chivalry and God nothing should become a veil.*[19]

The following excerpts from Suhrawardi's second, and longer, treatise on chivalry, are divided thematically by subtitles.

MERCY AND TOLERANCE

Although many things are permissible according to the Shari'a, but forbidden according to manliness [*muruwwa*] and chivalry [*futuwwa*], this does not mean that chivalry and the Shari'a are opposed to each other. However, the character of the adherents of chivalry is that if someone does ill to them, they do something good to that person in response, while according to the Shari'a, one requites evil with evil.

It is true that there are several moral traits that the Law approves of and condones but that chivalry forbids. Chivalry's disapproval of these moral traits is positively good, for they all relate to sacrificing one's own self-interest and personal share for the sake of another's comfort and convenience. . . . Thus, adherents of chivalry believe that if someone insults you, you should pray for him; if someone deprives you of something, give him something when he is in need; if someone severs his ties with you, adhere to him faithfully and never desert him. If someone hits you, gouges out your eye, or breaks your tooth, forgive him. This is the [true] chivalry and manliness and the essence of God's Word, the Qur'an, for forgiveness stems from divine Mercy while [the seeking to exact] justice belongs to the Law.[20]

Medieval chivalry was clearly and directly modeled on the practice of the companions of the Prophet, in particular, 'Ali, who consistently stressed the spirit of the Law over the letter, thus attempting to defuse conflict and foil litigation that could cause permanent injury to the accused party. Commenting on the altruistic character of 'Ali in various passages of his second treatise, Suhrawardi elaborates this further:

... The Word of God declares, "Retaliation is prescribed for you in the matter of the murdered: freeman for freeman, slave for slave, female for female" [2:178]. Thus, in the era of the Prince of the Believers, 'Ali—may God be content with him—a man who had unjustly slain another man was brought by some people before 'Ali. 'Ali said, "You tell me that the punishment of 'Retaliation . . . in the matter of the murdered' is necessary to be meted out to him as commanded by the Word of God. But you could have interceded for him yourselves, saying, 'Do not take him to task for this crime. This man's destiny was so ordained: in Pre-eternity the Divine Pen had written down this deed; it was the hand of Fate. The Angel of Death arrived, and mounted this person on the horse of ignorance [so that he performed this deed]. Forgive him and let me atone for the blood he has spilled.'" 'Ali himself went to great lengths to intercede for the man, such that if the wounded party refused to accept his intercession, he would offer to pay his blood-money in order to satisfy them. . . . In the end, he made peace between all the opposing parties and resolved the problem.[21]

. . . And if a person had committed theft and was brought before the Commander of the Faithful ['Ali] with proof of his theft, he would first order that his hand be cut off according to the text of the Word of God:

"As for the thief, both male and female, cut off the hands of both. It is the reward of their own deeds, an exemplary punishment from Allah" [5:38], saying, "It is correct that his hand be cut off, but [let us not do so and] forgive him for my sake anyway. Let me atone for his crime, for this thing that he stole was not your divinely allotted portion. This poor man has been afflicted by the tides of fate, and destiny did him a bad turn. Satan tempted him and drove him from the straight path of piety. I myself will pay you back for all the goods he has stolen."

And if they brought a woman to him with the accusation of immoral behavior, 'Ali would never accept anyone's testimony until four just witnesses were produced. However much the witnesses testified against the woman, 'Ali still rejected the testimony and would always demand greater analysis of the evidence. Of course, he would always strive to free the woman from accusation of sinful behavior, although he would go after her, admonish her, and make her afraid. And if, after all, it became necessary to administer the legal punishment required to a woman, he would always revile those who gave witness against her and refuse to ever accept their testimony again, saying, "You have previously given witness to adultery [and legally should not do so again]."[22]

. . . One day, the Commander of the Faithful said to the Prophet: "O Prophet of God, certain people came to visit you today, bringing with them another Muslim. On encountering me, they offered their salutations and stopped. I asked after their business. They told me they were on their way to see you. Again I asked them their business.

"'A man and a woman have committed adultery. We are going to testify against them to the Prophet of God, so that they can be stoned— so that the legal penalty may be properly administered,' they declared.

"'Begone,' I said, 'forsake your testimony! Busy yourselves in some other occupation that gives you some merit in this world and some benefit in the hereafter. What sort of business is it anyway, that you intend?'

"'But,' they contested, 'the command of God is that the adulterer should be scourged by the lash' [cf. 24:2].

"I said, 'Yes, I believe in the Word of God and I verify the word of the Prophet, but if you shut your eyes and turn a blind eye to this, and withdraw your testimony, the spiritual reward will be much greater.'" In this manner I discouraged them, and would not allow them access to the Prophet.

When I had related all of this to the Prophet, he commented: "Your behavior in this matter was delightful to God and myself who am his Prophet. You will receive your just reward for this deed both in this world and in the hereafter on the Plain of the Day of Resurrection when all humankind is denuded [before God]. Because you covered over the sins of those two Muslims, and refused to rend their veil, you will be garbed in the robes of paradise."[23]

HUMANISM, CULTURAL DIVERSITY, AND ARTISTIC SENSITIVITY

One who is a master of chivalry should be well read and a writer, because those who read and write immediately note down whatever they hear and thus advance in understanding, more quickly becoming masters in various branches of knowledge. In this fashion, if such a person is ignorant of a certain subject, he can examine the books of the authorities in the field, studying and learning what he needs to know thereof, educating himself by relying on himself, so that without recourse to anyone else or succumbing to bearing the burden of obligation to another temporal being, he may become an authority in that science and attain all his objectives. However, when he doesn't know how to read and write, he will not reap any advantage from written materials and books and be obliged to learn everything by ear. Even if he is very clever, intelligent, understanding, and intuitive, only a tenth part of what he hears will he remember, and one who lacks understanding and intuition will only recollect one hundredth of what he hears, such that were he to spend his entire life absorbed in learning by ear, his knowledge would still remain incomplete. From the foregoing it is obvious that the foundation of all the arts is the clerical discipline or secretarial art [*dabiri*], for no other art is as highly regarded and appreciated among the kings and princes as this art.

Furthermore, the man of chivalry should strive to learn words in various languages: Arabic, Farsi [*parsi*], Turkish, Persian [*'ajami*], Greek, and Hindi, because the philosophers [*hukama'*] reckon a man by the

number of languages he knows, and this is a commendable art. It always
happens that a man needs to know a certain word, and if he knows that
word and understands its meaning, he accrues great benefit, for it often
happens that one can save oneself from being hurt by an evil or impure
person by use of a single word, while without knowing this word, one is
in danger of losing his head and life.[24]

CHIVALRY AND SUFI CONTEMPLATIVE DISCIPLINES

. . . The master chevalier must be a complete adept in many diverse
arts so that if he finds himself in the company of scholars ['ulama'] and
other professors of chivalry and someone challenges him verbally he can
quickly mount a response to the query such that no one will be able to
find fault with, assail, or belittle his reply. Now, one cannot attain this
except by means of freedom from temporal distractions and total devotion to the effort of realization of these qualities.

[To that end one must be endowed with "eight types of soundness":]

Soundness of soul implies that the knight have control over himself,
that his soul be subject and tame to his command and will, so that the
reins of his soul lie firmly in his grip, being restrained from following
its whims, desires, lusts, and pleasures, else it will become distracted and
accustomed [to following bad habits].

Soundness of the heart is to maintain its conscious presence, while
arrayed with its diverse arts and required virtues, immune from whatever
is impious or outside the bounds of its required obligations, so that it may
be filled with sentiments of love and yearning for God. Now, soundness
of the heart can only be realized when the eye is not permitted to chase
after vain temptations. The eye is the spy of the heart: as long as the eye
does not look, the heart does not know or think. Thus it is apparent that
the malaise of the heart springs from the eye, and whoever can keep his
eyes downcast and prevents himself from staring about wantonly will
keep his heart secure and sound.

Soundness of the tongue is realized through submission to God and
patience. The one who possesses submission to God and patience will be
forbearing and not tremble at every wind, nor become piqued and upset

when he hears angry words. . . . When his tongue is safe and sound, his whole being will be likewise. However, if his tongue is not under control, he will be upset by everything he hears and will lose control of himself with every torment or injustice that he experiences and bewail every hardship or sickness that befalls him. To a question that calls but for a sole reply, such a person provides ten odd answers, and he engages everyone in disputation. Foes of equal mettle he will but goad and prod, while inferior opponents will be abused and suffer from his lack of chivalry, and when confronted with one [who is] superior, he may lose his head. Thus it is evident that the soundness of the tongue arises from patience and submission.

Now, soundness of the ear lies in adherence to the performance of supererogatory works, humility, and presence of the heart, because through prayer and reflection a man remains safe and secure and sound. When an individual is inwardly occupied [with God in his inner being], he will not hear the sound of the harp, cymbals, lute, flute, or organ, for his hearing and consciousness will all be inwardly concentrated on himself. When he passes through some place where lies, calumny, facetious jokes, idle chatter, and tall tales are told—being occupied inwardly with himself, he will hear nothing and, consequently, will hold his peace of mind. However, if a man is lacking in his performance of supererogatory works, humility, and presence of the heart, he will, of course, hear whatever is said, and fresh desires will crop up in his breast with every word he hears, so that every moment he will be inspired to pursue a different whim and satisfy every caprice. Every second he will get offended and will be constantly full of anxiety and grief, forfeiting both his faith and the world.

Another is soundness of the hand. For when the knight is contented, his hand will be safeguarded and under control, and as we said in the beginning, he must arm himself all his days with patience, endurance, and submission. He will be safe from harm as long as patience, endurance, and submission are his raiment, since some of the chevaliers have said: "Chivalry is abandoning pretension; veiling of spiritual truth; and patience under afflictions." In this fashion, he will realize the virtue of contentment without any pain or stress. Hence, it is obvious that the chief [of all the virtues] is endurance. . . .

The soundness of the foot also resembles that of the hand, for the foot is the body's means of conveyance; the hand is the body's servant; the eyes, ears, and sense of touch are the body's spies, whilst the tongue is its interpreter and the heart its sultan. When the spies cease their work of gathering information, the sultan is undisturbed by strangers. However, whenever any of the spies bring him reports and rumors, the sultan becomes anxious and fearful. As a result, sometimes he is full of spite, vengeance, inflamed with wrath. Sometimes he seeks to expand the borders of his kingdom. Sometimes he is ruled by anger and wrath; sometimes by desire for pleasure. Sometimes he gives himself over to enjoyments, glamor, and wealth, and other times he is totally immersed in avarice, greed, and jealousy.

Another requirement is soundness of thought. Thought is the secretary of reason, appointed by the sultan [the heart]. The work of thought is concentration and observation. Although the eye perceives, the heart meditates, thought apprehends, and the understanding retains—while all of these are occupied in their individual affairs—they still need a mount to carry them to their destination. First, the foot becomes a mount and goes along, while the hand grasps and the understanding collects. Again, they need a mount to carry them while [they remain] occupied in their individual affairs. All these functions are interlinked, and the commander of them all is Reason. Reason commands, the heart meditates; thought voyages and brings together; [the power of] judgment retains; Love constructs; and taste receives. Hence, it is obvious that the soundness of all these functions derives from the eye.

Now, whoever possesses soundness of the eye also enjoys ease and security in regard to all the above, whereas if the eye is ailing, then all these other functions suffer, being afflicted with anxiety and fear. As long as the eye does not deliver any news, the body will be safe and sound, but when the eye gazes wantonly about, the entire body will be moved. Reason, however, does not trail behind the eye, since it provides itself with independent instruction without perceiving anything externally; it passes judgment and puts thought into motion and quickens [the power of] Love.[25]

PATRONAGE AND THE ARTS

Women as Patrons of Architecture

In virtually every cultural and political setting, women have been influential patrons of the arts. Islamic law's provision for women's ownership of personal resources has been one ingredient in the mix. Patronage of the arts in general, and of architecture in particular, has on the whole been the province of the wealthy. Women of ruling or princely families have left an impressive, if little-known, record of achievement. Here is a small sample of their impact on material culture in thirteenth-century Ayyubid Syria, fifteenth-century Timurid central Asia, and sixteenth-century Ottoman Turkey.

✳ Sitt ash-Sham of Damascus

STEPHEN HUMPHREYS

Sitt ash-Sham (d. 1220), a sister of the Ayyubid sultan Salah ad-Din (Saladin), endowed two madrasas and a khanqah in Damascus during the late twelfth and early thirteenth centuries. So important was she in the life of the city that she merits the direct attention of one of the age's most famous chroniclers, Abu Shama. Sitt ash-Sham achieved a level of fame unusual even for a royal woman of her day, perhaps as a result of her thirty-five-year widowhood, during which she apparently maintained a good deal of personal independence. Abu Shama's biographical notice accords Sitt ash-Sham a degree of attention equal to that typically lavished on emirs (commanders, princes) or high-ranking legal scholars.

In [the month of] Dhu 'l-Qa'da of this year [1220], Sitt ash-Sham, the daughter of Ayyub ibn Shadhi and the sister of the kings Salah ad-Din and al-'Adil, passed away in Damascus. . . . She is the one after whom the two madrasas in Damascus are named: one of them lies south of the hospital of Nur ad-Din; the other is outside Damascus in the 'Awniya Quarter. The latter is also known as the Husamiya, taking its name from her son Husam ad-Din ibn Lajin. She had buried him there, and she herself was interred in the grave in which he had been placed. Among

Figure 37. The courtyard of the Mevlevi *tekke* (13th–16th cent.) in Konya, Turkey. Conical chimneys mark the individual residential cells of the dervishes. The fountain, originally for ritual ablutions, stands just outside the entrance to what was once a mosque and is now a museum housing the community mausoleum of the seven-hundred-year-old Mevlevi order. Atop the free-standing pillar on the right sits a miniature model of the fluted green conical cupola over the tomb of the order's founder, Jalal ad-Din Rumi. (See also SD figs. 12, 33.)

the three graves, it is the one next to the doorway. . . . Sibt ibn al-Jawzi says: She was first in rank among princesses, intelligent, deeply pious, and greatly devoted to prayer, good works, and alms. Every year thousands of dinars were expended in her residence on the manufacture of potions and medicinal plants, and she would distribute these to the people. Her gate was a refuge of seekers and a sanctuary for those who mourn. She provided a generous endowment for the two madrasas, and she received an impressive funeral.[26]

✳ Works of Timurid and Ottoman Women

During the fourteenth- and fifteenth-century Timurid regime in Iran and central Asia, a number of women commissioned important architectural works or

Figure 38.   Double-domed mausoleum (ca. 1425) in the Shah-i Zinda in Samarkand.

had major monuments named after them. In the city of Samarkand, not far from the properties described in the waqf of Khwaja Ahrar above, a curious necropolis called Shah-i Zinda ("The Living King") includes some two dozen funerary structures dated 1360–1405, most of which were built by and for women. Tradition had long ago identified one double-domed structure, built ca. 1435 (fig. 38), as the tomb of Timur's wet nurse, Ulja Aym, and her daughter, Bibi Seneb. Although in more recent times scholars declared the inhabitant to be Qazizada Rumi, one of Ulugh Beg's astronomers, excavations made in this century discovered only the bodies of women buried there, restoring credibility to the ancient tradition. The inscription on the drum of the larger dome is a hadith: "The Prophet said, upon him be prayer and peace, 'The tomb is the least dwelling of the dwellings of the Afterlife, and the best of the dwellings in this world.'"[27]

In the same city, tradition has it, Timur Lang named one of the largest mosques ever constructed (1399–1404, approx. 350 by 500 feet) in honor of his Chinese princess, Bibi Khanum (fig. 39). Actually, the building was constructed under Timur's first wife, Saray Mulk Khanum.[28] Around the tiled drum run the repetitive phrases "God alone endures" (lit., "To God [belongs] survival") in large Kufic script and, in smaller script, "To God [belongs] power."

Women of sixteenth- and seventeenth-century Ottoman Turkey made major contributions to the history of religious architecture. Sultan Suleyman the

Figure 39.   Mosque of Bibi Khanum in Samarkand (ca. 1399).

Magnificent's daughter Mihrimah Sultan was one of the world's richest women in the late 1500s. She was not only a princess, but functioned as *valide sultan* (equivalent to "Queen Mother") to her younger brother Selim II (r. 1566–1574) after their parents had died. In Ottoman Turkey, the valide sultan traditionally had access to considerable economic resources and often funded major architectural projects. Mihrimah Sultan's most famous foundations are the two Is-

Figure 40.   Mihrimah Sultan Mosque (1565–1570), Istanbul.

tanbul-area mosque complexes that bear her name, both designed by her father's chief architect, Sinan. Mihrimah's mosque at the Edirne Gate, at the western wall of the old city of Istanbul, was one of Sinan's most imaginative de-
signs, using new support systems and lateral spaces to increase the area available
for windows (fig. 40).

Safiye Sultan, wife of Murad III (r. 1572–1595) and mother of Mehmet III
(r. 1595–1603), also made an important contribution to the architectural heritage of Istanbul. With Safiye, moreover, begins the "Era of Women's Reign"
in Ottoman history. At the edge of the Golden Horn stands the Yeni Valide
("New Sultan-Mother's") mosque complex, designed by Sinan's successor as
imperial architect, Davut Agha, begun in 1598 and completed in 1663 (fig. 41).
The last of the monumental mosques designed in the classical style, the Yeni
Valide had a long genesis: it took three valide sultans and three chief architects
to see it to completion. Ülkü Bates sums up architectural patronage by Ottoman
women this way: "While the buildings commissioned by women lacked the
grandiose dimensions of buildings commissioned by men and were built in less
important sections of the city, they are significant in number and in innovations not generally found in the more monumental but conservative royal structures undertaken by men."[29]

Figure 41.   Yeni Valide Mosque (ca. 1625–1650), Istanbul.

Building Community and Community Patronage

✳   Architectural Past, Present, and Future in America

New Muslim communities continue to spring up all over the world. One can get a good sense of how this trend is manifested by looking at the architectural history of relatively recent American Muslim communities, such as that of Toledo, Ohio. The local Muslim community there began with a simple structure with a modest dome in the heart of the city (fig. 42), but has grown into the new Islamic Center of Greater Toledo on Interstate 75 in Perrysburg, Ohio (fig. 43). When circumstances allowed for a grander design, architects looked to Turkey for inspiration. The classic Ottoman mosque of Selim I (fig. 44), with its large central dome over a roughly cubic hall and twin minarets flanking the prayer hall, suggests itself as one of many possible models. Plans for the future envision a complete mosque complex, not unlike the great Ottoman architectural ensembles, including residential and educational facilities. An architectural model (fig. 45) shows the existing mosque in the foreground, a planned educa-

Figure 42.   An early mosque (mid–20th cent.) in Toledo, Ohio.

tional facility on the left, residential facilities on the right, and a multipurpose building in the background.

Chronicles of Royal Patronage

Accounts of the accomplishments of men with political power are by far the most numerous records of patronage. From fourteenth-century North Africa comes the following chronicle of the achievements of the chronicler's own patron. The works of fifteenth-century Timurid princes of central Asia, one extolled by a later historian and the other speaking for himself, are the subject of this part's final entries.

✳ Ibn Marzuq
Sultan Abu 'l-Hasan 'Ali's Architectural Patronage

JONATHAN M. BLOOM

Shams ad-Din Abu 'Abdallah Muhammad ibn Marzuq al-'Ajisi at-Tilimsani was born in the city of Tilimsan (now Tlemcen in western Algeria; see map) in 1310

Figure 43.   New Islamic Center of Greater Toledo (1980s), Perrysburg, Ohio.

or 1311 to a family of distinguished clerics who had been active for centuries in the religious, political, and literary life of North Africa. As a youth he traveled widely with his father throughout the great cities of the central Islamic lands, studied in Cairo, and preached his first sermon extemporaneously at the age of nineteen in the mosque of Alexandria. At the age of twenty-two or twenty-four he returned to the land of his birth and was appointed preacher in the mosque of al-ʿUbbad, the shrine outside Tlemcen associated with the famous North African Sufi Abu Madyan Shuʿayb (commonly called "Sidi Bu Medienne," d. 1197–1198) and private secretary to the sultan. After a brief exile in Granada, Ibn Marzuq was recalled to the Marinid court at Fez in 1353 and made a court official. During the following two decades he served in various capacities as he went in and out of favor with rulers.

One of his most important works, *The Correct and Fine Traditions About the Glorious Deeds of our Master Abu ʾl-Hasan (Musnad as-sahih al-hasan fi maʾathir mawlana Abi ʾl-Hasan)* discusses the distinguishing qualities of the sultan, his court, and the works undertaken during his reign. Following contemporary practice for this genre of literature, each chapter is usually divided into two or three parts, the first almost always containing examples drawn from the life of the Prophet and the early caliphs as well as general observations about the quality under discussion. Ibn Marzuq's text presents a contemporary ap-

Figure 44.   Mosque of Selim I (1522), Istanbul.

preciation of the patronage of religious architecture in the Muslim west of the fourteenth century. It is unusually valuable because many of the examples he cites as glories of Marinid art are those that survive to this very day.[30]

THE MUSNAD OF IBN MARZUQ

Chapter 40: His Construction of Congregational
Mosques, Mosques, and Minarets

[Section 2] On the importance that he—may God be pleased with him—

Figure 45.   Architectural model of future plans for the Islamic Center of Greater Toledo.

gave to construction of this type and on the considerable expenses that he incurred.

This was his [i.e., Abu 'l-Hasan's] preoccupation during his emirate and his caliphate. He is responsible for splendid monuments and numerous constructions in the city of Fez, may God protect it! such as the Mosque of the Coppersmiths[31] and the mosque known as "Shave the Sheep,"[32] both of them quite big, spacious, and having very high and handsome minarets, as well as several [other] mosques and minarets. The same was the case in the White City [New Fez], in al-Mansura near Ceuta,* where he had a magnificent congregational mosque and minaret built adjacent to the auspicious palace. He also erected innumerable smaller mosques in Tangier, Sale, Chella (which was particularly fine),[33] the Qasba of Taza, Meknes, and Marrakesh.

As for the monuments that he erected in the city of Tlemcen, they are such that one hopes God will preserve their forms and rejuvenate their

* A new city that Abu Saʿid began to build in 729/1328–1329.

remains; their like was not previously seen nor their form heretofore obtained in any land.[34] Among them is the congregational mosque of the Qasba, the incomparable qualities of which include the beauty of its placement, excellence of its form, organization of its galleries, equilibrium of its courtyard, handsomeness of the views, running waters, spaciousness of its courts, elegance of silver and copper fittings, and its splendid *minbar* [pulpit].

As for the Great Mosque [of al-Mansura outside of Tlemcen], all those who have traveled agree that they never saw anything like it; this mosque is not a bit inferior to the perfect beauty of the Umayyad mosque [in Damascus]; and if the Mosque of al-Mansur in Marrakesh, the fame of which is proverbial, covers a larger area, the richness of the marbles and the equilibrium of its proportions make it more marvelous and more beautiful. No other minaret in the east or the west can be compared to it. I have ascended it several times with the emir Abu ʿAli an-Nasir, the latter—may God have mercy on him!—on horseback and I on my mule, from the bottom to the top: one would have said that we were riding on flat ground. This minaret stands above the north portal of the mosque and contains two passages by which one ascends to the top. It was constructed with skill, from cut stone sculpted with different motifs on each side. I saw the shaft on which the globes [above the lantern] are mounted: it is of iron and resembles the mast of a ship. As for the chandelier [in the mosque], it was I who was charged with having it made and who inscribed the date on the lower part of it, in my own handwriting, as one can still see in the congregational mosque of Tlemcen. This chandelier contains approximately one thousand oil lamps. I believe that the total weight is inscribed on the base, as well as an estimation of its volume.[35]

As for the minbar, all craftsmen at that time declare that nowhere in the world was the equivalent ever made. They agree that the minbar of [the mosque of] Cordova and the minbar of the Booksellers' [Mosque] in Marrakesh are the most remarkable in craftsmanship, because it is not customary for easterners to have fine woodwork in their buildings.[36] A number of fragments from the Cordova minbar have appeared [in the Maghrib] and these have been compared with those from the Tlemcen

minbar. The latter does not suffer in comparison. It has carved pieces
of wood the size of a hazelnut or a chickpea, and encrustation's of about
the size of a grain of wheat: to see it, one is amazed. God will demand an
account of one who causes the ruin of his masterpieces and chastise him
because he destroyed monuments in which all the people of Islam took
glory and which would have illustrated religion for eternity.

[Abu 'l-Hasan also had] many mosques [built in Tlemcen]. Among
them are the mosques at the gates of al-Maghaz, Hunayn, and Fez.
For the aforementioned Great Mosque, he ordered a water channel that
passed underground in a conduit from the outskirts of town and at the
same time fed several fountains.

Among the mosques is the one that he had built in the city of
Hunayn.* The site was purchased under my supervision; it was a congregational mosque and the minaret there was high and elegant. We bought
the necessary land for a considerable sum from the surplus of the former
mosque; [the land destined for] the extension of the congregational
mosque of Algiers was similarly purchased.

As for the mosque that Abu 'l-Hasan had constructed near the tomb
of the Shaykh of Shaykhs, the Model of the Modern Imams among Sufis,
Abu Madyan Shu'ayb ibn al-Hasan—may God have mercy on him!—it
is of splendid form and imposing and solid aspect.[37] Abu 'l-Hasan spent
an enormous sum on this purpose. And it was built under the supervision
of my paternal uncle, the twin of Abu Salih, Abu 'Abdallah Muhammad
ibn Muhammad ibn Abi Bakr ibn Marzuq, and me. It had the most marvelous details of construction: in fact its entire ceiling is composed of
interlocking forms of stamps and woodwork motifs, every design different from the other [fig. 46]. The whole is carved in the fashion of mar-
quetry panels of such a sort that one does not doubt it for a moment and
one truly imagines that these motifs were worked in wood and put into
place when finished, when in fact they are entirely made of solid masonry
of brick and plaster.

This mosque also contains a minbar of remarkable form: it is made of
sandalwood, ivory, and ebony, the whole gilded. I have already described

* Abu 'l-Hasan's army took this city in 736/1336.

Figure 46.   ʿUbbad Mosque prayer hall, Tlemcen, Algeria (early 14th cent.). Photo by Jonathan Bloom.

the ornament on the base of this minbar. As for the northern door that opens on the stairs by which one descends to the tomb of the shaykh—may God have mercy on him!—and to the street, it is a portal of bronze, comprising two valves [i.e., halves of a double door] each of which is plated with bronze, pierced and engraved with polygons combining one with the other; different colors of bronze were used. It is a marvel that travelers do not neglect to notice. To make these two valves, the copper-smiths had to use about 700 dinars of gold coin. That is at least how much I had to provide myself, quite apart from the cost of the copper, iron, timber and colors. Above the stairs is a vault of *muqarnas* [stalactite] work [fig. 47]; it is of unusual form with few parallels. The minaret is also most handsome. Each of its four faces presents decoration different from that on the three other sides. The making and gilding of the balls on its finial cost 370 gold dinars. May God give the sultan the profit of these constructions, cover him with his favors and recompense!

As for mosques in *zawiyas* [see below] and in all other cities and stations, there is no exact count [because they are so numerous]. Let us confine ourselves to the several monuments of which we have spoken, because our desire is to be brief in this work!

Chapter 41: Construction of Madrasas by Abu 'l-Hasan

[Section 2] We have already said that the construction of madrasas was unknown in the Maghrib up until the time when our master, the Warrior for the Faith, the Pious King [Abu Yusuf] constructed that of the Halfaʾiyyin in the Qarawiyyin quarter of Fez.[38] Then our master the sultan Abu Saʿid, father of our Imam—may God have mercy on him!—constructed the ʿAttarin madrasa and the madrasa of New Fez with the help of his son—may God have mercy on him. The latter—may God the Almighty profit from it!—then founded an elegant madrasa in the ʿAdwa, that is the Andalus quarter of Fez; it is known as the Sahrij madrasa.* Then he erected the large madrasa known as the Madrasat al-Wadi [i.e., of the river valley] because its center crosses the principal stream of the ʿAdwa [river]. Then he erected the madrasa standing to the north of the Qarawiyyin mosque and which is known as the Madrasa Misbah after the person charged with instruction there.† This man—may God have mercy on him!—was also known as al-Kurras ["the note-

---

* It is thus known because of the pool (Ar., *sahrij*) in the center of the courtyard. It was completed by Abu 'l-Hasan in 1323, while his father was still living.
† It is also known as the Madrasa Misbahiya and the Madrasat al-Rukham, because of its white marble basin; it was completed in 747/1346–1347. The teacher, Abu 'd-Diyaʾ Misbah ibn ʿAbdallah al-Yalsuti, died at Fez in 750/1349–1350.

Figure 47.   'Ubbad Mosque, portal dome, Tlemcen, Algeria. Photo by Jonathan Bloom.

book"], because during his class every morning he read his citations from a notebook [instead of reciting them from memory].

Then Abu 'l-Hasan—may God have mercy on him!—built madrasas in every city of the far and central Maghrib. He first built the fine madrasa in old Taza, and in Meknes, Sale [fig. 48],* Tangier, Ceuta, Anfa, Azemmour, Safi, Aghmat, Marrakesh, al-Qasr al-Kabir, al-'Ubbad outside of Tlemcen near the mosque which we have already described, and at Algiers, the madrasas being of different importance depending on the size of the locality. The madrasa of Ceuta is beautiful, but the finest is that of Marrakesh, followed by that of Meknes.† All of them have wonderful construction, marvelous workmanship, numerous masterpieces, carved plasters, pavements of varicolored fine tiles, varied marbles, artistically carved wood, and abundant water.

One must also add the endowments he established to keep up and

* Opposite the Great Mosque, it was constructed in 742/1340–1341.
† The madrasa of Ceuta, like all that city's Islamic monuments, has disappeared. The madrasa in Marrakesh was replaced in the sixteenth century by the beautiful Ben Yusuf Madrasa. That of Meknes is known today as the Bu 'Inaniya after Abu 'l-Hasan's son Abu 'Inan, who completed it.

Figure 48.   Madrasa, Sale, Morocco (early 14th cent.). Photo by Jonathan Bloom.

maintain each of these madrasas in the best condition, for repairs, for salaries for the professors, fellows, manager, doorman, muezzin, imam, administrator, witnesses, and servants. That which remained after these were paid was set aside. This enumeration allows the reader to understand the sums necessary for each of these madrasas. With that, he also gave to most of these establishments a selection of precious [i.e., religious] books and literary works. There is no doubt that this was the reason that knowledge grew and its practitioners flourished during his reign. The rewards of the master and of the disciple will be weighed in the scale of good deeds, may God make it so! Furthermore, in the east a single madrasa or similar foundation preserves the memory of a sovereign; but how many individuals did he support until their end by these foundations? An authentic tradition of the Prophet—may God bless him and save him!—on this subject states: "When a man dies, his earthly deeds are over except in three cases: perpetual alms, a pious work from which others derive good, and a good son invoking God in his father's favor." Nothing is better than the perpetual works he left. May God Almighty accept them and grant him mercy!

Chapter 42: Abu 'l-Hasan's Construction of Zawiyas

[Section 3] A zawiya is known as a ribat or a khanqah in the east. This last term, which has the same meaning as ribat, is a Persian word. In the terminology of ascetics, the word *ribat* has the connotation of devoting oneself entirely to jihad and guarding the frontiers [of Islam]. For Sufis, the word has a different meaning, namely the place where one retreats to worship God.

[Section 4] It is clear that among us in the Maghrib, zawiyas are places designed to shelter travelers and to nourish voyagers. As for ribats, in the sense in which this term is employed in the east, I have only seen two in the Maghrib: the ribat of Sayyidi Abu Muhammad Salih [at Safi]* and the zawiya of Sayyidi Abu Zakariya Yahya ibn 'Umar† —may God benefit

* This mystical figure, a disciple of Abu Madyan of Tlemcen, died in 631/1234.
† This man, better known by his common name, Sidi Buzekri, died in the first half of the eighth century at his zawiya in Sale.

him!—in Sale, to the west of the Great Mosque. I have not seen a third foundation of the same type in the country, with men staying there to live, and resembling, by the life they lead, those of whom I have already written.

Chapter 43: Construction of Hospitals by Abu 'l-Hasan

Our Imam—may God have mercy on him!—completely restored the hospital of the city of Fez as well as others. This is a place for the treatment and care of the sick. The men of the east take a great interest in these establishments. Our master—may God have mercy on him!—was very interested in them, and after him, his son Mawlay Abu 'Inan—may God have mercy on him!—took up the tradition. And in this, the son was the worthy successor to his father.

✳ Khwandamir
The Rediscovery and Refurbishment of 'Ali's Tomb
WHEELER M. THACKSTON

From what Ibn Marzuq calls "the East" comes another historical chronicle of royal patronage. Timurid-era historian Ghiyath ad-Din Khwandamir's (1475–ca. 1535) universal history *Beloved of Careers on the History of Human Individuals (Habib as-siyar fi akhbar afrad al-bashar,* 1523–1524) represents a distillation of the major histories and chronicles of the period, including that of his grandfather Mirkhwand (ca. 1433–1498), the *Garden of Purity (Rawdat as-safa).* Khwandamir includes accounts of scores of famous figures, religious and political, as well as anecdotes about important events and places. The following story describes the patronage of the Timurid ruler Sultan-Husayn Mirza (1438–1506) and Prince Mirza Bayqara (d. 1486) in the renovation of a holy site, the tomb of Muhammad's son-in-law 'Ali, the first Shi'i Imam. The events take place in the environs of the Timurid capital of Herat, in present-day Afghanistan (see map). By including an anecdote about a charlatan intent on exploiting people's faith for his own gain, Khwandamir highlights the religious importance of the place by situating it in the context of the life and practice of believing Muslims of his day. The story also suggests the importance of local patronage in the form of spontaneous generosity on the part of pilgrims to the shrine.[39]

THE DISCOVERY OF THE HEAVENLY SHRINE ATTRIBUTED
TO THE KING OF MEN IN THE VILLAGE OF KHWAJA KHAYRAN

In the year 885 [1480], when Mirza Bayqara had unfurled the banner
of rule and governance in Balkh, there emerged from the realm of the
unseen a wonderful occurrence, a compendious description of which
follows.

A mystic, Shams ad-Din Muhammad by name, whose lineage went
back to the great saint Abu Yazid Bistami [d. 874], went during the
aforementioned year from Kabul to Balkh [see map]. There granted an
interview with Mirza Bayqara, he produced a history composed during
the time of Sultan Sanjar ibn Malikshah the Saljuqid, in which it was
written that the tomb of the King of Saints, the Conquering Lion of
God, the Prince of the Faithful, 'Ali ibn Abi Talib, was in a certain place in
the village of Khwaja Khayran. Accordingly Mirza Bayqara gathered the
sayyids, qadis, and nobles of Balkh and, taking counsel with them, went
to that village, which was three parasangs* from Balkh. In the very place
indicated in the book he found a dome in which there was a tomb. He
ordered the tomb excavated, and when, in obedience to his command,
a little had been dug away, suddenly a tablet of white stone appeared on
which was written: "This is the tomb of the Lion of God, brother of God's
Apostle, 'Ali Friend of God." Of course, great shouts from all present
went up to highest heaven, and everyone rubbed the forehead of supplication in that sacred dust and distributed alms to the poor.

As the news of this [discovery] spread far and wide, those afflicted
with chronic disease turned hopefully to that threshold to paradise. As
related by those who were there, many of that group were immediately
cured, and returned to their homes with their wishes fulfilled. Naturally,
more throngs of commoners and elites alike gathered at that sacred spot
than could be imagined, and so much money and valuables were brought
as propitiatory gifts that the mind would be dazzled by the very existence
of so much gold and jewelry.

When Mirza Bayqara realized the situation, he sent a courier on wings

---

* Parasang: an ancient Persian measure equivalent to about 3.4 miles.

of lightning to the capital, Herat, to give a report to the court officials.
When His Victorious Majesty learned of the contents of the report,
he was astonished by such an occurrence and, girding his loins with a
pilgrim's garb, set out for that focal point of hopes and desires with a host
of officials. Upon arrival he performed the rites of supplication and devotion and had a dome of consummate height and vastness built over that
holy tomb. Around it he caused gates and outbuildings to be constructed,
and in the village he founded a market containing shops and a bath. One
of the canals of Balkh, which is now called Nahr-i Shahi [Royal River],
he endowed to the shrine. As dean of the shrine he appointed Sayyid Taj
ad-Din Hasan Andkhuyi, a relative of Sayyid Baraka known for his piety
and lofty station, and the office of shaykh he delegated to the Shaykhzada
Bistami* to supervise the endowments and donations. Thereupon His
Majesty returned to the capital, safely reaching Herat, where he opened
the gates of liberality and generosity to military and civilian subjects alike.

To return to the narrative, when the discovery of the royal tomb by
virtue of His Majesty's going there and the establishment of structures
and the appointment of endowments became known far and wide, everyone who was in the least able set out for that place, and for a while the
coming and going of people to that "threshold of the Ka'ba" was such
that every year nearly one hundred Kepeki tumans in cash and goods
were brought in donation; and the dean, shaykh, and employees of the
shrine spent all the money in housing and feeding those who came, in
salaries, and in maintaining the buildings. The village of Khwaja Khayran
flourished until it became a veritable metropolis, and in a short time the
environs of the shrine became so populous that there is no way to say or
write a description of it.

However, a master of deceit and deception, a carriage driver in Herat,
imagined that he would fabricate a vision and, deceiving the people,
would acquire gold and gems by means of a fake shrine and thus attain
the ranks of the wealthy. One evening at Gazargah, near the shrine
of [Khwaja 'Abd Allah] Ansari, he began to shout and tear his clothing.
People gathered around him and asked what the matter was.

* The Shams ad-Din mentioned at the beginning of the text.

"Just now four men in the guise of Arabs on Arabian horses appeared to me in the fields. They said that the tomb of the King of Saints was in that place," he said as he indicated a platform near the enclosure of Shams ad-Din Sangtarash. The people accompanied the carriage driver to the platform, and immediately a large group of qalandars* and tabara'is† gathered around and, making the platform in the form of a grave, began to cry out and shout. The next day when the news reached Herat, everybody, men and women alike, headed out to Gazargah, where they treated the carriage driver like a saint. They showered him with all they had, and that deceiver, taking dirt from the grave, bestowed a little upon all he wished to, taking in exchange a lot of gold and jewelry. When people heard that the Imam's tomb had been discovered, a huge throng, especially the sick and ill, came to that spot to present gifts and make supplication. When a lame or blind person came to the grave and threw himself upon the ground, the qalandars and followers of the carriage driver would ask him whether his illness had been cured. If he said yes, they would cry out in thanksgiving, raise him up, and shout at the top of their voices. If, however, he said that his affliction was unchanged, they would kick and stomp on the poor fellow, saying, "He is a skeptic, a hypocrite, and should be executed and burned!"

In short, within ten or fifteen days the carriage driver had amassed in donations more gold, gems, and valuables than could be imagined and had become the spiritual leader of vast numbers of commoners and nobles alike. Other dishonest people, too, had like notions of fabricating such visions, and each of them, in some place or other, both inside and outside of Herat, as well as in other provinces, broadcast news of the discovery of the Imam['s bones]. The carriage driver, realizing how things were and fearing disgrace, withdrew.

The falsehood of those people was clear to His Victorious Majesty and the nobles of Herat, and Mawlana Kamal ad-Din Shaykh Husayn was charged with chastising them. He arrested most of them and had them flogged. Some he jailed until the brouhaha died down. Never again did

* Antinomian dervishes, generally considered disreputable.
† The ill and afflicted who seek healing at a shrine.

the embers of such a false notion sparkle in idle minds. However, the holy shrine at Khwaja Khayran flourishes until today and is circumambulated by throngs of people from near and far. And God knows best the truth of all affairs.

✳ Sultan-Husayn Mirza
Apologia
WHEELER M. THACKSTON

Rulers also occasionally composed their own accounts of their patronage. Sometime in the late fifteenth century (between 1485 and 1492), Sultan-Husayn Mirza, the last effective Timurid sovereign, wrote a defense of his regime. The text, written in Chaghatay Turkish, reviews his patronage of all the arts, from literature to painting to architecture. In this excerpt the shah reflects on the architectural glories of his time:

In the time of some, tyrannical ministers and wrong-thinking potentates wrecked the pious foundations and, spending the proceeds on debauchery and entertainment, have indulged in ungodliness and sacrilege. However, the overseers appointed to the foundations have repaired all the damage and gladdened the people of merit. Because in former times the foundations were in ruins, students were aggrieved and teachers deprived; but now, thank God, there are in the capital [Herat] nearly one hundred educational institutions where religious learning and certain knowledge are to be found. From the farthest reaches of Anatolia to the borders of China, capable students from all the lands of Islam, hearing of the limitless [opportunity for] study, choose the hardship of exile from their homes and turn their faces to this imperial city. Of God's favor all expenses are met by the income of the foundations, and they pass their days in freedom from want. Near the above-mentioned places is a khanqah, in every corner of which those in need are tended to and those deserving receive a portion [of good things].

If, in former days, traveling merchants, other strangers and wayfarers had insurmountable difficulty going from their homes to their destinations because of brigands and highway robbers, now swift retribution has rid the realm of the chaff of that God-forsaken group's existence and dispatched them to hellfire. At every stage there are lofty caravanserais for travelers and towering fortresses to provide safety for wayfarers where they may find protection from the cold and shade from the heat. . . .

If, during the time of some, mosques were allowed to go to rack and ruin, and the congregations were held captive by brutes, in my time the amount [spent] on mosques would be beyond reckoning of accountants, and the congregations can scarcely fit inside, every spot therein being as resplendent as the sanctuary at the glorious Ka'ba.[40]

Figure 49.   Dara Shikoh with Mian Mir and Mulla
Shah, album painting, India (ca. 1635, Mughal). Mulla
Shah (d. 1661) was a disciple of Mian Mir (d. 1636); the
Mughal prince Dara Shikoh met Mulla Shah when the
prince and his wife took counsel with Mian Mir in 1635
after their first child died. Dara and his sister thereafter
became disciples of Mulla Shah. Washington, DC: Sackler
Gallery, Smithsonian Institution, S86.432.

6 Pedagogy
Fanning Spark into Flame

ADVANCED INTERPRETATION OF FOUNDATIONAL ISSUES

Muslims have addressed pedagogical concerns on several levels. Even the most fundamental tenets of the faith require further exploration into their deeper meanings. Part 2 above includes several texts whose content is clearly pedagogical, affording Muslims basic information about a variety of topics and activities. Part 3 illustrates the role of exemplary figures in moral exhortation and religious education generally. The first selection below combines both of these elements within a cultural setting already long and deeply Islamicized. It teaches theological and devotional fundamentals by reflecting on one of the divine names, All-Forgiving, whose meaning is essential to spiritual well-being, and it illustrates those reflections by showing the implications of an understanding of that divine name in the lives of two paradigmatic individuals, Adam and Muhammad. The second selection sets out to instruct Muslims about God and about the meaning of Adam as well, but it does so within a cultural context that poses major challenges for the teacher, requiring him to "translate" concepts into terms his fellow Chinese will recognize from their ancient heritage. Then from Southeast Asia comes still another example of pedagogy across cultures, a text that translates Islamic teaching from Arabic into Javanese.

* Teaching Islam in Medieval Iran
Ahmad Sam'ani's Refreshment of Spirits

WILLIAM C. CHITTICK

Ahmad Sam'ani, who died in 534/1140, belonged to a family of famous scholars from Nishapur in Iran. Little is known of his life, though he is reported to have been an eloquent preacher. His eloquence comes out strongly in the one work that he is known to have written, *The Refreshment of Spirits in Explain-*

ing the Names of the All-Conquering King (Rawh al-arwah fi sharh asma'al-malik al-fattah.) This six-hundred-page Persian work fits into a long line of commentaries on the "most beautiful names of God." These are works written by Muslim scholars with the aim of explaining the significance of the many names that are attributed to God in the Qur'an, names such as Merciful, Majestic, Powerful, Loving, and Forgiving. By stressing God's softness and gentleness rather than his rigor and might, Sam'ani brings out an aspect of Islamic teachings that is often missed in theological works. His constant appeal to God's mercy, along with his frequent use of anecdotes and poetry to make his point, brings him into line with many of the great Sufi teachers of Islamic history, such as his contemporary Rashid ad-Din Maybudi, author of a major Persian commentary on the Qur'an, and Jalal ad-Din Rumi. The following is a complete translation of Sam'ani's commentary on one divine name.[1] The author's occasional use of various forms of rhetorical address ("O noble youth," for example) connects this piece formally with pedagogical genres to be exemplified later in Part 6.

The famous hadith "God's mercy takes precedence over His wrath" sums up the theme. Sam'ani asks his readers to recognize their own nothingness in the face of God. Human poverty and indigence is a great saving grace, for it calls down God's mercy. When people recognize their own nothingness, they can simultaneously recognize God's blessings and kindness toward them, even in the midst of the inevitable suffering they undergo in the world. In Sam'ani's view, the real significance of Adam's fall is that he prepared the way for all his children to enter into God's mercy and kindness. Sam'ani illustrates the parallels between Adam in his fall, Muhammad in his hijra, and the individual spirit of each and every one of us in its descent into this world—all this has occurred so that God can spread his mercy and forgiveness. The text begins:

God is "the Ever-forgiving" [*ghaffar*] and "the Forgiver" [*ghafir*]. Both "All-forgiving" [*ghafur*] and "Ever-forgiving" [*ghaffar*] denote intensive meanings, like "Ever-knowing" [*'allam*]. The literal meaning of [the Arabic word for] "to forgive" is "to cover."

God's forgiveness is that He covers His servants, conceals their misdeeds, and pardons their sins. This concealing and pardoning is through an excellence of God, not an excellence of the servants. Moreover, in reality, just as your acts of disobedience need concealing, so also your acts of obedience need concealing. If the blights of your acts of obedience were brought forward, you would fear obedience more than you fear disobedience.

Muhammad said, "Verily I ask forgiveness from God one hundred times a day." The skirt of prophecy was far too pure for the dust of disobedience and the dirt of slips to settle upon it, so he asked forgiveness [even] for his obedience.

Rabi'a 'Adawiya used to say, "I ask forgiveness from God for my lack of truthfulness in saying, 'I ask forgiveness from God for my lack of sincerity in my activity.'"

'A'isha the truthful relates as follows: "I asked Muhammad the meaning of the verse 'Those who give what they give, their hearts quaking' [23:60]. Is that someone who fornicates, steals, drinks wine, and then fears? He replied, 'No, that is someone who prays, fasts, gives alms, and then fears that these will not be accepted.'"

O noble youth! There are two veils. One is lifted—and may it never be let down! The other is let down—and may it never be lifted! The veil that is lifted is the veil of disavowal. It has been lifted from the hearts of those who profess unity [*tawhid*] and from the breasts of the faithful. The veil that is let down is the veil of generosity before the acts and works of the disobedient, the obedient, the ever-truthful, the God-wary, and the sincere.

O poor soul! Because of the decree of the eternal severity, the veil of generosity was lifted from before the works of Iblis, and they all became disobedience. All his knowledge was made deaf and dumb, and God's beginningless knowledge began to speak. But because of the decree of sheer gentleness, the veil of pardon was let down over Adam's slip and God spoke in intercession for him: "Adam forgot, and We found in him no constancy" [20:115].

O noble youth! It is His concealment that allows us to greet each other and pass our days with each other. God forbid that He should lift this concealment! Fathers would cut themselves off from their sons, and mothers from their children.

> Were the veil to be lifted from our activities,
>   I fear we would not be let into the brothels.

I wonder at the sanctimonious empty-head who recites two cycles of prayer at night and the next day knits the knot of self-satisfaction in his brow and acts as if heaven and earth are beholden to his existence. The atoms of existence say to him, "What a simpleton you are! It is here that they make a Kaʿba into an idol-temple, turn a seven-hundred-thousand-year worshipper into a Satan forever accursed, and bind in a kennel for dogs Balaam son of Beor—who had God's greatest name in his breast and whose every prayer was answered."*

> O you who have no clue to the work of this turning world!
> You're a drunken fool who knows Me not for who I am.

What is needed is someone who verifies the Truth, not someone who is obnoxiously sanctimonious. Anyone who speaks about his own works and looks at them for a single day will not achieve what we are speaking of. The obnoxiously sanctimonious recite two cycles of prayer at night and the next day want the whole world to hear about it. As for those who verify the Truth, they fill the east and the west with sincere prostration and then sink back into the water of displaying no needs.

A great one said, "I examined all my days, and in my whole life I had not committed more than forty sins. I repented from each sin three hundred thousand times, but I still walk in danger."

If you could ascribe nothing to yourself, you would be fine.

Abu 'l-Hasan Kharraqani[†] has some astounding words. He said, "If tomorrow You raise me from the earth and make the creatures present in that standing place, I will go to the Ocean of Oneness and dive into that Ocean so that the One may be, and Abu 'l-Hasan may not be."

Strive so that you may be angry with yourself for one day from morning till night, and see what the day will bring! These great men who came into this path fought a war with their own egos, a war that had no way to peace, for they found their egos opposed to religion. How can those who have religion be at peace with those who are opposed to it? Sometimes they described the ego as a dumb beast, sometimes as a

---

* The story of Balaam, a diviner whose prayers were always answered and who was asked by the king to pray against Moses and the Israelites, is found in the Hebrew Bible (mainly Numbers 22–24). The reference to Balaam entering among the dogs is derived from commentaries on a brief reference to him in Qurʾan 7:175–176.

† Abu 'l-Hasan (d. 1033) was a Sufi teacher known for his bold sayings addressed to God.

serpent, sometimes as a dog, sometimes as a pig. Every picture with
which they painted it was correct, save the picture of religion.

> O vile ego, you are lost and deranged—
> against whatever touchstone I scratch you, you come up false.

You must see your own acts of obedience in the color of disobedience
and count all your own meanings as empty claims. You should make
your own ego a broom for the dustbin, and see mangy dogs better than
yourself. You should sweep the doorstep of the infidels with your virtues
and walk a million deserts of disappointment to the end. Otherwise you
are simply a knocker on a door. Keep dust for the dust, and remain pure
from all claims!

Those belong to Him who, from the first day of their existence, have
placed their heads on the threshold of nonexistence with the attribute of
poverty and indigence, so as never to lift their heads from that threshold.
They will rise up from the earth, come to the resurrection, pass over the
Narrow Path, and go on to paradise without ever lifting their heads from
this threshold.

O noble youth! A man who comes to the market by day puts on
clothes, and at night he goes back home and takes them off. But what can
he do with his own skin? If they put a thousand kingly crowns on your
head and a thousand royal belts on your waist, what will you do with
your own beggarly face and the color of your poverty?

Tomorrow, those dear ones who had news of these words will be made
present in the private chamber of the elect. They will be given flagons of
Lordly gentleness one after another, and the breeze of Arrival will blow
against them from the direction of prosperity. But those dear ones will
themselves say, "I am that same beggar that I was on the first day."

O poor soul! Poverty, indigence, abasement, and lowliness are the
fundamental attributes of dust and clay. True, dust sits on the face and can
be washed off with water, but you cannot take away the color of your face
with water.

Yahya Mu'adh Razi said, "My argument is my need, my capital my
indigence."

No glance causes greater loss than the glance that rises from you and then falls upon you. Such a glance is the foundation of all loss. As for the glance that is far from you, that is the foundation of all gain.

Sahl ibn ʿAbdallah Tustari* said, "I looked at this affair and turned the eye of insight upon the realities, and I saw that no path takes one nearer to God than need, and no veil is thicker than making claims."

Look at the path of Iblis, and you will see nothing but making claims. Then look at the path of Adam, and you will see nothing but need. O Iblis, what do you say? "I am better than he" [7:12]. O Adam, what do you say? "Our Lord, we have wronged ourselves" [7:23]. God brought all the existent things out from the cover of nonexistence into the open plain of His decree, but the plant of need grew only in earth. When this hand-ful of earth was molded, it was molded with the water of need. It had everything, but it had to have need as well, so that it would never cease weeping before God's court.

Adam's disposition was molded of need, and he received help from need. The angels had to prostrate themselves before him, and he was placed on the throne of kingship and vicegerency, while the angels near to God were placed next to him. But his need did not decrease by a single dust mote. He was taken to paradise, and this proclamation was made: "Eat thereof easefully, you two, wherever you desire" [2:35]. "The eight paradises belong to you; wander freely as you wish." But his poverty did not disappear.

By God the Tremendous! They placed the worth of paradise in the palm of Adam's hand. Among all the existent things, there was no bride more beautiful than paradise. Despite a face of such beauty and an adornment of such perfection, the ruling authority of Adam's aspiration came down from the world of the unseen jealousy and placed its worth on his palm and its splendor in the scales! Paradise began to shout, "I cannot put up with this brazen man!"

O noble youth! If tomorrow you go to paradise and you look at para-dise from the corner of your heart's eye, in truth, in truth, you will have

---

* Sahl (d. 896): an early Sufi of Baghdad, author of one of the first Sufi Qurʾan commentaries.

fallen short of human aspiration. Something your father sold for a grain of wheat*—why would you want to settle down there?

Adam says, "O Lord, what You have said—'I am placing in the earth a vicegerent' [2:30]—this is correct. This is a great eminence deriving from Your bounty. But our right is this: 'Our Lord, we have wronged ourselves' [7:23]. That sofa of vicegerency is Your gift, but the right of our disposition is 'Our Lord, we have wronged ourselves.'"

"O Adam, of all the blessings, why did you choose the grain of wheat?"

He replied, "Because I found the scent of need in it."

Adam was shaped from need, and in the wheat was the scent of need. They brought the one who was shaped from need together with the scent of need. That is why wherever they placed Adam's throne, the stalk of wheat grew up before it—it had an affinity with his shape. Wherever Adam went, need came in his tracks. From paradise came everlastingness, blessing, kingdom, and good fortune, but from that grain of wheat came the station of being chosen and selected, of pain and sorrow. Lovers enjoy sorrow's sweetness more than kings enjoy the good fortune of power. In paradise, Adam was an exile, and that grain of wheat was also an exile. An exile gets along only with an exile.

> Are you then our neighbor? We two are strangers here,
> 　　and every exile shares with the exiles.
> Mercy on the exile in the land!
> 　　The far traveler can do nothing for himself.
> He has parted from his friends, so after his leaving
> 　　they have no pleasure in him, and he has none in them.

O poor soul! Do you think it was the unbelievers who drove Muhammad out of Mecca? No, it was not they who brought him out. He was a man sitting safely in his own homeland. Then the words of exile came, took him by the hand, and drew him out of his own homeland and domicile, giving him their attribute.

> I am an exile in the city and among its people,
> 　　even though my clan is among them, and my family is here.

---

* Islamic tradition says Adam was tempted to eat wheat rather than fruit.

A man's exile is not in distance from his home,
  rather, by God, in the lack of resemblance.

Adam had two existences—the first and the second.

The first existence belonged to this world, not to paradise, and the second belonged to paradise.

"O Adam, come out of paradise and go into this world. Lose your crown, belt, and hat in the way of love! Put up with pain and affliction. Then tomorrow, We will bring you back to this precious homeland and this domicile of subsistence, with a hundred thousand robes of gentleness and every sort of honor, as the leader of the witnesses and in the presence of the one hundred twenty and some thousand prophets, the possessors of purity and sources of lucidity. Then the creatures will come to know that, just as We can bring Adam's form out of paradise through the attribute of severity, so also We can bring him back through the attribute of gentleness."

Tomorrow, Adam will go into paradise with his children. A cry will rise up from all the particles of paradise because of the crowding. The angels of the World of the Dominion will look with wonder and say, "Is this that same man who moved out of paradise a few days ago in poverty and indigence?"

"Adam, bringing you out of paradise was a curtain over this business and a covering over the mysteries, for the loins of your good fortune were the ocean of the one hundred twenty and some thousand pearls of prophethood. Suffer a bit of trouble, then in a few days, take the treasure!

"O Muhammad! When We put the Meccans up to throwing you out of Mecca, We also commanded you—'Make the hijra, go to Medina, put on the clothing of exile, and go to the corner of the sorrow of Abu Ayyub Ansari.'* All this was the preparation. The goal was to bring you back to Mecca on the Day of Conquest along with ten thousand sword-wielding,

---

* When Muhammad entered Medina on his camel, he refused to accept the hospitality of any of those who offered it and instead let his camel wander until it found a place that suited it. It finally knelt down near the house of Abu Ayyub Khalid ibn Zayd, who took the saddle into his house. It was there that Muhammad lived until he built his own house and a mosque on the site where his camel had knelt. Abu Ayyub participated in most of the early battles of the Muslim community and was finally killed in the year 52/672 on the outskirts of Constantinople (Istanbul). His tomb there is an important site of pilgrimage.

spear-throwing, armored warriors, the like of whom had never been seen, while the nobles of Quraysh and the leaders of the unbelievers were standing by astonished: 'Is this that man who fled!?'"

God has a secret in your elevation—
the words of the enemies are senseless ravings.

"O precious spirit! You are the source of subtleness and the spring of refreshment and ease! It is We who sent you away from your homeland as an exile, made you the companion of the troublemaking ego, and imprisoned you in this dustbin. The goal is to call you back at the end of this business to Our own Presence with a hundred thousand robes of gentleness, kindly gifts, and secret bestowals. 'O soul at peace, return to your Lord, well pleased, well pleasing!' [89:28].

"O Adam! Although We sent you from paradise in the company of the serpent and Iblis, We will bring you back in the company of forgiveness and mercy and with the escort of good fortune and prosperity.

"O Muhammad! Although We brought you out of Mecca with the attribute of abasement and We made you a witness of struggle and kept you in the company of 'Abdallah ibn Ubayy ibn Salul* and the other unbelievers and hypocrites, We brought you back to Mecca in the company of conquest, victory, and divine help.

"O precious spirit! Although We have afflicted you for a few days in this dustbin, this domicile of grief, and this house of sorrowful separation, and although We have made you a companion of the vile ego for a time, in the end We will bring you back in the company of Our good pleasure and along with the escort of the exaltation of 'Return!' into the neighborhood of generous giving."

---

* 'Abdallah ibn Ubayy was the leader in Medina of the nominal Muslims known as the "Hypocrites," who were opposed to Muhammad's teachings and policies.

Teaching across Cultures

✳ Islam in China
Wang Daiyu's Real Commentary on the True Teaching

SACHIKO MURATA

Islam arrived in China over a millennium ago and remains quite visible in some areas (fig. 50). Nevertheless, *The Real Commentary on the True Teaching* (*Zhengjiao zhenquan*), the first book in Chinese on Islam written by a Muslim, did not appear until 1642. Its author, Wang Daiyu (d. ca. 1657), is considered by Chinese Muslims—who today number in the tens of millions—as the father of Chinese Islam. Wang tells us in the introduction to the book that his ancestor had come to China three hundred years earlier from Arabia to serve the Chinese emperor as an astronomer. Wang himself studied Arabic and Persian as a youth, but he did not begin studying literary Chinese until he was in his twenties. He wrote the book mainly with the aim of presenting authentic Islam to those Muslims who did not know the languages of their own heritage. He is thoroughly familiar with the Chinese classics and freely employs terminology drawn from Confucianism, Taoism, and Buddhism. Thus, for example, he refers to the angels as the "heavenly immortals" and the creatures of the world as "the Ten Thousand Things." He presents Islam's essential teachings as harmonious with the teachings of the Chinese traditions, though at times he is also critical of specific beliefs and practices of those traditions. The book is divided into two parts of twenty chapters each. The first part is devoted mainly to theological principles, such as the divine attributes, predestination, creation, and human nature. The second part focuses more on spiritual attitudes, ethics, and various commandments of Islamic law. What follows is taken from Chapter 2, which is called "The Original Beginning."

ADAM AND EVE

On the sixth day [of creation], at the time of the monkey [3:00–5:00 P.M.], for the first time the Real Lord commanded the heavenly immortals to bring the soil of the five directions. He created the form of Adam, the ancestor of human beings, and this is the form that people have had from ancient times until now. He completed the body in forty days. Hence, from the creation of the heaven, the earth, and the Ten Thousand Things to the end of Adam's creation it took forty-six days. This is the time scale of the permanent world, where every day is one thousand years of our time [cf. 22:47].

Figure 50.   Great Mosque, Taipei, Taiwan (mid–20th cent.). Many of the mosques in mainland China imitate traditional Chinese architectural styles. Unlike them, this mosque betrays features of the Ottoman style, especially in the central domed prayer hall with the windowed tympanum between the two towers.

Someone may say that all things live in one world, so why should there be different lengths of time? I would reply as follows: [As is well known in Chinese folklore,] if a worldly prince sets out to become an immortal, he will be transformed into a crane, and then length of time will be different. Like a crane, which lives a thousand years, he will have no awareness of the length. So also a mayfly, which is born in the morning and dies in the evening, does not know the shortness [of time]. In the same way, as long as the saltiness of the sea has not met the freshness of the river, the things in salt water are not aware of the saltiness and the things in fresh water are not aware of the freshness.

How can any of these transcend salt and fresh, long and short, so as not to be confined by the relationships before the eyes?

When the Real Lord completed the human ancestor's body through His own original real nature, the two sources, which are life and wisdom, wandered until combining with the body. After that, the four limbs and the one hundred bones, the eyes, the ears, the nose, and the tongue, all started to move mysteriously. The Lord gave the ancestor caps and robes and made him ascend the throne. He commanded all the heavenly immortals to prostrate themselves before him and to rise up while carrying him around the heavenly spheres, and all of them obeyed the command.

Then the Real Lord granted the ancestor great wisdom and real knowledge, so the principle of the heaven and earth and the nature of the Ten Thousand Things all became clear to him. Thus every name of each kind of thing was established [cf. 2:30]. However, when the ancestor remembered that the origin is pure and clean, and when he also considered that the body belongs originally to muddy dirt, he became modest and pride did not appear in him.

When Adam was sleeping deeply, the Real Lord created his wife from his left rib and named her Eve. The reason for the intimacy of husband and wife is that originally they derive from one body. Hence they should love and respect each other. The wife appeared from the husband, and the husband is the origin of the wife, so she should listen to his commands.

Thus you should know that the ancestor of human beings is one body, and this body became man and woman. From this we come to know the yin and yang of the Great Ultimate, the life and wisdom of the Beyond-Ultimate, the mercy and majesty of the Real Lord, and the ultimate high and ultimate low.[2] The subtleness of the Original Beginning without end left nothing unprovided for human beings. If one fails to grasp this principle, one's whole life will be wasted in drunken sleep, and that would be a great pity.

The Real Lord himself commanded Adam and Eve to live in paradise forever and to enjoy bliss everlastingly. However, a tree of wheat had grown up there, another name for which was "the tree of cause and effect." The Lord forbade them to take from this tree. Unexpectedly, the leader of the devils and his followers came up stealthily to paradise and tempted them to eat from the tree. At this time it happened that they became confused for a moment, and finally they were influenced by the devil's temptations and broke their promise with the Lord. Although we call it "breaking the promise," in reality they could not fail but hit the target. At its origin, their passion harmed them, but this was turned into an advantage. Here there was a secret that could not be known by the devil.

At this time the couple's caps and robes fell off and they became naked, so they covered their bodies with the leaves of the fig tree of the upper world. They did not look at each other, and they descended to the earthly world.

Someone may say that human beings are the most spiritual and the most noble of all things. Why should they fall into trouble like this at the very beginning? I would reply that there are two reasons for this. At the time of the creation of human beings, the heavenly immortals and the various spirits did not know the reason for their creation. Because of this, the Real Lord issued a clear proclamation saying, "Truly I want to create human beings to represent me in the world of existence." The heavenly immortals protested and said, "Their body is earth, water, fire, and air. These four elements were gathered together and became the body, but they are opposed to each other, so they will perhaps cause disorder in the future" [paraphrasing 2:30].[3] The leader of the [fiery] spirits [i.e., the jinn] said, "These human beings have passion, and tempting them is very easy" [cf. 15:39], so all the spirits despised the human beings. Hence the Real Lord issued another proclamation and said, "Truly, what I know, you certainly do not know" [2:30].

The first reason for the descent of the human ancestors was that paradise might become the place of pleasure and bliss for good people. From ancient times to the present, myriads of people have been brought into existence through the one body of the human ancestor, and they include two kinds—good and evil. If the ancestors had not descended and had not grown up here, good and evil would not have become separated from each other. Moving to this earthly world is coming down to live among good and evil. After that, people follow their own kind. Good people go up, but evil people descend further.

The second reason for the descent was so the Real Lord could reject the protest of the heavenly immortals and shame the empty effort of the devils, because He desired noble people from the very beginning. By making people suffer, He made them reach this situation. The human ancestors knew rightly the compassionate mercy of the Real Lord. At the beginning they realized their own wrongdoing and became more modest and humble. They became upset at the heavenly immortals' protest and guarded themselves against the devils' deception. They followed the clear heavenly mandate and conquered their own selves. They entrusted their bodies and lives to the Real Lord through faith, and from the ultimate lowness they ascended again to the ultimate highness. Naturally, the protest of the immortals and the deception of the devil came to nothing, and the Real Lord's skillful contrivance shone forth with unique brilliance. When we understand this, we see that although the name is "falling into trouble," in reality this was an increase in perfection.

For three hundred years after the descent, heaven was dim and earth dark. Adam and Eve lamented all day long and repented their mistake. The Real Lord accepted their real sincerity and forgave their unintentional offense. Heaven and earth became clear, the sun and the moon became bright, and the husband and the wife met again and started to follow the clear mandate to establish the teaching and to govern the world.

When you meditate on this situation, you will certainly come to know that the Beyond-Ultimate is the seed, the Great Ultimate the tree, and the human ultimate the fruit. The seed is the fruit, the tree is concealed in the fruit, and the fruit is concealed in the tree, which embraces everything, with no exceptions.

The Classic says, "Those who are attached to the letter and separated from the substance are only talking about the principle. All this is caused by the fact that the ego has not yet been purified and the eyes of the heart have not yet been opened. How could a breast filled with dregs reach the Original Beginning of the great transformation?!"

What I have explained here is for the most part nothing more than the superficial meaning. The subtle, ultimate principle can certainly not be described with inexact writing.

From Arabic into Javanese
The Gift Addressed to the Spirit of the Prophet

ANTHONY H. JOHNS

Recalling Sam'ani's reflections on one of the names of God, here is an extract from a rendering in traditional Javanese verse of an Arabic work with the title *The Gift Addressed to the Spirit of the Prophet* (*At-tuhfat al-mursala ila ruh an-nabi*).[4] The author of the rendering is a court poet, and in the opening stanzas, following the convention of the time, he tells of the heaviness that lies on his heart because of his sense of inadequacy to fulfill worthily his royal patron's command to translate the *Gift* into Javanese. He is not skilled at writing verse, he claims, and he has little knowledge of Arabic or the intricacies of the subject matter.

The Arabic original was written by an Indian scholar, Muhammad ibn Fadl Allah, who lived and taught at Burhanpur in the north Deccan (south central India) and died in 1620. He completed the work in 1590, and it rapidly established itself as a convenient summary of the basic theosophical ideas of the Ibn 'Arabi tradition. By 1610 at the latest the book was known in Sumatra and soon became a basic text for the study of Sufism in the madrasas of Sumatra, Java, and elsewhere in the Indonesian archipelago, as well as on the Indian subcontinent, and is still popular in Sufi circles. It also became well known in the Middle East. The Medinan scholar Ibrahim al-Kurani (d. 1691) wrote a long commentary on it in 1675 at the request of Sumatrans studying in Medina, and the Syrian scholar 'Abd al-Ghani an-Nabulusi (d. 1730) also commented on it.

Muhammad ibn Fadl Allah arranged his Javanese rendering in four cantos of different meters, intending that it be sung. Each of the meters had a variety of beautiful melodies that would carry this element of Islamic spirituality deep into the heart of the Javanese through a cultural medium widely known and loved.

This court poet who so humbly professed his inadequacy was no mere translator. He put his own stamp on the work. When Islam came to Java, the Indonesian archipelago had been under the pervasive influence of Hinduism and Buddhism for a millennium, and the gods and demons of the Hindu tradition, thanks to the influence of the shadow theater, were household names among the Javanese. Thus our author presents the concept of God as one, hidden, and unknowable in Himself, yet manifest in the world in a plurality of shapes and forms, in terms of Krishna revealing himself as an avatar of Vishnu. Such familiar names would be a reassurance to the Javanese, helping them to feel at home with the doctrines being taught, notwithstanding that religious ideas are at the core of the Ibn 'Arabi "reading" of the Islamic revelation.

The first part of the text is a presentation of Sufi theosophy, conveniently summarized in a schema of seven grades (*martaba*) of existence, at the head of which is God as essence, unknown, unknowable, and unmanifest. The remaining six are grades of manifestation. The last, that of the Perfect Man, is the point of return to God's thinking, knowing of Himself. The conclusion is spiritual counsel with the achievement of a state of perpetual prayer as its goal. The following excerpt is from Canto 3. In the interests of space, each stanza is reduced to paragraph form:

15. The prophet of God—may the Most High[5] cherish him—declared: The truest of all sayings is that of Ki Labid* who said, "Everything other than God is false. . . . "

16. The meaning of "false" is "nonexistent," for every individual thing is nonexistent in that it exists not through itself, but through the existence of God, just as reflections in a mirror exist not in themselves, but through the one to whom the mirror belongs [and who looks into it].

17. If the mirror is broken, the determinations [reflected in it] return to the Reality.[6] Shaykh Yusuf† declares: Be sure you understand correctly the word "return." Do not claim to become God, for this is wrong according to all four [Sunni legal] schools. The meaning of "return" is, as one says, "go back to a prior state."

18. One of the masters of Unity, Shaykh Bayazid [al-Bistami],‡ says: I believed it was I who praised and honored the Most High, but then an inspiration came to me and I realized that my words were God's own words of praise that came before my own, and this was how I praised and worshipped Him.

---

* Labid was a pre-Islamic poet, author of one of the seven classical Arabic odes known as the *Mu'allaqat*.

† Yusuf of Makassar, exiled by the Dutch East India Company from West Java to the Cape, where he died in 1697.

‡ Persian mystic Bayazid al-Bistami (d. 874) is most famous for his saying "Glory be to me!" which this text explains in the present verse.

19. Many proofs have been given to establish the Unity of the Reality [*al-Haqq*], in both the Qur'an and the Sunna. Many of the masters of Sufism, too, give proofs of this Unity. The Most High declares, "East and west are God's,

20. and whichever way you turn, there you behold the face of God" [2:115] manifest in existing things. He exists in Himself, they exist through Him as through a "substrate." A substrate is not changed by, but rather is manifest through accidents.

25. Among the sayings of Shaykh Muhammad [the author of the Arabic *Gift*] are many proofs of the Unity of Being, as there are likewise among the sayings of the mystics not set down here. They are so numerous that it would be impossible to count the proofs of this Unity: they are beyond counting.

26. But if this is what you wish, meditate constantly on the words of the masters of Unity, the guidance that the Sufis have to give concerning the Reality. One who does this, through the help of God's guidance together with good instruction will achieve intimate knowledge of God.

27. If you wish to reach the Reality, follow the example of the Prophet. Never forget this! Follow the example of the prophets and saints, both in what is prescribed and in what is hallowed by tradition. Fulfill it with all your heart. Never let your meditation be interrupted; throughout day and night, never slacken in meditating on the Subtle One.⁷

28. Keep this fixed in your heart, inscribe it in your mind alongside the name *Jalala* [the Beautiful].⁸ Never slacken in this. Never interrupt your gaze on the beauty of the Most Great.⁹ Let the vision of the heart's mental striving be beheld in the name Jalala as a word written in gold.

29. Once this is fixed in your mind, meditate on this name of the Reality, the name Jalala beheld in your heart. In your heart of hearts this name is revealed, yet as a manifestation, not a reality. Nothing of this may you forget, standing, sitting, or sleeping. Never abandon,

30. day or night, the essence of this teaching; devote yourself to it with all your heart; keep it in your mind; never forget the Most High. Whenever you look on any phenomenal thing, never regard it as having a self in its own right. Neither now nor previously had it a self, and in eternity, surely, it is within the Subtle One.

31. Understand thoroughly the sense of what is written here. Never fall away from God [*yang*]. Understand fully what I have here composed on kingly [i.e., divine] matters, for one who does this will gain the status of a friend of God whose belief is true, and will be called perfect in faith.

FROM THE GREAT TEACHERS

Since the eleventh century the institution known as the madrasa has provided the context for much of Islamic higher religious education (see figs. 51–53). But great teachers have worked their magic in a wide variety of other settings as well, often somewhat less formal than the circles of the madrasa (see fig. 49). Here are some of those teachers and some insights into their methods.

Between Sermon and Seminar

✳ Women as Scholars and Teachers

JOHN RENARD

For a variety of complicated social and cultural reasons, premodern Muslim women have left very few complete writings or collections of texts. The lack of material by no means implies that women have not been actively involved in the religious sciences. Their contributions are simply less visible than those of women involved in the arts and architecture, and one has to look very deliberately for evidence of their scholarly and pedagogical accomplishments.[10] A number of women, such as Khadija bint al-Baqqal (d. 1045) and Khadija ash-Shahjaniya (d. 1068), are known to have been prominent preachers and teachers.[11] Fortunately, at least some of what these women have thought and said has been preserved, however fragmentarily, in their notices in biographical anthologies such as that of ʿAbd ar-Raʾuf al-Munawi.

We begin with a complete biographical notice of one woman and continue with briefer examples of pedagogically memorable sayings attributed to several other women. The first woman, Fatima bint ʿAbbas, receives approval posthumously even from the redoubtable Ibn Taymiya, whose treatise on tafsir is given in part 1. Fatima (d. 1314–1315) was the shaykha of the "Baghdadi" ribat in Cairo, founded by a daughter of the Mamluk sultan Baybars (r. 1260–1277), one of many such institutions established to shelter and educate widows and other women impoverished or divorced and without family support. As shaykha, Fatima's duties included preaching to the women and teaching them jurisprudence (*fiqh*).[12]

Figure 51.   The Saljuqid Karatay Madrasa in Konya, Turkey (1253), though elaborately decorated on the interior, is, with only twelve residence rooms, an example of a smaller school. Named for the minister who built it, the Karatay is one of a number of early Turkish madrasas featuring a central domed chamber flanked by residential cells for students and teachers and, in some cases, by services facilities (such as kitchens) and funerary chambers. (See SD fig. 1 for another Saljuqid madrasa.)

FATIMA BINT ʿABBAS

Fatima bint ʿAbbas, the shaykha and legal counsel [*muftiya*], madrasa professor [*mudarrisa*], and legal scholar [*faqihiya*], devout in deed, the ascetic Sufi and spiritual combatant [*mujahida*], mother of Zaynab, originally from the city of Baghdad, [of the] Hanbali [*madhhab*], and preacher [*waʿiza*]. She used to ascend the pulpit and exhort the women, so that her encouragement gave them strength and those who were distressed gained confidence. All of the women benefited from her instruction, their hearts softened. How many [her] eloquent counsel touched!

Figure 52.   The Shir Dar ("Lion-bearing") Madrasa (1616–1636), one of three
madrasas framing the Registan plaza in Samarkand, arranges double rooms by
the dozens around a large central courtyard, with teaching facilities located in
iwans. This is the entry portal iwan.

What tears of sadness and weariness were shed! She was learned in the
recondite intricacies and most vexing questions of fiqh. Ibn Taymiya and
others were impressed with her knowledge and unstinting in their praise
of her brilliance, her humility, and [the abundance of] her tears. She
debated [the legal ramifications of] menstruation and other [questions of
religious law] with Ibn al-Wakil [d. 1389, a Shafiʻi jurist]. The swells of
the ocean of her learning roiled and surged. Her being a woman stood out
in [people's] mention of her, but awareness of [that fact] was no detri-
ment to her reputation.

   Thus did she live along the path of propriety, gathering provisions
[in preparation for the time] of her being weaned [from the verb *fatima*,
punning on her name] from the breasts of [this] life for her journey
from this world. She died in Cairo on the day of ʻArafa,* 714 [1314/15].

---

* During the month of pilgrimage, the twelfth lunar month, part of the ritual extending from the eighth to the thirteenth day includes a day (the ninth) on which

Figure 53.   The Safavid Madar-i Shah ("King's Mother") Madrasa, Isfahan, Iran (1706–1715), shows two-tiered student cells flanking the minaret-framed iwan at the main dome chamber. Each cell has a small porch opening onto the enclosed courtyard. (See fig. 36 for another view; also SD fig. 22 for a Mamluk madrasa.)

---

pilgrims visit Mount 'Arafa in the valley outside Mecca; tradition holds that Adam rediscovered Eve there after their expulsion from paradise. It was also the site of Muhammad's Farewell Sermon, and the place on which Abraham was commanded to sacrifice his son.

Ibn Taymiya said, "I have a vivid memory of her ascending the pulpit [to preach]; I was tempted to prevent her. Mustafa [i.e., Muhammad] appeared to me and said, "Fatima is a righteous woman."[13]

In shorter notices about four other women Munawi also includes material germane to the present topic:

[Umm Sufyan ath-Thawri said one day to her son, Sufyan ath-Thawri, who went on to become a noted scholar]: My son, devote yourself to the quest for knowledge, and I will make that possible for you with my spindle. [And she said to him]: My son, after you have written ten letters [of the alphabet], look within yourself for any improvement in your way of living, your spiritual state, your forbearance, and your reverence; and if you see none, know that [this learning] is harmful and worthless for you.[14]

[Ruqayya of Mosul (in Iraq) said]: Study fiqh in the madhhabs of sincerity, rather than exercising your mind about the [ritually] proper method of mounting a she-mule or a young camel.[15]

[Fatima of Nishapur (in northeastern Iran, d. ca. 850) said]: The authentic [seeker] who is close to God is [like one] on an ocean whose waves buffet her and who petitions God with the cries of a drowning person, begging his aid and salvation. [And she said]: One who labors for God with the goal of contemplating him is a person of intimate knowledge ['arif], and that person who acts as though God were watching is pure of heart.[16]

['A'isha bint Abi 'Uthman Sa'id al-Khayri (d. 864) said]: Educate yourself both inwardly and outwardly. One who lacks training in outward behavior suffers the outward consequences physically, and one who lacks proper demeanor in her interior life suffers the inner [spiritual] consequences.[17]

* Teaching with Pictures
Three Paintings of Bawa Muhaiyaddeen
GISELA WEBB

Muhammad Raheem Bawa Muhaiyaddeen (d. 1986), known to his followers as Bawa Muhaiyaddeen, had been known in Sri Lanka as a sage and "holy man" since the 1940s. He was invited to the United States in 1971 by a group of mostly young spiritual seekers from the Philadelphia area; this was the beginning of the Bawa Muhaiyaddeen Fellowship. His teachings focused on themes of remembrance of God, acquiring the divine qualities, attaining wisdom, and ultimately the experience of union with God (and for the hippies of the era, cleaning up and getting off drugs). Bawa Muhaiyaddeen's teachings emphasized the goal of attaining the "state of Islam," in which one surrenders to God and experiences the primordial state of unity with God (Day of the Covenant, *yawm al-mithaq*; the first, *al-awwal*) and with all human beings without distinctions of caste, race, religion, and nation.

His early years in America did not emphasize Islamic ritual and religious practices beyond Sufi themes of remembrance (*dhikr*) and divine unity, but over the years a more outward connection with Islamic practices emerged, particularly with the building of a mosque at the Fellowship headquarters in the Philadelphia neighborhood of Overbrook in 1984. Mosque attendance (mainstream Sunni congregational prayers, Hanafi madhhab) on Fridays has grown significantly, particularly with the increase of immigrant and African-American Muslim populations. Bawa Muhaiyaddeen had his followers buy land in Coatesville, Pennsylvania, for farming and for ritual burials. The land is also used for retreats and family dhikr weekends. The community built a *mazar* (place of visitation) for their shaykh in Coatesville, which has become a pilgrimage site for Sufis from a number of orders around the world.

The original pieces of Bawa Muhaiyaddeen's art work (which he referred to as "heartwork") are located in the Mosque-Fellowship complex in Overbrook, where Bawa Muhaiyaddeen lived and taught through the 1970s and early 1980s. The community reproduces them as posters, and Fellowship members often have reproductions in their homes. They are delightful in their bright color, directness, and intricate design. All are symbolic representations of particular dimensions of the shaykh's teachings as communicated in his discourses and songs. Indeed, the following descriptions must be seen as quite cursory in relation to the many layers of association these images carry in the shaykh's teachings. The pieces function as tools of remembrance.

THE INNER HEART

At the top of figure 54 is a star. In many discourses, Bawa Muhaiyaddeen associates the star with the inner form (*surat*) of humanity, fashioned from the twenty-eight letters of the Arabic language. The inner form of the human person "exists as the [eternal, inner] Qurʾan, imperishable and indestructible. . . .

Figure 54. *The Inner Heart;* painting by Bawa Muhaiyaddeen. This and the following two figures reproduced courtesy of the Bawa Muhaiyaddeen Fellowship, 5820 Overbrook Drive, Philadelphia, PA 19131.

If he can make these . . . letters speak here, within his body on earth, . . . he will transform into light and lose himself in the light of God"; "He must make the power of God speak within his own form; he must make God speak from within himself."[18] Therefore, the small star refers to the transformed human being, within whom the power of God speaks. Under the small star is a crescent moon. The moon with its "arms" upward is the heart turned toward God, the hands in supplication. The *bismillah* ("In the name of God, the Compassionate and Merciful") is written on the moon.

The primary symbolism of this piece is the heart-encompassed star, that is, the inner heart as the "house of Allah." The central star primarily represents Allah, the origin of creation and the human being, *insan*. However, the heart-encompassed star also represents the state of unity and intimate colloquy, in which God speaks through the human being and the human being speaks through God; that is the form of unity Bawa Muhaiyaddeen describes as the faith-surrender (*iman-islam*) of the perfected person (*al-insan al-kamil*).

Contained in the star are the Arabic letters *alif, lam, mim, dal,* and *ha.* There is double significance here. First, the alif, lam, and mim are most often used by Bawa to signify the macro- and microcosmic processes of generation and knowing, from Allah through Muhammad to Muhaiyaddeen, that is, God-in-Himself, the hidden treasure from which the first resonance emerged; the Light (*nur*) of Muhammad, "without which nothing would have been made"; and Muhaiyaddeen, the primal state of axial presence (*qutbiya*), the eternal revivifier of faith and explainer of wisdom within the heart of the insan (the human being). The state of "muhaiyaddeen" (revivifier of the faith) is manifested in history through the *qutbs*, the poles of wisdom, and Friends of God in the Sufi tradition. Those same letters—alif, lam, mim—along with dal and ha, form the letters of *al-hamd* (praise), that quality that is both cause and result of the heart's transformation.

The star is encompassed by the heart, that is, the human heart melted in love, praise, and union. The heart contains the salutation *As-salam 'alaykum* (Peace be upon you), *La ilaha illa 'llah, Muhammad rasul Allah* (There is no god but God, and Muhammad is the messenger of God), and *Allahu akbar* (God is supreme).

The moon represents the outward flow of breath in the dhikr, symbolic of the emptying of the world and the nafs from oneself; the sun represents the inward flow of breath of the dhikr (the intaking of the purity of divine wisdom and sustenance).

The heart is surrounded by a circle of "Allahs" written in Arabic, and a second circle (actually a crescent moon shape) of "Muhammads." To the right and left of the encircled heart are leaves and circles, each circle containing one of the Ninety-nine Names, or Qualities of Allah, the "fruits" of the transformed heart of the insan. Below the leaves and circles are repeated inscriptions of "Muhaiyaddeen." Radiating from—or toward—the heart are four columns, or "supports," of the insan al-kamil, the remembrance of "Allahu akbar," "La ilaha illa 'llah, Muhammad rasul Allah," and "As-salam 'alaykum."

FOUR STEPS TO PURE IMAN

Bawa Muhaiyaddeen's explanation of figure 55 was published in a slim volume, *Four Steps to Pure Iman [Faith]*.[19] The painting reflects the shaykh's teachings on the stages of prayer and religion; it consists of four ascending circles, each one smaller than the preceding, each one containing a set of doors. In the last circle there is an open space above the doors; above the space is an arc-shaped opening with "Allah" written above it. This four-stepped tower is surrounded by a garden filled with flowers, vines, fruits, trees, sky, and stars. The painting is meant to convey Bawa Muhaiyaddeen's teachings on the meaning of "the

Figure 55. *Four Steps to Pure Iman;* painting by Bawa Muhaiyaddeen.

four religions." A small part of this complex theory may be summarized in the following manner:

1. The four major religions are Hinduism, Hanal (Zoroastrianism), Christianity, and Islam. Bawa Muhaiyaddeen includes Judaism with Islam, since they are "brothers."

2. These four religions, while having their own specific societal manifestations, also have an existence in each human being as (a) the tendency to form idols both in the world and in oneself (Hinduism); (b) the tendency of the nafs toward the fires of anger, lust, infatuation, impatience (Hanal); (c) the tendency to focus on the realm of the "spiritual" (Christianity), a tendency, however, that may be informed by the mind and imagination rather than by the inner light within, the "pure soul," which is identified with Jesus; and (d) the tendency toward, or capacity for, *furqan* (discernment) and the constant awareness of both this world and the hereafter (Islam).

3. These four religions symbolize the deepening of religious experience as *shariʿa, tariqa, haqiqa,* and *maʿrifa.* Shariʿa (revealed law) signifies coming to know the most basic distinctions of right and wrong, permissible and impermissible. Tariqa (path) signifies the strengthening of determination, the understanding of intentions, motivations, and good qualities. Haqiqa (ultimate reality) is the beginning of communication and union of the soul with God. Maʿrifa (intimate knowledge) is a more perfected state of union with God. In the painting, the empty space above the fourth door represents the state of *sufiya* (being a Sufi), which Bawa described as transcending all four religions; it is the state of constant remembrance (*dhikr*) and contemplation (*fikr*) of God, in which the heart prostrates to God with every breath. Thus, "pure iman" is seen as a culmination, maturing, and perfection of the "four religions" as they are understood in terms of the development of historical religions, the human tendencies within us all that are represented by these religions, and the deepening states and stages of faith.

THE ROCKY MOUNTAIN OF THE HEART

Figure 56 represents the human mind as a huge, hard mountain formed by the solidification and encrustation of categories of difference, such as race, religion, philosophy, and ego. The mountain is even more impenetrable because of the outside forces of the world, which cause forgetfulness, and the inner jungle of the mind, which causes confusion and ignorance. The inner qualities and traits of human character, both positive and negative, are represented through images

Figure 56.   *The Rocky Mountain of the Heart;* painting by Bawa Muhaiyaddeen.

of plants and various animals. Therefore the mind, with its tendencies toward forgetfulness, illusion, and confusion, cannot discover, or recover, the unity between God and the human soul, or unity among human beings.

The water channels running down through the mountain, with fish swimming in them, represent both the path of following the shaykh and the disciples' absorption of the shaykh's qualities and wisdom. The "fish" finally enter the state of wisdom represented by the swan, symbol of the creature who moves gracefully and undisturbed on the ocean of being, taking into its mouth the mud, water, and other elements of the pond, sifting out the pure water and nourishment (God's wisdom, truth, goodness, peace, patience). The sifting out of wisdom is the beginning of the transformation of the inner heart of the insan, which is represented by the five-step tower—the stages and states—of the path to union with God.

Borrowed Notes

Insights and memorable quips from sessions of spiritual consultation like that depicted in figure 49 have been recorded frequently in a literary genre known as *malfuz* (pl. *malfuzat*, utterances). Collections made by students of the great teachers have preserved the best of the masters' originally oral discourses.

* ## Muhammad Husayni Gesu Daraz on Love

BRUCE B. LAWRENCE

Muhammad Husayni Gesu Daraz (d. 1422) was a major figure in the Chishti order. His malfuzat appear in *Collected Discourses* (*Jawamiʿ al-kalim*), the last major biographical work about early Indian Chishti shaykhs. It records his conversations following his departure around 1400 from Delhi, where he had lived some forty years, for Gulbarga in the Deccan (southern India). The work stands in the line of a number of major writings of the same genre by members of several Sufi orders, dating from at least the late thirteenth century. Here Gesu Daraz reflects on the pitfalls along the path of mystical love:

Every activity has its attendant perils. In love there are two dangers—one at the beginning, and another danger at the end. The initial danger is that the grief of love and pain from seeking the Beloved might overwhelm the lover suddenly and engulf him. After he remains in this state for some time, he finds complete contentment in it and no longer pursues union with God. He assumes that apart from pain and anxiety there are no other fruits of the spiritual life. But after some time, pain and affliction become second nature to him, almost a habit. The taste for more pain disappears, and he is left with neither the pleasure of union nor the pain of separation. Passion dies, and he becomes cold and unmoved. He has nothing to show for his troubles, ending his life in sorrow and without hope. From this [misery] we take refuge in God!

The danger at the end is that when one is at the point of union with the Beloved, he may become so absorbed in the pleasure of union that the pain of the agony of separation disappears. After some time, he becomes accustomed to union and loses his taste for it, but the goal in both conditions should be nothing other than a taste for, and contentment with, the Beloved. Union without continuing desire and separation without either pleasure or pain—what use are they? Again, the man becomes cold, and nothing remains. He is deprived of his taste for the beauty of the Beloved. May God prevent this [from happening to us]! For though in union there is invariably a sense of the beauty of the Beloved, where is the taste that allows enjoyment of it? Union with stasis—what use is it?

As for the fortunate lover, he is the one who in the initial state is absorbed in the pleasure of separation, the taste of its pain, and the passion of distant adoration. In the last state, the more united he becomes, the greater his taste for union, and the more eagerly he seeks it. Pain upon pain and taste upon taste appears. They say of this lover that he comes to a happy end; he finds contentment in love, and a full measure of life. Although the knowers of God would call this deficient, yet the taste of this stage is beyond the point where gain or loss can be reckoned.

In *The Benefits of Intimate Knowledge* [*Awarif al-ma'arif* by Shihab ad-Din 'Umar Suhrawardi, d. 1234] it is stated that the perfected Sufi no longer has any taste for sama', but this is the sort of "perfected Sufi" who has fallen prey to the danger at the end of the Way. Having been transported [to the presence of God], he becomes accustomed to union in such a way that it becomes a habitual state and he grows cold. The commendable Sufi is the one who avoids such a danger, and it is to him that the following couplet [of Sa'di; see fig. 58] alludes:

> It is not strange that the seeker of the Friend loses his head.
> What is strange is that I have found union and still my head is
>   spinning.[20]

Keeping in Touch

Letters have also been an important medium for disseminating central Islamic teachings. Part 2 reproduced a letter of Sharaf ad-Din Maneri, and another of his missives will appear in part 7. Here is a sample from a spiritual descendant of Maneri's.

* ### Shaykh Husayn
  A Letter on the True Names of God

  BRUCE B. LAWRENCE

Shaykh Husayn Mu'izz Balkhi (i.e., of a family that originated in Balkh in central Asia, d. 1440) was a master of the Firdawsi order, to which Maneri also belonged. Husayn was a grand-disciple of Maneri's through his uncle Muzaffar Shams Balkhi (d. 1400). Shaykh Husayn's large collection of letters (*maktubat*) was among several volumes he wrote on a wide range of topics; his works include treatises, collections of prayers, an edition of his malfuzat, and instructional manuals. In the following letter the theme of the divine names is reminiscent of the piece by Sam'ani with which part 6 opened.

It is known, dear brother, and it has also been attested in the commentary on *The Conduct of Seekers* [*Adab al-muridin*] by our esteemed Shaykh (who speaks from the stations of the travelers on the Path), that the real name is identical with the one named, that is, according to the technical usage of those who profess the divine unity. So long as you do not understand their usage, you will not be able to comprehend the real names. We will endeavor to shed some light on this subject, God willing.

You should know that "water" is a simple expression, but that water has its essence [*dhat*], appearance [*wajh*], and nature [*nafs*]. To examine the existence of water is one thing; to examine its general and inclusive qualities with respect to all plant life is another thing. Know, therefore, that the existence of water is the essence of water, that the general and inclusive qualities of water with reference to plant life is the appearance, and that the conjunction of both the existence and the inclusiveness of water is its nature. Water has a special relationship, a special method, and a special quality for each plant, and that relationship and quality of water is called its appearance.

Know also that the qualities of water exist already in its essence, so that the soundness and capacity of different trees, different roses, and different fruits as well as the stages of growth of trees and their capacity for coloration—all reflect attributes of water and have names that pertain to water at its apparent level. Just as all the shapes and parts of the tree can be distinguished—i.e., bark, flower, branch, fruit, and thorn—so the attributes of water, when they emerge from the world of prototypes into the world of forms and assume those inclusive and productive qualities that are the special feature of water, take on numerous forms and project a variety of distinctions. Distinctions require names, and there can be no doubt that names pertain to the appearance [of a thing]. Those names are real names that distinguish one aspect from another, and indeed, that is how one determines the real names of water. Hence the name is no different from that which it names.

As for the effects of water, they pertain to its nature. The conjunction of the effects and the names of water is called the essence of water. It is undifferentiated, whereas the appearance is always differentiated. The essence belongs to the realm of prototypes, the appearance to the realm of forms. Since water has come into existence in many forms, the sum total of all of them is the perfect expression of water. In every plant that you see, therefore, observe the appearance of water, for it is through plants that water attests to the beautiful secret of "Wherever you turn, there is the face of God" [2:115].

Once you have understood this analogy, then know that God Almighty has no height and depth, no right and left, no behind and before. He is a light unlimited in both its horizontal and vertical dimensions. He is an ocean without shore or floor. He has neither beginning nor end, nor width nor length, nor is he compounded of elements. He is not capable of change or exchange: He cannot be partitioned or divided. He does not disappear, nor does he dissolve. He is truly one in his essence; in no sense is he plural.

When you have understood this much, then know further that God is a light, a real light, that has no limits, nor does it diminish. Free of all deficiency, the divine light has its distinctive essence, appearance, and nature. If you examine the mere existence of this light, that is one thing; but if you look at it in the sense in which it encompasses all that exists, that is another thing. And if you examine it in the sense in which its existence and its universality are conjoined, that is something else. After you have grasped these three perspectives, then know that the essence of light is its existence, that the manner in which light is common to, and includes, all existing things, is its appearance. Know further that what comprises both these aspects of light is its nature. The qualities of the divine light that have the capacity to produce multiple forms pertain to the aspect of essence, while its names pertain to its appearance, its actions to its nature.

O brother, the divine light is universal with respect to all of existence, and the existence and continuation of all existence derives from this same light. There is no particle of the particles of existence but God is with it and surrounds it and is conscious of it. This universal, inclusive, comprehensive quality of light is called its appearance; hence, whoever has come face to face with God worships God. In the technical language of the people of unity [i.e., the Sufis], however, such a person is a heretic. "Most of them do not believe in God; are there no polytheists among them?" Why? Because every day such a person makes war on his fellow human beings and, therefore, opposes God and denies him. But everyone who passes beyond the appearance and arrives at God sees the divine essence and worships it. Such a one is a true monotheist. He is free from opposition and denial, and he is at peace with the people of the world.

O brother, you must arrive at this encompassing sea and this boundless light. You yourself must see this light. Observing it in the world, you will be free of polytheism, incarnationism, and other heresies; you will cease to deny or oppose God; you will bring about peace in your fellow human beings. Ponder all that I have written. In my instructions you will discover true joys and in time you will come to understand the real names of God.

REQUIRED READING FOR MYSTICS

Three further types of literature have become standard sources for Muslim spiritual seekers: didactic treatises on various aspects of the spiritual journey, texts designed to help readers interpret the inner meaning of their guidebooks, and dictionaries explaining the hidden meanings of metaphorical terminology.

Advice for Inexperienced Travelers

Here is a foundational text on the spiritual quest. This Persian treatise by Majd ad-Din Baghdadi (d. 1219) sets out the basic principles of spiritual wayfaring on three levels: that of the masses, that of the elite, and that of the elite of the elite.

✳ Majd ad-Din Baghdadi
Treatise on Journeying
FATEMEH KESHAVARZ

Of Majd ad-Din Abu Sa'id Sharaf ibn Mu'ayyad Baghdadi (1159–1219) only a few short treatises and a handful of poems have survived. The following is one such treatise, edited from two Tehran manuscripts copied almost two centuries after the author's death.[21] Majd ad-Din was a major shaykh of the central Asian Kubrawi Sufi order, founded by Najm ad-Din Kubra (d. 1221).

In the Name of God, the Compassionate, the Merciful. Praise be to the Lord and greetings to his Messenger. And then said the Lord, glory be to Him: "Say: roam the earth" [see 6:11, 27:69, 29:20, 30:42]. Similarly, stated God's Messenger, may the Lord bless him and grant him peace: "Travel, improve your health, and gain profit."²² The essence of existence, and the one selected over all created beings, the beloved of the Lord and the one sought in the realm of eternity, crowned with the divine address "By your life!,"* the bestower of sainthood through "Follow me. God will love you" [3:31], the utterer of "Say: I am but a mortal like your-selves" [18:110], and alien to claims such as "I am not like any of you" threw such a gem as "travel!" on the shore of worship through the fervor of the waves of prophethood that if it lands by the side of any fortunate person, it will be treasured by him. I am a slave to that seer of the truth and possessor of spiritual insight who would truly investigate [the idea of traveling], begging aid from the Lord, so that at the time of inner explo-ration it might be revealed to him that the journey of the masses is other than the journey of the elect, which, in turn, is other than the journey of the elect among the elect. [And so he may find out] the reward of each journey and the profit inherent in this enterprise.

The *Journey of the Masses* is the venture into new lands, and these masses are of two different ranks: one group are those who are restrained behind the veil of their nature, who have lost the property of humanity in the darkness of their mortal nature. Allured with the seed of lust they have fallen into the trap of misery and entered the rank of beasts accord-ing to the phrase "They are like beasts—indeed, they are more misguided" [7:179]. The benefit of their journeying in the land and visiting places is related to human pleasure. [They make these journeys] in order that they may nourish their senses by seeing and hearing things, gratify effortlessly their nature with such nourishment, and boast to one another on account of the frequency of such journeys and abundance of the cities visited.

Another group [among the masses] are those whose souls have tasted the aroma of intimacy. The awakening of the hearts of these, whose inner selves are aware of calamities, has opened their fleshly eye to learn les-

---

* A phrase addressed to prophet Muhammad in Q 15:72.

sons [from their surroundings]. The events of this world have enriched their minds with experience [so that] wherever they travel, and whatever ancient erected foundation they observe, they will think of the owner of the edifice and appreciate the suffering and the copious effort he has put into building it. [They would realize] how endless desires, this-worldly pride, the devil's temptation, and self-related concerns have buried each of them [the building owners] in the contemplation of the [appearance of] the building and kept them heedless of the truth of that structure built upon the fleeting breeze of impermanence—the foundation of life is on that breeze, how can a building be otherwise? [The traveler will wonder,] How have the owners of such buildings lost awareness so that the inner lust and the accusations of the animal soul have occupied their spiritual will with the building of an outer structure? Finally before the ending of that palace or garden they have tasted the assault from the angel of death with their building enterprise, leaving no lasting results behind:

> Where are the Khusraws, the tyrants of the past?
> They collected treasures. [The treasures] did not remain, nor did they.*

Or, [the traveler observes that the owner] might have according to his wish completed the building, nourishing in it for a short period of time his own Pharaonic nature. In the end, however, he has slipped back into the hidden realm of nonexistence, taking with him a thousand sufferings and unfulfilled wishes. At the time of departure, he has suffered the pain of separation from all kinds [of things], each inflicting a separate injury on his heart and soul. Forced to meet an unfortunate end, he has been held accountable for the lawful and unlawful amounts spent on that [building], whereas others have benefited from using it, taking pleasure in their benefit. The enemies, despite the owner's wish, have gained control of it [the building], spending time with their friends at their heart's desire without ever praying to God once for his [the owner's] salvation.

When they [the second category among the traveling masses] study this state of things, and ponder over the disloyalty of the world, and discover the benefit in the weariness of the heart from its affairs, they no longer put

* This verse, written by the Arab poet Mutannabi (915–955), alludes to kings such as Khusraw as examples of mortality.

their heart into that from which they necessarily must depart. They do not allow themselves to be afflicted with the love of an unfaithful beloved and divorce her, an irrevocable divorce, before she leaves them to unite with another [lover].* The infidel, the Muslim, the Christian, and the Jew equally share in this state [of awareness], for this basic perception by the intellect may be achieved in the first state of its [the intellect's] freedom from the calamitous ways of the nature. It is for this reason that the Sabians,† although they do not believe in spiritual ranks and in the day of resurrection, all used their will to free themselves from worldly attachments and pleasures, still more from the pleasure-seeking calamities of the brutal world:

> When the wise see through the appearances in this world,
>> They do not spend a grain of barley to buy worldly good fortune.
> Their unceasing effort throughout their lives
>> Is to free themselves from this calamitous snare.

The *Journey of the Elect* is the journey from earth to heaven, from the outer to the inner, from form to meaning, and from the apparent to the hidden according to the phrase "Thus did we show Abraham the kingdom of the heavens and the earth" [6:75]. This is because the earthly realm is shared by beasts as well as human beings. In fact, in the satisfaction drawn from that which is perceived by the senses, erotic pleasure, and the pleasure pertaining to form, the share of the beasts is bigger than that allotted to the human being, [even though the human being is] elevated through the ornament of intellect and venerated with the adornment of understanding and perception. As far as the eyesight is concerned, a vulture sees further than a human being; with regard to smelling, a dog or a wolf smells better; and in relation to the pleasure drawn from intercourse there is no comparison between a human being and a donkey. Other sensual desires may be compared to the instances enumerated here.

What sets human beings apart, then, is in the elevation through the adornment of intellect and veneration through the integrity of understand-

---

* This is a kind of divorce called *talaq al-hasan*, which involves three consecutive pronouncements and may not be revoked.

† According to Q 2:59, the Sabians belong among receivers of a revealed religion, along with Jews, Christians, and Muslims.

ing and perception. To discover the attributes of [the qur'anic assertion] "We have bestowed blessings on Adam's children" and to manifest the secret truth in [the other qur'anic text] "I breathed of my spirit into him" [17:70, 15:29], he must seek for himself a pasture other than that of the animals and a scenery beyond the scene of this world. He must ponder over that which he has in common with the beasts so that he may abandon it and observe that which gives him the privilege over the beasts in order to nurture it. It is in this fashion that in the dark night of the senses he will come to see [the truth in the dicta] "By the stars are human beings directed" and "When night drew its shadow over him, he saw a star" [16:16, 6:76].

Because a human being is used to the world of appearances and has grown accustomed to sensual life, when awareness is heightened unexpectedly to observe the hidden realm, and the eye of intellect opened to behold the perfection of the sovereign governance, they presume the luminous world of mysteries revealed to the inner self to be the divine dominion embracing him or Godly perfection being displayed before his eyes [as in the qur'anic verse] "This is my Lord" [6:77–78]. [This will be his state] until the divine grace nurtures and guides him to perfection, treating his inner shortcomings by putting the collyrium of guidance in his internal eyes, and awakens him from the state of slumber by uncovering his sainthood, sprinkling his mind with refreshing drops of kindness. He may, in this manner, observe [in his own nature] the affliction of instability and the unfortunate events in the outside world. Consequently, he would beg forgiveness reciting [the qur'anic passage] "I will not worship gods that fade," and to identify the ailment that hinders true worship he would examine the pulse of seeking. Understanding "He [Abraham] lifted up his eyes to the stars," he would observe the symptoms and recognize the malady in his own nature [as Abraham did], admitting, "I am sick" [6:76, 37:88–89]. Owing to the sense of pity for one's own state, and because of the natural desire to seek self-perfection, he delves into the concealed pharmacy in search of the antidote of knowledge, begging [for divine assistance and] saying, "I will take refuge with my Lord; He will give me guidance" [37:99]. Because God's grace is without cause, and because of the constant emanation of the light of his generosity, before he [the

human being] opens his mouth to utter the request, the cup-bearers of
his kindness and mercy would have filled the magic cup* of his heart with
the wine of knowledge [as Abraham did in the qur'anic example] "I will
turn my face to Him who has created the heavens and the earth" [6:79].

The journey of the elect is in two realms: the first is the realm of
worship. When the traveler ends the duty of studying the world [accord-
ing to the qur'anic text] "We will show them Our signs in all regions of
the earth" and steps into the dominion of [the ending of the same verse]
"And in their own souls" [41:53], he realizes that the vastness of this
world, which includes the seven climes, the seas, the mountains, the seven
heavens, and the throne, is a thousand times smaller compared to the
amplitude of the realm of sovereignty. So are the mysteries revealed
through earthly signs in comparison to those of the world within.
Lessons should be learnt from each earthly clime.

Knowledge concerning the properties and the true meaning of animal,
savage, and demonic concepts should be acquired, and the particulars of
good and bad human habits which are jewels in the mine of nature and
pearls in the sea of humanity must be recognized. Then, to make the
journey upward, he must ascend with the power of will through the
seven heavens of the heart. [Here,] each heaven has a different property,
and each sphere a different star. In one sphere there is the star of trust,
in another submission, in another resignation, in another knowledge, in
another contentment, and in yet another the star of love. In this fashion,
each sphere is illuminated with a star and each sky adorned with one.

After one has observed the state of the heavens of the heart, which
has reached the "two bows' length" in the realm of spiritual sovereignty,†
the manifestation of the lights emanating from the pure spirit begins to
appear to him and the secret of the placing of the spirit on the throne of
the heart is revealed [in line with the qur'anic dictum] "The Merciful sits
enthroned on high" [20:5]. [At this stage] the calamity of [addressing

* Literally the "world-depicting cup" (*jam-i jahannuma*), a goblet that belonged
to the ancient Iranian king Jamshid.
† A reference to the Prophet Muhammad's proximity to God in his nocturnal
journey in Q 53:9.

objects with] "This is my Lord" [6:77–78], which in the extrinsic world has a ring of infidelity to it, is, in the sovereignty of the heart, transformed to the secret of "I am the Truth."* That is, when that skin is shed, "I am the Truth" becomes visible.

This is still a preliminary state and a sign of crudity. If the wayfarer is protected by the grace [of God] and follows the innocence of the master of existence,† the ascendance of the sun of the spirit, which is referred to [in qur'anic terms] as "the light of God" [9:32], will be revealed to his inner eye. As long as the light of the intellect interferes, whatever is beyond the authority and endurance of the intellect appears as a manifestation from God. Still, the danger of [claims such as] "I am the Truth" and "Glory be to me" remains, and the principles of resemblance [*shubha*] and incarnation [*hulul*] may prevail.‡

With fine teachings of the Muhammadan pure spirit, the way would be cleared of doubts. Otherwise, residents of convents and monks come as far as the beginning of this domain but beyond that they lose their way, for their way is closed to lights emanating from God as well as to his magnetic attraction. God's predetermined will, which accorded the religion of Muhammad the right to abolish all other religions, made from the truth of that abrogation a barrier on [other] roads to God. That is, the followers of his [Muhammad's] way with the pure light of the first and last master [i.e., the Prophet] have opened the window in the house of devotion, so that the rays of the sun of Truth may fall into the house and clean the interior with the sanctity of that sacred world. He [the servant] brings his existence into annihilation in God's light, and in the perfection of the spiritual light he perceives the imperfection of [his] bondage, poverty, and need. He keeps saying, "Do not reject me as the Christians rejected Jesus, son of Mary."²³ Secretly he must declare, "I am the Truth," and in the open recite, "I am dust." He must observe the blemish of

---

* An ecstatic saying attributed to the mystic and martyr Hallaj (d. 922).
† *Sayyid-i ka'inat*, a title frequently used for the Prophet.
‡ "Glory be to me": attributed to Bayazid Bistami, the ninth-century mystic; *shubha* and *hulul* are technical theological terms referring, respectively, to the principles of similarity of God to human beings and incarnation.

createdness in the beauty of the spiritual world so that his face may
turn in the direction of the realm of spirit.

While he was in the domain of the heart, his learning from the
attributes of the outer world led to the manifestation of the spiritual
light. When he reached the spirit, the mysteries of spiritual manifestations led to the manifestation of the Truth. When his traveling in this
[the spiritual] domain has attained perfection, form, which covers the
mysteries, will be removed and the manifestations of the attributes of the
spirit will be revealed [according to the qur'anic decree] "Say: Truth has
come and Falsehood has been overthrown" [17:81]. The Moses-like spirit,
in the covenant of bondage on the Mount Sinai of the heart, continues to
cry out, "Lord, reveal Yourself to me, that I may look upon you." The
soul of his soul will be stricken with "You shall not see Me" [7:143], for
seeing presupposes a seer, whereas in [God's] eternal light the attributes
of servitude may not continue to exist. However, "I am you, otherwise
there would be no union" alludes to the sovereignty of the heart, which is
the site for the manifestation of the secret of his presence, whereas "But
look upon the mountain; if it remains firm upon its base, then only shall
you see Me" [7:143] speaks to the hellish nature of the seeker, which has
the characteristic of insatiability [as does hell in the Qur'an, asking:] "Are
there any more?" [50:30].

Here the sweetness of the conversation adds to the [lover's] desire so
that he sacrifices the moth of his life for the candle of the face of the desired
beloved. The scent of his sincerity rises up from the incense burner of his
soul and his sad murmur of "Are there any more?" reaches the Lord. The
lightening of the manifestation of His glory flashes at Moses and Sinai like
a thunderbolt [as in] "And when his Lord revealed Himself to the mountain, He leveled it into dust. Moses fell down senseless" [7:143]. Just so the
ultimate stage in the realm of sovereignty led to repentance and asking for
forgiveness [as in case of Abraham:] "I will not worship gods that fade"
[6:76]. When, after annihilation, the help of [divine] kindness restores signs
of subsistence and refreshes the face of nonexistence, sprinkling it with
his grace [which is] like the water of life, the secret of [the qur'anic state-
ment] "And they grow as do gardens as a result of floods" is revealed and

the effect of "When he came to" becomes apparent [7:143]. The way to ask for forgiveness, in this state, is to get away from oneself and to befriend Him [as in the case of Moses:] "He [Moses] said Glory be to you! Accept my repentance. I am the first of believers" [7:143].

[As for] the *Journey of the Elect Among the Elect*, the early manifestations of the signs of attraction occurred in the realm of the divine ['*alam-i uluhiyat*]. The realm of divinity, despite its boundlessness in comparison to the domains of humanity ['*alam-i mulk*] and sovereignty ['*alam-i malakut*], does in fact reach an end. The realm of lordship ['*alam-i rububiyat*], however, is infinite. The difference between the wayfarers who complete the journey becomes evident in this domain. The wayfarer will not be qualified for leadership until he learns from [God's] attributes. The truth of "As one soul" is revealed here.* The attributes of humanity will cease, the difference between natures will be obliterated, and the homogeneity of unity [*tawhid*] will arise. The real difference between sainthood and prophethood will become apparent, and absorption [to God] will turn into endeavor.

Furthermore, because pious conduct is like a skin covering the attraction [to God] and a curtain hiding the lady of the concealed world, just as the divine attraction continues uninterrupted so does the pious conduct, and each hour a new attribute manifests itself. The life [referred to in] "We shall grant him a happy life" [16:97] is here established. For [in this stage] if the eye looks, "it sees with me"; if the ear hears, "it hears with me"; if the tongue speaks, "it speaks with me"; if the hand and the foot move in the realm of sovereignty, "they move with me"; and if the heart engages in transformative action in the unseen or visible world, "it perceives through me."† [As in the poem] "I am the one who desires, and the one whom I desire is me," here the mistaken assumption of incarnation is dispelled because incarnation requires a place. Similarly, the doubt concerning [the Jewish and the Christians claims that] "the Messiah is

---

* "He created you only as one soul, and only as one soul will He bring you back to life" (31:28).
† A reference to the sacred "hadith of supererogatory works." See SD 16–17.

the son of God, and Ezra is the son of God" [9:30] is removed, for duality
[of God and His messenger] is inherent in the concept of prophethood.*

This much of the description of the excellence of this journey was here
put into writing. The details of the lodgings [*manazil*] on the way is based
on the ninety-nine names, perhaps even on a thousand and one names [of
God]. "Travel, improve your health, and gain profit."† Physical journeying does not lead to bodily health, because when nature and temperament
get accustomed to a certain climate, changing that climate leads to illness.
This is caused by the fact that each land has a different climate, and each
climate is suitable to a different temperament. The climate in the land
known as Turkistan is suited to the health of the Turks. If you take a Turk
to hot climate, it will lead to his illness and death. The same is true of
Indians who are taken to Turkistan. It is, therefore, clear that [the saying]
"Travel, improve your health . . . " refers to the journey, which is hoped
to lead [those described in the Qur'an with the words] "There is a
sickness in their hearts" [2:10, 5:52] to the health of intimate knowledge,
just as Abraham—God's blessings upon him—said, "I am sick" [37:89],
then turned to medicine for recovery. He understood the [meaning of]
good health intended by "Travel, improve your health, and gain profit,"
which led to [his declaration] "I will take refuge with my Lord; He will
give me guidance" [37:99]. Good health is in the domain of the heart,
and profit in the domain of Lordship and the realm of [divine] absorption,
because health and profit exist, and that is the opposite of [the state of
those in the fire of hell described in the Qur'an as] "It leaves nothing, it
spares no one" [74:28].

May God—may he be exalted and glorified—through His benevolence
and amplitude of generosity, grant his brokenhearted lovers perfect
satisfaction from this reservoir of sweet water and protect them from
calamities. May the Lord bless our master Muhammad, his family,
companions, and descendants, and grant them endless peace.

---

* The continuation of the poem attributed to Hallaj is as follows: "We are as two
souls who have entered one body." The qur'anic text is here quoted in reverse order.
† A saying attributed to the Prophet and quoted in the opening paragraph of the
text.

The treatise on journeying by the accomplished mystic Majd ad-Din Baghdadi—may God sanctify his secret—is finished with God's help and benevolence.

Mystical Geography

A sixteenth-century Turkish work by Vahidi takes this interpretation of the journey metaphor further. Addressed to the generality of seekers, the text spins an elaborate allegory of the quest. Vahidi stands in the tradition of such great authors as Farid ad-Din 'Attar, whose *Conference of the Birds* takes the seekers through seven valleys in search of their king (see fig. 57). But here the author probes more deeply into the psychological aspects of the journey, juxtaposing the seven ritual invocations to the seven levels of spiritual wayfaring.

✳ ## Vahidi
The Seven Invocations and the Seven Journeys

AHMET T. KARAMUSTAFA

The Book of the Master of the World and the Offspring of the Soul (*Menakib-i hvoca-i cihan ve netice-i can*), written in Ottoman Turkish by Vahidi in 1522, is a didactic treatise of mystical guidance addressed to the uninitiated. It introduces the basic doctrines of the "correct" Sufi path and provides interested readers the criteria with which to discover, to understand, and eventually to adopt the "right" path. Vahidi, himself a Sufi, discusses such topics as the identification of true Sufi masters, the conditions required to become wayfarers on the Sufi path, the ranking of wayfarers, and the topography of the path. Cast in the form of an extended allegorical tale, the work is notable for its literary qualities as well as for the wealth of social realistic information it preserves on Sufi life in Ottoman society.

This selection gives a sevenfold account of travel on the Sufi path known to be characteristic of the Halveti (Ar., *Khalwati*) order. Under this scheme, the wayfarer traverses seven stages under the supervision of a Sufi director: journey to God; journey for the sake of God; journey toward God; journey with God; journey in God; journey through God; and journey by God.[24] The seven "journeys" correspond to seven stages of the human soul: the commanding soul; the blaming soul; the inspiring soul; the pacified soul; the contented soul; the agreeable soul; and the perfect soul.[25] The wayfarer travels on this path with the help of a spiritual technique known as *zikr* (Ar., *dhikr*), "remembrance or mention

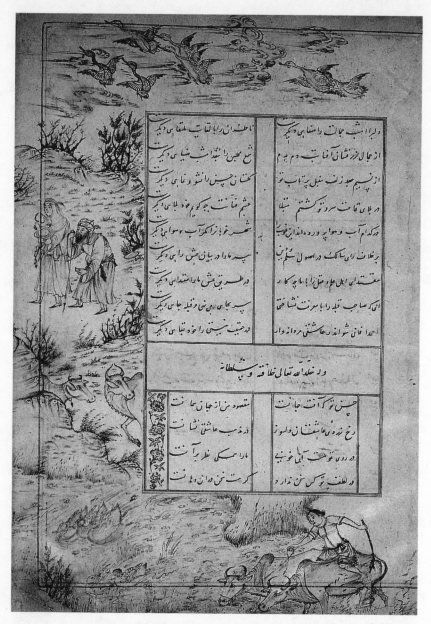

Figure 57. In the margin of the *Divan* of Sultan Ahmad Jalayir (1406–1410), a text of Persian lyric poems, the artist depicts "The Valley of the Quest," the first of a series of drawings showing six of the seven "valleys" through which the birds of 'Attar's didactic *mathnawi, The Conference of the Birds*, must travel in their spiritual quest. The drawings function as visual gloss to the religious poems, interpreting them by means of visual allusion to a work of mystical poetry that was by then already a classic. Washington, DC: Freer Gallery of Art, Smithsonian Institution, 32.30–1. (See also SD fig. 18.)

of God" (here translated as "invocation"), the regulated repetition of certain formulae by the aspirant. Each stage has its distinctive dhikr, which, though not specified in Vahidi's account, are known to be *Tahlil* (the witness to faith: *La ilaha illa 'llah*), followed by six names of God: Allah, *Hu* ("He"), *Hayy* ("the Living"), *Haqq* ("the True"), *Qayyum* ("the Self-standing" or "the Subsistent"), and *Qahhar* ("the Conqueror")—recalling the reflections on divine names with which part 6 began.[26]

ON THE SEVEN INVOCATIONS AND THE SEVEN JOURNEYS

Concerning the First Invocation and the First Journey, Which Is the Journey to God

Upon hearing the first invocation from his director, the serious aspirant should rest neither day nor night and should turn this invocation into a constant companion for his tongue and an occupation for his heart and soul. The initiated know well that this stage [of the path] is [called] the journey to God and is the beginning of the road for the wayfarer. In this portico, the commanding soul is dominant. It demands and desires the opposite of renunciation and abstinence. The wayfarer is here a helpless sinner, out of his senses, bewildered, and wretched. Yet, if he persists in his invocation day and night, the partial intellect appears, the light of admonition becomes manifest in the kingdom of the heart, and the ray of [the] blaming [soul] shines forth. The wayfarer then howls and groans. Some [wayfarers] experience disclosures and [work] saintly miracles, while others are content with a single ray. The soul is situated in between these two [options]. He who is in this [state] is possessed at times by splendor and at others by darkness. Continuous invocation of God is necessary for the invocation to find a point of entry to the heart in order to subdue it and take possession of it.

Concerning the Second Invocation and the Second Journey, Which Is the Journey for the Sake of God

Once the director detects receptivity in the aspirant, he inculcates in him the second invocation, and the aspirant becomes thoroughly engrossed [in the invocation]. The initiated know well that this stage [of the path] is [called] the journey for the sake of God. Here, private invocation is required for the grace of that Gracious One to reach [the aspirant] from time to time and for the wayfarer to start serving the Creator. The wayfarers on this [stage] are known as the people of love, and the Beloved's present [to them] is always "invocation by the heart." The partial intellect finds its perfection here and exhausts its powers. For this reason, some wayfarers develop a penchant for working saintly miracles, while others grow fond of taverns. Here, the sun of the sky of the world of love emits a ray that illuminates the heart of the wayfarer, who [thus] acquires the knowledge of certainty and reaches his desire. If he does not neglect his private invocation and persists in it, endless mystical knowledge appears, and he becomes a possessor of intimate knowledge and a knower of the secrets of the heart and the soul.

Concerning the Third Invocation and the Third Journey, Which Is the Journey Toward God

When the master director sees the aspirant to be agreeable, he inculcates in him the third invocation. The aspirant here becomes deserving of approbation and begins to see the Desired One. The initiated know well that this stage [of the path] is [called] the journey toward God. On this [station], one kind of wayfarer is overcome by love, [his] partial intellect dissipates, and his spirit departs, while another kind of wayfarer says to his spirit "God is not contained in the heavens and His earth, but is contained in my heart."* Still another kind of wayfarer crosses from this determined world to that absolute world, and he boasts [saying in Hallaj's words,] "I am the Truth." Doubt, opinion, and phantasy are removed from him, and he attains to the station of knowledge of certainty. From every direction, manifestations of [God's] essence pour [toward him], and he finds solace at times in the manifestations of [God's] actions and at others in the manifestations of [His] attributes. Then, the inspiring soul appears to the wayfarer and brings to him the fragrance of the rose of reality.

---

* This is an inversion of the well-known hadith *qudsi,* "My heavens and My earth do not embrace me, but the heart of my believing servant does embrace Me."

Concerning the Fourth Invocation and the Fourth Journey,
Which Is the Journey with God

When the master sees the outside of the aspirant decorated with invocation and his inside adorned with meditation, he inculcates in him the
fourth invocation. An intense desire arises within the aspirant's heart. He
becomes occupied with invocation day and night and attains to certainty.
He grows aware of the internal states of things [around him] and becomes a traveler on the journey with God. He is now a knower of the
divine knowledge and one with intimate awareness of the ancient secret.
His cheeks turn pale and he begins to cry and to wail day and night. Like
a mad lover, he ceases to care about all creatures, and talks about [what is]
above the sky and brings information about [what is] underneath the
earth. He thinks himself to be at the final degree and conceives himself to
be at the ultimate rank. The sun of love manifests itself to his heart from
the curtain of benevolence, and he becomes a pacified soul. All thoughts
that visit him depart [immediately]. There is much danger on this station,
and wayfarers should exercise caution. This station is the place of the
people of sincerity and the courtyard of select wayfarers. Here, it is
imperative to hold onto the religious law tightly and to invoke the Truth
constantly in order for a ray of the light of Muhammad, peace and
blessings upon him, to be cast into the heart [of the wayfarer]. Then,
the eye of certainty appears [to him], and he reaches [his destination].
His intimate knowledge increases, he is detached from his self, and he
becomes unique in the way he travels. At this point, [divine] attraction
manifests itself to the wayfarer.

Concerning the Fifth Invocation and the Fifth Journey,
Which Is the Journey in God

When the master sees the aspirant to be capable and eager for wayfaring,
he inculcates in him the fifth invocation. The initiated know well that this
stage [of the path] is [called] the journey in God. On this station, the
wayfarer loses his self and is no longer aware of his nature and his behavior. Friend and enemy appear the same to him. He is bold on the path
of God the Absolute Agent and sees his Friend clearly everywhere. He

gives up his existence altogether, clings firmly to the rope of the love of invoking God, and walks on the road of nonexistence. At this station, the invoker, the invoked, and the invocation are one and the same. The wayfarer here attains to the degree of immersion in unity, becomes solitary, and possesses the dominion of [the hadith] "I am his hearing. . . ."* If there is any trace left of his existence, he destroys his self, and if his self is totally annihilated, his soul becomes content. The secret of the heart comes into being and the heart becomes the treasury of the ocean of generosity. Yet in this station there are traces of deficiency in the wayfarers. They should exercise caution, remedy [these deficiencies], and provide information [on these difficulties] to those who cannot so remedy [their shortcomings].

Concerning the Sixth Invocation and the Sixth Journey, Which Is the Journey Through God

When the master sees the aspirant to be quick and nimble in invocation and intelligent in his work, he inculcates in him the sixth invocation. The initiated know well that this stage [of the path] is [called] the journey through God and it is the closest path for the wayfarer. In this station, bewilderment manifests itself to the wayfarer and induces his heart to cry and to wail, and the hadith "The tongue of whoever possesses intimate knowledge is long" takes effect.[27] Then, knowledge of prophethood reaches [the wayfarer]. Here, the soul of bad habits is totally annihilated, and the wayfarer attains to perfection. This is the station of select servants at the court of the Possessor of Majesty. It is here that service to God is perfected, that prophethood is granted to prophets, and that wayfarers turn into directors. Also, the soul is here transformed into [the] agreeable [soul], and the first [stage of] poverty becomes manifest; the hadith "Poverty was almost like unbelief" was uttered here.[28]

Concerning the Seventh Invocation and the Seventh Journey, Which Is the Journey by God

When the master sees the aspirant to be surefooted in [traversing] the stations, he inculcates in him the seventh invocation. The initiated know

* Another reference to the "hadith of supererogatory works."

well that this stage [of the path] is [called] the journey by God and it is the last of the stations. Here, existence is not appropriate. It is best to achieve complete annihilation within nonexistence, since such is the true goal. All [divine] names appear in this [station]. The saying "Poverty is the blackness of the face in the two worlds" was uttered here, and that sultan of the prophets [Muhammad] commanded his hadith "Poverty is my pride" here.[29] Also in this [station], the heart of the believer becomes the exalted throne [of God], the wayfarer achieves perfection, the perfect human being is constituted, and the light of unity shines forth so that desired, desirer, and desire as well as beloved, lover, and love all become one. Here, [everything] difficult becomes easy, and the hadith "The tongue of whoever possesses intimate knowledge is slow" manifests itself to the wayfarer, totally annihilates him from his own existence, and makes him enter the realm of subsistence in God.[30] The meaning of the hadith "He who knows himself knows his Lord" is then realized.[31] The wayfarer implements the hadith "Die before you die."[32] Since the origin of numbers was one, [everything] returns to its origin, otherness is removed, and only "one" subsists. This is because even though it starts the numbers, "one" itself is not to be reckoned a number: it is beyond numbers. Everything other than the essence of God perishes completely, and only the Absolute One remains. Peace!

Languages of the Spirit

When traveling in a foreign land, one needs to know the language of the territory. Jaʿfar Sajjadi's twentieth-century Persian *Lexicon of Mystical Language, Technical Terms, and Expressions* represents a contemporary development in the ancient genre of mystical lexicography.

✳ ## Sayyid Jaʿfar Sajjadi
Lexicon of Mystical Terms
FATEMEH KESHAVARZ

In his mystical dictionary, Jaʿfar Sajjadi (d. 1996) brings together examples of the usage of Sufi terms and concepts in the works of Persian mystics from the earliest examples to Jami (d. 1492). Among his Persian sources, the poetry of

'Attar (d. 1220), 'Iraqi (d. 1289), and Rumi (d. 1273) appear most frequently. Among the Arabic sources, the *Generations of the Sufis* (*Tabaqat as-sufiya*) by 'Abd ar-Rahman Sulami (d. 1021) stands out. In keeping with the theme of journeying, here is Sajjadi's entry on the various meanings of the term "Sea," proceeding from a definition of the term by itself.[33]

The sea refers to the essence and the infinite attributes of God [*Haqq*, "the True"]. The entire universe is the waves in this boundless sea. This world is [the world of] absolute existence. 'Iraqi:

> That sea of which the sea is a wave
> > That light to which all things are shades.

[He then includes several compound usages of the term: boundless sea, sea of God's generosity, sea of manifestation, and manifest sea. Here are his entries on the sea of existence, the sea of fire, the sea of friendship, and the engulfing sea:]

The sea of existence [*bahr-i hast-i*] is the divine celestial manifestations.

> They plunge in the sea of existence
> > As the heart plunges in the love of a beauty.

Quatrain:

> I melted in the sea of nonexistence like salt.
> > Nothing remained of me: [not] infidelity, faith, certitude, or doubt.
> A star appeared in my heart;
> > The nine spheres get lost in that one star!

O, wayfarer! one must first be cleansed of the impurity of nature in the salt mine of religious practice [*shari'a*], then plunged into the water of truth [*haqiqa*]. That is why it has been said that without perfection in the outward practice of the religion of Muhammad, you will not reach the truth of the oneness [of God]. 'Attar:

> It is a colossal task: to break away from oneself
> > To see the self completely annihilated
> To appropriately practice his [Muhammad's] shari'a
> > Then, arriving at its [the religion's] truth
> Like the reed pen with a tongue cut out
> > Running, head down, on the tablet of nonexistence

Being free in the wine house
　Drinking with the cup-bearer of the soul
[It is a colossal task] to leave one's own existence behind
　To find tranquillity in the existence of the Friend.

In experiential philosophy and in Sufism, existence is described as the sea
of being [*darya-yi hasti*] and this expression is based on the view of the
absoluteness of existence. (As I have explained under the term *vujud* in
my dictionary of rational sciences), according to the view of the absoluteness of existence, existence is like a boundless sea, and quiddities
[*mahiyat*] are all waves in this sea. This is the meaning of the contin-
gency of the quiddity and the absoluteness of existence. The movement
and change in the sea lead to creation of the waves of multiplicity that
appear but do not last. All waves eventually return to the sea just as He
said, "We are from God and to Him we return." Jami:

It is a sea that does not diminish or expand;
　On its face, waves are busy coming and going.
Since the world consists of these very waves,
　It doesn't last over time, not even for moments.

The world—if you are not incapable of learning lessons!—
　A river flowing in unexpected fashions.
And in each of the different kinds in which this river flows
　There flows a secret! Which is the truth of all truths.

Which means that the world and the people in it are all one truth dressed
in different forms. The accidental qualities of the world and the beings
make them look numerous. He [God] does not have a manifestation in
ranks of existence except through these forms and accidental qualities
just as these will not have an existence without His.

The Sophist who is deprived of wisdom
　Says the world is imagination in flux.
Yes, the world is all imagination, but
　There is always a truth manifested in it.

Finally, the people of spiritual unveiling and witnessing see that the Lord,
may He be exalted and glorified, in each moment manifests Himself in a

different manner. There is no repetition in His manifestations. That is to
say, He would not appear in one state and with one specification in two
moments. In each breath He manifests himself in a different nature with
a different disposition.

> The existence that does not keep one disposition in two moments,
>   Each instant displays a different nature.
> See this point in "each day some mighty task engages Him" [55:29]
>   If you need to find evidence [for this argument] in God's words.

The secret of this is in the fact that God has opposite [*mutaqabila*] names,
some pertaining to his grace and some to his wrath, which are all ceaselessly at work. When a possible reality, as a result of attaining desirable
conditions and removing the barriers, becomes suitable for existence, the
mercy of the merciful engulfs him and brings him into being. The manifested existence, according to the rules and conditions of that reality, takes
a specific disposition. Subsequently, God's wrath abolishes the specific
disposition that gives the reality its particular nature and an apparent
multiplicity of form, while at the same time God's grace endows him
with a new but resembling disposition which will again be abolished in
the next moment. This will continue as long as God wills. So, there are no
two moments in which the same manifestation occurs. In each moment,
the world goes to nonexistence and another like it [the world] comes into
being as do the waves in the sea.

> Existence is a sea ceaselessly fermenting;
>   The inhabitants of the world have not seen but waves from that sea.
> See the visible waves coming from the unseen of the sea!
>   [And see] how the sea itself is hidden by its own waves.

Jami:

> Existence that is the essence of the dear God,
>   All things are in it, and it is in all things.
> This is the explanation for the Sufi belief
>   "Everything is in everything."

Just as existence, through its specific application, is current in the essence
of all beings as if it were the very essence of those beings, [in the same

manner] those essences are waves of that current. The perfect attributes of existence are the origin and fountainhead of all attributes.

> Existence, with the attributes it has hidden in it,
> Is flowing visibly in all specific beings.
> Each attribute in the suitable being
> Is manifested as much as particularities of the being allow.

The sea of fire [*bahr-i atash*]. Love is a burning sea. The condition of union is that the sincere lover steps into this sea of fire and fearlessly allows himself to be devoured by the sea monster of love, and still enjoys all this hardship. Sa'di:

> If you call me kindly from the other end of a burning sea,
> Walking on fire will be more pleasant to me than sailing on water.

The sea of friendship [*bahr-i mavaddat*]. [This] is limitless love, and that is the perpetual love of God who said: "Say: If you love God, follow me. God will love you" [3:31]. For the Messenger is the perfect manifestation of God's love. Then there is the hadith "I stipulated my love on those who share in my love, who exchange it, who separate and unite in me, and who trust in me."[34] Sa'di:

> Do not blame the one drowned in the sea of friendship,
> For anyone away from the shore struggles [to save himself].

The engulfing sea [*bahr-i muhit*]. This is an allusion to God's unlimited light, to which he referred [in the qur'anic dictum] "God is the light of the heavens and the earth" (24:35). Sadr ad-Din Shirazi* has sometimes interpreted "the light" as the absolute existence; so has the Shaykh Shihab ad-Din Suhrawardi [Maqtul]. . . . † 'Aziz ad-Din‡ says: "The Indian Sufis have considered the world of existence as the sea of light." He says: "The innermost [core] of existence is light, one must reach this light. One must see this light and see the world through this light so that one may be freed from associating others with God, and [the illusion of] multiplic-

---

* Sadr ad-Din: philosopher from Shiraz (d. 1640), often referred to as Mulla Sadra.
† Suhrawardi: founder of the philosophy of Ishraq, "the monism of light"; he was executed in 1191.
‡ 'Aziz ad-Din Nasafi: a shaykh of the Kubrawi tariqa (d. 1300), author of *The Perfect Person* (*Insan-i kamil*), an influential work of mystical theology.

ity disappears. Our Shaykh said, 'I have reached this light and seen this brilliant sea. It was a boundless light, a shoreless sea that did not have up, down, right, left, front, or back. I was bewildered in this light.' O, Sufi! any wayfarer who did not reach this sea of light and did not plunge into this sea will never approach the station of unity. The one who did not reach the station of unity, and was not exalted through beholding God, did not see and know anything as it is. He was born blind and died blind. The sign of the one who has plunged into this sea is that he is in peace with all people of the world, looks at them with tenderness and love, does not deny anyone friendship and support, does not consider anyone to be lost, and regards everyone to be traveling on the road to God. A dear [friend] has said: 'For several years I called people to God. No one accepted my invitation. I despaired, stopped calling, and turned to the Lord. When I reached his abode, I found everyone present.' This is the meaning of the engulfing sea and the sea of existence."

Figure 58. Muslim artists have often fashioned visual metaphors for the experience of dreams or visions. According to the text of Jami's (d. 1492) *math-nawi The Rosary of the Pious* (*Subhat al-abrar*), included in this miniature, a student (*lower right*) dreams that his master, the poet Sa'di (reclining with a book), is composing poetry in praise of God while angels descend with heavenly gifts of light. Relieved of some unspecified doubt, the student rushes to Sa'di's house to see him and appears again at the door (*lower left*). Washington, DC: Freer Gallery of Art, Smithsonian Institution, 46.12.147a. (See also SD figs. 34, 36.) Thanks to Fatemeh Keshavarz for reading the text.

7 Experience
Testimony, Paradigm, and Critique

Accounts of "religious experience," however peculiar they may sound at first, open a window into the soul. Whether expressed as first-person recollections or as third-person descriptions, records of encounters with mystery also tap the wellsprings of imagination. Because they often use the language of feeling rather than that of reason, reflections on experience are notoriously difficult to explain and evaluate. Even so, believers and outsiders alike have never ceased trying to unravel the intricacies of inner experience that spiritual seekers have chronicled. The three main sections of part 7 offer rare glimpses of the interior lives of a dozen fascinating Muslims of both ancient and modern times.

HEART SPEAKS TO HEART

The diary of a late-twentieth-century Indonesian exemplifies a major genre of religious literature. Then an extended hadith narrates the details of what has become the classic description of Muhammad's paradigmatic sojourn in the realm of spirit.

Soul on Pilgrimage

✳ The Diary of Ahmad Wahib

ANTHONY H. JOHNS

The spiritual diary of Ahmad Wahib offers an unusual and moving entree into the struggle of a contemporary Muslim seeking to find a balance between the faith and tradition passed down to him and an honest, open desire to bolster the spirit amid the confusion of the twentieth-century world. Ahmad Wahib was born on the Indonesian island of Madura in 1943. His father was head of a local religious school, called a *pesantren*, and followed the reformist tradition of

Muhammad 'Abduh.* Wahib received a secular education, and in 1961 enrolled in the Faculty of Mathematics and Physics at Gadjah Mada University in Yogyakarta. A committed Muslim, he played a leading role in the local Islamic Students Association. The attempted coup in 1965, and the mass killings that took place in central Java, affected him deeply and set him on a troubled search for a personal understanding of Islam that would enable him to cope with the fragmented and disordered world around him.

Wahib had close associations with a number of religious institutions and traditions, including a Jesuit community. His mind in turmoil, he increasingly followed a path of his own choosing; as a consequence, he was forced to resign from the Islamic Students Association, which had been the center of his life for almost a decade. He left Yogyakarta to work for a news periodical in Jakarta. In 1973 he was killed in a traffic accident. The diary from which these extracts are translated was discovered after his death. A friend and close colleague edited and published it in Jakarta in 1980. It created widespread sympathy and interest, but was bitterly condemned by a number of traditionally inclined religious scholars. It is no longer available in Indonesian bookshops, although the ideas that it expresses have a wide circulation. The excerpts are arranged here in topical fashion.[1]

THE SPIRITUAL QUEST

Human beings are enriched by constant questioning. To reject or kill questions means to make our life barren. The problem is: how are we to be able to raise questions of which we are unaware from the subconscious to put them forward clearly at the level of consciousness.

I do not yet understand what Islam really is. So far I have only understood Islam according to Hamka,† according to Natsir,‡ according to 'Abduh . . . and frankly I am not yet satisfied. What I seek I have not yet found, not yet discovered, and that is Islam according to Allah who made it. How can I do so? By direct study of the Qur'an and the Sunna? I can try. But others may think that all I will end up with is Islam according to myself. Never mind. The important thing is the conviction in my sound

---

* Muhammad 'Abduh (1849–1905) was an Egyptian reformer widely regarded as the father of Muslim "modernism."
† See part 2 above on Hamka's tafsir.
‡ Mohammad Natsir (1908–1993) was a European-educated Indonesian nationalist whose works exemplify tensions between fundamentalism and modernism.

mind that the understanding I achieve is Islam according to Allah. This is what I have to be sure of. [28 March 1969]

God, I come into your presence not only at those times when I love you, but also at those times I do not love you and do not understand you, at those times when it is as if I want to revolt against your power. This being so, my Lord, I hope that my love for you will again be restored. I cannot wait for love for the length of a ritual prayer. [18 May 1969]

God, [I beg you] to understand me!

God, how can I accept your laws without first having doubts about them? Therefore, God, be understanding if I still have doubts about the truth of your laws. If you do not like this, give me such an understanding of them that my doubts vanish, and I [will] be swiftly brought from the level of doubt to acceptance.

God, are you angry if I speak to you with a free mind and heart, the mind and heart that you yourself have given me, with a great capacity for freedom? God, are you angry if the mind, with the capacity for knowledge that you have given it, is used to the extent of that capacity?

God, I long to speak with you in an atmosphere of freedom. I believe that you hate not only hypocritical utterances but also hypocritical minds, minds that do not dare to reflect on the ideas that rise within them, minds that pretend not to know their own thoughts. [9 June 1969]

Indeed, there is no end to thinking. One can never be satisfied. To think, get it wrong, to think again, be wrong again, think again. To seek, to seek and . . . keep on seeking. And perhaps the arguments that I have put above will sometime change? Perhaps individual motives will be formulated differently? If humankind must be continually questioning, is it possible that in the end I will come to ask whether this questioning is always necessary? And isn't this last itself a question about questioning? And how, if this last question is itself questioned? In that case, there is no question that can ever be settled, because the word "question" itself can never be absent. And humanity's discontent grows ever deeper. And thus we draw ever closer to the absolute.

By such a dialectic does life progress. [26 October 1969]

I do not know whether I am accurst for thinking in this way, involving myself in questions to which there are no answers. Is it possible that all this is going to plunge me into an eternity of wandering? Ah, thousands of issues arise in my heart. Hundreds of questions spring up in my mind, and no answer can be found to them. Alas, there is no one who understands that such a turmoil cannot possibly be resolved at an internal forum [of the association that wishes to expel me]. [29 November 1969]

I am not Hatta, not Sukarno, not Shahrir, not Natsir, not Marx, and not anyone else either. Indeed . . . I am not even Wahib. I am becoming Wahib, I am seeking, continually seeking, on the way toward trying to become Wahib. Truly I am not I. I am becoming me, am continually in the process of becoming I. Only in my death agony will I be I! [1 December 1969]

Heaven and hell are spiritual situations that constantly pursue and exist in the life of an individual. Thus heaven, or a heavenly state and avoidance of hell, is something to be struggled for second by second in this life. We must try to fashion heaven every moment. [22 April 1972]

My Lord, if this spiritual emptiness I feel can be the beginning of a new insight into your secret self, then plunge me deeper into this emptiness so that I may the more single-mindedly search for its meaning. [18 January 1973]

FAITH AND DOUBT

The human capacity to think is indeed limited, but we do not know what that limit is. The question is whether we make use of this limited capacity to the fullest extent, or whether we use it only halfheartedly.

To understand the Absolute [God] is the summit, not the middle or the bottom of intellectual endeavor, relative as its capacity may be. Therefore, strive continually to raise the summit of this capacity, relative as it is. Strive constantly for the utmost that this relative capacity can achieve. It is only by so doing that we can draw closer to the absoluteness of the Most Absolute.

What, then, is the content of belief? This is what we have to discuss together, because we have not yet agreed upon it. Does belief forbid the presence in the mind of any question that puts part of the content of belief in doubt? This is the point on which we differ. Perhaps, subconsciously, there are some who say that belief is against anything that opposes belief. In my view, belief is democratic; it loves and appreciates unbelief, even though belief does not accept the content of that unbelief. It is only in this way that one can reach true belief as opposed to pseudo-belief, or a belief that can be reduced to slogans. Let all the old 'ulama' and aspirant 'ulama' disagree with me. I want to speak directly to God, and to know Muhammad personally. I am sure that God himself loves and appreciates those thoughts that doubt part of His teaching. God gives the right to life, and gives the opportunity to "His enemies" to think, so that later they may become "His friends."

Indeed, how can people be told to believe in God of their own free will if they are forbidden to consider the possibility of the "belief" that God does not exist. How can we be convinced that the whole of the teaching of Islam is true, if the possibility of there being a weakness in the teaching of Islam never crosses the mind, a mind that later may consider the possibility of what was thought a weakness being correct. Especially if a desire to think through the issue is denounced as wrong and forbidden.

If A, for example, is stated to be in error, then it may follow that every question raised as to the possibility of A's not being in error is regarded as error. In that case, not only A is in error, but also anyone who questions whether A is in error. How heartless! I believe that God does not approve of this attitude of such heartless people, even if God himself regards A as in error. God may regard A as in error, and yet smile on those who query whether in fact A is or is not in error.

I am of the opinion that reason cannot be taken out of our life. One can abandon the use of one's intelligence. But one has to use one's intelligence to do so, to use reason to abandon reason. To use reason to abandon objectivity and use subjectivity as a means of arriving at the truth. [15 October 1969]

THE ROLE OF REASON

Some people ask me to keep my thinking within the limits of Tawhid, for this is the ultimate point of the universality of Islam. That's strange! Why should thinking be under constraints? Is God fearful of reason that he himself created? I believe in God, but God is not a no-go area for thought. God does not exist so that he should not be thought about. God has the attribute of existence not in order to be invulnerable to critical scrutiny. Indeed, those who claim to have a God, but refuse freedom of thought, are in fact despising the rationality of [belief in] the existence of God. In fact, they are despising God, because their professed belief is a hidden pretense.

If Islam really restricts freedom of thought, it is best that I reconsider my commitment to Islam. And there are only two alternatives: to be a partial and halfhearted Muslim, or simply to be an unbeliever. But up to the present I am still convinced that God does not put thought under constraints, and that God is proud that my mind should always be asking about him. I believe that God is full of vigor, alive, not static. He does not wish to be reduced to a stasis.

In my view, those who think in this way, even if their conclusions may be wrong, they are still far better than those who never make mistakes because they never think. And I simply cannot understand why people are so scared of freedom of thought. Even though there is the possibility that the effect may be bad, the benefit is much greater than the harm. Rather, those who fear to think freely in this way will be overwhelmed by fear of the pretense and uncertainty they are attempting to hide, afraid to admit an idea that may be buried in the subconscious and forbidden to emerge into consciousness. Whereas by thinking freely, human beings would know more about themselves, would know more about their own humanity. Some may say there is a danger in freedom of thought, in that one who indulges in it may incline towards atheism, or even become an atheist. Is that so? Even people who don't think at all can become atheists. It is better to become an atheist as a result of using the mind freely, than an atheist who never uses his mind at all.

The results achieved by uninhibited thought may be wrong. But not to think at all can also lead to wrong conclusions. So where is the greater potential to be preserved from error? And where is the greater potential to discover new truths?

I believe that those who do not exercise freedom of thought are wasting the most valuable gift that God has given them, namely their minds. I pray that God will guide those who do not use their minds to the fullest. Yet I realize that anyone who does think freely is seeking the restlessness [I feel], a restlessness that leads him to reflect on all kinds of issues, above all basic issues, as he attempts to establish a position based solely on intellectual objectivity. [17 July 1969]

INTEGRITY

Sometimes my heart tells me that in several respects, the teaching of Islam is bad. Thus God's teachings in several respects are bad, and some of the teachings of men, of great men that is, are far superior. It is my unfettered mind that speaks, a free mind that struggles desperately to bring itself to dare to think as it wills, without fear of incurring God's anger. It is only because of my belief in the existence of God, and the Qur'an is truly from God, and that Muhammad is truly a perfect man, that in the final analysis I still believe that Islam in its totality is good and perfect. It is only my mind that cannot grasp this perfection. [9 March 1969]

No matter how pointed our criticism of the general attitude of the community, we should never fall into the error of judging anything *a priori* wrong any more than [into] that of judging it a priori right. We must genuinely be able to avoid making use of a double standard, a double standard that takes either the side of the Muslim community or that of the non-Muslim community.

It is well for us to remember that to say *as-salam 'alaykum* is not necessarily Islamic; to recite the Qur'an so loudly that it can be heard far and wide is not necessarily Islamic; to write using the Arabic script is not necessarily Islamic; to put on a show of sincerity or religious devotion is not necessarily Islamic; to lace one's conversation with verses of the Qur'an is not necessarily Islamic; to invoke blessings upon the Prophet when making a speech is not necessarily Islamic.

By the same token, to denounce a girl for wearing a head shawl is not
necessarily modern; to defend atheism, to reject formalism, to criticize the
Islamic community, to defend those who dance in the Western manner,
are not necessarily modern. These are matters in which we must exercise
great care lest we fall into the trap of making a show of being Islamic, or
a show of being modern.

This does not mean that a priori I do not approve of people who regularly say *as-salam ʿalaykum*, write using the Arabic script, lace their
conversations with verses from the Qurʾan, et cetera. Likewise, it does
not mean that I do not approve of those who denounce the wearing of the
head shawl, attack the Muslim community, reject formalism, and the like.

The important thing in exercising freedom of thought is to free
ourselves from two tyrannies within ourselves. We have to dare to free
ourselves from the tyranny of pride—pride at being supposedly genuinely Muslim or sincerely modern, or intellectual, or moral, or pure, or
authentic, and the like—and the tyranny of fear—fear of being regarded
as conservative, atheistic, out of date, unbelieving, Muʿtazilite,* disori-
ented, ideologically weak, suspect as to faith, secularist, westernizing,
and the like. [3 August 1969]

THE RELIGIOUS ESTABLISHMENT

Now is the right moment for me to try to promote a democratic attitude,
even though I am not of the opinion that Islam is not completely democratic. I frankly admit that in this matter I am, up to the present, not a complete Muslim. I am not going to pretend to deny that I reject the ruling
of an Islamic law that a Muslim who does not pray should be punished.
I believe that one of the characteristics of a democrat is not to inflict
psychological terror on anyone who disagrees with him. [8 June 1969]

Just see how the ʿulamaʾ attempt to impose specific laws on mankind.
Alas, the fact is that here they spread abroad only the words of the Law,
and make little effort to understand and analyze the human problems to
which the Law is addressed. What possibility is there, by such means, to

---

* Muʿtazilites: a school of philosophical theology most famous for its role in the
intellectual life of ninth-century Baghdad.

transform the Law into an interior awareness? The result is rather the reverse. People increasingly disregard the laws they formulate.

In my view our leading 'ulama' . . . have no right to lay down the law on matters of morality and government. How can they make the right decisions when they have no grasp of the issues in human society and the like? They are not doing anything creative. They are [acting] only at the level of interpretation. . . .

As far as I have studied it, the language our 'ulama' use in their preaching is quite inadequate. They are so poor in the use of language that they are incapable of expressing the meaning of God's utterances— their language is totally barren.

If they speak of human love for God or the love of God for human-kind, the most their language of love can do is make sense to the intellect; it has no power to touch the heart. They speak of love, but they do not understand by it that love which is present like a seed in every human heart. It is not surprising that their call is rejected by every heart to which it is directed. [29 March 1970]

ISLAM AND CHANGE

What ought to be is that the philosophy of Islam is universal and eternal; the reality is that it is continually changing—which simply indicates that the philosophy of Islam is not yet perfect. Never mind! We strive to get as close to perfection as we can. Thus it does not matter that there is one philosophy according to Mawdudi,* another according to others. Uniformity of opinion throughout space and time is difficult to achieve, even though it ought to exist. It doesn't matter. Let it be. But even if we don't agree on it, what at least is the philosophy of Islam according to ourselves? Are not we ourselves the young thinkers of Islam?

As to which is the true religion, the problem is the same. There ought only to be one religion. The fact is that there are many sorts of religion. Every religion has to feel that *it* is God's religion. That it is the one that is universal and eternal. [8 March 1969]

* Mawlana Sayyid Abu 'l-'Ala' Mawdudi (d. 1979): an influential Pakistani intellectual.

God, I wish to ask whether the standards set by your religion are fixed or changing. God, just what is it in your teaching that is really fundamental, which cannot change, which has to be a guide for the development of social standards? I believe it is no longer right to include *ijmaʿ* [consensus] in the array of sources from which the Law is derived, an array that consists of the Qurʾan, the Sunna, and ijmaʿ [Wahib omits *qiyas*, analogy]. In a world that is rapidly changing, and in which individualism is becoming increasingly prominent, the Qurʾan and the Sunna are enough. Let everyone understand the Qurʾan and the Sunna in his or her own way.

Now then, as the standards that apply in society develop, so the laws of Islam must develop. The *haram* [forbidden] and *halal* [permissible] of today cannot be the same as the haram and halal of three or four centuries ago, let alone what they were when the Prophet was still alive. Therefore, there must be many hadith of the Prophet and even verses of the Qurʾan itself that no longer apply, simply because they are no longer necessary, and the harm that was once feared (and to avoid which they were promulgated) no longer exists, owing to the new standards that now apply in society.

I am aware that changes in moral standards will certainly bring about changes in the possibilities for the occurrence of harm and benefit that they allow. Because the Law of Islam, in my view, takes as its point of departure matters relating to harm and benefit, moral laws in Islam must also change *pari passu* with changes in the moral standards of society. Well, then, will not this situation cause confusion and even conflict within Islamic circles, because it appears that there is no legal certainty? Yet confusion and conflict are commonplace enough, and do not need to be avoided, for they are symptomatic of a society in flux, striving to realize better values. [8 September 1969]

CONSCIENCE

In making use of *ijtihad* [independent investigation] in relation to individual issues such as belief, law, and a number of ethical issues, actually every individual has the right to participate, and every individual has the obligation to exercise that right. Ijtihad in such issues cannot be handed over entirely to an institute of adjudication, even if highly competent, which can then produce a decision that is valid in general. The human conscience, to be specific, every human being, has to take part in discussions about what is right for him, and in the last resort, it is the human conscience that has the right to make decisions after considering the opinions of expert 'ulama'.

Belief, law, and part of ethics are matters of *private concern*. It is every individual, in accordance with his uniqueness, who in the last resort has the right to determine and to interpret God's determinations as they apply to himself. The privatization of ethical questions in this way is formally different from the moral position in the secular community, even though possibly, materially, in practice, the result may be the same. In this kind of privatization, a Muslim is nevertheless still taking as his point of reference religious principles. It is only the interpretation of such principles that may differ, according to the conscience of each individual. In the secular community however, such matters are morally neutral. As Bryan Wilson writes in *Religion in Secular Society*:

> Many aspects of behavior which were once moral matters supported by religious attitudes are now morally neutral. Thus, for instance, the matter of dress was in various societies and at various periods regulated by religious conception. The early Methodists went so far as to specify numbers of petticoats and their height from the ground, and the Scriptures themselves make prescriptions about a woman's head and a woman's arms. Today, with certain reserves about public decency (and these are subject to open disputation), dress has become a morally neutral matter.

Thus once again, it is necessary to remember that possibly the dress of a pious Muslim woman may be as modern as that of a woman who accepts secular ideas. The difference is in the point of departure of the mind in question; that is to say, the one, in deciding on her dress, does not omit reference to the teaching of religion, whereas the other has let go all contact with the teaching of religion. The one feels that God has blessed her choice of dress, whereas the other has no concern for whether it is blessed by God. [20 March 1970]

The sole authority in Islam for the life of a Muslim is conscience, not the *fatwa* [legal advisory] of a religious scholar, not what books on religion have to say, or the decisions of friends, colleagues, and others. All of these are simply considerations to be taken into account, and indeed they must be taken into account. Islam is conscience, after one has carefully taken into account the opinions, the interests, the ideals of others and the social environment. Thus the final measure is Conscience. [6 August 1972]

In the final analysis, it is the conscience that has the right to decide whether a particular attitude in one's personal life is right or wrong. But before a decision is taken, every individual has the duty to study what views there are, that is to say the opinions of fellow human beings who, *nota bene*, also have consciences, and especially the opinions of God as revealed by inspiration. Simply to submit the data one has collected to the capacity of one's own conscience reflects an arrogant attitude, one at odds with an attitude that is authentically human, that is an open attitude in a life shared with others. [3 April 1970]

Muhammad as Mystical Model

Tabari
Muhammad's Night Journey and Ascension
REUVEN FIRESTONE

Ahmad Wahib's record of soul searching is that of an articulate, sensitive man who did not shrink from the anguish and exhilaration in store for one willing to risk deep self-knowledge. His is a struggle with which many readers will identify. Islamic tradition includes a vast range of accounts of remarkable experience, all the way to the clearly mystical. If one can speak of an Islamic exemplar of the ultimate spiritual experience to which a human being might arrive, it is the story of Muhammad's Night Journey and Ascension. Tabari's commentary on Qur'an 17:1 represents one of several extended narrative versions of Muhammad's paradigmatic experiences, whose general outline provided various mystics with a pattern by which to explain their experiences. Another version included in Tabari's work narrates the experiences in the first person, as though Muhammad were speaking; the present version was chosen because it includes a greater number of story elements. Note especially how the story treats Muhammad's relationship to the other prophets.[2]

'Ali ibn Sahl related to me from Hajjaj, from Abu Ja'far ar-Razi, from ar-Rabi' ibn Anas, from Abu 'Aliya ar-Riyahi, from Abu Hurayra and others regarding God's words "Praised be He who caused His servant to make a night journey from the Sacred Mosque to the Distant Mosque, the environs of which We blessed, to show him some of Our signs. He is the Hearer, the Knower" [17:1]. Gabriel came to the Prophet with [the angel] Michael. Gabriel said to Michael: Bring me a bowl of water from Zamzam so that I may purify his heart. He cut open his chest. [The narrator] said: Then he cut down to his belly and washed him three times as Michael exchanged three basins of water from Zamzam. He then opened up his chest, extracted the malice that was inside him, and filled him with gentleness, knowledge, faith, certitude, and submission, and he put the mark of prophecy between his shoulders.* Then he brought him a horse and placed him on it, each of [the horse's] steps reaching the utmost limit of its eyesight. [See fig. 59.]

[Here the hadith tells of how, apparently en route from Mecca to Jerusalem, Muhammad experienced some of the torments of the damned in hell and of the rewards of the righteous in the Garden. We move now to the scene in Jerusalem.]

Then he came to Jerusalem, dismounted and tied his horse to the Rock,† entered, and prayed with the angels. When the prayers were completed, [the angels] said: O Gabriel, who is this with you? He answered: Muhammad. They asked: Was he sent to you? He answered: Yes. They said: Greetings, and may God preserve the brother and great ruler. [May God grant] goodness to the brother and great ruler, and goodness to the newcomer. [The narrator] continued: Then he met the spirits of the prophets, who praised their Lord. Abraham said: Praised be God who took me as a friend‡ and gave me great wealth, who made from me a community obedient to God following my example, and who saved me from the

---

* The opening of Muhammad's chest and the cleansing of his heart are part of an ancient purification legend, the general thrust of which finds parallels in other religious traditions as well, and it serves as a basis for the Islamic doctrine of *'isma* or "protection" of the Prophet Muhammad from sin.
† At the center of the Dome of the Rock; see fig. 23.
‡ *Khalil*: the honorific name for Abraham in Islamic tradition (*al-khalil*), and the Arabic name of the city of Hebron, traditional site of the burial cave of Abraham.

Figure 59.   This unusual version (16th cent., Safavid) of the often-depicted Ascension of Muhammad shows a lion floating at upper left; it is a symbol of 'Ali, the "Lion of God," a clue to the Shi'i origins of this illustration of a work attributed to the sixth Shi'i Imam, Ja'far as-Sadiq. Washington, DC: The Sackler Gallery, Smithsonian Institution, S86.253a. (See also SD fig. 35.)

fire and made it cool and peaceful.* Then Moses extolled his Lord and
said: Praise be to God who spoke to me in words, who caused the destruction of the family of Pharaoh and the redemption of the people of Israel
through my hand, and who made some of my people a righteous group
guided by truth.

Then David praised his Lord, saying: Praise be to God who gave me
great wealth and taught me the psalms, who softened iron for me,† who
made available to me the mountains for the birds to sing praises,‡ and
who gave me wisdom. Then Solomon extolled his Lord, saying: Praise
be to God who made the winds and the demons obey me and who made
prayer niches for me and examples [of erudition] and generosity as
answers; [who made me] cooking pots [like] towering mountains and
taught me the language of the birds [27:16, 19]; who gave me all good
things, made armies of demons, men, and birds available to me [27:17],
and blessed me with many of His believing worshippers; and who gave
me great wealth inappropriate to anyone after me and impossible to
reckon.

Then Jesus extolled his Lord, saying: Praise be to God who made me
His word, who fashioned me out of earth like His creation, Adam, and
then said: "Be," and I became; who taught me Scripture and wisdom,
the Torah and the Gospel [3:48]; who made me the most adequate creator
from clay in the form of a bird, who blew into it and it became a bird by
God's will [3:49]; who made it possible for me to cure the blind and the
leprous [5:110] and who enabled me to bring back to life after death by
God's will [3:49, 5:110]; and who raised me up and purified me, who
protected me and my mother from the accursed Satan, and who gave
Satan no power over us.

[The narrator] said: Then Muhammad extolled his Lord, saying: Each
of you extolled his Lord, and I extol my Lord. Praise be to God who sent

---

* This is a reference to the fire into which Abraham was thrown by the tyrant
Namrudh (Nimrod) for refusing to bow down to idols, and from which he was saved
by God.
† David is known as the one who, with God's help, invented armor (Q 34:10–11).
‡ God makes the birds and mountains David's servants so they may unite in prais-
ing God (21:79, 34:10, 38:19–20).

me compassion for the worlds and sufficiency for the people as a bringer
of good tidings and as a warner; who revealed to me the *furqan** in which
is clarification of all things, made my community "the best community
ever brought forth for humanity" [3:110], and made my community one
of the "golden mean" [2:143]; who [made] my people the first and the
last, cut open my chest [to] remove from me my crime and increase my
renown, and who made me the opener and the sealer. Abraham said: With
this, Muhammad has surpassed you [earlier prophets]. Abu Ja'far said,
this being ar-Razi: [Sealer means] seal of prophecy, and [opener means]
opener of intercession and advocacy on the Day of Judgment.

Then he brought him three containers wrapped in spices. [The first]
was a container of water. He was told: "Drink!" So he happily drank from
it. Then another container was brought to him containing yogurt and
he was told: "Drink!" So he drank from it until he was satisfied. Then
another container was brought to him in which was wine and he was told:
"Drink!" He replied: I do not want to, for I am satisfied. Gabriel said to
him: This will be forbidden your community. Had you drunk from it,
then only a few of your community would follow you.†

He then brought him up into the nearest heaven and Gabriel requested
that one of its doors be opened. He was asked: Who is this? He answered:
Gabriel. He was asked: Who is with you? He answered: Muhammad.
They asked: Was he sent to you? He answered: Yes. So they said: Greetings, and may God preserve the brother and great ruler. [May God grant]
goodness to the brother and great ruler, and goodness to the newcomer.
He entered and suddenly came upon a perfect man who was without any
of the flaws that humanity has. On his right was a door from which a
wonderful scent wafted, and on his left was a door out of which came a
foul smell. When [the man] looked toward the door on his right he smiled

---

* Usually translated as "proof"; this has become a synonym for the Qur'an.

† Muhammad is being tested with the three (or in some versions, four) liquids
that correspond with the rivers that flow out of Paradise, according to the Qur'an
(47:15, 85:11; and see below). The motif finds parallels in Persian religious custom
as well as certain Christian baptismal customs and ancient Indo-European libations
for the dead; in the Islamic narrative, however, Muhammad is always tested and
proves his innate inclination to follow the will of God by refraining from drinking
wine.

and was happy, but when he looked to the door on his left he cried and was sad. He [Muhammad] said: O Gabriel, who is this perfect and flawless gentleman and what are these two doors? He answered: This is your father, Adam, and the door to his right is the door to the Garden. When he sees one of his progeny entering it, he smiles and is happy. The door to his left is the door to hell. When he sees one of his progeny entering it, he cries and is sad.

Then Gabriel brought him up to the second heaven and requested to enter. He was asked: Who is it? He answered: Gabriel. He was asked: Who is with you? He answered: Muhammad, the Apostle of God. They asked: Was he sent to you? He answered: Yes. They then said: Greetings, and may God preserve the brother and great ruler. [May God grant] goodness to the brother and great ruler, and goodness to the newcomer. [The narrator] said: [After having entered] he was suddenly alongside two young men. He asked: O Gabriel, who are these two young men? He answered: This is Jesus, son of Miriam, and John [the Baptist], son of Zakaria, his maternal cousin.

Then Gabriel brought him up to the third heaven and requested to enter. He was asked: Who is it? He answered: Gabriel. He was asked: Who is with you? He answered: Muhammad. They asked: Was he sent to you? He answered: Yes. They then said: Greetings, and may God preserve the brother and great ruler. [May God grant] goodness to the brother and great ruler, and goodness to the newcomer. He entered, and suddenly he was next to a man who was more beautiful than all other men, just as the moon is more beautiful than all other stars on the Night of Power.* He said: O Gabriel, who is this most beautiful man? He answered: This is your brother Joseph.

Then he brought him up to the fourth heaven and requested to enter. He was asked: Who is it? He answered: Gabriel. He was asked: Who is with you? He answered: Muhammad, the Apostle of God. They asked: Was he sent to you? He answered: Yes. They then said: Greetings, and may God preserve the brother and great ruler. [May God grant] goodness to the brother and great ruler, and goodness to the newcomer. He entered

---

* The 27th of Ramadan, date of Muhammad's inaugural revelation.

and found himself next to a man. He said: Who is this, Gabriel? He answered: This is Idris,* whom God raised up.

Then he brought him up to the fifth heaven and requested to enter. He was asked: Who is it? He answered: Gabriel. He was asked: Who is with you? He answered: Muhammad, the Apostle of God. They asked: Was he sent to you? He answered: Yes. They then said: Greetings, and may God preserve the brother and great ruler. [May God grant] goodness to the brother and great ruler, and goodness to the newcomer. They entered and saw a man sitting down and speaking to a tribe of people around him. He said: Who is this, Gabriel, and who are all these people around him? He answered: This is Aaron who is beloved by his people, and these are the Children of Israel.

Then he brought him up to the sixth heaven and requested to enter. He was asked: Who is it? He answered: Gabriel. He was asked: Who is with you? He answered: Muhammad, the Apostle of God. They asked: Was he sent to you? He answered: Yes. They then said: Greetings, and may God preserve the brother and great ruler. [May God grant] goodness to the brother and great ruler, and goodness to the newcomer. [They entered] and he suddenly found himself beside a man sitting down. When he passed by him, the man cried. He said: Gabriel, who is this? He answered: Moses. He asked: Why is he crying? [Moses himself] answered: The Children of Israel claim that I am the most noble of men in the eyes of God, but this man [Muhammad] just replaced me in the world of the living, while I am in this world. If it were [only] him, I would not mind, but his entire community [surpasses me].

Then he brought him up to the seventh heaven and Gabriel requested to enter. He was asked: Who is it? He answered: Gabriel. He was asked: Who is with you? He answered: Muhammad, the Apostle of God. They asked: Was he sent to you? He answered: Yes. They then said: Greetings, and may God preserve the brother and great ruler. [May God grant] goodness to the brother and great ruler, and goodness to the newcomer.

---

* Idris: a prophet whose name occurs in 19:56–57 and 21:85–86. In Sunni tradition he is usually placed chronologically between Adam and Noah. In Shiʻi tradition, the figure of Idris is reminiscent of the biblical Elijah and Elisha.

When he entered, he found himself beside a gray-haired man sitting on a chair at the door to the Garden. With him was a group of people with white faces like [the color of] paper and [another] group with some color [in their complexion]. The group with some color rose, entered a river, and were washed by it, and when they came out a little color was gone. Then they entered another river and were washed by it, and when they came out a little [more] color was gone. Then they entered another river and were washed by it, and when they came out a little [more] color was gone until their [color] became like that of their companions. They then came and sat with their companions. [Muhammad] said: O Gabriel, who is this gray-haired man, who are these with the white faces, who are those with some color, and what are these rivers into which they entered and had their color cleaned? He answered: That is your father, Abraham, the first on earth to become gray. As for those with the white faces, these are people who have not overlaid their belief with iniquity. As for those with some color, they are people who have confused righteous actions with evil. They have repented, and God has turned toward them. As for the rivers, the first is the Mercy of God, the second is the Goodness of God, and the third their Lord gives them to drink and become pure.

[The narrator] continued: Then he arrived at the Lotus Tree* and was told: Every member of your community who restricts himself to your Sunna will reach this Lotus Tree, from the essence of which flow rivers of pure water, rivers of milk all of the same flavor, rivers of wine of delight to those who drink of it, and rivers of pure honey. It is a tree that makes happy those who bask in its shade for seventy years without interruption. One of its leaves can envelop the entire community of believers. [The narrator] said: The light of the Creator envelops [the tree], and the angels cover it like ravens when they alight on a tree. [The narrator] said: [God] spoke to him at that point, saying: "Ask!" [Muhammad] responded: You

---

* Lotus Tree: According to Muslim cosmology, paradise is described almost like a pyramid rising above the heavens in stages. At the top of the pyramid, at the apex of the highest heaven, grows the "the farthest lotus tree" (*sidrat al-muntaha*). It is said to shade all of the heavens and the waters that flow from them. Neither angel nor prophet can pass beyond this tree, which marks the boundary between all creations and the Divinity. This is where, according to Q 53:13–18, Muhammad actually beheld God.

took Abraham for a friend and gave him great riches; You spoke to Moses
in words; You gave David great riches, softened iron for him, and made
the mountains serve him. You gave Solomon riches and made the jinn,
humankind, and the demons serve him; you made the winds serve him,
and you gave him such riches that have never been equaled by anyone
since him. You taught Jesus the Torah and the Gospel, enabled him to
cure blindness and leprosy and to bring back to life after death with God's
permission, and protected him and his mother from the accursed Satan,
not allowing Satan a way with him.

His Lord responded: I have taken you as a friend and companion, as it
is written in the Torah, "Beloved of God" [*habib Allah*]. I have sent you
to the people to be sufficient as a bringer of good tidings and as a warner.
I cut open your chest, took from you your sin, and increased your renown. You will always be remembered in reference to Me. I made your
community a "middle community" [2:143] and made it the first and the
last, and I made it such that whenever anyone makes a speech in your
community, that person will bear witness that you are My servant and
apostle. I made the people of your community with hearts of the Gospel,
and I made you the first prophet created, the last one sent, and the first
completed. I have given you the seven *mathani*,* which no prophet has
received before you [see 15:87]. I have given to you Abundance.† I have
given you eight shares of Islam: the Hijra, Jihad, righteousness, prayer,
the fast of Ramadan, the command to do good, and the prevention of evil.
I have made you the opener and the sealer.

The Prophet said: My Lord has singled me out with six things: He has
given me the opening of words and their conclusion, the collection of
tradition, sent me to the people, made me sufficient as a bringer of good

---

* The term *mathani* traditionally refers to either the first seven verses of the
Qur'an, seven long chapters, or seven famous qur'anic passages that are often repeated.

† The name of Sura 108, "Kawthar," is translated in various ways. Its root meaning is "abundance," but in Islamic tradition it often refers to a magnificent river or
pool in paradise at which believers quench their thirst (e.g., 9:72, 47:15, 77:41–44,
88:10–16). Because desert aquifers are often polluted from the high concentration
of salts, the significance of such a motif is not lost on desert peoples whose very survival depends on potable water.

news and a warner, has discarded from the hearts of my enemy the fright of a month's journey, has permitted me spoils [of religious war], which was not permitted to anyone before me, and made the entire land pure as a place of prayer.

BEYOND STORYTELLING

Descriptions of religious experience are inevitably laden with metaphor and subject to varied interpretation. Muslim artists have often sought to tell in pictures stories too large for words. They have depicted visionlike scenes of journeys through the heavens (fig. 59), and of paradise itself (fig. 61); individuals of introspective and meditative demeanor (figs. 63 and 65); and people apparently experiencing the effects of some sort of ecstasy (figs. 58 and 64). Some images, such as that on the lusterware plate in figure 60, seem to probe several levels beneath the surface of the human psyche. One of several possible interpretations of the thirteenth-century Kashani plate is that of a reading through the lenses of Sufi symbolism. Beginning with the lower quarter: The fish are symbols of the mystic swimming in the ocean of God's unity. The woman to whom the fish seem attracted may be a reflection of divine beauty. In the upper half the horse may symbolize the body with its five senses, or perhaps the aggregate of lower tendencies called nafs. In the middle, the youth asleep may be either lost in ignorance and ensnared by appearances, or lost in an inner vision of the realities depicted in the lower quarter of the plate. All together the image may suggest the liberation of a mystic from the world of appearances and lower tendencies in the ecstatic vision of divine realities.[3] Somewhat easier to interpret, but still defying ordinary language, are explicit accounts of dreams and visions.

Saying the Unsayable

From earliest times Muslims have been recording their dreams and visions, though they themselves are not always certain to which category the experiences belong. Islamic tradition considers the prophet Joseph the foremost interpreter of dreams (see fig. 62). Here are remarkable accounts from five sources: a ninth-century Arab woman mystic, two Indian men of the thirteenth and fourteenth centuries, a nineteenth-century Egyptian man, and a twentieth-century Indonesian man.

Figure 60.   Lusterware plate, Kashan, Iran (1210, Saljuqid), by Shams ad-Din al-Hasani. Washington, DC: Freer Gallery of Art, Smithsonian Institution, 41.11.

✳ Rabiʿa's Dream

JOHN RENARD

Rabiʿa al-ʿAdawiya is among the most famous Muslim women of all time. In the classic biographical anthologies that include notices on women, accounts of Rabiʿa are frequently among the more detailed entries. ʿAbd ar-Raʾuf al-Munawi's *Shining Stars* includes a dream narrative in which Rabiʿa recalls:[4]

One night just before dawn I had said some prayers of praise and dozed off. I saw [in a dream] a coolly verdant tree of immeasurable height and beauty. Upon it were three kinds of fruit, unlike any of this world's fruits, the size of a maiden's breast: one white, one red, and one yellow, shining like moons or suns against the green background of the tree.

As I marveled, I asked, "Whose tree is this?"

[A voice] said: "It grows from your prayers of praise."

Then I walked around [the tree] and spied some golden fruit that had fallen on the ground. "It would be much better if this fruit were on the tree with the others," I said. Came the response, "This fruit was on the tree, but during your prayer of praise, you thought about whether the dough was rising, and [at that moment] it fell."

✳ Amir Khusraw of Delhi's Poetic Vision

BRUCE B. LAWRENCE

Amir Khusraw Dihlawi (1254–1325), disciple of the Chishti leader Nizam ad-Din Awliya', was one of the greatest Indo-Muslim Sufi poets. Many of his lyric poems, from among the various divans he composed, remain popular today. The following poem is one of the most famous of the classic texts still performed in Indo-Pakistani songs called *qawwali*, and one of Amir Khusraw's best-known poems. He recounts an indescribable moment with the dramatic refrain "in that place where I was last night," alluding to the spiritual transport often experienced by participants in the mystical "audition" called *samaʿ*.[5]

I do not know what abode it was, that place where I was last night.
On every side I saw the dance of the *bismil*,* in that place where I was
    last night.
I saw one with the form of an angel, the height of a cypress, cheeks like
    tulips,
From head to toe I quivered, my heart astir, in that place where I was last
    night.
Rivals, listen to his voice, the voice which calms my raging fright.
The words he spoke left me in awe, in that place where I was last night.
Muhammad was the candle illumining the assembly, O Khusraw, in that
    place which was no place.

---

* The words "In the name of God, the Compassionate and Merciful," beginning in Arabic *bi 'smi 'l[lahi]*.

Figure 61.   As early as the fourteenth century, artists began depicting
angels (as well as fairies, or peris) and houris, the dark-eyed maidens
of the Garden. Angels, usually distinguished by their crowns, often
play important roles in accounts of extraordinary religious experience
(such as the Mi'raj narrative, below, and Amir Khusraw's vision [16th
cent.], above), as do the houris (in the vision of Gesu Daraz, below).
Washington, DC: Freer Gallery of Art, Smithsonian Institution, 50.2.

And God Himself was the head of that gathering, in that place where I
   was last night.

✳ Gesu Daraz's Vision of Jesus

BRUCE B. LAWRENCE

Sayyid Gesu Daraz (d. 1422) was an important member of the Indian Chishti
tariqa. In the 114 "night discourses" in his Persian work *Night Discourses on
the Secrets* (*Asmar al-asrar*) he recalls the 114 suras of the Qur'an, but the content of the discourses is highly symbolic. Here the writer recounts a mysterious dreamlike vision in which Jesus appears. Perhaps this is the reverie of an
old man who knows his end is near. Perhaps the bride is spirit (*ruh*), the groom
the lower soul (*nafs*), and Jesus the heart over which they struggle. But one could
also interpret the characters as aspects of the nafs, as described by Vahidi in part
6: the young woman as the recalcitrant (*'ammara*) soul, the interlocutor as the
blaming (*lawwama*) soul, and Jesus as the peaceful (*mutma'inna*) soul. The
shaykh recalls:[6]

One time it happened that I saw a lake the length and depth of which
only God knows, but it was no more than waist deep. Some people were
wading into it, and I was among them. There was also a girl of about
fifteen years among the waders. The strange thing is that we were all
naked up to the waist. This young girl was a beauty such that if the
houris had been created from the reflection of [her] light they would have
claimed to be gods. Between us there was a distance of about one farsang.
She beckoned me to her. In the same manner that they bring a bride-
groom to the bride, they brought me a distance of one farsang to be
united with her. A man from the world of the unknown was a witness to
this. He threw a cloak over us, as though to hide us, and at that moment I
saw myself clothed in the same beauty and grace as she. From between us
the prophet Jesus arose and cried out, "I am the Son of God." The two of
us began to quarrel, I saying that Jesus was my child and she saying, "No,
he is mine." Jesus was complaining and leaping about and denouncing
both of us. "I am neither your son nor hers," he would say. "I am only of
myself and with myself." And when the girl again said, "Jesus is mine,"

I remarked, "I find myself to be just like him and just like that water; I am everything." And God knows [the truth of the matter].

✳ ## Visionary Experiences of 'Ali al-Bayyumi

WILLIAM SHEPARD

From the historian al-Jabarti's life of 'Ali al-Bayyumi (see part 3 above) come these descriptions of several of the Sufi's visionary experiences, taken from the end of his treatise on the Khalwatiya Sufi order. It is not always clear whether he is talking of dreams or of visions; what is clear is the prominence of Muhammad in the experiences.[7]

Among God's gifts and favors to me is that I saw Shaykh Dimirdash in heaven and he said to me, "Have no fear either in this world or the next." I also used to see the Prophet [Muhammad] (may God grant him blessings and peace) while in seclusion during the *mawlid* [birthday celebration], and he said to me one year, "Have no fear in this world or the next." I saw him say to Abu Bakr (may God be pleased with him), "Let us go and observe the zawiya of Shaykh Dimirdash," and they both came and entered my cell and stood by me while I was reciting, "Allah, Allah." An [uncanny] foreboding came over me at seeing the Prophet (may God bless him and grant him peace), but I saw the great shaykh [Dimirdash standing] by his tomb and saying to me, "Extend your hand to the Prophet (may God bless him and grant him peace), for he is here with me."

I [also] had a vision, half-waking, half-sleeping, in the cell [*khalwa*] of al-Kurdi, that is, Shaykh Sharaf ad-Din, who is buried in the Husayniya, and I woke up and saw that light had filled the place. I rushed frantically out of [the cell] but some [or one] of those who were there stopped me, so I spent the rest of the night at [the tomb of] the shaykh, but I was too terrified to go back into the cell. One time he [the Prophet] smiled at me and gave me a signet ring and said to me, "By the One who has my soul in his hands, tomorrow what has passed between us will become known." Then Shaykh Kurdi took me and transported me to Mecca and made me

Figure 62. This early-seventeenth-century Mughal album painting of the prophet Joseph interpreting dreams is a good example of the influence of European style on Indian miniature painting. St. Louis: St. Louis Art Museum, 403.52.

see it with my own eyes. I entered where Sayyid Ahmad al-Badawi*
was, and the Prophet (God bless him and grant him peace) was with him.
[Sayyid Ahmad] passed [a harsh] judgment on me because I had delayed
attending his mawlid, and I appealed to the Prophet for aid. So then God
helped me by the grace [*baraka*] of the Prophet (may God bless him and
grant him peace), who said, "Go to al-Kurdi." He had twice previously
dressed me in the red garment, once in Birket al-Hajj† and once in his
place in the mausoleum.‡ [Al-Bayyumi] continues: Once I saw myself
outside of Medina and I said, "I will not enter until I know that [the
Prophet] is pleased with me and has accepted me." Then he sent to me a
man having a fan with which he fanned me and said, "You are accepted." I
saw [the Prophet] say to me, "I would like to talk to you," and he made me
stand before him and said to me, "Do you question the divine judgment?"
Then I woke up and felt the effects of that and did not know the reason.

[Jabarti comments:] On the margin of this treatise I also saw what
I took to read: I saw [the Prophet] (may God bless him and grant him
peace) on Monday evening at the end of Ramadan in the year 1157
[=1743–1744] hastening along just outside the student quarters [of al-
Azhar] [lit., "at the level beside the *riwaq* (portico around the courtyard)"], and I ran after him and said, "Do not pass me by, O Apostle
of God," and we stopped in a wide open place and I came up to him and
stood beside him and said to one who was present, "Look at his noble
beard and count the white hairs in it."

✳   Ahmad Wahib's Dream

ANTHONY H. JOHNS

In one of his diary entries, Ahmad Wahib recounts the following dream and wonders what its origin might have been:

***

* The most popular wali in Egypt; his mawlid in Tanta in the Delta attracts thousands each year. He is the "founder" of the Ahmadiya tariqa, mentioned at the beginning of al-Jabarti's text in Part 3 above.
† About eleven miles from Cairo, the second-to-last stopping place before Cairo
of the returning hajj caravan.
‡ Very likely the Prophet's mosque in Medina.

Last night I dreamt that I met with mother Mary. She was dressed in
white, and her face, so full of holiness, impressed me deeply. She smiled
and gazed at me, and her loving look brought me comfort and happiness.
I myself am not a Christian, so I do not know why I found such peace and
inner tranquillity while face to face with her. Could I ever know such
peace in daily life? I long for her, she who is full of wisdom, whose gaze
is gentle and tender. Every expression of her personality fills me with
wonder and reverence. [13 December 1971]

Explaining the Unexplainable

✳ Tabari
The Correct Interpretation of the Mi'raj Narrative
REUVEN FIRESTONE

Attached to the account of Muhammad's Night Journey and Ascension given
above Tabari includes the following explanation on how one ought to interpret
the narrative. Tabari gives here what later mystics would refer to as a "literalist" interpretation, for he explicitly rules out the view that Muhammad's was
a purely spiritual experience. Note especially the distinction he makes between
dream or vision and the experience of physical locomotion:[8]

The correct view is that God took His servant Muhammad on a night
journey from the Sacred Mosque to the Distant Mosque just as God has
told His people [in the Qur'an] and just as the reports on the authority
of the Apostle of God demonstrate [in the Hadith]. God carried him on
al-Buraq when he brought him [to Jerusalem]. He prayed there with the
prophets and messengers, and [God] showed him some of His wonders.
There is no substance to the opinion that He brought [only] his soul
and not his body, for if that were the case it would contradict the [other]
evidence about his prophethood, and there is no proof of that with regard
to his apostleship. It is not that those who dispute the truth of this are
idolaters, but they [nevertheless] oppose the truth, for it cannot be
unknown to them or to anyone who has any truthful instinct that
[Muhammad] could see a vision in his sleep without journeying for

a year. How could he have journeyed even for a month or less? Furthermore, God communicated in His book that He took His servant on a night
journey. He did not tell us that He took his soul on a night journey, and it
is not permissible to anyone to go beyond [the simple meaning] of what
God said [in the Qur'an] and change it. Some think that it is permissible
because the Arabs did that in their own communications, as it is said [in
an old poem]:

> I reckoned the cry of my she-camel to be that of a she-goat;
>   It is not so extraordinary for you to change it to a she-goat.

That is, I reckoned the cry of my she-camel to be the voice of a she-goat.
The sound [of the she-camel] was short[er than usual] and [therefore]
acceptable [to be considered] as [that of] a she-goat. The Arabs do that,
as is known, by the design of the one speaking the words [in oral poetry].
But there is no proof other than visible proof, and no connecting to what
is known of the intent of the speaker except what he makes clear. Do not
cut it short, for there is no evidence that the intent of God in His words
"who caused His servant to make a night journey" was that He caused
the soul of His servant to make a night journey. On the contrary, the
clear evidence and the reports on the authority of the Apostle of God
which follow prove that God caused him to make a [corporeal] night
journey on the riding animal called al-Buraq. If the night journey were
of his soul, the soul would not have been carried on al-Buraq, for riding
animals only carry corporeal beings. If one said that the meaning of our
statement is: He caused his soul to make a night journey and he saw in
his sleep that He caused his body to make a night journey on al-Buraq, he
would contradict the meaning of the reports that were transmitted on the
authority of the Apostle of God, that Gabriel put him on al-Buraq. This
is because if [Muhammad] were sleeping [during the time of his night
journey], according to this view his soul would not be with him if it were
riding the animal. But the body of the Prophet would not have ridden al-
Buraq, so the Prophet could not have been carried on al-Buraq, and that
was not so. The situation would then be simply one of a dream, which
contradicts the revelation and the reports which follow on the authority

of the Apostle of God and the evidence that has come on the authority of the leaders of the Companions and Followers [of the Prophet].

✳ ## Al-Ghazali
Treatise on the Intimate Knowledge of God
WILLIAM SHEPARD

Al-Ghazali's *Treatise on the Meaning of the Intimate Knowledge of God* (*Risala fi bayan ma'rifat Allah*) represents a major theologian's attempt to establish principles from which one might interpret accounts such as these above. Part 1 presented Ghazali's views on interpreting Scripture. Here he argues for a theoretically consistent way of approaching the issue at the heart of many of these accounts, namely, in what sense one speaks of having an intimate knowledge (*ma'rifa*) of a God who is by definition beyond human knowing.[9]

1. In the name of God, the Merciful, the Compassionate. The treatise of the Imam, the Proof of Islam, Muhammad ibn Muhammad ibn Muhammad al-Ghazali on the meaning of the knowledge of God.

2. You have asked me—may God grant you success—concerning a matter on which you have doubts. This is that no one, however great his knowledge and understanding, has attained complete knowledge of all bodily and spiritual entities, nor does he know them as they really are. If so, then how can we accept anyone's claim to know God as He really is along with [or: by means of] His attributes? The one who makes such a claim limits God and makes Him finite, since his knowledge would have to encompass God's essence, and whatever encompasses something must be before it and after it, outside of it and within it. But God Almighty says, "He [God] is before everything and after everything. . . . "*

3. The answer. We must know, first of all, that no one has true knowledge of God Almighty except God Almighty Himself, nor does anyone but Him know the secret essence of His sublimity. One should not be

---

* Q 57:3. The full verse in a more literal translation reads: "He is the first and the last, the outward and inward, and He knows everything." I have modified the translation in the text to show the relevance of the verse to Ghazali's argument.

surprised at this, for I say that no one truly knows an angel except an angel, and indeed no one truly knows a prophet except a prophet, and indeed no one truly knows a scholar except a scholar. In fact, if a student has not attained his teacher's level of scholarly knowledge, he does not truly know his teacher, and if he has attained his teacher's level he still does not know the teacher as the teacher knows himself.* For he first comes to know what his teacher knows, and perceives that within himself, then he knows his teacher by analogy with himself since he knows that he has the same knowledge as his teacher has. Indeed, I say it is inconceivable that the condition experienced by one who has slaked his desire in sexual intercourse be truly known by someone else because complete knowledge of that condition comes only by direct experience. Nor is it conceivable that anyone should know what he essentially is before he is completely like him;† the most that can be conceived is that he can affirm the existence of something whose essence and true nature are unknown to him.

4. How can a human being aspire to know God Almighty when he cannot truly know his own soul, but only knows his soul, in most states, by its actions and its attributes, and does not perceive its essence. Indeed, if a human being wanted to perceive completely the true nature and essential attributes of an ant or a bug, he could not do so. The most he could attain would be to know by sight their shape, their color, their bodily composition and how they differ in external matters. As for the various ways in which the soul of a bug differs from the soul of an ant, and from which the differences in bodily composition and attributes arise, he cannot know them.

5. If one could conceive that there was someone or something that was like God (may He be exalted above that), one could say that one knows God with true knowledge by analogy with his own self, which he has first known and to which he compares the inner nature of someone else, just as a scholar knows another scholar by analogy with himself.

---

* Or possibly: he does not know the teacher as the teacher knows him (the student).

† More literally: that anyone should know his quiddity or essence (*mahiya*) before he has his attributes.

6. I say that humankind exists in different stages: the first stage is that of a fetus, then that of an infant, then that of one at the stage of discrimination, then that of one at the stage of reasoning, then that of one of the Friends of God Almighty. The fetus does not perceive the states of its soul, nor can it know the state of the infant; nor does the infant know the state of one who has reached the level of discrimination; nor does the latter, as long as he has reached only the level of discrimination, know the state of one who can reason; nor does the one who perceives the objects of reason by reason know the Friend of God's state of mystical revelation other than by inference. Nor does the Friend of God know the state of the prophet, since the stage of prophecy is beyond that of *wilaya* [sainthood]; nor does the prophet know the angel as the angel knows himself; nor does the angel know God as God knows Himself. Each stage has its own perfection, and one from whom the next stage is veiled cannot know the essential nature of that stage.

7. At most, he may have a logical proof that confirms its existence. If you know this, then know that the furthest possible extent of the creatures' knowledge is that they know that this marvelous, ordered universe needs a Director who is living, powerful, and knowing, who does not resemble the universe, and whom the universe does not resemble. Thereby the creatures prove the existence of something from which creation has issued, but this is knowledge of His action and not knowledge of His essence.

8. Also, they prove the existence of the attributes of life, knowledge, and power, but this is knowledge of the attributes and not knowledge of the true nature. It is not even knowledge of the true nature of the attributes, but rather a kind of analogy, for if humans did not label them as knowledge, life and power, they could not recognize the evidence that proves the fact of their existence.

9. Likewise, they prove that it is impossible for God to be originated, have a body, have accidents, and so forth, but this is knowledge of what God is not, not knowledge of what He truly is.

10. The creatures' knowledge of God is only in these three ways, though they may differ in the degree and manner of knowledge,[10] and in the amount known, but all of that derives from knowledge of the need

of the universe for a maker, not knowledge of the true nature of His essence.

11. At this point, if the mystic [*'arif*] penetrates further, what he comes to know by a way that it would take too long to present here is the impossibility of the creatures' attaining true knowledge of God's essence; that is as far as the mystics can go. Then they say: the failure to attain is itself an attainment. For when a person knows that, of necessity, one cannot attain to the essence of God's sublimity, then he has attained to his greatest possible perfection, for this is the highest degree of human perfection.

12. At this point, if the mystic says: I do not know Him, he is telling the truth in one sense; and if he says: I know Him, he is telling the truth in another sense. He is like a person who is shown some handwriting and is asked whether he knows the one who wrote it. He knows that the writer exists, is living, able [or powerful], knowing, hearing, and seeing, since one cannot produce writing without these qualities. He also knows that he is not an inanimate thing, a plant, or a beast. So he says: Yes, I know him. But he could also say: Even though I know all this, I do not know him.

13. This mystic has two conditions. In one condition he says: I do not know God Almighty; in the other he says: I know only God. He is telling the truth in both conditions. In the first, when his mind attempts to grasp the essence of God he is overcome with bewilderment and at that point he says: I do not know Him.

14. In the second condition, when he looks at His works as His works, he sees nothing in existence except God, may He be revered and exalted, and His works, and then he says, I know nothing except God Almighty and there is nothing on earth except Him, and properly speaking, He is everything. Now, if one looks only at the sun and its light spread throughout the universe, and his mind does not observe the things lit up by it insofar as they are things or animals, it is as if he sees only the sun. In such a condition the mystic experiences "expansion" [*bast*] as a result of the divine lights he beholds which have radiated their effects onto him. The other condition is that of "contraction" [*qabd*]. Therefore the master of the Apostles and leader of the mystics, may God bless him and grant

him peace, said: Reflect on the creation of God, do not reflect on His essence.

15. This is a matter we could discuss for a long time, since the mystic would never exhaust the oceans of knowledge that God has poured forth into him even if he should live as long as Noah, upon whom be peace. All the knowledge of the mystics is in relation to the knowledge of God Almighty less than a drop of water in relation to all the oceans of the world. Indeed, in relation to God it is infinitesimal. But this answer is enough to resolve the doubt. It has been shown in what sense a human being can undertake to know God. The original question was wrongly put; if this is recognized, then nothing should seem strange.

EVALUATING EXPERIENCE

Muslims have written extensively on two dimensions of the search for clarity upon which all seekers must embark in view of the human proclivity for self-deception. The first dimension is the theory of spiritual guidance, or Science of Hearts, as it was called; the second is the actual experience and practice of spiritual direction that affords spiritual companionship for journeyers on the inner path.

The Science of Hearts

Here are samples of the views of two influential South Asian Muslims on preliminary concerns and theoretical aspects of spiritual guidance.

✳ ### Sharaf ad-Din Maneri
A Letter on the Qualities of Spiritual Guides
PAUL JACKSON

Muslim authors since Tabari and Ghazali have developed extraordinarily sophisticated canons and methods by which to evaluate the most subtle of spiritual experiences. Because of the inherent difficulty in this "science of hearts," Muslim spiritual tradition has held in high esteem the role of the shaykh/*pir* or spiritual guide in assisting seekers to plumb the depths of their own souls. Maneri, introduced along with one of his letters in part 2, writes again, this time about how one recognizes an authentic spiritual guide. He touches on various

Figure 63.   Scenes of solitary religious seekers have been popular
subjects for artists; in this Safavid ink drawing, a dervish meditates
in the mouth of a cave. St. Louis: St. Louis Art Museum, 83.42.

related issues, such as the nature of a guide's spiritual authority and how to deal
with the fact of every guide's sinful humanity. Like his earlier-quoted letter, this
one is sprinkled with citations from various Persian teachers and mystical poets. Maneri deals with several aspects of the theme in turn, referring to specific
questions raised by his addressee.[11]

God Most Exalted has said: "You [Satan] shall have no authority over My servants" [15:42]. Whoever has entered the world of the heart has escaped from the clutches of being a worshipper of Satan and has become a religious leader fit to be imitated. Spiritual guidance is entrusted to such a person, not to someone who is still enmeshed in the world of the selfish soul [*nafs*] and has not yet reached the world of the heart. Men of God are of one kind, while Satan's minions are of another. Do you know what the virtues of men of God are?

> Since they are placed in the divine presence,
>> Anything unsuited to Him is trampled under foot.
> Everybody's desire arises from his conscience:
>> He who embraces God and abandons others becomes a guide.
> You quaffed one draught in front of the cup-bearer:
>> Whatever is left, let it remain behind.

Anyone who is caught up in the darkness of the selfish soul is an abode of demons. Whatever makes its appearance from him is for the sake of his prone-to-evil soul. Even if he looks devoted, nevertheless demons reside within him. Whatever he turns his hand to will be tainted by what is within him. If he wants to come up with some work untainted by any demon, then he will have to entrust the bridle of his own work into the hands of one whose name is inscribed in "You shall have no authority over My servants" [15:42]. So if he says, "Do this, but don't do that," then his command would not be that of Satan, for there is no way by which Satan can enter his heart. Whatever emerges from a heart closed to Satan would be divine, not devilish.

> Consider his every word a powerful secret:
>> Consider his every action a deed of God.
> Become his dust and you will be a king:
>> Become his, and do whatever you wish.

You might ask at this stage, "Was there ever anybody in this world to whom Satan had no access?" O brother, there is nobody whom Satan did not seek to influence! There were a hundred and twenty thousand examples of prophethood. All of them were wounded by him. It is one

thing, however, to be his special tenant, and quite another to be occasionally wounded by him, by way of testing, and to arise lion-hearted.

> Give me your heart and see how you capture mine:
> Read my face for yourself and see a lion.

If you had your very own horse and your slave mounted it in order
to take it to water, would you say that it had become his? No, by God, not
at all!

With regard to the sin of Adam all persons are equal, but "the best of
those who sin are those who repent." What distinguishes and is necessary
for a guide is not that he should be sinless. Rather, what is necessary is
that spiritual guides should have trodden the Way to God and become
aware of the reality of what is involved. For example, if you wish to
acquire knowledge from someone, it is not necessary for him to be
sinless. What is needed is that he possess that knowledge. Sinlessness is
required for prophets, not for spiritual guides. Prophets have trodden the
Path of God in sinlessness and with His grace because Divine Wisdom has
made this demand with regard to prophecy, no matter how difficult or
dangerous this Way may be. What would you say to the Distinguished
One who is endowed with the quality of "He guides whom He will and
leads astray whom He will" [39:24]? It would not be difficult or dangerous to associate as a disciple with that Distinguished One.

> What safety is there on a path of fire?
> What blame is there for a mad man?

It is for the moth to associate with the candle and cotton in the
production of fire. You know how dangerous this is. "The sincere ones
are in great danger."

> On this side, need: on that, utter needlessness:
> On what basis do You play the lover with me?

Moreover, for others, a guide who has fully trodden the Path of God
and seen the reality of the work or a prophet needs to be present. This
way of proceeding would be without danger, for spiritual guides have
nothing more than the quality of guidance, yet it suffices.

If you have pain, a guide will appear:
His words will be a key to unlock your pain.
An intermediary has arisen for this people:
What he says will naturally be correct.

This is the meaning of those who say that worshipping a spiritual
guide is better than worshipping God. By way of explanation they say
that a guide is a better protector for someone than God is, but we do not
know whether they understand the meaning of this or not.

O brother, do you have any idea of what is meant by "the qualities
of men," for they eat and sleep and put on clothes; they have wives and
children and go to the bazaar. "What kind of a messenger is this who eats
food and walks through the bazaars" [25:7] is the criticism of the worshippers of external form by way of blame. Moreover, they know in their
hearts things to which, for you and me and the likes of us, there is no
access. Khwaja Sana'i* has praised them thus:

Those who sell their lives are almost nothing:
Those in Sufi garb are the ancient meeting place.
We devoted ones are fully engaged in striving:
We intimate knowers are all belief.
"God does whatever He wills" with a sense of care:
It is up to the servant to be fully obedient.

It is seen in alchemy that, in the presence of an elixir, copper becomes
gold. Everyone with a heart who receives a love-filled glance from that
Heart is endowed with eternal life.

One glance from the Friend equals happiness untold:
I am waiting to feel such a glance.

It has also been said:

I do not know what sort of men these were:
Work never satisfied them for a moment.
Inevitably they became the King's servants:
The elite of the people became their world.
Their pain is not acquired: it is bestowed:
For such pain could not possibly be acquired.

* The Persian poet whose parables appeared in part 4.

O brother, on the Day of Resurrection such a heart will appear like the sun in today's world. Anybody who performs some service for one of them, no matter what, or has a good opinion of one of them, will be under his protection in the age to come. The work of masters of the human heart is greater than can be expressed or put into writing and be comprehended by your feeble intellect or mine. Listen to how a poet has put it:

> I sat at the head of the table of generosity,
>   Having kindled a fire of both worlds.
> There is a place at the head of the Path for the best of them,
>   While the path to [God's] throne and footstool is a couch.
> Say: "What can a member of this group say and what can he write?"
>   Of what use is the sun to the eyes of a bat,
> Or a rose garden for an imprisoned cock?

It is not necessary that there be one in the whole world but it is fitting that there be ten, or twenty, or a hundred. Nor is it necessary for him to be in a city. It is fitting that he be in a village. Abu 'l-Hasan Kharaqani was from a village but had the perfection acquired by traveling a thousand years along the Path. It is said that if someone reaches that perfection or not, "God gives His grace to whom He wills." If someone says, "Assuredly one of them will be the most perfect," then say: "This is to be expected." It is also proper that ten, twenty, thirty, or forty, more or less, should be in one stage and this cannot be known, except by a distinguished person who has been honored above all men. At that time he will consider how many they are and which stage each one is in. Investigators of reality, however, say that the Prophet spoke in this fashion: "The thought had not occurred to me on any day that I have met all the saints of God. On that day, however, I saw a saint I had never seen before." How can this control apply to anyone else? There is a hint in this tradition that you should pass beyond your knowledge and come to your helplessness. It would be better for you that you be one of the saints of the Lord or men of God to whom speech has come. They have been praised thus:

> Do away with everything connected with self-esteem,
>   Then you will acquire the knowledge of needlessness.

Figure 64. *Sama'* showing dervishes in various states, ecstatic dancing, weeping, and fainting; from the *Divan* of Hafiz (ca. 1490, Timurid). New York: Metropolitan Museum of Art, Rogers Fund, 1918 (17.81.4).

Their eyes are fixed upon the sanctity of Adam;
Their names extend to the ends of the earth.
In ecstasy, ecstasy itself has passed away:
Why and wherefore no longer find a place.
One in seclusion, in the abode of every secret,
Is without need of all needlessness.

Don't you see that the joy of all mystics, the most excellent of the

Arabs and Iranians [i.e. Muhammad], on the Night of the Ascension reached the stage of proximity to God and of miracles. He came forward with "I cannot praise You as You have praised Yourself." Moreover, the one who, after the prophets, was the most favored and perfect of all the people, namely the Righteous One par excellence, Abu Bakr, said: "I understand my Lord by means of my lord." My appointed guide said: "Helplessness in understanding is understanding." Whenever a disciple is one in reality, not merely in outward form, then this occurs.

> In love of You, helplessness is the master's secret:
> In your land bondage is the doorway to freedom.
> Being a guide along Your Path is common:
> Grief for You is gladness for Your lovers' souls.

In what has been described above, one question claims our attention: How can a helpless beginner know that a particular person is a master of the heart and is of that group whose name, "My devotee is not for you like a king over them," has gone ahead, or is nothing but a pretender?

O brother, in tracing back this question one ends up at the problem of what is preordained and measured out. There can be no anxiety along his path for a person who, from the beginning, has been clothed with the robe of felicity and union as perfectly as Bayazid or Uways Qarani. As for another one without any wealth, has not a black blanket been woven for him? All these things are a form of restriction for him, and they will all be found on his path. "All things for which he has been created are rendered easy" is fulfilled.

> The future of two men is settled in heaven:
> One becomes a lord, and the other, a weaver.
> He knows no increase apart from the garments of kings,
> While the other weaves nothing except a black blanket.

Khwaja 'Attar has said:

> Whatever the master puts in writing
> Can be read by a child at school.
> Speech is necessarily cut short there:
> Escort and traveler fall behind: the Way remains.

As it is said, the pen reached this point and broke. This is what is meant.

Another matter you raised is this: Would you say a devotee can acquire intimate knowledge of God by himself, without a guide, or not? The answer is: If by this knowledge you mean that he knows about the being and oneness of God, then this is attainable by means of his own intellect without a guide. Yet if by this knowledge you mean the perfection of the travelers in their knowledge of the Lord Most Exalted, such as the perfection of Bayazid or that of Uways Qarani or of Khwaja Ma'ruf Karkhi, then there is an agreement that this also, through self-struggle and asceticism, is also attainable alone, without a guide or escort, but it is rare, and of a low degree.

> How can a blind man walk straight?
>> It is dangerous for him to proceed without a staff.
> If you come to the Way without an escort,
>> Then all will say: "You will fall along the Way."

In *The Ornament of the Friends of God*[12] it is related that the Apostle said that in every age there will be forty persons with hearts like that of Moses; and seven persons with hearts like that of Abraham. At the end of the tradition, he says that there will be one person with a heart like that of Israfil.* There will also be a community known as Uwaysians. They will not have any need for a guide. Prophecy, [such] as was bestowed upon Khwaja Uways Qarani, nourishes them in their cells without the intermediary of a guide. Even though he had not seen the Lord of the prophets in his external appearance, nevertheless he obtained instruction from him. This, however, is a rarity.

At the very least, such aptitude and ability are not often found. What is mostly found and more customarily seen is that it is acquired in the shape of the spiritual wealth of a guide and escort. Every perfection that you would like to acquire is a perfection of the travelers [themselves]. What I say in this matter is to study methodically and with great attention what pertains to the world of the heart, not the explanation of those caught up in custom and habit, for they come out with stories and fables—but God knows best! The result of the words of that group is no

---

* Israfil is the angel who will sound the final trumpet.

more than the words and explanations that roll off their tongues. On
the other hand, the words of this group are from the heart, not acquired;
from the world of "my Lord trained me," not that of "my Lord taught
me" [12:37]; from the revelation of secrets, not the abundance of repetition; and from what has been seen and tasted, not what has been read
or heard. The insight of masters of the heart is an understanding and
appreciation of another kind, which is hidden from externalist scholars.

> The taste and grasp of masters of the heart is special,
>> For their knowledge exceeds that of both worlds.
> Whoever is immersed in understanding that work
>> Throws himself into an ocean of mysteries.
> When that understanding arises like revelation
>> Whatever he writes will reflect what is correct.

It has also been put thus:

> "He shows His face to them along the Way":
>> Who can explain well what this means?

✳ ## Sayyid Ahmad Khan
Treatise on Visualizing the Shaykh
BRUCE B. LAWRENCE

Sir Sayyid Ahmad Khan (d. 1898) was a major religious and intellectual figure
in nineteenth-century Delhi. He came from a long line of Muslims affiliated
with the Mujaddidi Naqshbandi Sufi tariqa, and was thus heir to a strong tradition of seeking spiritual guidance. His father was even buried adjacent to the
grave of his spiritual mentor, his shaykh. In 1852 Sir Sayyid wrote a short Persian treatise called the *Epistle Explaining the Practice of Visualizing the Shaykh*
(*Namiqa dar bayan-i mas'alat-i tasawwur-i shaykh*). Ahmad Shahid, a prominent reform-minded neo-Sufi leader, had condemned the practice of visualization as tantamount to idolatry, and Sir Sayyid set out to defend the practice as
theologically acceptable. Using a type of deductive argument, he begins with
the proposition that keeping good company brings about good results in an individual, and then argues that meditating on the image of the shaykh is a form
of spiritual companionship. It should be noted that this text represents earlier
views of the author, and is included here because of its thematic interest, not as
a key to Sayyid Ahmad Khan's overall system of thought. After a brief self-
effacing introduction, the author continues:[13]

FIRST PREFACE

It is the unanimous opinion of both the elect and the common people that company produces an effect. If you sit with a good person, you yourself become good. If you sit with an evil person, you raise the veil from the face of that which is abhorrent. This is a fact which from one corner of the world to another no one will deny—whether you ask a Parsee or a Christian, a Sufi or a strict Muslim. On this point the poet has said:

> The company of the righteous will make you righteous [*salih*].
> The company of the wicked will make you wicked [*talih*].

Sufficient for me in this matter is the tradition of the Prophet, in whose path my heart has become dust, even as my life has been sacrificed upon that throne of heaven. Imam Bukhari* has related on the authority of Abu Musa [a transmitter of hadith] that the Prophet of God once said:

> The company of good and evil persons is like the difference between the seller of musk and the blower of bellows. The seller of musk comes to you and you buy from him, and you find in what you have bought a pleasant odor. But the blower of bellows burns your clothes with his bellows, and leaves behind a disgusting odor.

Hence, about the effect of company, commonly known as the benefit of company, no one can add to what the Prophet has already said on this subject.

SECOND PREFACE

When you have enjoyed the benefit of company you will know that this benefit neither resides in the physical parts of the body, nor is it related to what you see with the outer eye or can identify by the eye, hand, or foot. Otherwise it would be impossible for the blind to accomplish anything, and likewise for the person who lacks hands or feet. But this is not the case. Whether one is learned or ignorant, if God unexcelled has opened the inner eye, what loss does that person suffer from the shutting up of these two piebald eyes? Similarly, one whose hand has been held by the hand of God cannot be a failure because he lacks a bodily hand or foot. In

---

* Muhammad ibn Isma'il al-Bukhari (d. 870) compiled one of the two most famous collections of hadith.

this dust-laden curtain and in this appearance without existence, that is, the body, there is a luminous witness to the One to whom pertains the basis of all that is, and all the marvels that we possess are from Him. The benefit of company is located in Him, just as it is derived from Him.

THIRD PREFACE

It is a matter of common agreement that as long as admiration of the doer is not implanted in you, whatever he does will not influence you. Moreover, people have given different names to that which is implanted according to the nature of their admiration for the doer. Those whose souls have been burnt in the fire of passion [*ishq*] call it love [*mahabbat*], while those who know the traditions of devotion [*adab-i iradat*] call it faith [*'aqidat*]. In truth, to receive the benefits of company you have to have faith in the doer. For the place where the pleasures of company may be obtained is the same for everyone, since the perceptive faculty is influenced by the amount of rain that God sends down, just as it is influenced by the seed and care that the tiller of the land provides. Above all, the perceptive faculty is influenced by the predetermined receptive capacity; for unless the receptive capacity—whether one calls it love or faith—has been created in you, love will not influence you. In the words of Sa'di:*

> Rain in whose nature there is no contradiction
>   Causes tulips to grow in the garden and thorns in the desert.[14]

(That is to say, the difference is not in the amount of rain, but in the capacity to receive.)

The last benefit of the company of the Prophet is to obtain perfect faith, but that is not possible without first possessing love. From Anas ibn Malik† it is related that the Prophet said: "No one believes until I become more precious to him than his soul, his family, and all the people in the world." In the same tradition, 'Umar‡ is reported to have said: "O Prophet

---

  * Sa'di of Shiraz (d. 1292) wrote poetry and didactic literature in Persian. (See fig. 58.)
  † Anas ibn Malik (d. ca. 710) was a Companion of the Prophet and noted Traditionist, or transmitter of hadith.
  ‡ 'Umar ibn al-Khattab (d. 644) was the second "Rightly Guided Caliph" and a Companion of Muhammad.

of God, you are more precious to me than everything except my soul which is lodged within me." Then the Prophet said, "You are not a believer until I have become more precious to you than even your soul!" Then 'Umar said: "O you to whom the Book was revealed, surely you are more precious to me than my soul which is lodged within me." Then the Prophet said, "O 'Umar, your faith has been perfected."

The early Muslims raised up Abu Bakr to the highest position, but they threw down Abu Jahl,* who always challenged the Prophet. The reason for that presence and absence of the gem of the evening light [i.e., Islam] was acceptance of the mark of love for the Prophet. The Prophet was the same to both, just as his company was available to both. The one took hold of the firm rope and progressed to the highest post. From the hand of the other the firmest hand slipped out [see Q 2:255, 31:21]; and he did not reach even the lowest rung of the ladder that leads to the attainment of perfect faith.

Hence the beneficiary should make love of the benefactor obligatory on himself so that between their two souls there may come into being a relationship the import of which will be evident to both. It is perhaps for this reason that Sufis have named this station "annihilation [*fana'*] in the shaykh." The disciple who does not achieve this station can produce no result, nor can he, in turn, influence others. We blind people grope our way into this worship, while it is left to the professional craftsmen to say what it really contains. In the words of the poet Sa'di:

> Kings know best the policy of government.
> Beggars sit in the corner; Ahmad, don't complain.

FOURTH PREFACE

The principal way to obtain the benefactor's love is to remember Him continually. As God says in the Qur'an: "Then remember me, even as I remember you" [2:152]. The traditions that support this line of thought are so numerous that space does not permit their citation. What is meant

---

* Abu Jahl (Father of Ignorance) was the nickname early Muslims gave to 'Amr ibn Hisham (d. 624), a Quraysh tribesman bitterly opposed to Islam.

can also be realized by the intellect. Who brought Layla before Majnun*
and who dressed Shirin in black out of grief for the death of Farhad?† For
those who are acquainted with physical love not a single day passes that
the pleasure of remembering the Beloved does not come to mind. Indeed,
it is this imagined embracing and this projected union which brings the
Beloved out into the marketplace and makes her so much like the Lover
that the Beloved, in fact, becomes the Lover. In the words of the poet:

> Love is that homeless creature
> Who brings you to my house.

Remembrance [*dhikr*] requires you to visualize that He is He, in order
that you do not become separate from Him. Look into yourself and
reflect. Then you will discover that He is in your heart, and that it is in
remembering Him that your love and your taste and your desire and
your passion become excited.

But the projected picture of the Beloved should not be fixed in your
mind or adorned with human attributes. Rather, visualization is necessary
for remembrance in the same way that remembrance is necessary for
visualization. The end result of both is Love.

There is a tradition in which Hasan ibn 'Ali‡ said: "I asked Khali Hind
ibn Abi Halah, since he knew the form of the Prophet, to describe something of his attributes to me, that I might become attached to him. That is
to say, I adopted love on account of that image of the perfect beauty of the
Prophet."

Now, when you have understood these Prefatory Remarks, understand
further that our Naqshbandi saints—may the mercy of God be upon all
of them—have ordered this same silent meditation [*muraqaba*], because
the visualization of the shaykh is necessary for the *murid* [seeker,
aspirant], both in the actual state of remembrance and otherwise. It is
through sincere and continuous remembrance alone that love of the

---

* Majnun (literally, be-jinned) was the moonstruck lover of the enchanting Layla
who went mad in his unrequited love.

† Farhad was a sculptor who fell in love with Shirin, wife of King Khusraw, and
flung himself from a mountain to his death in desperate longing.

‡ Hasan ibn 'Ali (d. 669) was the second Shi'i Imam, brother of Husayn, the pro-
tomartyr (d. 680).

Figure 65.   Pensive dervish with begging bowl and staff (Iran, late
15th cent., Timurid). New York: Metropolitan Museum of Art,
Bequest of Cora Timken Burnett, 1956 (57.51.30).

shaykh wells up in the heart of the murid, till gradually the stage of
annihilation in the shaykh takes place. At that stage there develops a
relationship between the perceptive faculty of the shaykh and the murid,
in which the benefit of the company and guidance of the shaykh takes
root in the perceptive self of the murid. The base perceptive self is then
purified and cleansed and brought to higher stages. In this station

whatever I might say about the image of the shaykh would be justified. If I say that the image of the shaykh is a cushion for receiving the mercy of God, I would have spoken the truth, and I presume to say that without the image of the shaykh I shall not find a way to God or the Prophet, then I would be right.

Now this love of the shaykh is probably of two kinds: inherited and intentional, the second coming by deliberate visualization and intentional remembrance. I call the first compulsory and the second voluntary, but with respect to the result there is no difference between them.

Nonetheless, liars have concluded that these saints in the state of muraqaba presumed the shaykh to be present and seeing and knowing and cognizant at all times and in every condition. And by muraqaba they mean the same thing, namely, that the shaykh is present and looking at us without intermediary and is aware of the condition of the one who remembers him without any intermediary or without any physical cause.

God forbid that the pure skirt of these saints should be stained with such belief. To the contrary, as you know, the state of muraqaba is derived from the state and special devotions [*waridat*] of the companions of the Companions and Followers and Followers of the Followers of the Prophet. The traditions of the Prophet are in support of this practice, and the 'ulama' attach the same meaning to the invocation [*khitab*]: Prayers and peace be upon you, O Prophet, together with the mercy of God and His blessing.

How then can this practice be an innovation [*bid 'at*] and proscribed by the shari'a, especially since these saints regard muraqaba as an instrument and intermediary for higher purposes? As long as purification of the soul is achieved, together with annihilation in the Prophet—which I hope it may be the good fortune of all true believers to attain—I have no objection against anyone following this practice. What we have known is enough for us, though the ignorant may beat their heads against the rock.

And what Mawlana Isma'il [Shahid]* has said in *The Straight Path* [*Sirat-i mustaqim*] is also worth noting in this connection. To my

---

* Shah Isma'il Shahid (d. 1831) was an important Naqshbandi author of Delhi, grandson of Shah Wali Allah (d. 1762).

knowledge he was a man of attainment, and however much his writing was like this [i.e., condemning muraqaba and those who practiced it], he was in the service of those who regarded diligence in muraqaba as a binding duty day in and day out, and to his last breath he viewed those same Naqshbandi saints as his own pride and he never walked on the path of doubt toward them.

And may peace be upon those who are obedient to the guide.

Traveling Companions

✳ Hasan Palasi's Encounter with Shaykh Kujuji

LEONARD LEWISOHN

Firsthand accounts of the experience of spiritual guidance provide unique insight into the practice of the science of hearts. The memoir Hasan Palasi composed in honor of his shaykh, Khwaja Muhammad Kujuji (d. 1279), is one such account. Palasi calls the whole work "A Gift for Novices and Largess for Adepts." Originally written in Persian, the work was translated into Arabic in hopes of wider circulation. After the Persian original was lost, it was retranslated back into Persian early in the fifteenth century. Shaykh Kujuji was a widely renowned spiritual director of his day. In a section of his work evidently referring to events of the early 1270s, Palasi has gone from his home city of Tabriz to the village of Kujujan, in present-day Azarbaijan in the Caucasus, for an extended visit with his spiritual guide. We join his narrative just after his arrival there. Palasi explains:[15]

Now, I had vowed to myself that I would eat nothing for the first three days of my visit to the master. When the time for the midday meal came, the servant brought in a tray of food. The master looked at the victuals and stretched out his hand and ate a few morsels. I ate nothing. He remained silent, partaking of a small bit of the food, and since I ate nothing, he motioned to the servant to collect the meal cloth.

When the servant had gathered up the cloth, the master began to speak, asking many strange and marvelous questions concerning the problematic passages and the deeper allegorical meanings of the Glorious Qur'an and the Prophetic traditions related to the divine Reality which is

Figure 66.   Seeker receiving spiritual direction: album painting (India, Jahangir's reign [1605–1627], Mughal). St. Louis: St. Louis Art Museum, 386.52.

the inner dimension of the religious Law. I answered these questions as best I could, according to what God vouchsafed me at that time.

The content of these answers I myself did not even understand, for they had never before occurred to me, nor had I ever heard their like from anyone else nor read them in any book! This experience reached such an intensity and degree during that time that from those words that sprung from my lips, such enthusiasm, purity of humor, and joy penetrated my heart that I wondered, "How is it that these divine mysteries are being expressed by *me?*"

Then I realized that in reality the source of these words and the elucidation and materialization of these mysteries and allegories by medium of my tongue was all due to the grace of the spiritual regard and blessed breath and the heightened willpower of the reverend master.

In this manner, I remained three days in the company [of the master] and ate nothing either day or night. When the servant brought us food, the master would eat a few small morsels and then tell him to take the rest away, since I was not eating anything.

The dawn of the fourth day broke. We said our morning prayers, following which, as was the master's custom, he lit a candle, lowering his head in meditation, and his disciples and companions followed suit, and an absolute vow of silence on everyone's part was observed, and no other litanies or invocations were recited until the sun had risen one spear's length above the horizon.

When the fourth day had dawned, raising his head forth from his meditation, he turned toward me and requested that I continue my discourse.

"Oh Mawlana, today, I will ask the questions and it is your turn to reply," I rejoined. "My speaking over the past few days has given you ample opportunity to become acquainted with my character. Now you should speak too, so that I can get to know you. As the adage goes: 'Speak until you make yourself known, for a man is hidden behind his tongue,' [and] 'Regard what is being said, not who is saying it.'"*

"The author of these maxims, whoever he was," interjected the venerable master, "spoke well. For a man's speech is a clear sign of his perfection. Yet when his discourse springs from his own heart's conviction and enthusiasm [not when it comes from books or when he quotes from others], those who are alien to his theosophical sensibility will not understand what he says simply by listening to him, nor will they recognize the measure and worth of his speech.

* The first sentence is a hadith of the Prophet and the second is a saying of 'Ali.

"In the workshop of spiritual poverty* paralogicality and sophistry abound, and this sort of discourse has upset and made unstable countless numbers of people. Each wise man has his own just 'measure' and each person's 'measure' is always changing and transforming according to his outer and inner conditions and states. However, the interior measure, when set on the balance, is far more reliable and superior [than that of the exterior] and the judgment made by the interior being is much more accurate and reliable than that which exterior being passes.

"Since the measure that one's interior being possesses rests upon a truthful and dependable basis, it is in this that the wise man trusts, for this inner measurement is steadier than the outer judgment. Now, the proper measure of things can be assessed in respect to four things:

"One relates to the spiritual station of the apprehension of the realities of Existence, in respect to which those who specialize in spiritual matters differ. Another relates to the means through which such apprehension is obtained, and again, the opinions and views of people differ in this matter. Another relates to how one should conduct oneself with God, the Creator. This, in turn, depends upon the amount of insight each person has, as well as upon his or her previous faith. Another relates to how one should conduct oneself with people, and this all depends upon how one considers each [social] context.

"From the foregoing it should be recognized that spiritual levels are quite varied. Therefore, if you find someone on a certain level, you shouldn't pass any definite judgment on him until you examine and test out his inner state and rub the circumstances of his temperament on the touchstone of what lies in the interior. . . .

"All that you have told me [Shaykh Kujuji says to Palasi] over the past few days, of occult sciences, exotic mystical lore, refined expressions, and sublime symbolic allusions, would make you—that is, if you yourself had been actually endowed with these same qualities, ethical character, social conduct, and mystical states—the leader, and leading light of this day. However, when I look at you from the standpoint of my own spiritual

---

* An apparent allusion to organized and institutionalized "Paths" or "Orders" of Sufism, another epithet for which was *faqr* (spiritual poverty).

insight, I must confess that all your words and deeds, and both your inactivity and motion stand in utter contradiction to your true talents and knowledge!

"Thus, it is now quite clear to me that wisdom is substantially different from inner reality of the sage, and that intimate knowledge [of God; *ma'rifat*] is substantially different from inner reality of the mystic, and theological knowledge [*'ilm*] is substantially different from inner reality of the knower. An exception to this rule would be, of course, the knowledge one ascribes to God, the Almighty. Although God's knowledge pertains to the Transcendent Oneness of his Essence, his attributes are neither in disparity with, nor separate from, his Essence, insofar as within his Essence there is absolutely no multiplicity.

"Now, it sometimes happens that one finds a person who is in reality a simpleton, narrating one of the questions pertaining to mystic-philosophical wisdom. On other occasions, one sees someone who is merely a scholar, rather than a mystic, relating something to do with intimate knowledge [of God]. On other occasions, you find a person who speaks of theological knowledge who is, in reality, an ignoramus himself!

[Shaykh Kujuji continues speaking to Palasi:] "Oh teacher, which of these two groups do you belong to? The first group, who are aware of their ignorance, or the second, who are not apprised of their ignorance?"

[Palasi then describes his reaction:] As soon as the Shaykh—peace be upon him—had uttered these words, every limb and muscle in my body began to shiver and tremble. All my hair stood up on its end. My heart suddenly felt drowned in woe and grief. I had never experienced the anguish with which at that moment my heart was filled.

"O Shaykh," I cried, "I belong to that group of scholars who are apprised of their own ignorance! What you said in regard to me is all completely true! You have truly recognized who I am. I realized then that I was a sick person and perceive now that there is no other clever physician, genuine master, or benign and responsive teacher to redeem me from this malady other than you. So heal me! My entire inner and outer being is devoted to and convinced of your love. I submit myself to you, so find the cure for my ailment!"

The master (may God sanctify his soul) replied: "The first medicine

you must take is Sincerity [sidq]. I have informed you of the psychological sickness that I observed in you. You too have confirmed my diagnosis,
saying that I spoke truly. If you are really sincere in validating my
assessment of your condition, then your cure is simple and the remedy
within reach."

"I am totally sincere, O Master," I hastened to say, "in my confirmation of your diagnosis, and anyway, your own heart is conversant enough
with my illness to ascertain this."

He said, "You have spoken truly—and have done well to have spoken
so. I myself witnessed the proof of your sincerity: for your very skin
crept and all the limbs of your body shook. That itself was a sign that
fear and awe of God touched your heart and proves the sincerity of your
engrossment in finding the object of your quest. Such fear also indicates
God's grace and solicitous regard for you, evincing the fact that the Light
of God is now focused on you and that God Almighty is Himself holding
parley with you—although of that you are as yet incognizant. This fear
and trembling is a definite sign of your certitude [yaqin] and spiritual
realization [tahqiq]. It is God's gauge and criterion, for in this state the
gates of hope and faith are opened unto the devotee by God.

"There is no other way to God, the Almighty, except by His Light.
The way toward Him can never be fared except through grace of His
Light. This Light derives from the lights of divine Union and Presence.
Whenever this Light is manifested to the heart of the faithful devotee,
everything besides God is consumed away. This Light is the natural result
of the dread that fills the heart of the faithful. [Then the shaykh cited
Qur'an 39:23–24:]

"'God has sent down the fairest discourse as a Book, consimiliar in its
oft-repeated pairs of truths whereat shiver the skins of those who fear
their Lord; then their skins and their hearts soften to the remembrance
of God. That is God's guidance, whereby He guides whomsoever He will;
and whomsoever God leads astray, no guide has he.'"16

And now I understood what it meant to taste directly the relish
and delight of mystical states. In fact, by means of his spiritual control
[ta'arrufat] the entire ground of my being began to quake and was stirred

to motion. Alternative mystical states and spiritual shapes were revealed to me, so that unto my spirit the window of imagination was opened. Then I heard an address that disclosed to me many mysteries and matters of the invisible realm, experiencing countless visions, dreams, and revelations, still without understanding their interpretation. Yet in none of this did I abide or rest, nor in any station did I pause or stop, until some time had passed and my commotion, agitation, and intoxication at last settled and became tranquil.

And then the venerable master—my God hallow his soul—exercised his spiritual initiative [*ta'arruf*] upon me once again. My spirit, which had been smothered in the placenta of interest and love for friend and kin, so that my body of light lay becalmed and immobile in the ocean of physical kinship, was then reawakened by him. I quickened. Just like a person bound in shackles, from whose feet chains are suddenly released, the bonds from the soul were unloosed and I began to stir. Although bold as a lion I set out on the quest, all the movement I made at this time was but total rest, my search appeared to me to be but utter serenity.

In this manner, I advanced from station to station until I had put both the "blessed" and the "wretched" behind me in the dust—until I reached a place where the light of divine unity enveloped my entire being and I passed away from my selfhood in the reality of detachment, and became so drunk that I was entirely bereft of self.

Now, the master was a clever physician, and was able to use the physic of his sainthood to effect my cure as soon as I experienced this state. While the eye of my heart was opened, he took care to safeguard my physical constitution so that my body did not become disabled. Although I was engaged in spiritual voyage and flight, he made me mount the litter of the body. While in this state, I rubbed the eye of my heart and opened the eye of spiritual insight when, glancing aloft, I beheld face to face the object of my quest and witnessed Reality.

At once I saw that I was myself my own leader and guide, and even if I was in bliss, much of the state to me was strange and wondrous.

Turning to my venerable and veracious master, I cried, "O master, what weird spectacles are these? What is the truth of these phantasies?"

But the master merely bid me be silent, causing me to be possessed by intensely tormenting fear and dread. Yet by the power of his inner being, I remained steadfast.

"You have studied the sciences of moral limitations and prophetic customs,"* he admonished me, "so bring to mind what you know, have studied and memorized. Confront the vision you are now witnessing with that knowledge. You are going to be annihilated from self. If you have really been burnt up and consumed, then that [knowledge] has also been consumed away. So ask from your own self the reality of what remains [of that knowledge]. For it will soon come to pass that you will learn everything you need to know from [within] yourself without ever asking anyone else."

So some of these matters I understood through the process of methodical progression on the Sufi Path [*suluk*], and others I verified by way of divine intimation and tutelage. Although luminous snares lay before me, I yet witnessed how the remainder of all living creatures and creation was annihilated in the reality of [the qur'anic dictum] "Everything is perishing but his Face" [28:88].

Then I saw that behind all my master's discourses lay the speech of God, and thus gained certitude of the fact that all his biddings and forbiddance during the stages where veils had beclouded me and on those levels where I was subject to secondary causes were true and correct. In this state, I also witnessed how everything was saying, "There is none like unto Him" [42:11], and God [in reply] was saying, "I am like unto no thing."

When I considered everything, I saw that all spiritual realities [*haqa'iq*] had a place within me—in such a manner that I could obtain the object I sought from them, and the goal which all things sought was also realized through me.

After that, I transcended the "realm of physical things" and found myself alone with nothing from the realm of things beside me. Now, at

---

* I.e., you are aware of ethical injunctions that determine a human being's relationship to God, and are aware of your obligation in respecting those who train you and lead you in prayer and the danger of transgressing these boundaries, even if your spiritual experience seems to lead you elsewhere.

this station, gazing within with the eye of spiritual insight, I beheld how every other spiritual guide [*murshid*] is always accompanied by his disciples and followers, with his regard focused upon his own states and circumstances, but that my own master (God's mercy be upon him) could not be classified by any description, nor did he fit under any rubric. That is to say, he was not within "direction" or "place," since he did not see with the eye nor hear with the ear.

Appendix 1: Text Distribution

Text/Author	Century	Place	Language	Literary Notes
Part 1				
Qur'an 12, 55	7	Arabia	Arabic	Rhymed prose
Hadith	9	Mideast	Arabic	Prose: text and transmission
Muqatil	8	Iraq	Arabic	Tafsir
Ibn 'Abbas	7/9–10	Arabia	Arabic	Tafsir
Suyuti	15	Egypt	Arabic	Tafsir
Ibn Taymiya	13–14	Iraq	Arabic	Treatise
Ghazali	11	Iraq	Arabic	Treatise
Nawawi	13	Syria	Arabic	Treatise
Part 2				
Maneri	14	India	Persian	Letter
Madjid	20	Indonesia	Indonesian	Treatise
Tabari	9–10	Iran/Iraq	Arabic	Hadith in tafsir
Epic of Moses	19	Mozambique	Swahili	Utenzi poetic form
Hamka	20	Indonesia	Indonesian	Tafsir
Women's Prayers	16–17	Egypt	Arabic	Hagiography
Marthiya	19	India	Urdu	Lyric, 6-line stanzas
Madih	20	Iran	Persian	Lyric, ghazal
Na't	19	India	Urdu	Lyric, ghazal
Ginan	16	India	Hindi/ Gujarati/ Braj Bhasha	Lyric, hymn form
Sermon	20	Egypt	Arabic	Khutba for radio

Text/Author	Century	Place	Language	Literary Notes
Part 3				
Acrostic Poem	19	Egypt	Arabic	Lyric/didactic naʿt
Naʿt	18–19	India	Urdu	Lyric
Hussein	20	Egypt	Arabic	Treatise
Thaʿlabi	11	Iran/Iraq	Arabic	Hagiography
Munawi	16–17	Egypt	Arabic	Hagiography
Women/Iberia	13	Spain	Arabic	Hagiography
Women/Morocco	13	Egypt	Arabic	Hagiography
Sufi Badhni	16–17	India	Persian	Hagiography
Jabarti	18	Egypt	Arabic	Hagiography
Surat Luqman	7	Arabia	Arabic	Qurʾan text
Aphorisms	16–18?	Mideast	Arabic	Brief maxims, acrostic
Sayings/Chishti	12–13	India	Persian	Varied maxims
Mulla Hadda	19–20	Afghanistan	Pakhtu	Oral folk tale
Nakhshabi	14	India	Persian	Literary moral anecdotes
Part 4				
Shir Nawaʾi	15	Central Asia	Chaghatay Turkish	Prose/verse preface to Divan
Lahiji	15	W. Iran	Persian	Commentary on poetry
Suhrawardi	12	Iran	Persian	Prose allegory
Sanaʾi	11–12	Iran	Persian	Didactic, mathnawi
Gayo Poetry	20	Indonesia	Gayo	Didactic saer verse
Ibn al-Farid	13	Egypt	Arabic	Lyric, ghazal, qasida, rubaʿiyat
Munawi	16–17	Egypt	Arabic	Literary hagiography
Rumi	13	Turkey	Persian	Lyric, ghazal
Maghribi	14	W. Iran	Persian	Lyric, ghazal
Nuri and Shad	20	India	Urdu	Lyric, naʿt, qasida
Bibi Hayati	19	Iran	Persian	Lyric, ghazal

Text/Author	Century	Place	Language	Literary Notes
Part 5				
Shaykh Luqman	20	Jordan	Arabic	Contemporary narrative
Ibn Barquq	15	Egypt	Arabic	Architectural epigraphy, historical
Sultan Barquq	14	Egypt	Arabic	Waqf document
Khwaja Ahrar	15	Central Asia	Persian	Waqf document
Suhrawardi	13	Iran	Persian	Treatise
Sitt ash-Sham	13	Syria	Arabic	Historical chronicle
Ibn Marzuk	14	Morocco	Arabic	Historical chronicle
Khwandamir	16	E. Iran	Persian	Historical chronicle
Husayn-Mirza	15	Central Asia	Chaghatay Turkish	Autobiography/ memoirs
Part 6				
Ahmad Sam'ani	12	E. Iran	Persian	Treatise
Wang Daiyu	17	China	Chinese	Treatise
Gift . . . Spirit	16–17	Indonesia	Javanese	Treatise, 10-line/ stanza verse
Women Scholars	16–17	Egypt	Arabic	Hagiography
Gesu Daraz	15	India	Persian	Malfuzat
Shaykh Husayn	15	India	Persian	Letter
Baghdadi	12–13	Central Asia	Persian	Treatise
Vahidi	16	Turkey	Ottoman Turkish	Treatise, prose/verse (mathnawi)
Sajjadi	20	Iran	Persian	Mystical lexicon

Text/Author	Century	Place	Language	Literary Notes
Part 7				
Ahmad Wahib	20	Indonesia	Indonesian	Spiritual diary
Tabari	10	Iran/Iraq	Arabic	Extended hadith in tafsir
Rabiʿa	16–17	Egypt	Arabic	Hagiography, dream account
Amir Khusraw	13–14	India	Persian	Lyric, ghazal
Gesu Daraz	15	India	Persian	Mystical treatise
ʿAli al-Bayyumi	18	Egypt	Arabic	Hagiography
Ahmad Wahib	20	Indonesia	Indonesian	Spiritual Diary
Tabari	10	Iran/Iraq	Arabic	Hadith commentary in tafsir
Ghazali	11–12	Iraq	Arabic	Treatise
Maneri	14	India	Persian	Letter
Ahmad Khan	19	India	Persian	Treatise
Hasan Palasi	13	Iran	Persian	Autobiography/ memoirs

Appendix 2:
Art Program Distribution

Fig.	Century	Place	Form	Function
1	20	Malaysia	Tiled dome (ext.)	Congregational mosque
2	9	Iraq (?)	Manuscript page	Qur'an text
3	14	Egypt	Manuscript page	Qur'an text
4	17	India	Marble facade	Funerary monument
5	17	W. Iran	Tiled facade, dome	Royal oratory/mosque
6	10	Spain	Mosaic ribbed dome (int.)	Mosque, over qibla
7	14	W. Iran	Tiled niche	Mihrab
8	16	Turkey	Tiled niche	Mihrab
9	14	W. Iran	Stucco niche	Votive Mihrab
10	12	Iran	Carved stone niche	Votive Mihrab
11	16	Turkey	Stone portal, fountain	Mosque courtyard, ablution
12	19	Turkey	Rug with niche design	Prayer carpet
13	14	Iran	Brass candle holder	Mosque lighting flanking mihrab
14	12	Central Asia	Tower of baked brick	Minaret
15	19	Malaysia	Stone/marble facade, domes	Congregational mosque
16	16	Mecca	Manuscript page	Pilgrim guide illustration
17	17	North Africa	Embroidered cloth banner	Pilgrimage ritual object
18	20	India	Calendar painting, color	Devotional image
19	15	Iran	Manuscript page	Illustration of mystical text
20	12	Iran	Marble slab, niche design	Tombstone
21	10	Central Asia	Baked brick dome chamber	Funerary monument
22	17	Turkey	Manuscript page, detached	Illustration
23	7	Jerusalem	Octagonal dome chamber	Sacred site, shrine

Fig.	Century	Place	Form	Function
24	17	Syria	Tile panel	Devotional image
25	20	India	Calendar painting, color	Devotional image
26	16	Iran	Manuscript page	Illustration of mystical text
27	16	Iran	Manuscript page	Frontispiece of text of poetry
28	15–16	Egypt	Domed bldgs., minarets	Funerary complexes
29	15	Egypt	Stone domed bldg., minaret	Funerary complex
30	15	Central Asia	Tiled domed bldg.	Funerary complex
31	8–17	W. Iran	Tiled facade, pishtaq	Mosque courtyard
32	17	India	Stone mosaic portal facade	Gateway, funerary complex
33	17	India	Stone, marble facade, dome	Mosque prayer hall and courtyard
34	15	Turkey	Stone domed bldg., minarets	Mosque prayer hall
35	16	Turkey	Stone domed bldg., minarets	Mosque
36	18	W. Iran	Tiled dome and facade	Madrasa courtyard and prayer hall
37	13–16	Turkey	Enclosed space with fountain	Courtyard of residential facility
38	15	Central Asia	Tiled domed chambers	Funerary monument
39	14	Central Asia	Tiled domed structure	Congregational mosque
40	16	Turkey	Painted domes, windows	Congregational mosque
41	17	Turkey	Stone domed bldg., minarets	Congregational mosque
42	20	USA	Brick bldg. with dome	Congregational mosque
43	20	USA	Brick bldg., dome, minarets	Congregational mosque
44	16	Turkey	Stone domed bldg., minarets	Congretational mosque
45	20	USA	Architectural model	Plans for future building
46	14	Morocco	Tile/stuccoed walls, arches	Prayer hall, congregational mosque
47	14	Morocco	Muqarnas vault, tiled piers	Portal, congregational mosque
48	14	Morocco	Stucco/tile room with font	Madrasa
49	17	India	Manuscript page	Album painting

Fig.	Century	Place	Form	Function
50	20	Taiwan	Tiled Dome, piers, minarets	Congregational mosque
51	13	Turkey	Inlaid stone facade, dome	Madrasa
52	17	Central Asia	Tiled pishtaq, fluted dome	Madrasa
53	18	W. Iran	Tiled dome, minarets, arcade	Madrasa
54	20	USA	Geometric-calligraphic painting	Didactic/devotional image
55	20	USA	Geometric-floral painting	Didactic/devotional image
56	20	USA	Geometric-figural painting	Didactic/devotional image
57	15	Iran	Manuscript page: text, marginal drawing	Visual gloss of poetry
58	16	Iran	Manuscript page	Illustration of mystical text
59	16	Iran	Manuscript page	Illustration of esoteric text
60	12	Iran	Ceramic plate, luster glaze, painted	Possible depiction of mystical moment
61	16	Iran	Miniature in ink	Album drawing
62	17	India	Miniature painting	Album page
63	16	Iran	Miniature in ink	Album drawing
64	15	Iran	Manuscript page	Illustration of mystical text
65	15	Iran	Miniature painting	Album page
66	17	India	Miniature painting	Album page

Notes

PREFACE

1. In that volume, a concern with form and function in textual and visual sources provided the chief organizational and structural considerations. Thematic content in the works studied was important, but generally remained a sometimes distant third. So, for example, chapter 6, on pedagogy, gathered various literary forms (letter, lecture later transcribed by a disciple, compendium, and lexicon) among whose principal functions pedagogy seems to dominate. Here I have modified that overriding concern with form and function somewhat. Now thematic content emerges as an organizational category in its own right. For example, while the Prophet's Hadith as a foundational source belong formally and functionally in part 1, I have here sometimes included selections from Muhammad's sayings in other parts when thematic content warrants. Part 2 thus includes a hadith on how the practice of five daily ritual prayers became the standard for the Muslim community. Part 3's section on wisdom literature includes a selection from the Qur'an's Surat Luqman as a scriptural paradigm of wisdom. And part 7 features an extended hadith narrative of Muhammad's Night Journey and Ascension as the exemplar of mystical experience. For pedagogical purposes, therefore, one can either pair the respective sections of the two volumes, or dip more selectively into the parts of this anthology to illustrate specific sections of volume one.

PART ONE

1. An earlier, more fully annotated version appeared in James W. Morris, "Dramatizing the Sura of Joseph: An Introduction to the Islamic Humanities," *Journal of Turkish Studies* (Harvard), 18 (1994): 201–224 (Annemarie Schimmel Festschrift issue). Note that, because of printer's errors, verses 12–14 and 33 are missing in that version.

2. Translated from the Arabic in Muhammad M. Khan, *The Translation of the Meanings of Sahih al-Bukhari* (Lahore: Kazi Publications, 1983), 4:283.

3. Translated from the Arabic in Ghazi Ahmad, *Sayings of Muhammad* (Lahore: Sh. Muhammad Ashraf, 1972), 42.

4. Ibid., 26.

5. Texts translated from the Arabic in William Graham, *Divine Word and Prophetic Word in Early Islam* (The Hague: Mouton, 1977), 117, 182–184; and adapted from Annemarie Schimmel, *And Muhammad Is His Messenger* (Chapel Hill: University of North Carolina Press, 1985), 86, 116, 131, 307.

6. Muqatil ibn Sulayman, *Tafsir al-Qur'an* (Cairo: n.p., 1979). On Muqatil, see *EI2* under Mukatil ibn Sulayman. On his tafsir, see John Wansbrough, *Quranic Studies: Sources and Methods of Scriptural Interpretation* (Oxford: Oxford University Press, 1977), sec. IV, passim.

7. Text is from a work printed in Cairo in 1951 under the title *Tanwir al-miqbas min tafsir Ibn 'Abbas,* ascribed to al-Firuzabadi (d. 1414), although this is likely a false ascription. On the text itself, see A. Rippin, "Tafsir Ibn 'Abbas and Criteria for Dating Early Tafsir Texts," *Jerusalem Studies in Arabic and Islam* 18 (1994): 38–83, 79–80. On Ibn 'Abbas as a commentator, see Wansbrough, *Quranic Studies,* sec. IV, passim, and the references to the *Tafsir al-Kalbi,* which is identical to this text.

8. *Tafsir al-Jalalayn* (Cairo, n.d.), 2:264–265.

9. Taqi ad-Din Ahmad ibn 'Abd al-Halim ibn Taymiya, *Muqaddimatun fi usul at-tafsir,* ed. 'Adnan Zurzur (Beirut: Dar al-Qur'an al-Karim, 1391/1971). Several sections have been abridged in the interest of space.

10. Variants of this hadith may be found in both the *Sunan* of ad-Darimi and the *Jami'* of at-Tirmidhi, two of the six most authoritative collections.

11. Translated by Annemarie Schimmel, *Islamic Calligraphy,* summer 1992 issue of the *Metropolitan Museum of Art Bulletin,* commenting on fig. 38 (p. 29).

12. See Mohamed Hosein Halimi, "Le Mihrab en Iran et sa décoration," in *Le Mihrab dans l'architecture et la religion musulmanes,* ed. Alexandre Papadopoulo (Leiden: E. J. Brill, 1988), 95–96.

13. Geza Fehervari, "Tombstone or Mihrab? A Speculation," in *Islamic Art in the Metropolitan Museum of Art,* ed. Richard Ettinghausen (New York: Metropolitan Museum of Art, 1972), 241–252; Sheila Blair and Jonathan Bloom, *Images of Paradise in Islamic Art* (Hanover, N.H.: Hood Museum, 1991), 96. Cf. Nuha N. Khoury, "The Mihrab Image: Commemorative Themes in Medieval Islamic Architecture," *Muqarnas* 9 (1992): 11–28.

14. The translation is based on the text of the work as edited by Muhammad Zahid al-Kawthari and published in Cairo in 1359/1940 under the title *Qanun at-ta'wil.* The work is listed by Carl Brockelmann (*Geschichte der arabischen Litteratur,* 1:539, no. 21) under the title *Al-qanun al-kulli fi 't-ta'wil.* An article on Ghazali's *Qanun al-kulli fi 't-ta'wil* with a partial Turkish translation was published by M. Serafeddin under the title "Gazalinin Te'vil Hakkinda Basilmamis bir Eseri" in *Darulfunun Ilahiyat Fakultesi Mecmuasi,* 1st ser., vol. 4, no. 16 (1930): 46–58. Passages cited from the Qur'an are taken from the English translation of Mohammed Marmaduke Pickthall.

15. Reading *fawq* instead of *mawqif.*

16. *Manazil al-qamar:* As explained by Paul Kunitzsch, "The stations of the Moon are a series of 28 positions in the heavens through which the Moon passes, in its cycle from new moon to new moon, during each of its 27 or 28 nights. Each individual station has a name and is identified with one or more fixed stars in its immediate vicinity." See Paul Kunitzsch, *Arabische Sternnamen in Europa* (Wiesbaden: n.p., 1959), 53. See also his article "Al-manazil" in *EI2,* 6:374–376.

17. Such as "Alif. Lam. Mim," the first verse of Sura 2.

18. A reference to a well-known tradition; see Graham, *Divine Word,* 202.

19. Nawawi, *At-tibyan fi adab hamalat al-Qur'an,* the Cairo edition of Mustafa al-Babi al-Halabi wa Awlad, 1379/1960.

PART TWO

1. Sharaf ad-Din Maneri, *Maktubat-i Sad o Panja*, unpublished MS, Asiatic Society of Bengal, letter 3.

2. Nurcholish Madjid, *Islam Doktrin dan Peradaban* (Jakarta: Yayasan Wakaf Paramadina, 1992), 57–71. The author's notes have been deleted and extensive citations of Qur'an have been replaced in some cases with a cross-reference to the passage in question.

3. 'Ali Ahmad al-Jurjawi, *Hikmat al-Tashri' wa Falsafa* (Cairo: Dar al-Fikr, n.d.), 119–120.

4. Abu Ja'far Muhammad ibn Jarir at-Tabari, *Jami' al-bayan 'an tafsir ay al-Qur'an* (Beirut: Dar al-Fikr, 1984), book 15, pp. 10–11.

5. The text, translated here for the first time, is one of three written in a copy book discovered by Prof. Eugeniusz Rzewuski of Warsaw University.

6. On snakes in hell, see Jan Knappert, *Traditional Swahili Poetry* (Leiden: E. J. Brill, 1967), 23.

7. Reading of inscriptions in fig. 17 taken from Anthony Welch, *Calligraphy in the Arts of the Muslim World* (New York: Asia Society, 1979), 76–77.

8. Text translated from Hamka, *Tafsir al-Azhar Djuzu'II* (Jakarta: Pembimbing Masa, 1965), 39–43.

9. 'Abd ar-Ra'uf al-Munawi, *Al-kawakib ad-durriya tarajim as-sadat as-sufiya (aw Tabaqat al-Munawi al-kubra)*, ed. 'Abd al-Hamid Salih Himdan, 4 vols. in 2 (Cairo: al-Maktabat al-Azhariya, 1994), 1:173. Nelly Amri and Laroussi Amri, in *Les Femmes soufies* (St. Jean-de-Braye: Editions Dangles, 1992), translate all thirty-five notices on Sufi women, in some cases rather freely; I have used a later edition than theirs, but have borrowed information from some of their notes.

10. Munawi, *Al-kawakib ad-durriya tarajim as-sadat as-sufiya*, 1:190.

11. Ibid., 200.

12. Ibid., 206.

13. Ibid.

14. Ibid., 264.

15. Ibid., 415.

16. Imam Husayn was the grandson of Muhammad who was killed with his small forces by the army of the Umayyad caliph Yazid and acquired the status of the most revered Shi'i martyr; see L. Veccia Valieri, "Husayn b. 'Ali," *EI2*, 3:607–615.

17. Translated from a collection of elegies in Urdu intended for recitation during Muharram ceremonies, entitled *Muntakhib-i Marasi-yi Muharram* (Hyderabad [India]: Maktab-i Turabiya, n.d.), 322–324.

18. Zabih Allah Safa traces the *manaqibyan* or *manaqib'khwanan* (reciters of praise) to the Buyid period in the early eleventh century when the Shi'a used trained reciters to memorize and recite publicly poems written in praise or lamentation of prominent Shi'i figures. The reciters themselves viewed their profession as stretching back in time to the first century of Hijra, when the death of Imam Husayn created the occasion for composing such poems; see *Tarikh-i adabiyat dar Iran* (Tehran: Intisharat-i Firdaws, 1369/1990), 2:192–195.

19. For a brief account of Riza's life, see Moojan Momen, *An Introduction to*

Shii Islam: The History and Doctrines of Twelver Shiism (New Haven: Yale University Press, 1985), 41.

20. *Qibla-yi haftum*, ed. ʿAbbas Mushfiq Kashani and Mahmud Shahrukhi (Tehran: n.p., 1993), 330–331.

21. Ibid., 236.

22. Ibid., 281–282.

23. *Armaghan-i naʿt*, comp. Shafiq Brelvi (Karachi: Maktaba-i khatun-i Pakistan, 1975), 117.

24. From the collection *Ginan-i Sharif*, vol. 1 (Karachi: HRH the Aga Khan Ismaʿilia Association for Pakistan, 1978).

25. Translated from a live broadcast over Egyptian State Radio, 22 September 1984; location: Mosque of Sidi ʿAbd ar-Rahman ʿUthman ash-Shahawi, Village of Shuha, in the district of Mansura, Daqahliya Governorate, Egypt.

PART THREE

1. This poem comes from a handwritten bound volume found in the library of the mosque in Tanta, Egypt. The text is directly connected to the famous Egyptian saint Ahmad al-Badawi (d. 1278), whose shrine in Tanta is a pilgrimage center. Entitled *An Ocean Overflowing with Blessings and Salutation to the Glorious Prophet* (*Al-bahr az-zakhir fi ʾs-salah wa ʾs-salam ʿala ʾn-nabi al-fakhir*), the book incorporates poems and meditations of one of Badawi's closest followers, Shaykh Ahmad Muhammad al-Hijab. However, the material found in the book may not all be his. This version was sponsored by a local leader, as a statement at the end of the book indicates: "Muhammad, from God Almighty and His Goodness, helped us to write and collect it to perfection, aided by the most revered of the people of his age, the most good, the most godly, the most knowledgeable, the most spiritually complete, who is called Hasan al-Fuʾad Basha al-Luqah, may God grant him the fullness of being and the highest of ranks" (569). It is dated 1273 (1856).

2. *Armaghan-i naʿt*, comp. Shafiq Brelvi (Karachi: Maktaba-i khatun-i Pakistan, 1975), 93.

3. Taha Hussein, *ʿAla hamish as-sira* (Cairo: n.p., 1933).

4. See Paul Losensky's fine new translation of ʿAttar in Michael A. Sells, trans. and ed., *Early Islamic Mysticism* (New York: Paulist Press, 1996), 151–170.

5. The edition gives *misriya* rather than *basriya*, probably owing to a scribal error.

6. Abd ar-Raʾuf al-Munawi, *Al-kawakib ad-durriya tarajim as-sadat as-sufiya (aw Tabaqat al-Munawi al-kubra)*, ed. ʿAbd al-Hamid Salih Himdan, 4 vols. in 2 (Cairo: al-Maktabat al-Azhariya, 1994), 200–202.

7. *The Precious Pearl Recalling Those Who Have Helped Me on the Path of the Hereafter* (*Ad-durrat al-fakhira fi dhikr man intafaʿtu bihi fi tariq al-akhira*) and *The Spirit of Holiness in the Counseling of the Soul* (*Ruh al-quds fi munashafat an-nafs*), from *Sufis of Andalusia*, ed. and trans. R. W. J. Austin (Berkeley: University of California Press, 1971).

8. Ibid., 142.

9. Ibid., 145–146.

10. Ibid., 154–155.

11. Denis Gril, *La Risala de Safi al-Din Ibn Abi l-Mansur Ibn Zafir: Biographies*

des maîtres spirituels connus par un cheikh égyptien du VIIe/XIIIe siècle (Cairo: Institut Français d'Archéologie Orientale, 1986), 89–90 (Arabic text).

12. ʿAbd al-Haqq Muhaddith Dihlawi, *Akhbar al-akhyar fi asrar al-abrar* (Delhi: Muhammad Mirza Khan, 1280/1863).

13. Translated from ʿAbd ar-Rahman al-Jabarti, *ʿAjaʾib al-athar fi tarajim wa 'l-akhbar*, ed. Hasan M. Jawhar et al. (Cairo, 1958–1965), 2:338–341, also consulting the French translation, *Merveilles biographiques et historiques*, trans. Shaykh Mansour Bey et al. (Cairo, 1888–1894), 3:60–64.

14. Translated by Victor Danner under the title *Sufi Aphorism* (Leiden: E. J. Brill, 1973).

15. Translation uncertain; literally "the way of the people" (*tariq al-qawm*).

16. Translation is a bit uncertain; "fully initiated Sufis" here translates *salikun*, "wayfarers."

17. *At-Tuhfat al-bahiya wa 't-turfat ash-shahiya*, ed. anonymous (Istanbul: Matbaʿat al-jawaʾib, 1884–1885), 107–114.

18. From Dihlawi, *Akhbar al-akhyar fi asrar al-abrar*. [I have omitted the repetitious phrase "He said. . . . "—Ed.]

19. Reprinted with permission from David B. Edwards, *Heroes of the Age: Moral Fault Lines on the Afghan Frontier* (Berkeley: University of California Press, 1996), 126–128.

20. Muhammad A. Simsar, trans. and ed., *Tales of a Parrot* (Cleveland: Cleveland Museum of Art, 1978).

21. Dihlawi, *Akhbar al-akhyar fi asrar al-abrar*, excerpted from secs. 30, 33, 75, 101, 105, 106.

PART FOUR

1. Reprinted with permission from W. M. Thackston, *A Century of Princes: Sources on Timurid History and Art* (Cambridge, Mass.: The Aga Khan Program for Islamic Architecture, 1989), 370–372.

2. The original Persian text is to be found in Muhammad Lahiji, *Mafatih al-iʿjaz fi sharh-i Gulshan-i raz*, ed. K. Samiʿi (Tehran 1337/1958), 638–648. For a further discussion of this text and Shabistari's views on idolatry, see Leonard Lewisohn, "The Transcendental Unity of Polytheism and Monotheism in the Sufism of Shabistari," in *The Legacy of Medieval Persian Sufism*, ed. Leonard Lewisohn (London: Khaniqahi Nimatullahi Publications, 1992), 379–406.

3. *Ghayr* literally means, "other," "alien," "else," "without," but it is also used in Persian to render the English prefixes "un-," "in-," and "non-." As the commentary indicates, the term here implies nonexistence or nullity.

4. On the theme of "real infidelity" in Shabistari's works, see Leonard Lewisohn, *Beyond Faith and Infidelity: The Sufi Poetry and Teachings of Mahmud Shabistari* (London: Curzon Press, 1995), 268–317.

5. Based on the Persian text, in Major J. Stephenson, ed. and trans., *The First Book of the "Hadiqatu 'l-haqiqat"* (New York: Samuel Weiser, 1972), 21–24.

6. Translated from ʿUmar Ibn al-Farid, *Diwan Ibn al-Farid*, ed. ʿAbd al-Khaliq Mahmud (Cairo: Dar al-Maʿarif, 1984), 177–178, 205–206, 213, 215.

7. Edited and translated from Muhammad ʿAbd ar-Raʾuf al-Munawi, *Al-kawakib*

ad-durriya fi tarajim as-sadat as-sufiya, MS. 1885 (Ta'rikh Tal'at), 561–567, and MS. 260 (Ta'rikh), fols. 354b–357a (Cairo: Dar al-Kutub al-Misriya, n.d.).

8. Rumi, *Kulliyat-i Shams ya divan-i kabir,* ed. Badi' az-Zaman Furuzanfar (Tehran: Amir Kabir, 1976), D 2997:1–10.

9. Reprinted with permission from Leonard Lewisohn, "Mohammad Shirin Maghrebi," *Sufi* 1 (1988): 34 (ghazal 8).

10. *Armaghan-i na't,* comp. Shafiq Brelvi (Karachi: Maktaba-i khatun-i Pakistan, 1975), 315.

11. From an anthology of na't poetry composed by Hindu poets compiled by Fani Muradabadi, *Hindu shu'ara ka na'tiya kalam* (Lyallpur: Arif Publishing House, 1962), 66.

12. Reprinted with permission from Javad Nurbakhsh, *Sufi Women,* 2d ed. (London: Khaniqahi Nimatullahi Publications, 1990), 244–245 (ghazal 38).

PART FIVE

1. See Richard Antoun, *Village Preacher* (Princeton: Princeton University Press, 1986), 99–100, for a listing of the books in his library.

2. Relying on David Mandelbaum's concept of life history as applied by James Freeman in *Untouchable: An Indian Life History* (Stanford: Stanford University Press, 1979); see Mandelbaum, "The Study of Life History: Gandhi," *Current Anthropology* 14, no. 3 (June 1973).

3. Mandelbaum, "Study of Life History," 377; see also Freeman, *Untouchable,* 376–377.

4. Mandelbaum, "Study of Life History," 180; see also Freeman, *Untouchable,* 378–379.

5. Mandelbaum, "Study of Life History," 180; see also Freeman, *Untouchable,* 383.

6. From the Arabic text in Saleh Lamei Mostafa, *Kloster und Mausoleum des Farag ibn Barquq in Kairo* (Glueckstadt: J. J. Augustin, 1968), 131–132.

7. Ibid., 132.

8. Ibid., 134.

9. From the Arabic text in Saleh Lamei Mustafa and Felicitas Jaritz, *Madrasa, Hanqah und Mausoleum des Barquq in Kairo* (Glueckstadt: J. J. Augustin, 1982), 126–129, with repetitive portions of headings omitted.

10. This is document 5 in *Samarkandskie dokumenty XV–XVI vv.,* a collection of endowment and purchase deeds concerning Khwaja Ahrar that was published in Persian with a Russian translation by the late economic historian Ol'ga D. Chekhovich in 1974 in Moscow.

11. All were published in Chekhovich's *Samarkandskie dokumenty XV–XVI vv.*

12. The Samarkand madrasa of Khwaja Ahrar, built in 1455–1456 in the southern part of the city, is no longer in existence. In document 10 from this same collection we learn that this madrasa had two floors, and according to document 5 it appears that the mosque was located in the southeast corner of the madrasa. See ibid., 386n.49.

13. M. Sarraf, ed., *Rasa'il-i javamardan* (Tehran: French-Iran Institute, 1973), 89–166.

14. C. Cahen, "Futuwwa," *EI2* 2:964. Also see H. Corbin's introduction to Sarraf, ed., *Rasa'il-i javamardan.*

15. Zarrinkub, "Ahl-i malamat va fatiyan," in *'Ayin-i javanmardi*, ed. Murtada Sarraf (Tehran: n.p., 1363/1984), 201.

16. Sarraf, ed., *Rasa'il-i javamardan*, 93.

17. "One cannot enter the Sufi Path except by way of the Canon Law; likewise, no one can comprehend the divine Reality except through the spiritual Path of Sufism; chivalry is a concomitant of the Path" (ibid., 93).

18. Ibid., 126. For other references to the connections of the two institutions, see 110–111.

19. Ibid., 116.

20. Ibid., 105.

21. Ibid., 106.

22. Ibid., 107–108.

23. Ibid., 114–115.

24. Ibid., 158–159.

25. Ibid., 152–155.

26. Reprinted with permission from R. Stephen Humphreys, "Women as Patrons of Religious Architecture in Ayyubid Damascus," *Muqarnas* 11 (1994): 47.

27. Lisa Golombek and Donald Wilber, *The Timurid Architecture of Iran and Turan* (Princeton: Princeton University Press, 1988), 1:250–52. See also Roya Marefat, "Timurid Women: Patronage and Power," *Asian Art* 6, no. 2 (spring 1993): 33.

28. Gawhar Shad (d. 1438), wife of Shah Rukh (d. 1447) and mother of Ulugh Beg (d. 1449) and Baysunghur Mirza (d. 1433), is another prominent example of Timurid patronage by a woman; she built a large mosque in Mashhad (1405–1419) and a madrasa and *musalla* (site for ritual prayer) in Herat (1417–1437). On Gawhar Shad's patronage in Mashhad, see Bernard O'Kane, *Timurid Architecture in Khurasan* (Costa Mesa, Calif.: Mazda Publishers, 1987), 119–129.

29. Ülkü Bates, "The Architectural Patronage of Ottoman Women," *Asian Art* 6, no. 2 (spring 1993): 64.

30. Text in E. Lévi-Provençal, "Un nouveau texte d'histoire merinide: Le Musnad d'Ibn Marzuk," *Hesperis* 5 (1925): 1–84.

31. The Mosque of the Coppersmiths (*saffarin*) in Fez is probably the Mosque of the Sharabliyin in the northwest of the city. It is known as the *jami' as-saffarin al-qudama'* (mosque of the old quarter of the coppersmiths). For the monuments of Fez, see A. Bel, *Inscriptions arabes de Fes* (Paris: n.p., 1919). A convenient introduction to Fez in this period is Roger Le Tourneau, *Fez in the Age of the Marinides* (Norman: University of Oklahoma Press, 1961).

32. *Halq al-na'am*: This is probably the small mosque now known as the Mosque of Abu 'l-Hasan, which lies about a hundred meters from the Bu 'Inaniya Madrasa on the Small Tala (*at-Tala as-saghira*).

33. For the royal necropolis at Chella, cf. Henri Basset and E. Lévi-Provençal, *Chella: Une nécropole mérinide* (Paris: Emile Larose, 1923).

34. The standard work on the monuments of Tlemcen remains William Marçais and Georges Marçais, *Les Monuments arabes de Tlemcen* (Paris: Fontemoing, 1903); cf. also Rachid Bourouiba, *L'Art religieux musulmane en Algérie* (Algiers: S.N.E.D., 1973).

35. Some idea of this chandelier can be gleaned from contemporary Marinid chandeliers in the congregational mosque at Taza, Morocco, and the Qarawiyyin

Mosque, Fez. The Taza chandelier, installed in the mosque in 1294, had 514 oil lamps and cost 8,000 dinars. See Henri Terrasse, *La Grande mosquée de Taza* (Paris: Editions d'art et d'histoire, 1943). For the chandelier in Fez, made from a Spanish bell captured at Gibraltar by Abu 'l-Hasan's son, Abu Malik, see Jerrilynn D. Dodds, ed., *Al-Andalus: The Art of Islamic Spain* (New York: Metropolitan Museum of Art, 1992), 278–279.

36. On these minbars, see J. M. Bloom in Dodds, ed., *Al-Andalus*, 362–367, with bibliography.

37. On the complex of Sayyidi Abu Madyan at al-'Ubbad, see, in addition to the works of Marçais and Bourouiba, Sheila S. Blair, "Sufi Saints and Shrine Architecture," *Muqarnas* 7 (1990): 35–49.

38. For the history of the madrasa as an institution, see *EI2*, s.v. "Madrasa"; for the history of the form in the Muslim West, see Robert Hillenbrand, *Islamic Architecture: Form, Function, and Meaning* (Edinburgh: Edinburgh University Press, 1994), 237ff.

39. Reprinted with permission from Wheeler M. Thackston, *A Century of Princes: Sources on Timurid History and Art* (Cambridge, Mass.: The Aga Khan Program for Islamic Architecture, 1989), 213–215.

40. Ibid., 375.

PART SIX

1. Najib Mayil Harawi, ed., *Rawh al-arwah fi sharh asma' al-malik al-fattah* (Tehran: Intisharat-i 'Ilmi wa Farhangi, 1368/1989), 87–92.

2. In Chinese thought, the "Great Ultimate" (*tai-chi*) is the origin of heaven, earth, and the Ten Thousand Things. Its activity becomes manifest through the complementary principles, yin and yang, which are receptive and active, or female and male. Here Wang understands the Great Ultimate as synonymous with the Islamic idea of "Creator." As for the "Beyond-Ultimate" (*wu-chi*), it is the Great Ultimate inasmuch as it remains nonmanifest. Wang understands it as synonymous with the Islamic concept of *dhat*, the "Essence," or God in Himself without regard to creation. Thus, in this passage, Wang is saying that the human differentiation into male and female reflects the fact that the Creator differentiated the world through yin and yang. This in turn illustrates the polarity between God's life (or Being) and His wisdom (or knowledge), which are the principles of receptivity and activity within God Himself. These in turn are parallel to the two basic types of divine attributes, the merciful and the wrathful (also known as the majestic and the beautiful), as well as with the highness and lowness that are the basic qualities of heaven and earth, the two poles of the universe. For a detailed explanation of these and other polar opposites in Islamic thought, see S. Murata, *The Tao of Islam* (Albany: State University of New York Press, 1992), esp. 66ff.

3. Muslim thinkers often see "corruption" and "shedding blood" as a necessary corollary of being created of the four elements; see, for example, W. C. Chittick, *The Sufi Path of Knowledge* (Albany: State University of New York Press, 1989), 68, 142.

4. Revisions from text in Anthony H. Johns, ed. and trans., *The Gift Addressed to the Spirit of the Prophet* (Canberra: Australian National University Press, 1965).

5. Taking the Javanese *widi* as a possible equivalent to the Arabic *'ali*.

6. Javanese *Sejati*, taken as equivalent to the Arabic *al-Haqq*.

7. Reading the Javanese *Yang Sukma* as equivalent to the Arabic *al-Latif*.

8. Possibly rendering the Arabic *al-jalil* for the sake of meter, or perhaps *dhu 'l-jalal*.

9. Reading Javanese *Yang Agung* as equivalent to the Arabic *al-Kabir*.

10. See Jonathan Berkey, "Women and Islamic Education in the Mamluk Period," in *Women in Middle Eastern History: Shifting Boundaries in Sex and Gender*, ed. Nikki R. Keddie and Beth Baron (New Haven: Yale University Press, 1991), 143–157.

11. See, for example, George Makdisi, *The Rise of Humanism in Classical Islam and the Christian West* (Edinburgh: Edinburgh University Press, 1990), 178, 187.

12. Jonathan Berkey, *The Transmission of Knowledge in Medieval Cairo* (Princeton: Princeton University Press, 1992), 173–174.

13. Muhammad 'Abd ar-Ra'uf al-Munawi, *Al-kawakib ad-durriya tarajim assadat as-sufiya (aw Tabaqat al-Munawi al-kubra)*, ed. 'Abd al-Hamid Salih Himdan, 4 vols. in 2 (Cairo: al-Maktabat al-Azhariya, 1994), 3:48.

14. Ibid., 1:167.

15. Ibid., 206.

16. Ibid., 474.

17. Ibid., 581.

18. M. R. Bawa Muhaiyaddeen, *A Contemporary Sufi Speaks: The True Meaning of Sufism* (Philadelphia: Fellowship Press, 1995), 9.

19. *Four Steps to Pure Iman: Explanations of a Painting* (Philadelphia: Fellowship Press, 1979).

20. Muhammad Akbar Husayni, *Jawami' al-kalim* (Hyderabad: n.p., 1937), 109.

21. Majd ad-Din Baghdadi, *Risala dar safar*, ed. Karamat Ra'na Husayni, in *Wisdom of Persia: Collected Papers on Islamic Philosophy and Mysticism*, ed. Hermann Landolt and Mehdi Mohaqqeq (Tehran: McGill University Institute of Islamic Studies, Tehran Branch, 1971), 179–190.

22. A. J. Wensinck, *Concordance et indices de la tradition musulmane* (Leiden: E. J. Brill, 1992), 2:468.

23. Source of the quotation is unknown.

24. In Turkish these are *seyr ile 'llah; seyr li 'llah; seyr 'ale 'llah; seyr ma'a 'llah; seyr fi 'llah; seyr 'an allah;* and *seyr bi 'llah*.

25. Turkish: *nefs-i emmare; nefs-i levvame; nefs-i mulhime; nefs-i mutmainne; nefs-i raziye; nefs-i marziye; nefs-i kamile*.

26. The selection is on folios 138b–142b of the text edited in Ahmet T. Karamustafa, *Vahidi's Menakib-i Hvoca-i Cihan ve Netice-i Can: Critical Edition and Analysis* (Cambridge, Mass.: Department of Near Eastern Languages and Civilizations, Harvard University, 1993).

27. On this hadith, see Hermann Landolt, *Correspondance spirituelle échangée entre Nuroddin Esfarayeni (ob. 717/1317) et son disciple Alaoddawleh Semnani (ob. 736/1336)* (Tehran: Département d'Iranologie de l'Institut Franco-Iranien de Recherche, 1972), 125.

28. For the hadith, see, for instance, Badi' az-Zaman Furuzanfar, *Ahadith-i Masnavi* (Tehran: Intisahrat-i Danishgah-i Tihran, 1344/1955), 45, no. 119.

29. The saying is recorded in 'Ali Akbar Dihkhuda, *Kitab-i aml va hikam*

(Tehran: Matbaʿa-i Majlis, 1310/1931), 1:265. For the hadith, see Furuzanfar, *Ahadith-i Masnavi*, 23, no. 54; and Dihkhuda, *Kitab-i aml va hikam*, 1:266.

30. For the hadith, see Furuzanfar, *Ahadith-i Masnavi*, 67, no. 179; and Landolt, *Correspondance spirituelle*, 125.

31. Famous hadith; see, for instance, Dihkhuda, *Kitab-i aml va hikam*, 4:1744–1745; and Furuzanfar, *Ahadith-i Masnavi*, 166–167, no. 529.

32. Dihkhuda, *Kitab-i aml va hikam*, 4:1753; and Furuzanfar, *Ahadith-i Masnavi*, 116, no. 353.

33. Jaʿfar Sajjadi, *Farhang-i lughat va istilahat va taʾbirat-i ʿirfani* (Tehran: Kitabkhana Tahouri, 1350/1971), 92–96.

34. Wensinck, *Concordance et indices*, 7:137.

PART SEVEN

1. From *Pergolakan pemikiran Islam: Catatan Harian Ahmad Wahib*, ed. Djohan Effendi and Ismed Natsir (Jakarta: n.p., 1983).

2. Abu Jaʿfar Muhammad ibn Jarir at-Tabari, *Jamiʿ al-bayan ʿan tafsir ay al-Qurʾan* (Beirut: Dar al-Fikr, 1984), book 15, pp. 6–10.

3. Grace D. Guest and Richard Ettinghausen, "The Iconography of a Kashan Luster Plate," *Ars Orientalis* 4 (1961): 25–64.

4. ʿAbd ar-Raʾuf al-Munawi, *Al-Kawakib ad-durriya tarajim as-sadat as-sufiya (aw Tabaqat al-Munawi al-kubra)*, ed. ʿAbd al-Hamid Salih Himdan, 4 vols. in 2 (Cairo: al-Maktabat al-Azhariya, 1994), 1:203.

5. Text copied from a *majlis-i samaʿ* in Delhi at Nizam ad-Din in September 1974. See also Regula Qureshi, "The *Mahfil-e-Sama*: Sufi Practice in the Indian Context," *Islam in the Modern Age* 17, no. 3 (Aug. 1986): 161–162.

6. Reprinted with permission from Bruce B. Lawrence, *Notes from a Distant Flute: The Extant Literature of Pre-Mughal Indian Sufism* (Tehran: Imperial Iranian Academy of Philosophy, 1978), 51–52.

7. From ʿAbd ar-Rahman al-Jabarti, *ʿAjaʾib al-athar fi tarajim wa ʾl-akhbar*, ed. Hasan M. Jawhar et al. (Cairo, 1958–1965), 2:341.

8. Tabari, *Jamiʿ al-bayan ʿan tafsir*, book 15, pp. 16–17.

9. Translated from Mahmud Hamdi Zaqzuq, ed., *Thalath rasaʾil fi ʾl-maʿrifa lam yunshar min qabl* (Cairo: Maktabat al-Azhar, 1399/1979); based on a photocopy (or microfilm copy?) of MS. Or. 177(7), sheets (or folios?) 103–106, at Leiden University (old number 1491 in the index of manuscripts at the Leiden library). Zaqzuq notes that Brockelmann mistakenly identified this treatise with Ghazali's *Risala fi ʾl-maʿrifa*. So far as he knows, this is the only manuscript of the treatise. This confirms Bouyges's suspicions; see *Essai de la chronologie des oeuvres de al-Ghazali*, ed. M. Allard (Beirut: Imprimerie Catholique, 1959), 123–124. Dr. Zaqzuq sees no reason not to attribute this treatise to Ghazali. He notes that its opening format is similar to that of writings such as *Al-munqidh min ad-dalal* and *Al-maqsad al-asna*, while its ideas are similar to those found in other works of Ghazali, such as *Al-maqsad al-asna*.

10. Literally: in the degrees of disclosure (*kashf*) and way of intimate knowledge (*maʿrifa*). I do not take *kashf* here to refer to a different sort of knowledge from *maʿrifa*.

11. Maneri, *Maktubat-i Sad o Panja*, letter 15.

12. *Hilyat al-awliya'*by Isfahani; see SD, 86.

13. Reprinted by permission of the editor and copyright holder from *The Rose and the Rock: Mystical and Rational Elements in the Intellectual History of South Asian Islam*, ed. Bruce B. Lawrence (Durham, N.C.: Duke University Programs in Comparative Studies on Southern Asia), 73–76.

14. *Gulistan*, chap. 1, story 4, end.

15. Excerpted with permission from Leonard Lewisohn, "Palasi's Memoir of Shaykh Kujuji, a Persian Sufi Saint of the Thirteenth Century," *Journal of the Royal Asiatic Society* 6, no. 3 (1996): 346–366; text translated from *Tadhkira-yi shaykh Muhammad ibn Sadiq al-Kujuji* (Tehran: Chapkhana Packitchi, 1947).

16. Translation by A. J. Arberry, *The Koran Interpreted* (Oxford: Oxford University Press 1983), with minor changes.

Suggestions for Further Reading

PART ONE

Burton, John. *An Introduction to the Hadith*. Edinburgh: Edinburgh University Press, 1994.

Goldman, Shalom. *The Wiles of Women/The Wiles of Men: Joseph and Potiphar's Wife in Ancient Near Eastern, Jewish, and Islamic Folklore*. Albany: State University of New York Press, 1995.

Haleem, Muhammad Abdel. *Understanding the Qur'an: Themes and Style*. New York: St. Martin's Press, 1995.

Hawting, G. R., and Abdul-Kader A. Shareef, eds. *Approaches to the Qur'an*. London: Routledge, 1993.

Kugel, James L. *In Potiphar's House: The Interpretive Life of Biblical Texts*. Cambridge, MA: Harvard University Press, 1994.

Lazarus-Yafeh, Hava. *Intertwined Worlds: Medieval Islam and Bible Criticism*. Princeton: Princeton University Press, 1992.

Schimmel, Annemarie. *Calligraphy and Islamic Culture*. New York: New York University Press, 1984.

Stowasser, Barbara F. *Women in the Qur'an, Traditions, and Interpretation*. New York: Oxford University Press, 1994.

PART TWO

Asani, Ali, Kamal Abdel-Malek, and Annemarie Schimmel. *Celebrating Muhammad*. Columbia: University of South Carolina Press, 1995.

Ayoub, Mahmoud. *Redemptive Suffering in Islam: A Study of the Devotional Aspects of 'Ashura in Twelver Shi'ism*. The Hague: Mouton, 1978.

Bowen, John R. *Muslims Through Discourse: Religion and Ritual in Gayo Society*. Princeton: Princeton University Press, 1993.

Chelkowski, Peter, ed. *Ta'ziyah: Ritual and Drama in Iran*. New York: New York University Press, 1979.

Elad, Amikam. *Medieval Jerusalem and Islamic Worship: Holy Places, Ceremonies, Pilgrimage*. Leiden: E. J. Brill, 1995.

Gaffney, Patrick D. *The Prophet's Pulpit: Islamic Preaching in Contemporary Egypt*. Berkeley: University of California Press, 1994.

Hunzai, Faquir M., comp. and trans. *Towards God: An Anthology of Isma'ili Poetry*. New York: St. Martin's Press, 1996.

Murata, Sachiko, and William C. Chittick. *The Vision of Islam*. New York: Paragon House, 1994.

Padwick, Constance. *Muslim Devotions: A Study of Prayer-Manuals in Common Use*. Oxford: Oneworld, 1996.

Smith, Grace M., and Carl W. Ernst, eds. *Manifestations of Sainthood in Islam*. Istanbul: Isis Press, 1993.

PART THREE

Alvi, Sajida Sultana. *Advice on the Art of Governance: An Indo-Islamic Mirror for Princes*. Albany: State University of New York Press, 1989.

Edwards, David. *Heroes of the Age: Moral Fault Lines on the Afghan Frontier*. Berkeley: University of California Press, 1996.

Guillaume, A., trans. *The Life of Muhammad*. Oxford: Oxford University Press, 1955.

Malti-Douglas, Fedwa. *Woman's Body, Woman's Word: Gender and Discourse in Arabo-Islamic Writing*. Princeton: Princeton University Press, 1991.

Peters, F. E. *Muhammad and the Origins of Islam*. Albany: State University of New York Press, 1994.

Phipps, William E. *Muhammad and Jesus: A Comparison of the Prophets and Their Teachings*. New York: Continuum, 1996.

Renard, John. *Islam and the Heroic Image: Themes in Literature and the Visual Arts*. Columbia: University of South Carolina Press, 1993.

Roded, Ruth. *Women in Islamic Biographical Collections: From Ibn Sa'd to Who's Who*. Boulder, CO: Lynne Rienner Publishers, 1994.

Rubin, Uri. *The Eye of the Beholder: The Life of Muhammad as Viewed by the Early Muslims*. Princeton, NJ: Darwin Press, 1995.

PART FOUR

Bürgel, Johann C. *The Feather of Simurgh: The "Licit Magic" of the Arts in Medieval Islam*. New York: New York University Press, 1988.

Hillenbrand, Robert. *Islamic Architecture: Form, Function, and Meaning*. New York: Columbia University Press, 1994.

Homerin, Th. Emil. *From Arab Poet to Muslim Saint: Ibn al-Farid, His Verse, and His Shrine*. Columbia: University of South Carolina Press, 1994.

Keshavarz, Fatemeh. *Reading Mystical Lyric: The Case of Jalal ad-Din Rumi*. Columbia: University of South Carolina Press, 1997.

Knappert, Jan. *Swahili Islamic Poetry*. Leiden: E. J. Brill, 1971.

Lewisohn, Leonard. *Beyond Faith and Infidelity: The Sufi Poetry and Teachings of Mahmud Shabistari*. Richmond, Surrey, Eng.: Curzon Press, 1995.

Schimmel, Annemarie. *A Two-Colored Brocade: The Imagery of Persian Poetry*. Chapel Hill: University of North Carolina Press, 1992.

Sperl, Stefan, and Shackle, Christopher, eds. *Qasida Poetry in Islamic Asia and Africa*. 2 vols. Leiden: E. J. Brill, 1996.

PART FIVE

Blair, Sheila S., and Jonathan M. Bloom. *The Art and Architecture of Islam, 1250–1800*. New Haven: Yale University Press, 1994.

Dumper, Michael. *Islam and Israel: Muslim Religious Endowments and the Jewish State*. Washington, DC: Institute for Palestine Studies, 1994.

Karamustafa, Ahmet T. *God's Unruly Friends: Dervish Groups in the Islamic Later Middle Period, 1200–1500*. Salt Lake City: University of Utah Press, 1994.

Lifchef, Raymond, ed. *The Dervish Lodge*. Berkeley: University of California Press, 1992.

Makdisi, George. *The Rise of Humanism in Classical Islam and the Christian West*. Edinburgh: University of Edinburgh Press, 1990.

McChesney, Robert. *Waqf in Central Asia: Four Hundred Years of the History of a Muslim Shrine, 1480–1889*. Princeton: Princeton University Press, 1991.

PART SIX

Berkey, Jonathan. *The Transmission of Knowledge in Medieval Cairo: A Social History of Islamic Education*. Princeton: Princeton University Press, 1992.

Farhadi, A. G. Ravan. *Abdullah Ansari of Herat (1006–1089): An Early Sufi Master*. Richmond, Surrey, Eng.: Curzon Press, 1994.

al-Ghazali, Abu Hamid. *Disciplining the Soul and Breaking the Two Desires*. Translated by T. J. Winter. Cambridge: Islamic Texts Society, 1995.

Jamali, Muhammad Fadil. *Letters on Islam*. London: World of Islam Festival Trust, 1978.

Maneri, Sharaf ad-Din. *The Hundred Letters*. Translated by Paul Jackson. New York: Paulist Press, 1980.

Netton, Ian Richard. *Seek Knowledge: Thought and Travel in the House of Islam*. Richmond, Surrey, Eng.: Curzon Press, 1994.

Nizam ad-Din Awliya'. *Morals for the Heart*. Translated by Bruce B. Lawrence. New York: Paulist Press, 1992.

al-Qushayri, Abu 'l-Qasim. *Principles of Sufism*. Translated by Barbara von Schlegell. Berkeley: Mizan Press, 1990.

Sells, Michael A., ed. and trans. *Early Islamic Mysticism*. New York: Paulist Press, 1996.

PART SEVEN

Arnaldez, Roger. *Three Messengers for One God*. Translated by Gerald Schlabach, Mary Louise Gude, and David Burrell. Notre Dame: University of Notre Dame Press, 1994.

Chodkiewicz, Michel. *The Spiritual Writings of Amir 'Abd al-Kader*. Translated by James Chrestensen and Tom Manning. Albany: State University of New York Press, 1995.

Dols, Michael W. *Majnun: The Madman in Medieval Islamic Society*. New York: Oxford University Press, 1992.

Ernst, Carl, trans. *Ruzbihan Baqli: The Unveiling of Secrets, Diary of a Sufi Master*. Chapel Hill, N.C.: Parvardigar Press, 1997.

Ernst, Carl. *Ruzbihan Baqli: Mysticism and the Rhetoric of Sainthood in Persian Sufism*. Richmond, Surrey, Eng.: Curzon Press, 1994.

Katz, Jonathan G. *Dreams, Sufism, and Sainthood: The Visionary Career of Muhammad al-Zawawi*. Leiden: E. J. Brill, 1996.

Massignon, Louis. *Essay on the Origins of the Technical Language of Islamic Mysticism*. Translated by Benjamin Clark. Notre Dame: University of Notre Dame Press, 1994.

Özelsel, Michaela M. *Forty Days: The Diary of a Traditional Solitary Sufi Retreat*. Brattleboro, VT: Threshold Books, 1996.

Tusi, Nasir ad-Din. *Contemplation and Action*. Translated by Seyyed Jalal Hosseini Badakhchani. New York: St. Martins/I. B. Tauris and Co., 1996.

About the Contributors

RICHARD ANTOUN is Professor of Anthropology at the State University of New York at Binghamton, specialist in Middle Eastern societies, and author of *Muslim Preacher in the Modern World*.

ALI ASANI is Professor of the Practice of Indo-Muslim Languages and Cultures at Harvard University, and co-author of *Celebrating Muhammad: Images of the Prophet in Popular Muslim Poetry*.

R. W. J. AUSTIN is Professor of Arabic and Islamic Studies in the School of Oriental and African Studies at the University of Durham, England. In addition to *Sufis of Andalusia* he has translated Ibn 'Arabi's *Bezels of Wisdom*.

JONATHAN M. BLOOM specializes in the architecture and art of medieval Egypt and North Africa. With his wife, Sheila Blair, he has been co-editor of the Islamic entries for the multivolume *Dictionary of Art* and co-author of *The Art and Architecture of Islam, 1250–1800*.

JOHN R. BOWEN is Professor of Anthropology and Chair of the Committee on Social Thought and Analysis at Washington University in St. Louis; he is the author of several books on Islam in Indonesia.

WILLIAM C. CHITTICK teaches religious studies at the State University of New York, Stony Brook. Among his books are *The Sufi Path of Love: The Spiritual Teachings of Rumi, Faith and Practice of Islam: Three Thirteenth-Century Sufi Texts*, and *Imaginal Worlds: Ibn al-'Arabi and the Problem of Religious Diversity*.

FREDERICK M. DENNY is Professor of Religious Studies at the University of Colorado, Boulder. A specialist in Qur'anic studies and American Islam, he recently published a revised edition of *Islam: An Introduction*.

DAVID EDWARDS is Associate Professor of Anthropology at Williams College, Williamstown, Massachusetts. Focusing on Islam in Afghanistan, he has written *Heroes of the Age: Moral Fault Lines on the Afghan Frontier*.

REUVEN FIRESTONE, Associate Professor of Medieval Judaism and Islam at Hebrew Union College in Los Angeles, researches early Islam and its relationship with other religions. He is author of *Journeys in Holy Lands: The Evolution of the Abraham-Ishmael Legends in Islamic Exegesis*.

PATRICK D. GAFFNEY is Associate Professor of Anthropology at the University of Notre Dame. Most recently he has concentrated on Islam in East Africa, and wrote *The Prophet's Pulpit: Islamic Preaching in Contemporary Egypt*.

JO-ANN GROSS is Associate Professor of History at Trenton State College in New Jersey. She has written on Islamic central Asia, and is editor of *Muslims in Central Asia: Expressions of Identity and Change.*

PETER HEATH is Associate Professor of Arabic Language and Literature and Chairman of the Department of Asian and Near Eastern Languages and Literatures at Washington University in St. Louis. His publications include *Allegory and Philosophy in Avicenna (Ibn Sina)* and *The Thirsty Sword: Sirat ʿAntar and the Arabic Popular Epic.*

NICHOLAS HEER is Professor Emeritus of Near Eastern Languages and Civilization at the University of Washington in Seattle. He has published a number of works on medieval Islamic thought and mysticism, including *The Precious Pearl,* a translation of Jami's *Ad-durrat al-fakhira.*

TH. EMIL HOMERIN is Associate Professor of Religion in the Department of Religion and Classics at the University of Rochester. Specializing in Islamic mysticism and classical Arabic poetry, he is the author of *From Arab Poet to Muslim Saint: Ibn al-Farid, His Verse, and His Shrine* and the forthcoming *Ibn al-Farid: Sufi Verse and Saintly Life.*

STEPHEN HUMPHREYS is Professor of History at the University of California at Santa Barbara and author of *Islamic History: A Framework for Inquiry.*

PAUL JACKSON, S.J., has worked in India for many years, where he specializes in Islamic spirituality and Muslim-Christian dialogue. His books include several on Sharaf ad-Din Maneri, among them *The Hundred Letters* and *A Table Laden with Good Things.*

ANTHONY H. JOHNS is Professor Emeritus of the Faculty of Asian Studies at the Australian National University in Canberra. He has published especially in qurʾanic studies in Arabic and Southeast Asian languages, and on Sufism.

AHMET T. KARAMUSTAFA is Director of the Center for the Study of Islamic Societies and Civilizations at Washington University in St. Louis, and author of *God's Unruly Friends: Dervish Groups in the Islamic Later Middle Period, 1200–1550.*

FATEMEH KESHAVARZ is Associate Professor of Persian Language and Literature at Washington University in St. Louis. She has written *Reading Mystical Lyric: The Case of Jalal ad-Din Rumi.*

JAN KNAPPERT has published over thirty books, including numerous translations of literature from Swahili and several Southeast Asian languages; among them is his two-volume *Islamic Legends: Histories of the Heroes, Saints, and Prophets of Islam.*

BRUCE B. LAWRENCE is Professor of Religious Studies at Duke University, focusing on Islam in the Indian subcontinent. His publications include *Notes from a Distant Flute: Sufi Literature in Pre-Mughal India.*

LEONARD LEWISOHN, assistant editor of *Sufi: A Journal of Sufism,* specializes in Persian literature and Islamic religious studies. His latest book is *Beyond Faith and Infidelity: The Sufi Poetry and Teachings of Mahmud Shabistari.*

JANE DAMMEN MCAULIFFE is Chair of the Department for the Study of Religion at the University of Toronto, Victoria College. Author of *Qur'anic Christians: An Analysis of Classical and Modern Exegesis*, she is currently editing an encyclopedia of the Qur'an.

THOMAS MICHEL, S.J., now working in Rome, has specialized in Muslim-Christian relations, Islam in Indonesia, and Islamic theology, and has published a major study of Ibn Taymiya.

MUSTANSIR MIR is Professor of Islam in the Department of Philosophy and Religious Studies at Youngstown State University in Ohio. His numerous studies of Islam's scripture include *Coherence in the Qur'an*.

JAMES W. MORRIS teaches Islamic studies and comparative religious studies at Oberlin College in Ohio. He has published studies and translations in many areas of Islamic thought, including philosophy, popular religion, and Shi'ism.

SACHIKO MURATA teaches Islam and the Far Eastern traditions at the State University of New York, Stony Brook. She is the author of *The Tao of Islam: A Sourcebook on Gender Relationships in Islamic Thought* and, with William C. Chittick, *The Vision of Islam*.

JOHN RENARD is Professor of Theological Studies at Saint Louis University. His publications include *Islam and the Heroic Image: Themes in Literature and the Visual Arts, All the King's Falcons: Rumi on Prophets and Revelation*, and the companion to the present volume, *Seven Doors to Islam*.

ANDREW RIPPIN is Professor of Religious Studies at the University of Calgary, Alberta, Canada, and is the author of the two-volume introduction to Islam, *Muslims, Their Religious Beliefs and Practices*.

WILLIAM SHEPARD is Senior Lecturer in the Department of Philosophy and Religious Studies at the University of Canterbury in Christchurch, New Zealand. His principal interests are modern Islamic ideology, especially in Egypt, and Sufism; he recently published a book on Sayyid Qutb.

WHEELER M. THACKSTON, Jr., is Professor of Persian Literature in the Department of Near Eastern Languages and Civilizations at Harvard University. He has published a number of translations of classic texts, including *The Tales of the Prophets of al-Kisa'i*.

EARLE H. WAUGH is Professor of Religious Studies at the University of Alberta, Edmonton, Canada. His publications include *The Minshidin of Egypt: Their World and Their Song*.

GISELA WEBB is Associate Professor of Religious Studies at Seton Hall University in South Orange, New Jersey, teaching Islamic studies and comparative religions. She writes on medieval Islamic mysticism and Islamic spirituality in America.

Index of Qur'anic Citations

Brackets [ ] indicate reference by sura and verse number only, without the text itself.
Asterisk * indicates the text is a near-quote of the scripture.

Sura:verse	Page	Sura:verse	Page
Sura 1	25–6, 29–34, [107], [136]	4:82	57
		4:104	[73]
2:10	310	4:105	36
2:28	[69]	5:38	239
2:30	275, [280], 281*	5:52	310
2:34	[166]	5:110	[339]
2:35	274	6:11	302*
2:57	[32]	6:75	304
2:59	[304]	6:76–78	305, 307, 308
2:81	235	6:82	[74]
2:111–12	5	6:101–2	28
2:115	285, 300	7:8–9	[53]
2:133	71	7:12	274
2:143	340, 344	7:23	274, 275
2:144–145	85	7:143	308, 309
2:146–148	224	7:175–176	[272]
2:152	371	7:179	302
2:153	[74], 87	8:2	[72]
2:158	85, 87, 90	8:53	[32]
2:177	[235]	9:18–19	27
2:178	238	9:18–22	[43]
2:197	115	9:30	310
2:255	82*, [371]	9:32	307
2:286	27	9:36	[14]
3:7	54	9:72	[344]
3:18	[104]	9:99	[69]
3:31	302, 321	10:62	114
3:37	44, 224	11:114	47
3:48–49	[339]	Sura 12	6–23
3:97	209	12:4	183
3:110	113, 340	12:37	368
3:187	43	12:87	[73]
3:191	173	13:2	51
4:29	111	13:11	133
4:59	46	13:28	[73]

Sura:verse	Page	Sura:verse	Page
14:37	90	30:30, 43	[14]
15:29	305	30:42	302*
15:30	[182]	Sura 31	144–49
15:39	281*	31:21	[371]
15:42	361	31:28	309
15:72	302	31:33	[69]
15:87	31, [344]	34:10–11	[339]
16:16	305	34:54	60
16:44	36	36:38	24
16:64	36	36:67–83	[26]
16:97	309	37:53	30
16:98	57	37:88–89, 99	310
16:128	47	38:11	131
17:1	337	38:19–20	[339]
17:44	178, 179	38:30	57
17:70	305	38:73	[182]
17:81	308	39:23–24	380
17:85	52	39:24	362
17:109	57	39:53	213
18:30	111	40:7–9	28
18:110	302	40:16	34
19:35	28	40:28	131
19:56–57	[342]	41:30	73
19:58	30	41:46	111
20:5	306	41:53	306
20:14	[72]	42:11	382
20:115	271	43:65–71	225
21:79	[339]	44:39	174
21:85–86	[342]	47:15	[340], [344]
21:107	123	48:1–4	88
22:47	[278]	48:4	[70]
23:60	271	48:10	51
23:101–104	[53]	50:16	82*
24:2	[239]	50:30	308
24:13	42	53:9	306
24:21	[71]	53:13–18	[343]
24:35	321	Sura 55	2–5
25:1	30	55:26–27	225
25:7	363	55:29	320
27:16–17	[339]	57:3	355
27:18	184	63:7	[17]
27:19	[339]	65:2	[74]
27:69	302*	66:5	30
28:88	382	66:11	130, 132
29:20	302*	70:19–23	[73]
29:45	[69]	72:16	[74]

Sura:verse	Page	Sura:verse	Page
74:28	310	89:28	277
Sura 76	[26]	Sura 91	[26]
77:41–44	[344]	96:19	[69]
82:19	30	Sura 98	[26]
83:18–36	[6]	98:5	55
84:1–3	[6]	101:6–11	[53]
85:11	[340]	Sura 108	[26], [344]
88:10–16	[344]	Sura 110	2
89:27–28	233	Sura 112	2

General Index

For further references to: dynasties and their works, see Illustrations (xiii–xvi); literary and visual forms, and languages, see Appendices (385–391).

ʿAbbasid dynasty, 98, 235
ʿAbduh, Muhammad (d. 1905), 85, 189, 326
ablution, 58, 78, 161, 245. *See also* fountain(s); purity, ritual
Abraham, 9, 10, 71, 76; builder of Kaʿba, 172; during Muhammad's Ascension, 337, 343; and Ismaʿil, 89; as model, 306; man of faith, 68; Muqatil ibn Sulayman on, 30; prayer at tomb of, 87; station of, 85. *See also* prophet(s)
Abu Ayyub Khalid ibn Zayd (d. 672), 276
Abu Bakr as-Siddiq (d. 634), in a dream, 350; and good intention, 62; on interpretation, 42; love for Muhammad, 271; on understanding, 366. *See also* caliph(s); model(s)
Abu Dharr (d. 653), 24
Abu Hanifa (d. 767), 92; law school of, 226, 291. *See also* law
Abu Hurayra (d. 678), 24, 30, 337
Abu Jahl, 371. *See also* unbelief
Abu Madyan Shuʿayb (d. 1198), 251
acrostic literature, 120, 149. *See also* genre(s)
Adam, 80, 84; in Chinese Muslim tradition, 278; creation of, 182, 274, 276, 280; discovers Eve, 289; exiled from paradise, 97, 164, 270, 275, 276, 277; and heaven and hell, 341; as model, 269; during Muhammad's Ascension, 341; sin of, 271, 362; as vicegerent, 275. *See also* prophet(s)
Africa, Islam in, 78, 251
Aga Khan, 103

Ahrar, Khwaja ʿUbayd Allah (d. 1490), 231, 246
ʿAʾisha (d. 678), 90, 271
ʿAʾisha bint Jaʿfar as-Sadiq (d. 762), 94
Ajmer, India, 156
Akbarabadi, Nazir (d. 1831), 123
Alexander the Great (d. 323 B.C.E.), 172
ʿAli, aphorisms of, 149; in an inscription, 26, 46; in miniature painting, 338; as model for Sufi chivalry, 238; on pilgrimage banner, 88; renovation of tomb of, 261; sayings of, 46, 377. *See also* caliph(s); martyrdom; model(s); Shiʿites
alms, commanded, 55, 80, 154; blessings of, 145; and faith, 74; and intention, 61, 64. *See also* five pillars; worship
Amir Khayrbak (16th c.), tomb of, 181
Amir Khusraw Dihlawi (d. 1325), 268, 303; dream of, 347
ʿAmr ibn Hisham (d. 624). *See* Abu Jahl
Amrullah, Haji Malik Karim (d. 1981), 85, 326
analogy. *See* qiyas
Anas ibn Malik (d. ca. 710), 370
angel(s), 15, 31, 34, 276; Adam, king of, 182, 274; creation of, 84; and daily life, 73; and death, 131, 166, 206; of death, 238; as "heavenly immortals," 278; Israfil, 367; Jibril, 80, 337, 340; at Judgment Day, 82; Michael, 337; in miniature paintings, 268, 324, 348; during Muhammad's Ascension, 340; worship God, 83. *See also* Israfil; Jibril; Michael; Munkar; Nakir

Anis (d. 1875), 95
Ansar, 90
aphorism(s), 149. *See also* genre(s)
apocalyptic, in Qur'an, 2, 4. *See also*
    eschatology; heaven; hell; judgment,
    Day of
arabesque, 168. *See also* art(s)
Arabic, 7; in China, 278; importance of
    studying, 240; and Javanese, 269,
    283; literature in, 126, 284; in paint-
    ing, 292; poetry, 119, 284; and Qur'an
    interpretation, 43. *See also* calligra-
    phy; interpretation; language;
    Qur'an
architecture, of American Muslims, 249,
    251, 253; of Chinese mosques, 279;
    dome, 141, 258, 262; and sacred text,
    26–28; Sufi, 231. *See also* 'Abbasid;
    art(s); arabesque; Ayyubid; dome(s);
    Il-Khanid dynasty; inscription(s);
    Mamluk dynasty; *mihrab*; minaret;
    Mongol dynasty; Ottoman dynasty;
    Safavid dynasty; Saljuqid dynasty;
    Timurid dynasty; tomb(s)
art(s), of the Book, 5; European influence
    on Mughal, 351; painting, 291; poster
    art, 93; rug(s), 66. *See also* architec-
    ture; calligraphy; rug(s)
Ascension of Muhammad, 76, 123, 139,
    325, 336, 366; Tabari on, 353. *See
    also* miracle(s); Muhammad
asceticism, 132, 367; of Ibn al-Farid, 203;
    spiritual, 150; of Sufi Badhni, 140.
    See also fasting; five pillars
Asiya, 130
association, as sin, 23. *See also* idolatry;
    sin
'Attar, Farid ad-Din (d. 1220), 64, 311,
    366; illustration from *Conference*,
    99; in mystical lexicon, 318, 319; on
    Rabi'a, 132
Ayyubid dynasty, 244
Azhar, al-. *See* Cairo, al-Azhar

Baghdad, 39, 63, 165, 166, 274, 287, 332
Baghdadi, Majd ad-Din (d. 1219), 301
Balaam son of Beor, 272

Balkh, 29, 262, 298
Balkhi, Husayn Mu'izz (d. 1440), 298
Balkhi, Muzaffar Shams (d. 1400), 298
baraka (blessing). *See* holy people,
    power of
Barquq, Faraj ibn (d. 1412), 180, 224, 225
Barquq, Sultan (d. 1399), 226, 227
bashar, 8. *See also* human nature
Basra, 29, 94, 132
Basri, Hasan al- (d. 728), 63, 132
Bawa Muhaiyaddeen (d. 1986), 290
Bayezid II (r. 1481–1512), 210
Bayqara, Prince Mizra (d. 1498), 261
Bayyumi, 'Ali al- (d. 1769), 141;
    dream(s) of, 350
Bayyumi order, 141
Bibi Hayati (19th c.), 214
Bibi Khanum (14th c.), 246, 247
Bible, 7. *See also* Christian(s); Jew(s);
    People of the Book
Bihjati, Muhammad Husayn (20th c.),
    100
biography, 92; collection of Gesu Daraz,
    297; by Ibn 'Arabi, 135; of Shaykh
    Luqman, 222; Taha Hussein's of
    Muhammad, 125; of women, 286,
    346. *See also* genre
Bistami, Bayazid al- (d. 874), 262, 284,
    307, 366
Buddhism, 278; and Javanese Islam, 283
Bukhara, 108, 231
Bukhari, Muhammad ibn Isma'il al- (d.
    870), on pilgrimage, 89; transmitter
    of traditions, 38, 55, 369
Buraq, al-, 122, 353. *See also* Ascension;
    Night Journey
Buyid period, 395n

Cairo, 203; al-Azhar University, 124,
    143, 194, 204; northern cemetery,
    180. *See also* Bayyumi order; Egypt;
    Ibn al-Farid; Mamluk dynasty
caliph(s), 42, 238, 249, 370; in art, 150;
    and interpretation, 37. *See also* Abu
    Bakr as-Siddiq; 'Ali; patronage;
    politics; 'Umar
calligraphy, Kufic, 5, 26, 27, 43, 46, 88,

104, 190, 246; *muhaqqaq*, 43; Naskhi,
47, 88, 104; *rayhani*, 6; *tawqiʿ*, 6;
thuluth, 26, 44, 46. *See also*
inscriptions; language(s)
candlestick(s), 45, 67
ceremonialism, and faith, 69. *See also*
faith; intention; reason; ritual(s)
Ceuta, madrasa of, 258
Charkhi, Mawlana Yaʿqub (d. 1447), 231
Chella, 253
China, 269, 278; and Islam, 400n
Chishti, Muʿin ad-Din (d. 1236), 155
Chishti order, 139, 140, 297, 347, 349
chivalry, fraternities of. See *futuwwat*
Christian(s), 5; Bawa Muhaiyaddeen on,
295; bearers of tradition, 38; and
faith, 68; heresy of, 173, 307; Ibn
ʿAbbas on, 33; Jesuits in Java, 326; and
morals, 335; and mosque of Cordova,
27; Muqatil ibn Sulayman on, 30; as-
Suyuti on, 34; Tabari on, 38. *See also*
Jesus; Jew(s); People of the Book
circumambulation, 87, 91; of a shrine,
265; spiritual, 101, 208. *See also*
Kaʿba; pilgrimage
Confucianism, 278
conversion, of all to Islam, 80
Cordova, 27; mosque of, 254
creation, 3; of Adam and Eve, 84, 280; in
Chinese Muslim tradition, 278; and
evil, 189; and God, 69, 71, 145, 180,
339; goodness of, 174; of heaven and
earth, 182; and human knowledge,
357; in Ibn al-Farid's poetry, 194; and
idolatry, 173; of Intellect, 180; of
Jesus, 339; in Swahili legend, 78, 83.
See also sign(s)

dalil (argument), 35. *See also* reason
Damascus, 35, 218, 244; Umayyad
mosque of, 254
darshan (sight), 105
David during Muhammad's Ascension,
339, 344
Davut Agha (d. 1597), 248. *See also*
architecture; Ottoman dynasty
death, 328; angels of, 131, 166, 206;

burial customs, 221; call of, 233. *See
also* heaven; hell; judgment; tomb(s)
deception, 42; of self, 359; in Sura of
Joseph, 7. *See also* Satan; sin
dervish, miniature painting of, 360, 365,
373; prayer of, 164. See also *murid*;
mystic(ism)
devotion, at ʿAli's tomb, 262; to
knowledge, 240; to Muhammad, 120;
and prayer, 59, 284; to spiritual
guide, 105; and worship, 74, 87. *See
also* holy people; model(s); worship
dhikr (recollection, Sufi ceremony), 120,
195, 295; of al-Bayyumi, 142. See
also *duʿaʾ*; meditation; prayer
diary, spiritual, 325. *See also* genre
didactic. *See* poetry, didactic
divan. *See* poetry, divans
Dome of the Rock, 83, 139, 337
dome(s), 26; over ʿAli's tomb, 262; of
Amir Khayrbak's mausoleum, 181; in
Chinese mosques, 279; of Congregational Mosque in Delhi, 202; double,
246; of Gur-i Mir mausoleum, 190; of
Mosque of Bayezid II, 210; of Tlemcen
mosque, 258; of the Toledo mosque,
249. *See also* architecture; mosque(s)
doubt. *See* unbelief
dream(s), of Ahmad Wahib, 352; of Amir
Khusraw, 268; of al-Bayyumi, 350; of
a deceiver, 263; of Ibn Taymiya, 290;
of Jesus, 349; and Joseph, 345; in a
miniature painting, 324; and mystical
experience, 345, 381; of Muhammad,
91, 350; vision of a shaykh, 368. *See
also* inspiration; revelation
duʿaʾ (personal prayer), 72, 92. See also
dhikr; intercession; prayer

Egypt, 7, 35, 107, 124, 137. *See also*
Cairo; Mamluk dynasty
endowment. See *waqf*
epigraphy. *See* inscriptions
eschatology, images of, 14; and Zulaykha's threat, 12. *See also*
judgment, Day of
ethics, 144. *See also* law; models

etiquette, in recitation, 55
Eve, 84, 289
exegesis. *See* interpretation

faith, consequences of, 2, 81; defined, 151; enjoined, 115; and intention, 62, 271; of Jacob, 9; lack of, 81, 329; and salvation, 83, 95; and worship, 65, 68, 74
Farid ad-Din Ganj-i Shakar (d. 1265), 141
fasting, of Ibn al-Farid, 204; and intention, 64, 271; of Shaykh Luqman, 219; of Moses, 78, 80; during Ramadan, 84, 218; and true health, 152; and worship, 73. *See also* asceticism; five pillars; intention; Ramadan
Fatima (d. 633), 98
Fatima bint 'Abbas, (d. 1314/15), 287, 290
Fatima of Nishapur (d. ca. 850), 290
Fez, 251, 253, 257
fiqh (jurisprudence). *See* law
Firdawsi order, 59, 298
five pillars, 59, 85, 92. *See also* alms; fasting; pilgrimage; prayer; Ramadan; ritual(s); *shahada*
forgiveness, of God, 2, 22, 116, 194, 270, 305; of Joseph, 22; Muhammad asks for, 271. *See also* grace
fountain(s), 58, 144, 259; at the Mevlevi tekke, 245. *See also* ablution; architecture; ritual(s)
Friends of God, 137, 138, 155, 357. *See also* holy people
funerary architecture. *See* tomb(s)
futuwwat (chivalry, Sufi), 235, 336

Gabriel. *See* angel(s), Jibril
Gayo language, 184, 189, 191
Genghis Khan, 141
genre. *See* aphorism(s); biography; diary; *ginan; ghazal(s); madih; marthiya; na't;* poetry; *qasida; ruba'iyat;* sermon(s); *tafsir;* wisdom literature
Gesu Daraz, Muhammad Husayni (d. 1422), 297, 349

ghayb, al- (the unseen), 16
ghazal(s), 170, 208. *See also* genre; poetry
Ghazali, Abu Hamid al- (d. 1111), 1; on interpretation, 48, 355; on recitation, 57
ginan, 92. *See also* genre; poetry
God, attributes of in Qur'an, 2, 104, 270; *al-'Aziz,* 12; condescension of, 76; as Creator, 71, 189, 343; existence of, 299; faithful, 188; gentleness of, 270; as Guide, 40, 79; all knowing, 43, 79; and law, 69; names of, 270, 285, 294, 299, 317; nearness to Muhammad, 121, 306; present in idols, 176; speaks to Moses, 78, 308; unity of, 30, 143, 144, 147, 284, 309, 317, 330
grace, and generosity, 158; of God, 25, 81, 84, 94, 97, 107, 270; of Qur'an, 36. *See also* God
Granada, 251
greed, 82. *See also* sin
grief, 97, 98, 99
guidance, brother over sister, 214; of enemies, 150; and evaluating experience, 359; of God, 26, 32, 40, 62, 88, 121, 123; of Islam, 110; and law, 111, 237, 376; in a miniature painting, 376; of Muhammad, 24, 290; and mystical experience, 359; of prophets, 362; rejection of, 62; on a spiritual journey, 311; of spiritual leader, 60, 105, 135, 182, 214, 311, 359, 373; through visions, 368, 372; by truth, 339. *See also* law; *murid;* prophet(s); Qur'an
guidebook(s), for pilgrimage, 86

Habiba al-'Adawiya (8th–9th c.), 93
hadith: and 'A'isha, 90; Barquq's shaykh of, 228; collections of, 55; companion to Qur'an, 36; examples of, 1, 25, 36, 38, 41, 43, 46, 57, 62, 72, 112, 129, 134, 145, 149, 192, 207, 260, 270, 271, 284, 302, 309, 317, 334; on good company, 369; and interpretation of Qur'an, 1, 24, 28, 50; on Muham-

mad's Night Journey, 325, 336; on
pilgrimage, 89; and revelation, 1; on
ritual prayer, 59; sayings of ʿAli, 46,
377. *See also* Muhammad; Sacred
Sayings
Hafiz (d. ca. 1490), 365
Hagar, 85, 89
hajj. See pilgrimage
Hajjaj, Shuʿba ibn al-, 337; on interpre-
tation, 40
Hallaj, al- (d. 922), 63, 307, 314
Halveti order, 142, 311, 350
Hamadhani, ʿAyn al-Qudat al- (d. 1132),
60
Hamka. *See* Amrullah, Haji Malik Karim
Hanafi law school, 226, 291
Hanbali law school, 35, 228; and Fatima
bint ʿAbbas, 287. *See also* law
Harran, 35
Hasan ibn ʿAli (d. 669), 46, 372
Hasan al-Basri. *See* Basri, Hasan al-
heaven, 4, 60; and Adam, 341; and ʿAli's
tomb, 262; described, 84; desire for,
135; and God's mercy, 79; and human
nature, 240; inhabitants of, 81, 132;
and intention, 63; personified, 274;
and prayer, 140; for righteous, 145;
spiritualized, 328. *See also* judgment
hell, 60; and Adam, 341; avoidance of, 80;
and mystical love, 94; spiritualized,
328; Swahili description of, 81; for
wicked, 145, 266. *See also* judgment
Herat, 261, 264
hermeneutics. *See* interpretation
hikma (wisdom), 10
Hindi, 103, importance of studying, 240
Hinduism, and Bawa Muhaiyaddeen,
295; in Java, 283; and praise of
Muhammad, 212, 213
holy people, Ibn al-Farid as, 202; Bawa
Muhaiyaddeen as, 291; and *mawlid*,
107, 109, 350; miracles of, 98, 136, 141,
157, 339; as models, 140, 285;
Muhammad on, 364; power of, 122;
remembrance of, 152. *See also* Friends
of God; *mawlid*; miracle(s); prophet(s)
hospital(s), construction of, 261

Hudaybiya, treaty of, 91. *See also*
Quraysh
human nature, Bawa Muhaiyaddeen on,
296; before God, 240, 270; created by
God, 3; false, 101; weakness of, 76, 119,
295, 303, 318, 360; and worship, 70
humility, blessings of, 156, 164; enjoined,
100, 105, 273; of Husayn, 98; of
Moses, 79; and prayer, 73; of Rabiʿa,
134, 271; and recitation, 57; of Sufi
Badhni, 140; and Sufi chivalry, 237.
See also intention
Husayn ibn ʿAli (d. 680), 46, 372; com-
memoration of, 395n; intercession
of, 95; shrine of, 143
Hussein, Taha (d. 1973), 124
hymn(s), 103; of Ibn al-Farid, 196. *See
also* music

Iblis. *See* Satan
Ibn ʿAbbas (d. ca. 687), 131; commentary
on Sura One, 31; on interpretation,
38, 40, 41, 43; on pilgrimage, 89
Ibn Abi Hajala (d. 1375), 205
Ibn ʿArabi (d. 1240), 135, 173; Javanese
summary of, 283
Ibn ʿAsakir (d. ca. 1203), 203
Ibn ʿAtaʾ Allah al-Iskandari (d. 1309), 142
Ibn al-Farid (d. 1235) 194; Munawi on,
202, and *Wine Ode*, 205
Ibn Hanbal (d. 855), 92
Ibn Hisham (d. ca. 830), 125, 130
Ibn Ishaq (d. 767), 39, 125, 130
Ibn Marzuq, Shams ad-Din Abu
ʿAbdullah Muhammad (d. 1379), 250
Ibn Saʿd (d. 845), 129
Ibn Sirin, Muhammad (d. 728), 63; on
interpretation, 42
Ibn Taymiya, Taqi ad-Din (d. 1328), 1; on
Fatima bint ʿAbbas, 288, 290; on
tafsir, 35
Ibn al-Wakil (d. 1389), 288
Ibn Yasar, Abu ʿUbaydallah ibn Muslim,
on interpretation, 42
Ibrahim ibn Adham (d. ca. 790), 166
idolatry, 173; non-existence of, 175. *See
also* sin

Idris, 342

ijma' (consensus), 334

ijtihad (independent investigation), 54, 334. *See also* interpretation; *mujtahid;* Qur'an

ikhlas (sincerity), 10. *See also* virtue(s)

Il-Khanid dynasty, 45, 173. *See also* Uljaytu

image(ry) in Bawa Muhaiyaddeen's art, 292; of judgment, 2, 3, 4, 14, 16; of Ka'ba, 86, 118, 272; of a lusterware plate, 346; and meanings, 169; of mystical experience, 345; of paradise, 4, 53, 292; and philosophy, 73; of sea of existence, 318. *See also* art; interpretation; poetry

Imam Riza. *See* Riza, 'Ali ar-

iman. See faith

India, 27; Sufism in, 139, 156, 159, 283, 297, 322

Indonesia, 59, 283, 325

insan (human being), 8

inscription(s), 'Ali mentioned, 26, 46; on buildings, 223, 246; of Faraj ibn Barquq, 224, 225; of hadith, 26, 43, 246; on mihrabs, 29, 44; Muhammad's name, 190; prayer of Joseph, 47; of Qur'an, 26, 27, 28, 29, 44, 224, 225; Throne mentioned, 28; on tombstone(s), 104. *See also* architecture; calligraphy

inspiration, ethical, 119; literature of, 130; of Qur'an, 36; spiritual, 206; knowledge, 284; of Sunna, 36. *See also* Qur'an; revelation; *tafsir; ta'wil*

intention, and acts of devotion, 271; of Adam and Eve, 282; and interpretation, 41, 54; and judgment, 41, 61; and law, 290; and pilgrimage, 61; and prayer, 59, 60, 79; of Rabi'a, 271; and recitation, 55, 331; of Scripture, 54; and spiritual sickness, 380; and worship, 71

intercession, and forgiveness, 238; of Husayn, 95; of Imam Riza, 102; of Moses, 131; of Muhammad, 120, 123;

of spiritual guides, 363. *See also* holy people; prayer

interpretation, and aesthetics, 173; and Companions, 37; and deeper meanings, 269; diversity of, 31, 39, 48; and the Divine Reality, 376; of dreams, 346, 353; epigraphic, 44; of fall into sin, 281; and Followers, 39; and Hadith, 1; Ibn Taymiya on, 36; and literalism, 353, 355; and opinion, 41; of Qur'an, 1, 35, 334, 354, 355; and reason, 48, 52; of religious experience, 345. *See also* Qur'an; *tafsir; ta'wil*

intoxication, spiritual, 63, 214, 215. *See also* Ibn al-Farid; mystic(ism); wine

Iran, 100, 163, 269, 306

'Iraqi (d. 1289), 318

Isaac, 9

Isfahan, 19, 216, 288. *See also* Madar-i Shah Madrasa; mosque of; Safavid dynasty

Iskandari, al-. *See* Ibn 'Ata' Allah al-Iskandari

Isma'il, 89

Isma'ili Shi'ism. *See* Shi'ites, Isma'ili

isnad (chain of transmitters), 24, 31. *See also* Hadith

Israfil, 367. *See also* angel(s)

iwan (vaulted hall), 26, 216, 226; picture of, 191; use of, 288

Ja'bari, Ibrahim al- (d. 1288), 205

Jabarti, 'Abd ar-Rahman al- (d. 1825), 141, 350

Jacob, 9; and worship, 71

Ja'far as-Sadiq (d. 765), 94, 338

Jahangir (r. 1605–1627), 376

jahiliya (age of ignorance), 90

Jalayir, Sultan Ahmad (fl. 15th c.), 312

Jama'a, Al-'Aziz ibn al- (d. 1416), 207

Jami (d. 1492), 317, 319, 320

Java, 65, 283, 326

Jerusalem, 83, 138, 337. *See also* Dome of the Rock

Jesuit(s). *See* Christian(s), Jesuits

Jesus, Bawa Muhaiyaddeen on, 295; creation of, 339; in Gesu Daraz's dream, 349; during Muhammad's Ascension, 339, 340, 341, 344. *See also* Christian(s); People of the Book; prophet(s)

Jew(s), 5; Bawa Muhaiyaddeen on, 295; bearers of tradition, 38; and faith, 68; Ibn 'Abbas on, 33; Ibn Taymiya on, 38; Muqatil ibn Sulayman on, 30; redemption of Israel, 339; and ritual prayer, 76; as-Suyuti on, 34. *See also* Christian(s); People of the Book

Jibril. *See* angel(s)

Jilani, Abd al-Qadir al- (d. 1166), 88

Jili, al- (d. ca. 1410), 142

John the Baptist, during Muhammad's Ascension, 341

Jordan, 217

Joseph, 2; and attributes of Intellect, 180; and beauty, 182; in miniature painting, 163, 351; as model, 119; during Muhammad's Ascension, 341; Sura of, 6–7, 145. *See also* prophet(s)

journey, depicted in miniature painting, 312; and God, 311; highest, 309; of the masses, 303; and mystical lexicon, 317; spiritual, 159, 198, 301, 304, 311. *See also* pilgrimage

judgment, 2, 3, 4, 14, 16; angel of, 82; based on Qur'an, 37; Day of, 26, 43, 79, 82, 134, 148, 194, 225, 364; of the inner meaning, 378; and intention, 41, 60, 82, 282; reasonableness of, 53; *waqf* in force until, 233. *See also* heaven; hell; intention; law

Junayd (d. 910), 166

Jurjawi, 'Ali Ahmad al-, on prayer, 73

Juwayni, al- (d. 1085), on ritual purity, 56

Ka'ba, 62, 85; and Abraham, 172; and 'Ali's tomb, 262; of desiring God, 186; glorious, 266; of the heart, 100; and Ibn al-Farid, 203; made an idol-temple, 272; picture of, 86, 93, 118. *See also* Abraham; Mecca; pilgrimage

karamat. See miracle(s), saintly

Karatay madrasa, 287

Karkhi, Ma'ruf. *See* Ma'ruf Karkhi

Khadija (d. 619), 130

Khadija bint al-Baqqal (d. 1045), 286

Khadija ash-Shahjaniya (d. 1068), 286

Khaliliyan, 'Ali (20th c.), 100

Khalwati order. *See* Halveti order

Khan, Sayyid Ahmad (d. 1898), 368

khanqah (Sufi residence), 159; endowed by a woman, 244; and Khwaja Ahrar's *waqf*, 232; of Faraj ibn Barquq, 180, 224, 225. *See also* architecture; mosque(s); *ribat; tekke; zawiya*

Kharraqani, Abu 'l-Hasan (d. 1033), 272

Khayri, 'A'isha bint Abi 'Uthman Sa'id al- (d. 864), 290

khutba. See sermon(s)

Khwandamir, Ghiyath ad-Din (d. ca. 1535), 261

knowledge, limitations of, 52; spiritual, 19. *See also* human nature; reason; science

Kubra, Najm ad-Din (d. 1221), 301

Kubrawi order, 301, 321

Kufa, 5

Kufic. *See* calligraphy, Kufic

Kufr al-Ma, 218. *See also* Jordan

Kujuji, Khwaja Muhammad (d. 1279), 375

Kurani, Ibrahim al- (d. 1691), 283

Labid (6th c.), 284

Lahiji, Shams ad-Din Muhammad (d. 1507), 172, 209

language(s), importance of studying, 240; Indonesian, 87; South Asian, 103, 269. *See also* Arabic; calligraphy; Gayo; Hindi; inscription(s); Persian; Swahili; Urdu

law, 'Ali's interpretation of, 238, 376; Christian, 335; doubt of God's, 327; as guide, 111, 284; and idolatry, 177; and intention, 60; and interpretation of Qur'an, 43, 238, 239, 334, 376; love

law (*continued*)
for, 82; of Muhammad, 122; and
pilgrimage, 92; and punishment, 142;
obedience to enjoined, 84; schools
pictured in guidebook, 86; and Sufi
chivalry, 237, 399; and the Sufi
path, 399n; and *waqf* documents,
226, 235; and wisdom literature,
144; women's issues in, 288; women
teachers of, 286; and worship, 69, 363.
See also Hanafi law school; Hanbali
law school; judgment; Maliki law
school; Shafi'i law school; sin; *waqf*
letter(s), 59, 298, 360. *See also* genre
lexicography, spiritual, 317
light, of the Creator, 343, 380; of
Muhammad, 293, 307, 315, 347
love, of God, 83, 93, 105, 135, 145, 208,
321, 363; in Ibn al-Farid's poetry,
194; images of, 208; Imam Riza, 102;
for law of God, 82; for Muhammad,
122; of parents, 84; personification of,
180; and sacrifice, 237; spiritual, 105,
155, 195, 297, 333; for spiritual guide,
374, 379; and Sufi chivalry, 244; unrequited, 195; for the world, 61, 80
Luqman, 144, 218–223

madih (praise), 92. *See also* genre; poetry
Madjid, Nurcholish, 65
madrasa, 216; in Barquq's *waqf*, 226;
construction of, 257; endowment
of by Mizra, 265; Karatay of Konya,
287; in Khwaja Ahrar's *waqf*, 232;
Madar-i Shah, 289; Shir Dar, 288.
See also architecture; teaching
Madura, 325
Maghribi, Muhammad Shirin (d. ca.
1408), 209
Mahalli, Jalal ad-Din al- (d. 1459),
commentary on Sura One, 33
maktubat. *See* letter(s)
Malaysia, 27; Jami Masjid in, 76. *See
also* mosque, in Shah Alam
malfuz (utterances), 297. *See also* genre
Malik ibn Anas (d. 795), 92
Malik ibn Dinar (d. ca. 750), 135

Maliki law school, 228
Maliki, Shams ibn 'Imara al- (d. 1440),
207
Mamluk dynasty, 35; inscriptions of,
224, 225. *See also* Abu Hanifa, law
school of; Cairo; Egypt
ma'na (meaning), 195
Manat, 90. *See also* idolatry
Maneri, Sharaf ad-Din (d. 1381), 299; on
intention, 59; on mystical experience,
359
Mansura, al-, 253; mosque of, 254
maqam (station, place), 195
ma'rifa (intimate knowledge), 157, 295;
al-Ghazali on, 355
Marrakesh, 253; glories of its mosque,
254
marriage, 161; of Joseph to Zulaykha,
163
marthiya (lament), 92; and Shi'ites, 95.
See also poetry
martyrdom, of Husayn, 95. *See also*
Shi'ites; suffering
Ma'ruf Karkhi (d. 815), 164, 367
Marv, 29
Marwa and Safa, 87
Mary, 10, 44, 130, 344; in Wahib's
dream, 353. *See also* holy people;
women
Mas'ud, Abdallah ibn (d. 653), on
interpretation, 37
mathnawi (couplets), 185; of Jami, 324.
See also poetry, didactic
Mawdudi, Mawlana Sayyid Abu 'l-'Ala'
(d. 1979), 333
mawlid (birth celebration), 107, 350. *See
also* holy people; miracle(s)
Mecca, conquest of, 276, 277; in a dream,
350; and hijra, 275; Mosque of, 27,
276; and qibla, 43, 85; as spiritual
home, 137, 199, 203; as symbol, 100;
and 'umra, 74. *See also* Ka'ba;
Quraysh
Meccan period, 144
Medina, 62; Islamic university in, 223;
Muhammad enters, 276; Sumatrans
in, 283

meditation, 105, 315. See also *dhikr;
du'a'*; prayer
Mehmet III (r. 1595–1603), 248
Meknes, 253
metaphor(s). *See* image(s)
Mevlevi order, 245. *See also* Rumi, Jalal
ad-Din
Michael. *See* angel(s), Michael
mihrab (prayer niche), 27, 43, 104; of
mosque of Isfahan, 45, 46; on rug(s),
66, 150; Turkish, 44. *See also*
architecture; inscription(s);
mosque(s); *qibla*
Mihrimah Sultan (16th c.), 247
milla (community, faction), 14. *See also*
Christian(s); Jew(s)
minaret, of Amir Khayrbak's mosque,
181; of Congregational Mosque of
Delhi, 202; on Faraj ibn Barquq's
khanqah, 180; in Fez, 253; glory of
Marrakesh mosque, 254, 258; of Jami
Masjid in Kuala Lumpur, 76; of
Kalyan mosque, 75; of Madar-i Shah
Madrasa, 288; of mosque of Selim I,
249, 252; of Selimiye mosque, 211.
See also architecture; mosque(s)
minbar (pulpit), 254, 287; picture of two,
46
miracle(s), attainment of, 313; of Jesus,
330; saintly, 143, 157; of Ibn al-Farid,
205; of God, 49; of holy people, 98,
136, 138, 141, 157, 160; of Muhammad, 366. *See also* holy people
Mirkhwand (d. 1498), 261
Mizra, Sultan Husayn (d. 1506), 261;
patronage of, 265
model(s), Abraham as, 306; early caliphs
as, 251; for good behavior, 223;
Muhammad as, 114, 119, 251, 269,
270, 285, 336; negative, 274; prophets
as, 162; women as, 130, 245, 271. *See
also* hadith; holy people; Muhammad
Mongol dynasty, 35, 141; and patronage,
236
Moses, 32, 130, 162, 308; during
Muhammad's Ascension, 339, 344;
and Muhammad, 76; and ritual

prayer, 59, 71, 72, 76. *See also* law;
prophet(s)
mosque, of Amir Khayrbak, 181; of
'Amr, 204; of Aqsunqur, 181; of
Bayezid II, 210; of Bibi Khanum, 246,
247; Congregational, of Delhi, 202;
of Cordova, 27, 254; Great Mosque
of Taipei Taiwan, 279; guide to the
construction of, 252; of Isfahan, 44,
45, 46, 191; of Mihrimah Sultan, 248;
of Muhammad, 93; of al-Mushtaha,
204; and patronage, 232; prayers in,
164; of Rustem Pasha, 44; of the
Sanctuary in Mecca, 27; of Selim I,
252; of Selim II in Edirne, 58, 211;
in Shah Alam, 27, 43; of Shaykh
Lutfullah, 26; of Toledo, Ohio, 250;
of 'Ubbad in Tlemcen, 256, 258;
Yeni Valide complex, 248. *See also*
architecture; dome; *mihrab*; minaret;
minbar; qibla
Mozambique, Islam in, 78
muezzin (person who makes call to
prayer), 110, 231, 232. *See also* prayer
Muhaddith, 'Abd al-Haqq (d. 1642), 139
Muhaiyaddeen, Muhammad Raheem
Bawa. *See* Bawa Muhaiyaddeen
Muhammad, Ascension of, 77, 306, 336,
340; creation of, 80, 83, 122; dream
of, 91; in a dream, 290, 350; on
endowments, 260; foretold to Moses,
80; as guide, 123; hijra of, 270, 275;
and Ibn al-Farid, 205, 208; in an
inscription, 190; as intercessor, 120,
133, 225; light of, 293, 307, 315, 347;
as model, 114, 119, 251, 269, 270,
285, 331, 336; as Mustafa, 103, 290;
painting of his Ascension, 338; and
other prophets, 336, 340; pilgrimage
of in painting, 118; praise of, 56, 98,
110, 120, 170, 208, 212, 310, 331;
praised by God, 80, 212; on prayer,
192; and the Qur'an, 36; and revelation, 1; Seal of Prophets, 121, 124, 340;
Taha Hussein on, 125; on tombs, 246;
in traditions, 76, 118, 195, 276, 364;
on travel, 302. *See also* Ascension;

Muhammad (*continued*)
　　Hadith; model(s); Night Journey;
　　Night of Power; prophet(s); Qur'an;
　　revelation
Muhammad ibn Fadl Allah (d. 1620), 283
Muhammadiya, reformist movement, 85
muhsinun (those who do good), 10
Mujahid ibn Jabr (d. ca. 720), 31; on
　　interpretation, 39, 41
mujtahid (legal scholar), 54. See also
　　ijtihad; interpretation
Mulla of Hadda, the. *See* Najmuddin
　　Akhundzada
Mulla Sadra. *See* Sadr ad-Din
Munawi, 'Abd ar-Ra'uf al- (d. 1621), 92;
　　on Ibn al-Faird, 202; on Rabi'a, 132,
　　346
Mundhiri al- (d. 1258), 203
Munkar, 166. *See also* angel(s)
Muqatil ibn Sulayman (d. 767),
　　commentary on Sura One, 29
muqri' (reciter), 107, 229. *See also*
　　recitation
Murad III (r. 1572–95), 248
murid (seeker, novice), 105; in a minia-
　　ture painting, 360, 376; and visu-
　　alizing the shaykh, 372. *See also*
　　guidance
music, 120, 347. *See also* hymn(s);
　　qawwali
Mutannabi (d. 955), 303
Mu'ayyiri, Rahi (20th c.), 101
Mu'tazilite philosophy, 332
mystic(ism), and architecture, 260;
　　defined, 157; etiquette of, 236; in
　　India, 139, 156, 159, 283, 297, 322;
　　Javanese, 65, 283; and literature, 120,
　　180, 301; of Luqman, 219; painting
　　of a, 360, 365; and theological proofs,
　　285; in the United States, 291. *See
　　also* asceticism; Bayyumi order;
　　devotion; *dhikr; du'a';* faith; Firdawsi
　　order; *futuwwat;* grace; guidance;
　　Halveti order; holy people; intention;
　　intoxication, spiritual; journey,
　　mystical; *khanqah;* love, of God;
　　malfuz; maqam; ma'rifa; Mevlevi

order; miracle(s), saintly; *murid;*
　　Naqshbandi order; poetry; prayer;
　　Qadiriya order; *qawwali; ribat; rizq;*
　　*sam'; Sufi(sm); *tekke; zawiya*

Nabulusi, 'Abd al-Ghani an- (d. 1730),
　　283
Nagauri, Shaykh Hamid ad-Din (d.
　　1276), 162
Najmuddin Akhundzada (19th c.), 159
Nakhshabi, Ziya' ad-Din (d. 1350), 162
Nakir, 166. *See also* angel(s)
Naqshbandi order, 231, 374; Mujaddidi,
　　368
Nasafi, 'Aziz ad-Din (d. 1300), 321
Nasir ad-Din Muhammad (d. 1356), 141
Naskhi. *See* calligraphy, Naskhi
na't, 92, 102, 103, 119, 212. *See also*
　　genre; poetry
Natsir, Mohammad (d. 1993), 326
Nawa'i, Mir 'Ali-Shir (d. 1502), 170
Nawawi, Abu Zakariya Yahya ibn Sharaf
　　ad-Din an- (d. 1278), 55
Night Journey, of Muhammad, 76, 123,
　　139, 325, 336; Tabari on, 353. *See
　　also* miracle(s); Muhammad
Night of Power, 138, 341. *See also*
　　Muhammad; Qur'an; revelation
Nimrod, 339
Nisaburi, Abu Ishaq Ahmad an-. *See*
　　Tha'labi
Nizam ad-Din Awliya' (d. 1325), 140, 347
Nizari. *See* Shi'ites, Isma'ili
Noah, 342
Nuna bint Fatima (13th c.), 136
Nuri. *See* Shafiq, Musarrat Jahan Begum

opinion, and interpretation, 41
Ottoman dynasty, governor of, 143,
　　mosque(s) of, 44, 248; pilgrimage
　　during, 86; Sufism in, 311. *See also*
　　Turkey
Oushi, Khwaja Qutb ad-Din Bakhtiyar
　　(d. 1235), 155

Pakistan, 333, 347
Palasi, Hasan (13th c.), 375

parable(s), 185
paradise. *See* heaven
patronage, 217, 223; of art(s), 67; of
    mosques, 46; royal, 170, 226, 236,
    244, 261, 265; of Sufis, 143, 231; by
    women, 46, 244, 246, 247, 248. *See*
    also politics
People of the Book, 38. *See also* Chris-
    tian(s); Jew(s)
Perrysburg, Ohio, 249; mosque of, 251
Persian, in China, 278; commentary on
    Qur'an, 270; importance of studying,
    240
Pharaoh, 130, 339
philosophy. *See* Mu'tazilite philosophy;
    reason
pilgrimage, to Abu Ayyub's tomb, 276;
    to 'Ali's tomb, 261; banner of, 88;
    to Bawa Muhaiyaddeen's tomb, 291;
    description of, 89, 288; enjoined by
    Moses, 80; and faith, 74; guidebook
    for, 86; of Ibn al-Farid, 194, 198; and
    intention, 61, 64, 73; from Jordan,
    221; spiritual, 74, 195, 208, 301; *tafsir*
    on, 59, 85; to tombs, 98, 122, 156. *See*
    also guidance; guidebook(s); tomb(s)
pillar(s). *See* five pillars
pishtaq (facade), picture of, 191; in
    Mughal architecture, 201. *See also*
    architecture
poetry, acrostic, 120; didactic, 185; divans
    of Nawa'i, 170; Gayo, 184, 191;
    ghazal, 101; Javanese, 283; lyric,
    185, 194; on pilgrimage banner, 88;
    Persian, 60, 64, 98, 170, 184; in praise
    of Muhammad, 119, 212; Swahili, 78.
    See also genre; *ghazal*; *ginan*; *madih*;
    marthiya; *na't*; *qasida*; *ruba'iyat*
politics, and community, 217, 236; and
    Sufi chivalry, 243. *See also* patron-
    age, royal
prayer, commanded, 55, 84, 87; of a
    dervish, 164; in an inscription, 47;
    and intention, 63, 64, 191; of Joseph,
    23; and purity, 56; reasons for, 76,
    87; and rug(s), 66, 150; and spiritual
    ascent, 284; of Sufi Badhni, 140;

Tabari on, 74, 76; at tombs, 87; of
    women, 92, 133, 245, 346; and
    worship, 70, 71, 84, 116, 191. See
    also *dhikr; du'a'*
pride, a disgrace, 152, 164; of much
    travel, 303; and poverty, 317; and
    prayer, 73; and revelation, 145; and
    ritual prayer, 271; tyranny of, 332.
    See also sin
prophet(s), and Adam, 276; favored by
    God, 32; inferior to Muhammad, 121,
    336; mark of, 337; message of, 10;
    Moses as, 78, 308; Muhammad as,
    1, 57; and reason, 49; and "skirt" of
    prophecy, 271; and spirituality, 8; and
    spiritual journey, 316; and tempta-
    tion, 361. *See also* Adam; David;
    Moses; Muhammad
prophetic sayings. *See* hadith
Psalms, and David, 339; and Moses, 80
purity, enjoined, 84; of God, 97; of heart,
    79, 81, 100, 290, 337; of Muhammad,
    337; ritual, 56, 78, 271. *See also* ablu-
    tion; intention; ritual

Qadiriya order, 88. *See also* mystic(ism)
Qalandars, 264
Qasba of Taza, 253; mosque of, 254
qasida (ode), 194–202, 205. *See also*
    genre; poetry
Qatada (d. 735), on interpretation, 40, 41
qawwali (devotional singing), 347
qibla (direction of Mecca), 29, 43; change
    of, 85, 91; of intellect, 186; Muham-
    mad as, 124; and recitation, 57. *See*
    also architecture; *mihrab*
qiyas (analogical reasoning), 334, 356
Qur'an, 1; authority of, 111, 144, 285,
    354; Barquq's shaykh of seven read-
    ings, 229; and Companions, 37; devo-
    tion to, 137; eternal, 170, 292; and
    Followers, 39; *as al-furqan*, 340; Ibn
    Taymiya on, 35; its own interpreter,
    36; literary styles in, 2; al-Mahalli
    on, 33; memorization of, 142, 228;
    and mercy, 238; Muhammad Abduh
    on, 85; Muqatil ibn Sulayman on,

Qur'an (*continued*)
    29; Persian commentary on, 270; in
    poetry, 213; questioning of, 326;
    reading enjoined, 84; and reason, 48,
    144, 331; recitation of, 7, 55, 56, 57,
    107, 160, 192, 331; scripts used for, 6,
    7; in a sermon, 107; and the Sunna,
    36, 285, 326, 334; as-Suyuti on, 33;
    Tabari on, 76; Taha Hussein on, 125;
    and wisdom literature, 144; and wor-
    ship, 71. *See also* calligraphy; inscrip-
    tion(s); interpretation; inspiration;
    recitation; revelation; *tafsir*
Quraysh, 91, 121, 277. *See also* Mecca
Qushchi, 'Ala' ad-Din 'Ali (15th c.),
    Timurid astrologer, 233
Qusi, 'Abd al-Ghaffar al- (d. 1309), 206
Qutb ad-Din Bakhtiyar Kaki (d. 1232), 141

rabb (Lord), 8, 9, 11, 13. *See also* God
Rabi'a al-Adawiya (d. 801), 63; dream of,
    346; on forgiveness, 271; loves God,
    165; as model, 132, 206; prayer of, 94
Ramadan, 84, 138, 218. *See also* fasting
ra'y. See opinion
Razi, Yahya ibn Mu'adh (d. ca. 871), 165,
    273
reason, abandonment of, 120; exclusive
    use of, 49, 128, 243; and faith, 62, 87,
    329; importance of, 51, 52; and
    interpretation, 48; language of, 325;
    and revelation, 144, 330; and Sufi
    chivalry, 243; Taha Hussein on, 128.
    See also science
recitation, 1; accuracy in, 7; of call to
    prayer, 162; etiquette in, 55, 56, 57; of
    God's name, 106; and intention, 192;
    and miracles, 136, 160; of prayers,
    157; of religious poetry, 395n; in a
    sermon, 107; seven ways of, 229. *See
    also muqri'; Qur'an
redemption, through suffering, 95; and
    truth, 153. *See also* grace; salvation
repentance, and God, 186; from sin, 114;
    and spiritual development, 157.
    See also forgiveness; grace; heaven;
    salvation

revelation, circumstances of, 37, 42; and
    creation, 2, 145; of Hadith, 1; on
    Night of Power, 135; and People of
    the Book, 38; of Qur'an, 1, 144; and
    reason, 144. *See also* inspiration;
    Night of Power; Qur'an; sign(s),
    of God
ribat (Sufi residence), 260. See also
    khanqah; tekke; zawiya
Rida, Rashid (d. 1935), 85
ritual(s), and faith, 59, 65; and prayer,
    43, 59, 74, 133; and purity, 56, 78; of
    Shi'ites, 95. *See also* alms; fasting;
    five pillars; pilgrimage; prayer;
    Ramadan; *shahada*
riwaq (portico), 352. *See also* architecture
Riza, 'Ali ar- (d. 818), 98
rizq (sustenance), 13
ruba'iyat (quatrain), 194. *See also*
    poetry, lyric
rug(s), 66. *See also* art
ruku' (bowing), 72
Rumi, Jalal ad-Din (d. 1273), 174, 178,
    208, 270; in mystical lexicon, 318;
    tomb of, 245
Ruqayya of Mosul (8th c.), 94, 290

sabr (patience), 10, 21
Sacred Hadith, 1, 25, 26, 80, 213;
    inversion of, 314. *See also* God,
    condescension; Hadith; mystic(ism)
Sa'di of Shiraz (d. 1292), 298; on good
    company, 370; in a miniature paint-
    ing, 324; in mystical lexicon, 321
Sadr ad-Din of Shiraz (d. 1640), 321
saer (didactic poem, Gayo), 191. *See also*
    poetry
Safa and Marwa, 87, 92
Safavid dynasty, 26
Safi ad-Din ibn Abi 'l-Mansur ibn Zafir
    (d. 1283), 137
Safiye Sultan (16th c.), 248
saint(s). *See* holy people
Sajjadi, Sayyid Ja'far (d. 1996), 317
Salah ad-Din (d. 1193), 244
salat (ritual prayer). *See* prayer
Sale, 253; madrasa of, 259

Saljuqid dynasty, 236

salvation, 83; and faith, 95; and mercy, 172; and sin, 152. *See also* grace; heaven; judgment

Sam'ani, Ahmad (d. 1140), 269

Samarkand, 190, 231, 288; mosque of Bibi Khanum, 246, 247; women patrons in, 246

sama', 120; of Amir Khusraw, 347; of Ibn al-Farid, 206; in a miniature painting, 365

Sana'i of Ghazna (d. 1131), 185, 363

Satan, 8, 49; as enemy of the faithful, 82, 84, 131, 277, 339; as deceiver, 147, 148, 281; as powerless, 361; and prayer, 57; sin of, 164; works of, 271, 274. *See also* hell; judgment; sin

Saudi Arabia, 223

Sayyid Khan (d. 1572), 103, 107

science, 67. *See also* reason

Selim I (r. 1512–20), 249, 252

Selim II (r. 1566–74), 211, 247

sense(s), weakness of, 51. *See also* human nature; reason

sermon(s), 28, 92; description of, 107; Egyptian, 108

Sha'bi, 'Abdallah ibn Abi as-Safar ash-, on transmission, 42

Shabistari, Mahmud (d. ca. 1340), 172, 209

Shad, Kishan Prasad (d. 1943), 213

Shafi'i, Abu 'Abdallah Muhammad ibn Idris ash- (d. 820), 92; on interpretation, 36; and Jariri school, 75

Shafi'i law school, 75, 142, 227, 288

Shafiq, Musarrat Jahan Begum (20th c.), 212

shahada (profession of faith), 110; and Moses, 80. *See also* five pillars

Shahawi, Sidi 'Abd ar-Rahman 'Uthman ash-, *mawlid* of, 109

Shahid, Shah Isma'il (d. 1831), 374

Shah Jahan (r. 1628–59), 202

Shah Wali Allah (d. 1762), 374

Sharaf ad-Din Maneri. *See* Maneri, Sharaf ad-Din

shari'a. See law

Shaykh Luqman (20th c.), 218

Shibli, Abu Bakr ash- (d. 945), 63, 165

Shi'ites, 95; Isma'ili, 103; *marthiya* of, 95; and miniature painting, 338; and praise of Shi'ite heroes, 395n; and renovation of 'Ali's tomb, 261; rituals of, 95; sayings of 'Ali, 46, 377; suffering of, 96; Twelver, 45, 98. *See also* 'Ali; Imam Husayn; Imam Riza

sidq (righteousness), 10, 11, 15

sign(s), of devotion, 87, 263; of God, 9, 17, 23, 34, 85, 148, 179, 306, 337; of idols, 173. *See also* creation; guidance; inspiration; Qur'an; revelation

sin, 120; and heaven, 84; and hope, 101; of Moses, 79; repentance from, 114; results of, 157; and justice, 238. *See also* hell; pride; unbelief

Sinan (d. 1588), 44, 58, 211, 248. *See also* architecture; Ottoman dynasty

sincerity. *See* intention

Sitt al-Muluk, 137

Sitt ash-Sham (d. 1220), 244

snake(s), in Afghan story, 160; in hell, 81; pride as, 273; Satan as, 277

Solomon, during Muhammad's Ascension, 339, 344

soul(s), creation of, 83; and God's love, 195; Muhammad more precious than, 370; mystical imagery of, 349; mystical states of, 357; as poetic symbol, 103; and renunciation, 150, 361; soundness of, 241. *See also* heaven; hell; judgment

Spirit of God, 21

spirituality. *See* mystic(ism)

Sri Lanka, 290

station. See *maqam*

suffering, and redemption, 95. *See also* hell; Shi'ites

Sufi Badhni (14th c.), 140

Sufi(sm), 69, 99, 121, 123, 135, 137, 139, 142, 159. *See also* mystic(ism)

Suhrawardi, Shihab ad-Din Abu Hafs 'Umar (d. 1234), 235, 298

Suhrawardi, Shihab ad-Din Yahya
Maqtul (d. 1191), 180, 321
sujud (prostration), 72
Sulami, ʿAbd ar-Rahman (d. 1021), 318
Sulayman the Magnificent (r. 1520–66),
44, 211, 247. *See also* architecture;
Ottoman dynasty; Sinan
Sultan Barquq (Abu Faraj). *See* Barquq,
Sultan
Sumatra, 85, 189, 283
Sunna, and interpretation, 36, 41, 285,
334. *See also* hadith; Muhammad
Suyuti, Jalal ad-Din as- (d. 1505),
collection of hadith of, 142; commen-
tary on Sura One, 33
Swahili, 59, 78, 81
symbol(s). *See* image(s)

taʿabbud (worshipfulness), 87
taʿaqqul (acts of understanding), 87
Tabari, Abu Jaʿfar Muhammad ibn Jarir
at- (d. 923), history of, 129; on interpretation, 37, 40, 43, 353; on Muhammad's Night Journey, 336, 353;
Qurʾan, commentary of, 76; on ritual
prayer, 74, 76
Tabriz, 173, 375
Tabuk, 61
tafsir (exegesis), 1; of Ibn Taymiya, 35;
Indonesian, 59, 85, 191; of al-
Mahalli, 33; of Muhammad ʿAbduh,
85; of Muqatil ibn Sulayman, 29; of
as-Suyuti, 33. *See also* Hadith;
interpretation; Qurʾan
Taipei, Taiwan, 279
Taj Mahal, 26, 27, 202. *See also* Shah
Jahan
takbir (pronouncing "Allahu Akbar"), 72
talismanic symbols, 88
Tangier, 253
Tanta, 352
Taoism, 278
taqwa. See devotion
taslim (invoking peace, saying "*as-
salam ʿalaykum*"), 72
tawatur (frequency, dispersion), 50. See
also *isnad*

taʾwil (interpretation), 1, 38, 49
taʾwil al-ahadith (interpretation of
events), 9
teaching, through art, 290–291;
informal, 286; and literature, 297;
moral, 69; of the Qurʾan, 55; and
women, 286, 287. *See also madrasa;
saer*
tekke, 236; Mevlevi, 245. *See also*
architecture; *khanqah*; mystic(ism);
ribat; zawiya
Tengku Mude Kala (20th c.), 191
Tengku Yahye (20th c.), 191
Thaʿlabi (d. 1036), 130
Thawri, Sufyan ath- (d. 767), 134
Thawri, Umm Sufyan ath- (8th c.), 290
throne, of God, 24, 78, 82, 83, 364; in an
inscription, 28
thuluth. See calligraphy, *thuluth*
Tilimsan. *See* Tlemcen
Timurid dynasty, 26, 232; and patronage,
245, 261; and Ulugh Beg, 233, 246.
See also patronage; politics
Timur Lang (Tamerlane, d. 1405), 246
Tirmidhi, Abu ʿIsa at- (d. 892), 192, and
interpretation, 40
Tlemcen, 250; mosque of, 256, 258
Toledo, Ohio, 249, 253
tomb(s), of Abu Ayyub, 276; of Akbar,
201; of ʿAli, 261; of Amir Khayrbak,
181; of al-Bayyumi, 144; of Chishti,
156; in a dream, 350; of Faraj ibn
Barquq, 180, 224, 225; and funeral
of Sitt ash-Sham, 245; of Gur-i Mir,
190; hadith about, 246; of Ibn al-
Farid, 207; of Ismaiʿl the Samanid,
108; of Joseph's brothers, 207; of
Muhammad, 122; and pilgrimage, 98,
122, 156, 195, 276, 291; prayer at, 87;
of Qurqumas, 180; of Rumi, 245; of
the Shah-i Zinda, 246; of Sultan Inal,
180; and tombstone(s), 104. *See also*
architecture; pilgrimage; Taj Mahal
Torah, and Moses, 80; and Muhammad,
344. *See also* Jew(s)
totemism, 69
tradition(s). *See* hadith

Turkey, 58, 245, 310; and Vahidi, 311.
  See also Ottoman dynasty
Turkish language, 240
Tustari, Sahl ibn 'Abdullah (d. 896), 274

'Ubayd Allah, 31
Udfuwi, Al-Kamal al- (d. 1347), 206
'Udhra clan, poetry of, 195, 198
Uljaytu (r. 1304–16), 45
Ulugh Beg (r. 1447–49), 233, 248
'Umar ibn al-Khattab (d. 644), 370
'Umar Khayyam (d. 1123), 194
umma (community), 217
'*umra* (lesser pilgrimage), 74, 85; description of, 89. *See also* pilgrimage
unbelief, consequences of, 2, 290; and
  despair, 73; and intimate knowledge,
  355; and opposition to Muhammad,
  277; and prayer, 151; as sin, 79, 146,
  224; and understanding, 36, 329. *See
  also* faith; hell; sin
United States, Islam in, 291
Urdu language, 95, 119, 212
Uways Qarani, Khwaja (d. 643), and
  intention, 62; on mystical union, 366,
  367

Vahidi (fl. 1500s), 311
virahini (yearning lover), 103
virtue(s), 10; lack of, 106; models of, 119,
  132, 151; of the righteous, 84, 111;
  spiritual, 23, 243; and Sufi chivalry,
  237, 243
vision(s). *See* dream(s)

Wahib, Ahmad (d. 1973), 325; dream of,
  352
wajd (ecstasy), 195, 197
Wang Daiyu (d. ca. 1657), 278
waqf (pious endowment), 226, 231
wine: and Ibn al-Farid, 195, 196, 205; and
  spiritual intoxication, 63, 195, 200,
  214, 215; as symbol, 14
wisdom, defined, 151; literature of, 119,
  144; and Sufi chivalry, 236
women, buildings commissioned by, 248,
  286; and law, 203, 239, 286; as

models, 130, 135, 245, 271; under
  Ottoman dynasty, 246; as patrons,
  46, 244, 246, 247, 248; prayers of, 92,
  93, 137, 245; and recitation, 56; and
  ritual purity, 56; in Sufi order, 214;
  as teachers, 286. *See also* 'A'isha;
  'A'isha bint Ja'far as-Sadiq; Asiya;
  Bibi Hayati; Bibi Khanum; Eve;
  Fatima; Fatima bint 'Abbas; Fatima
  of Nishapur; Habiba; Khadija;
  Khadija bint al-Baqqal; Khadija ash-
  Shahjaniya; Mary; Mihrimah Sultan;
  Nuna bint Fatima; Rabi'a al-'Adawiya;
  Ruqayya of Mosul; Safiye Sultan;
  Sitt ash-Sham; Zulaykha
worship, of Asiya bint Muzahim, 130; and
  community, 69; and divine signs, 306;
  out of love, 135; and faith, 65; of God,
  32, 33, 83; and human nature, 70;
  and intention, 64, 192; and prayer,
  84; proper, 65; of Satan, 361; of a
  spiritual guide, 363. *See also* alms;
  fasting; pilgrimage; prayer; ritual(s)

Yalsuti, Misbah ibn 'Abdallah al-
  (d. 1350), 257
Yarmouk University, 223
Yarmuk, Battle of, 38
Yemen, 62
Yogyakarta, 326
Yusuf of Makassar (d. 1697), 284

Zahra' the Mournful (9th c.), 94
Zakaria, 10, 44, 341
zakat. See alms
Zamzam, of the heart, 100; in Ibn al
  Farid's poetry, 198; and Muhammad,
  123, 337; origins of, 89; picture of, 86,
  118
zawiya (shaykh's residence), 257, 350;
  construction of, 260. See also
  khanqah; ribat; tekke
Zoroastrianism, and Bawa Muhaiyaddeen, 295
Zulaykha, 12, 182; in a miniature
  painting, 163

Compositor: Integrated Composition Systems
Text: 10/15 Aldus
Display: Aldus
Printer and binder: BookCrafters, Inc.